A COMMENTARY
ON THE MANUSCRIPTS AND TEXT
OF THE NEW TESTAMENT

A COMMENTARY
ON THE MANUSCRIPTS AND TEXT
OF THE NEW TESTAMENT

PHILIP WESLEY COMFORT

Kregel
Academic

Published by Kregel Publications, a division of Kregel, Inc., 2450 Oak Industrial Dr. NE, Grand Rapids, MI 49505-6020.

Some text in chapters 1–2 and the appendix originally appeared in the author's book *Encountering the Manuscripts.* It is used with permission of B & H Academic, Broadman and Holman Publishers, Nashville, TN. Where appropriate, the text has been revised and updated.

The image of lines 1–26 of Ephesians (1:1–11) from $\mathfrak{P}^{46}$ is reproduced with the permission of the Papyrology Collection, Graduate Library, University of Michigan.

Some text in chapters 3–9 originally appeared in the author's book *New Testament Text and Translation Commentary*. It is used with permission of Tyndale House Publishers, Carol Stream, IL. All notes on specific verses were completely rewritten.

The translation of the New Testament portions used throughout the commentary is the author's own English rendering of the Greek.

The Hebrew font NewJerusalemU and the Greek font GraecaU are available from www.linguistsoftware.com/lgku.htm, +1-425-775-1130.

ISBN 978-0-8254-4340-4

Printed in the United States of America
15 16 17 18 19 / 5 4 3 2 1

Contents

Introduction

This commentary focuses on the textual readings in the many manuscripts of the New Testament. There are nearly 6,000 manuscripts, and just as many textual variants. Thousands of manuscripts of the New Testament have been discovered since the time of the Textus Receptus and King James Version, which were printed in the sixteenth and seventeenth centuries. And hundreds of New Testament manuscripts have been discovered in the past 100 years. Many of these are quite early—as early as the second, third, and fourth centuries. Some of the most important early manuscripts are the Beatty Papyri ($\mathfrak{P}^{45}$, $\mathfrak{P}^{46}$, $\mathfrak{P}^{47}$), the Bodmer Papyri ($\mathfrak{P}^{62}$, $\mathfrak{P}^{72}$, $\mathfrak{P}^{75}$), and the Oxyrhynchus Papyri ($\mathfrak{P}^{1}$–$\mathfrak{P}^{126}$).

Most commentaries usually adhere to a certain English translation, and the commentators refer to an edition of the Greek New Testament (such as *Novum Testamentum Graece* or the United Bible Societies' *Greek New Testament*), diverging from it when they deem it necessary. These two Greek editions (which have the same text) were compiled according to the eclectic method, which means that various readings from various manuscripts were selected for the text on a verse-by-verse basis. In this commentary readers will be reading commentary on actual manuscripts, such as $\mathfrak{P}^{75}$ for most of the Gospel of Luke, $\mathfrak{P}^{66}$ and $\mathfrak{P}^{75}$ for the Gospel of John, $\mathfrak{P}^{46}$ for nearly all of Paul's Epistles and Hebrews, and so on. (These are all second-century manuscripts). No other Bible commentary does this.

The early papyrus manuscripts (second and third century) cover nearly two-thirds of the New Testament (see the front section "Early Manuscripts"). The text of all these manuscripts is freshly presented in *The Text of the Earliest New Testament Greek Manuscripts* (Comfort and Barrett). The remaining one-third is found in codices Vaticanus (designated as codex B) and Sinaiticus (designated as codex א), both from the mid-fourth century. And there are several other manuscripts that are dated c. 400—namely, codex Alexandrinus (A), codex Ephraemi Rescriptus (C), codex Bezae (D), and codex Washingtonianus (W). And there are many more significant manuscripts. Chapter One provides an annotated list of the most significant manuscripts of the New Testament. This chapter also has discussions about how to assess the manuscripts and the canons of textual criticism.

There is another feature of this commentary that is found in no other commentary. English readers of the Bible, as well as those who read editions of the Greek New Testament, do not see that the New Testament manuscripts (from earliest times) were filled with nomina sacra (sacred names) written in a special way. In all the manuscripts, scribes presented the divine names with special calligraphy to distinguish these names as being sacred; the sacred names were written in contracted form with an overbar.

Certain divine names were almost always written as nomina sacra in the ancient manuscripts: God (*theos*), Lord (*kurios*), Jesus (*Iesous*), and Christ (*Christos*). There are a few occurrences where they are not written as nomina sacra; these are noted throughout. Special attention is given to the word "Lord" (*kurios*) when people are addressing Jesus. The nomina sacra form indicates that people, in several instances in the Gospels, were calling him "Lord," not just "sir" (or "lord"). There are notes on this.

Other divine names are "Father" (*pater*), "Son" (*huios*), and "Spirit" (*pneuma*). In most instances, these were written as nomina sacra by the ancient scribes. However, the name was sometimes written in full (in *plene*; i.e., not in nomen sacrum form—not contracted with an overbar) when the scribe wanted to indicate a human father (or the "father" as the originator of something), an earthly son, or the human spirit. These are noted throughout. It must also be said the titles "Son of God," "Son of Man," and "Son of David" were written as nomina sacra in the ancient manuscripts—so as to indicate these are not to be translated as "a son of God," "a son of man," or "son of David." These are noted throughout. The words "cross" and "crucify" were also written as nomina sacra in several early manuscripts, as well as the words "spiritual" and "Christian." These are noted throughout the commentary. The Appendix provides a full discussion of the nomina sacra.

More than anything, this commentary is filled with notes on significant textual variants. Several of the notes on textual variants pertain to the fact that the earliest manuscripts often have shorter texts than what is found in later manuscripts. Throughout the history of textual transmission, the text grew larger by scribal additions. The earliest manuscripts have hundreds of readings that are shorter than what appears in later texts. This pertains to phrases, words, and entire verses. Indeed, the early text has over 60 verses not present in what many translations include today. This exclusion of verses is evident in the following places: Matthew 6:13b; 7:13; 12:47; 16:2–4; 17:21; 18:11; 21:44; 23:14; 26:49–50; Mark 7:16; 9:44, 46; 11:26; 15:28; 16:9–20; Luke 9:54–56; 17:36; 22:43–44; 23:17, 34a; John 5:3b-4; 7:53–8:11; 9:38–39a; 13:23a; Acts 8:37; 15:34; 24:6b-8; 28:29; Romans 16:24; Galatians 1:9; Hebrews 2:7b; 1 Peter 5:14b; Revelation 20:5a. There are notes throughout the commentary on these verses that are not included.

I also refer the reader to two other books I have written for further discussions on texts and the nomina sacra: *New Testament Text and Translation Commentary* and *Encountering the Manuscripts*, which are quoted in this book.

The translation of the New Testament portions used throughout the commentary is my own English rendering of the Greek.

Early Manuscripts

This list presents the earliest manuscript(s) for each chapter of the New Testament.

Matthew

1: $\mathfrak{P}^{1}$
2: $\mathfrak{P}^{70}$
3: $\mathfrak{P}^{64+67}$, $\mathfrak{P}^{101}$
4: $\mathfrak{P}^{101}$, $\mathfrak{P}^{102}$
5: $\mathfrak{P}^{64+67}$
6: $\mathfrak{P}$. Antinoopolis 2.54; $\mathfrak{P}$. Oxyrhynchus 655
7–9: א (codex Sinaiticus), B (codex Vaticanus)
10: $\mathfrak{P}^{19}$, $\mathfrak{P}^{110,\,0170}$
11: $\mathfrak{P}^{19}$, $\mathfrak{P}^{70}$
12: $\mathfrak{P}^{70}$
13: $\mathfrak{P}^{103}$
14–18: א, B
19: $\mathfrak{P}^{25}$
20: $\mathfrak{P}^{45}$
21: $\mathfrak{P}^{45}$, $\mathfrak{P}^{104}$
22: א B
23: $\mathfrak{P}^{77}$
24: $\mathfrak{P}^{70}$
25: $\mathfrak{P}^{35}$, $\mathfrak{P}^{45}$
26: $\mathfrak{P}^{37}$, $\mathfrak{P}^{45}$, $\mathfrak{P}^{53}$, $\mathfrak{P}^{64+67}$
27–28: א B

Mark

1: א, B
2: $\mathfrak{P}^{88}$
3: א, B
4–9: $\mathfrak{P}^{45}$
10: א, B
11–12: $\mathfrak{P}^{45}$
13–16: א, B

Luke

1–2: $\mathfrak{P}^{4}$
3–5: $\mathfrak{P}^{4}$, $\mathfrak{P}^{75}$
6: $\mathfrak{P}^{4}$, $\mathfrak{P}^{45}$, $\mathfrak{P}^{75}$
7: $\mathfrak{P}^{45}$, $\mathfrak{P}^{75}$
8: $\mathfrak{P}^{75}$
9–14: $\mathfrak{P}^{45}$, $\mathfrak{P}^{75}$
15–16: $\mathfrak{P}^{75}$

17: $\mathfrak{P}^{75}$, $\mathfrak{P}^{111}$
18: $\mathfrak{P}^{75}$
19–21: ℵ, B
22: $\mathfrak{P}^{69}$, $\mathfrak{P}^{75}$, 0171
23–24: $\mathfrak{P}^{75}$

John

1: $\mathfrak{P}^{5}$, $\mathfrak{P}^{66}$, $\mathfrak{P}^{75}$, $\mathfrak{P}^{106}$, $\mathfrak{P}^{119}$, $\mathfrak{P}^{120}$
2: $\mathfrak{P}^{66}$, $\mathfrak{P}^{75}$, 0162
3: $\mathfrak{P}^{66}$, $\mathfrak{P}^{75}$
4: $\mathfrak{P}^{45}$, $\mathfrak{P}^{66}$, $\mathfrak{P}^{75}$
5: $\mathfrak{P}^{45}$, $\mathfrak{P}^{66}$, $\mathfrak{P}^{75}$, $\mathfrak{P}^{95}$
6: $\mathfrak{P}^{28}$, $\mathfrak{P}^{66}$, $\mathfrak{P}^{75}$
7: $\mathfrak{P}^{66}$, $\mathfrak{P}^{75}$
8: $\mathfrak{P}^{39}$, $\mathfrak{P}^{66}$, $\mathfrak{P}^{75}$
9: $\mathfrak{P}^{66}$, $\mathfrak{P}^{75}$
10–11: $\mathfrak{P}^{45}$, $\mathfrak{P}^{66}$, $\mathfrak{P}^{75}$
12–14: $\mathfrak{P}^{66}$, $\mathfrak{P}^{75}$
15: $\mathfrak{P}^{22}$, $\mathfrak{P}^{66}$, $\mathfrak{P}^{75}$
16: $\mathfrak{P}^{5}$, $\mathfrak{P}^{22}$, $\mathfrak{P}^{66}$
17: $\mathfrak{P}^{66}$, $\mathfrak{P}^{107}$, $\mathfrak{P}^{108}$
18: $\mathfrak{P}^{52}$, $\mathfrak{P}^{66}$, $\mathfrak{P}^{90}$, $\mathfrak{P}^{108}$
19: $\mathfrak{P}^{66}$, $\mathfrak{P}^{90}$, $\mathfrak{P}^{121}$
20: $\mathfrak{P}^{5}$, $\mathfrak{P}^{66}$
21: $\mathfrak{P}^{66}$, $\mathfrak{P}^{109}$

Acts

1: $\mathfrak{P}^{56}$, ℵ, B
2–3: $\mathfrak{P}^{91}$
4–6: $\mathfrak{P}^{8}$, $\mathfrak{P}^{45}$
7: $\mathfrak{P}^{45}$
8: $\mathfrak{P}^{45}$, $\mathfrak{P}^{50}$
9: $\mathfrak{P}^{45}$, $\mathfrak{P}^{53}$
10: $\mathfrak{P}^{45}$, $\mathfrak{P}^{50}$, $\mathfrak{P}^{53}$
11–17: $\mathfrak{P}^{45}$
18–19: $\mathfrak{P}^{38}$
20–22: ℵ, B
23: $\mathfrak{P}^{48}$
24–25: ℵ, B
26: $\mathfrak{P}^{29}$, ℵ, B
27–28: ℵ, B

Romans

1: $\mathfrak{P}^{10}$, $\mathfrak{P}^{40}$
2: $\mathfrak{P}^{40}$, $\mathfrak{P}^{113}$
3: $\mathfrak{P}^{40}$
4: $\mathfrak{P}^{40}$, 0220
5: $\mathfrak{P}^{46}$, 0220
6: $\mathfrak{P}^{40}$, $\mathfrak{P}^{46}$
7: ℵ, B
8: $\mathfrak{P}^{27}$, $\mathfrak{P}^{46}$
9: $\mathfrak{P}^{27}$, $\mathfrak{P}^{40}$, $\mathfrak{P}^{46}$
10–16: $\mathfrak{P}^{46}$

1 Corinthians

1–6: $\mathfrak{P}^{46}$
7–8: $\mathfrak{P}^{15}$, $\mathfrak{P}^{46}$
9–16: $\mathfrak{P}^{46}$

2 Corinthians

1–13: $\mathfrak{P}^{46}$

Galatians

1–6: $\mathfrak{P}^{46}$

Ephesians

1–3: $\mathfrak{P}^{46}$
4–5: $\mathfrak{P}^{46}$, $\mathfrak{P}^{49}$
6: $\mathfrak{P}^{46}$

Philippians
1–2: $\mathfrak{P}^{46}$
3–4: $\mathfrak{P}^{16}$, $\mathfrak{P}^{46}$

Colossians
1–4: $\mathfrak{P}^{46}$

1 Thessalonians
1–2: $\mathfrak{P}^{46}$, $\mathfrak{P}^{65}$
3: א, B
4: $\mathfrak{P}^{30}$
5: $\mathfrak{P}^{30}$, $\mathfrak{P}^{46}$

2 Thessalonians
1–2: $\mathfrak{P}^{30}$
3: א, B

1 Timothy
1–6: א

2 Timothy
1–4: א

Titus
1–2: $\mathfrak{P}^{32}$
3: א

Philemon
1: $\mathfrak{P}^{87}$

Hebrews
1: $\mathfrak{P}^{12}$, $\mathfrak{P}^{46}$, $\mathfrak{P}^{114}$
2–5: $\mathfrak{P}^{13}$, $\mathfrak{P}^{46}$
6–8: $\mathfrak{P}^{46}$
9: $\mathfrak{P}^{17}$, $\mathfrak{P}^{46}$
10–12: $\mathfrak{P}^{13}$, $\mathfrak{P}^{46}$
13: $\mathfrak{P}^{46}$

James
1: $\mathfrak{P}^{23}$
2: $\mathfrak{P}^{20}$
3: $\mathfrak{P}^{20}$, $\mathfrak{P}^{100}$
4–5: $\mathfrak{P}^{100}$

1 Peter
1: $\mathfrak{P}^{72}$
2–3: $\mathfrak{P}^{72}$, $\mathfrak{P}^{81}$
4: $\mathfrak{P}^{72}$
5: $\mathfrak{P}^{72}$, 0206

2 Peter
1–3: $\mathfrak{P}^{72}$

1 John
1–3: א, B
4: $\mathfrak{P}^{9}$
5: א, B

2 John
1: 0232

3 John
1: א, B

Jude
1: $\mathfrak{P}^{72}$, $\mathfrak{P}^{78}$

Revelation
1: $\mathfrak{P}^{18}$, $\mathfrak{P}^{98}$
2: $\mathfrak{P}^{98}$, $\mathfrak{P}^{115}$

3: $\mathfrak{P}^{115}$, 0169
4: 0169
5: $\mathfrak{P}^{24}$
6: $\mathfrak{P}^{24}$, $\mathfrak{P}^{115}$
7: א
8: $\mathfrak{P}^{115}$
9–15: $\mathfrak{P}^{47}$, $\mathfrak{P}^{115}$
16–17: $\mathfrak{P}^{47}$
18–22: א

Abbreviations and Works Cited

BAGD: *A Greek-English Lexicon of the New Testament and Other Early Christian Literature*, Bauer, Ardnt, Gingrich, Danker.

DJG: *Dictionary of Jesus and the Gospels*, Green, McNight, Marshall.

ESV: English Standard Version

KJV: Authorized King James Version

Lit.: Literally

LXX: Septuagint

Maj: Majority of Manuscripts

Maj^{A}: Majority of Manuscripts according to Andreas' commentary in Revelation

Maj^{K}: Majority of Koine Manuscripts in Revelation

mg: marginal reading

Moffat: The Bible, James Moffatt translation

Moulton and Milligan: *The Vocabulary of the Greek New Testament*, Moulton and Milligan.

MS: manuscript

MSS: manuscripts

NA^{27}: *Novum Testamentum Graece* (27th edition), Nestle-Aland.

NASB: New American Standard Bible

NEB: New English Bible

NIV: New International Version

NJB: New Jerusalem Bible

NLT: New Living Translation

NRSV: New Revised Standard Version

NT: New Testament

NT Text and Translation Commentary, Comfort

NU: Nestle-Aland and United Bible Society text

OT: Old Testament

REB: Revised English Bible

RSV: Revised Standard Version

TCGNT: *Textual Commentary on the Greek New Testament*, Metzger.

TEV: Today's English Version

Text of the Earliest NT Greek MSS, Comfort and Barrett.

TR: Textus Receptus

UBS[3] and UBS[4]: *Greek New Testament* (United Bible Society, third and fourth editions).

vid: videur (= it appears [to read so])

WH: *The New Testament in the Original Greek*, Westcott and Hort.

Chapter One

Introducing the Manuscripts, Text, and Nomina Sacra of the New Testament

Prior to the fifteenth century when Johannes Gutenberg invented movable type for the printing press, all copies of any work of literature were made by hand (hence, the name "manuscript"). We have over 5,500 manuscript copies of the Greek New Testament or portions thereof. No other work of Greek literature can boast of such numbers. Homer's *Iliad*, the greatest of all Greek classical works, is extant in about 650 manuscripts; and Euripides's tragedies exist in about 330 manuscripts. The numbers on all the other works of Greek literature are far less.

Furthermore, it must be said that the period of time between the original composition and the next surviving manuscript is far less for the New Testament than for any other work in Greek literature. The lapse for most classical Greek works is about eight hundred to a thousand years; whereas the lapse for many books in the New Testament is around one hundred years. Because of the abundant wealth of manuscripts and because several of the manuscripts are dated in the early centuries of the church, New Testament textual scholars have a great advantage over classical textual scholars. The most important manuscripts are presented in chapter two in detail.

The New Testament Papyri

Generally speaking, the papyrus manuscripts are among the most important witnesses for reconstructing the original text of the New Testament. It is not the material they are written on (papyrus) that makes them so valuable, but the date in which they were written. Several of the most significant papyri are dated from the second century to the early third. These manuscripts, therefore, provide the earliest direct witness to the autographs. The papyri can be placed in four large categories: (1) the Oxyrhynchus papyri, (2) the Beatty papyri, (3) the Bodmer papyri, and (4) other significant papyri.

The Oxyrhynchus Papyri

Beginning in 1898 Grenfell and Hunt discovered thousands of papyrus fragments in the ancient rubbish heaps of Oxyrhynchus, Egypt. This site yielded volumes of papyrus fragments containing all sorts of written material (literature, business and legal contracts, letters, etc.), along with several biblical manuscripts. Over half of the 127 New Testament papyri have come from Oxyrhynchus. The Oxyrhynchus papyri were discovered between the years 1898–1907 by Grenfell and Hunt, and then by the Italian exploration society from 1910 to 1913, and 1927 to 1934. Of the 50 Oxyrhynchus papyri, about half were published between 1898 and the 1930s. These include $\mathfrak{P}^{1}$, 5, 9–10, 13, 15–18, 20–24, 27–30, 35–36, 39, 48. In addition to the 25 New Testament papyri they published in the early part of this century, they have given us another 25 in the second part of the century—(as numbered by Aland): $\mathfrak{P}^{51}$, $\mathfrak{P}^{65}$, $\mathfrak{P}^{69}$, $\mathfrak{P}^{70}$, $\mathfrak{P}^{71}$, $\mathfrak{P}^{77}$, $\mathfrak{P}^{78}$, $\mathfrak{P}^{90}$, $\mathfrak{P}^{100}$–$\mathfrak{P}^{115}$, $\mathfrak{P}^{119}$–$\mathfrak{P}^{127}$ (these last 28 have come out in the late 1990s and early 2000s.

Some of the more significant Oxyrhynchus papyri are as follows: $\mathfrak{P}^{1}$ (Matt. 1), $\mathfrak{P}^{5}$ (John 1, 16), $\mathfrak{P}^{13}$ (Heb. 2–5, 10–12), $\mathfrak{P}^{22}$ (John 15–16), $\mathfrak{P}^{77}$ (Matt. 23), $\mathfrak{P}^{90}$ (John 18), $\mathfrak{P}^{104}$ (Matt. 21), $\mathfrak{P}^{115}$ (Rev. 3–12).

The Chester Beatty Papyri

The Beatty papyri were purchased from a dealer in Egypt during the 1930s by Chester Beatty and by the University of Michigan. Quite possibly the manuscripts came from the ruins of the library of some church or library of a Christian scholar or monastery—perhaps in the Fayum or the east bank of the Nile near Atfih, the ancient Aphroditopolis, from which Antony, the founder of Egyptian monasticism, came. Among the New Testament manuscripts are $\mathfrak{P}^{45}$ (Gospels and Acts, c. 200), $\mathfrak{P}^{46}$ (Paul's Epistles, c. 150–200), and $\mathfrak{P}^{47}$ (Revelation, late third). The substantial content of these papyri and their early dates made them immediately significant, so much so that the translators of the RSV claimed that their revision of the ERV was prompted by these manuscripts (see Introduction to the RSV). And, for the first time, these papyri (and those published earlier) were cited in the Nestle text in significant fashion (see 16th edition, 1936). Detailed studies of these papyri followed in suit, by such scholars as Kenyon, Zuntz, Schofield, Schmid, Aland, Colwell, and Royse.

The Bodmer Papyri

The Bodmer Papyri (named after the owner, M. Martin Bodmer) were purchased from a dealer in Egypt during the 1950s and 1960s. The Bodmer biblical papyri (or Dishna Papers) were discovered seven years after the Nag Hammadi codices in close proximity (in the Dishna plain, east of the Nile River). (Dishna is midway between Panopolis and Thebes.) In 1945 the Nag Hammadi manuscripts were found in Jabal al-Tarif (just north of Chenoboskion—near Nag Hammadi, the city where the discovery was first reported). In 1952 the Bodmer papyri were found in Jabal Abu Manna, which is also located just north of the Dishna plain, 12 kilometers east of Jabal al-Tarif. It is quite likely that all these manuscripts were part of a library of a Pachomian monastery. Within a few kilometers of Jabal Abu Manna lies the ruins of the ancient basilica of Pachomius (in Faw Qibli). The New Testament papyri in this collection are as follows: $\mathfrak{P}^{66}$ (c. 150, containing almost all of John), $\mathfrak{P}^{72}$ (third century, having all of 1 and 2 Peter and Jude), and $\mathfrak{P}^{73}$ (Matthew, seventh c.), $\mathfrak{P}^{74}$ (Acts, General Epistles, seventh c.), and $\mathfrak{P}^{75}$ (Luke and John, c. 175–200). These manuscripts were studied extensively by such scholars as Colwell, Fee, Kubo, Aland, Porter, and Royse. I also did an extensive study of $\mathfrak{P}^{66}$ and $\mathfrak{P}^{75}$ for a doctoral dissertation (see bibliography: Comfort 1997).

Other Significant Papyri

A few significant New Testament papyri were also published in the early part of this century. One notable manuscript is $\mathfrak{P}^{4}$, having portions of Luke 1–6. It was later realized that this manuscript is part of the same codex as $\mathfrak{P}^{64}$+$\mathfrak{P}^{67}$. Another is $\mathfrak{P}^{32}$ (dated late second century by Roberts and Skeat); it contains a portion of Titus 1–2. Another small but significant papyrus, known as $\mathfrak{P}^{52}$, was published. In 1935, Colin Roberts announced that he had found a small codex fragment of John 18, which he dated to c. 125 (a date that was confirmed by other eminent papyrologists such as Kenyon, Bell, and Deissman). As the earliest extant New Testament papyri, this manuscript challenged theories about the fourth Gospel being composed in the early second century. It also opened the way for dating New Testament papyri earlier than they had been up until then because it was now clear to paleographers that the Christian codex must have existed in the first century. A few other significant, early papyri are $\mathfrak{P}^{87}$, an early copy of Philemon; $\mathfrak{P}^{91}$, a third-century fragment of Acts 2; $\mathfrak{P}^{92}$, a third-century codex of Ephesians and 1 Thessalonians; and $\mathfrak{P}^{98}$, a late second-century fragment of Revelation 1.

Finally, it should be mentioned that new fragments of already published manuscripts and fresh reconstructions of previously published manuscripts have gone to press in recent years. Kurt Aland identified new fragments of $\mathfrak{P}^{66}$ and $\mathfrak{P}^{75}$. Two additional leaves of $\mathfrak{P}^{45}$ were published—one by Zuntz and another by Skeat and McGing. Three small fragments of $\mathfrak{P}^{4}$, one new fragment of $\mathfrak{P}^{30}$, two new fragments of $\mathfrak{P}^{40}$, and several new fragments of $\mathfrak{P}^{66}$ were published for the first time in a work I edited (with Barrett), *The Text of the Earliest New Testament Manuscripts*. This work also includes several new reconstructions, especially of $\mathfrak{P}^{46}$ and $\mathfrak{P}^{66}$. Some of the same reconstructions of $\mathfrak{P}^{46}$ appear in Aland's *Das Neue Testament Auf Papyrus*, volumes 2 and 3. The actual papyrus manuscripts I have personally seen and studied are as follows: $\mathfrak{P}^{1}$, $\mathfrak{P}^{4}$, $\mathfrak{P}^{9}$, $\mathfrak{P}^{10}$, $\mathfrak{P}^{24}$, $\mathfrak{P}^{37}$, $\mathfrak{P}^{38}$, $\mathfrak{P}^{46}$, $\mathfrak{P}^{64}$, $\mathfrak{P}^{66}$, $\mathfrak{P}^{69}$, $\mathfrak{P}^{71}$, $\mathfrak{P}^{72}$, $\mathfrak{P}^{75}$, $\mathfrak{P}^{90}$, $\mathfrak{P}^{100-115}$. As for the others, I have studied photographs or transcriptions.

Significant Uncial Manuscripts

In addition to the papyri, there are several uncial manuscripts that are extremely important in studying the text of the New Testament. (They are detailed in chapter two.) The two most significant manuscripts are codex Vaticanus (designated B) and codex Sinaiticus (designated א). Both of these fourth-century manuscripts were studied extensively in the 1800s and were responsible for the creation of new editions of the Greek New Testament by such scholars as Tischendorf, Tregelles, Westcott and Hort. These editions completely overthrew reliance on the Textus Receptus, and they paved the way for revisions of the Authorized King James Version, as well as several new translations. The two editions used by most scholars today (*The Greek New Testament* and *Novum Testamentum Graece*), which both have the same text, are significantly influenced by the readings in codex Vaticanus and codex Sinaiticus.

Other important uncial manuscripts are codex Alexandrinus (designated A), codex Ephraemi Rescriptus (designated C), codex Bezae (designated D), codex Freerianus (designated I), codex Guelferbytanus B (designated Q), codex Borgianus (designated T), and codex Washingtonianus, also known as the Freer Gospels (designated W). These, and several other uncial manuscripts, are discussed in chapter two.

Assessing the Manuscripts to Establish the Text of the New Testament

Westcott and Hort, followed by Colwell,[1] urged that knowledge of documents must precede all decisions about textual variants. They asserted that a textual critic must know the scribal tendencies at work in each manuscript before using that manuscript to make a decision about a reading. For example, if a scribe was prone to prune phrases, a textual critic should be wary about citing this manuscript in support of a shorter reading as being original.

I would also urge that knowledge about the reader-reception tendencies of the scribes who produced the earliest extant documents must also precede all decisions about readings, and that a well-developed theory of scribal-reception could help us understand the dynamics that created changes in the New Testament text during the stages of transmission from the second century to the fifth. This does not call for a new canon of textual criticism, but it does call for a new awareness of the reception tendencies of each New Testament scribe. Of course, since these tendencies can be ascertained only through a study of individual variants, the variants themselves are usually not the original text. But the sum total of these variants for each manuscript displays the tendencies of the scribe who produced them. A textual critic can then take this knowledge and apply it to the task of textual criticism.[2]

In recent years, textual critics have been able to identify some of the very best manuscripts—with respect to textual purity. At the top of the list is $\mathfrak{P}^{75}$. It is a well-known fact that the text produced by the scribe of $\mathfrak{P}^{75}$ is very pure. It is also well-known that $\mathfrak{P}^{75}$ was the kind of manuscript used in formulating Codex Vaticanus—the readings of $\mathfrak{P}^{75}$ and B are remarkably similar (see discussion above on $\mathfrak{P}^{75}$). Prior to the discovery of $\mathfrak{P}^{75}$, certain scholars thought Codex Vaticanus was the work of a fourth century recension; others (chiefly Hort) thought it must trace back to a very early and accurate copy. Hort said that Codex Vaticanus preserves "not only a very ancient text, but a very pure line of a very ancient text."[3] $\mathfrak{P}^{75}$ appears to have shown that Hort was right.

Prior to the discovery of $\mathfrak{P}^{75}$, many textual scholars were convinced that the second- and third-century papyri displayed a text in flux, a text characterized only by individual independence. The Chester Beatty Papyrus, $\mathfrak{P}^{45}$, and the Bodmer Papyri, $\mathfrak{P}^{66}$ and $\mathfrak{P}^{72}$ (in 2 Peter and Jude), show this kind of independence. Scholars thought that scribes at Alexandria must have used several such texts to produce a good recension—as is exhibited in Codex Vaticanus. But we now know that Codex Vaticanus was not the result of a scholarly recension, resulting from editorial selection across the various textual histories. Rather, it is now quite clear that Codex Vaticanus was simply a copy (with some modifications) of a manuscript much like $\mathfrak{P}^{75}$, not a fourth-century recension. This was argued very effectively in an article appropriately titled "$\mathfrak{P}^{75}$, $\mathfrak{P}^{66}$, and Origen: The Myth of Early Textual Recension in Alexandria" by Fee, who said that there was no Alexandrian recension before the time of $\mathfrak{P}^{75}$ (late second century) and Codex Vaticanus (early fourth) and that both these manuscripts "seem to represent a 'relatively pure' form of preservation of a 'relatively pure' line of descent from the original text."[4]

Some scholars may point out that this does not automatically mean that $\mathfrak{P}^{75}$ and B represent the original text. What it does mean, they say, is that we have a second-century manuscript showing great affinity with a fourth-century manuscript whose quality has been highly esteemed. But various scholars have demonstrated that there was no Alexandrian recension before the time of $\mathfrak{P}^{75}$ (late second century) and B (early fourth) and that both these manuscripts represent a relatively pure form of preservation of a relatively pure line of descent from the original text.

The current view about the early text is that certain scribes in Alexandria and/or scribes familiar with Alexandrian scriptoral practices (perhaps those in Oxyrhynchus) were probably responsible for maintaining a relatively pure text throughout the second, third, and fourth centuries. The Alexandrian scribes, associated with or actually employed by the scriptorium of the great Alexandrian library and/or members of the scriptorium associated with the catechetical school at Alexandria (called the *Didaskelion*), were trained philologists, grammarians, and textual critics. Their work on the New Testament was not recensional—that is, it was not an organized emendation of the text. Rather, the work of purification and preservation was probably done here and there by various individuals trained in text criticism. This is apparent in the production of $\mathfrak{P}^{66}$, which contains the Gospel of John. This manuscript was probably produced in an Egyptian scriptorium by a novice scribe who made many blunders, which were subsequently corrected by another scribe working in the same scriptorium. The first text produced by the novice could be classified as being very "free," but the corrected text is far more accurate. (See the discussion on $\mathfrak{P}^{66}$ above.)

But one dilemma still remains for some textual critics. They cannot explain how a $\mathfrak{P}^{75}$/B-type text coexisted with a D-type in the second century. All that can be said is that the D-type text generally appears to be inferior to the $\mathfrak{P}^{75}$/B-type text. Of course, this kind of judgment troubles certain scholars, who point out that the esteem given to B and $\mathfrak{P}^{75}$ is based on a subjective appreciation of the kind of text they contain rather than on any kind of theoretical reconstruction of the early transmission of the text. This same subjective estimation was at work when Westcott and Hort decided that B was intrinsically superior to D. Yet the praxis of textual criticism time and again demonstrates that the $\mathfrak{P}^{75}$/B-type text is intrinsically superior to the D-type text.

In the final analysis, the manuscripts that represent a pure preservation of the original text are usually those called "Alexandrian." Some scholars, such as Metzger, have called the earlier manuscripts "proto-Alexandrian," for they (or manuscripts like them) are thought of as being used to compose an Alexandrian-type text. However, this is looking at things backwards—from the perspective of the fourth-century. We should look at things forward—from the second century onward and then compare fourth century manuscripts to those of the second. The second-century manuscripts could still be called "Alexandrian" in the sense that they were produced under Alexandrian influences. Perhaps a distinguishing terminology could be "early Alexandrian" (pre-Constantine) and "later Alexandrian" (post-Constantine). Manuscripts designated as "early Alexandrian" would generally be purer, less editorialized. Manuscripts designated "later Alexandrian" would display editorialization, as well as the influence of other textual traditions.

The "early Alexandrian" text is reflected in many second and third-century manuscripts. As has been mentioned previously, on the top of the list is $\mathfrak{P}^{75}$, the work of a competent and careful scribe. Not far behind in quality is $\mathfrak{P}^{4}$+$\mathfrak{P}^{64}$+$\mathfrak{P}^{67}$, the work of an excellent copyist. Other extremely good copies are $\mathfrak{P}^{1}$, $\mathfrak{P}^{20}$, $\mathfrak{P}^{23}$, $\mathfrak{P}^{27}$, $\mathfrak{P}^{28}$, $\mathfrak{P}^{32}$, $\mathfrak{P}^{39}$, $\mathfrak{P}^{46}$, $\mathfrak{P}^{49+65}$, $\mathfrak{P}^{66}$ (in its corrected form), $\mathfrak{P}^{70}$, $\mathfrak{P}^{77}$, $\mathfrak{P}^{87}$, $\mathfrak{P}^{90}$, $\mathfrak{P}^{91}$, $\mathfrak{P}^{100}$, $\mathfrak{P}^{104}$, $\mathfrak{P}^{106}$, $\mathfrak{P}^{108}$, $\mathfrak{P}^{111}$, $\mathfrak{P}^{115}$, $\mathfrak{P}^{119}$, $\mathfrak{P}^{120}$, and $\mathfrak{P}^{125}$ (all of the second and third centuries). The "later Alexandrian" text, which displays editorial polishing, is exhibited in a few manuscripts, such as T (fifth century), Ψ (seventh century), L (eighth century), 33 (ninth century), 1739 (a tenth-century manuscript copied from a fourth-century Alexandrian manuscript much like $\mathfrak{P}^{46}$) and 579 (thirteenth century).

Beginning in the fifth century, Byzantine-type manuscripts began to make their influence in Egypt. Some manuscripts dated around 400 that came from Egypt clearly reflect this influence. Codex Alexandrinus (A), in the Gospels, is probably the best example. Other Egyptian manuscripts of this era, such as Codex Sinaiticus (א) and Codex Washingtonianus (W) display large-scale harmonization in the Gospels, which cannot be directly linked to any kind of recension.

The Alands have categorized manuscripts without using geographical labels, such as "Alexandrian" or "Western." They have noted four kinds of manuscripts in the early New Testament manuscripts, which they call "strict," "at least normal," "normal," and "free."[5] In a sense, these categories speak not only of how a scribe produced a manuscript but indicate how much or how little the scribe allowed himself to interact with the text he or she was copying —in the sense of making changes.

The Alands indicate that the "strict" text is found in those manuscripts in which the scribes reproduced the text of an exemplar with greater fidelity than in the "normal" text—although still with certain characteristic liberties. The "strict" text is the best copy in that the scribe who produced it allowed for little variation from his exemplar in the copying process. The "strict" manuscripts are those that were usually produced by professional scribes or those attuned to Alexandrian scriptoral practices. The second category, called "at least normal," includes those manuscripts that are "normal" but also display a distinct tendency toward a "strict" text. The Alands say the "normal" text is found in manuscripts in which the scribes transmitted the exemplar with a limited amount of variation characteristic of the New Testament textual tradition. Other papyri, however, display a very "free" rendition of the text—that is, they are characterized as having a greater degree of variation than the "normal" text.

Using these four categories, the Alands classify the following papyri as follows:

strict

$\mathfrak{P}^{1}$
$\mathfrak{P}^{23}$
$\mathfrak{P}^{27}$
$\mathfrak{P}^{35}$
$\mathfrak{P}^{39}$
$\mathfrak{P}^{64}$/67
$\mathfrak{P}^{65}$

$\mathfrak{P}^{70}$
$\mathfrak{P}^{75}$

at least normal
$\mathfrak{P}^{15}$
$\mathfrak{P}^{22}$
$\mathfrak{P}^{30}$
$\mathfrak{P}^{32}$
$\mathfrak{P}^{49}$
$\mathfrak{P}^{72}$ (with peculiarities)
$\mathfrak{P}^{77}$

normal
$\mathfrak{P}^{4}$
$\mathfrak{P}^{5}$
$\mathfrak{P}^{12}$
$\mathfrak{P}^{16}$
$\mathfrak{P}^{18}$
$\mathfrak{P}^{20}$
$\mathfrak{P}^{28}$
$\mathfrak{P}^{47}$
$\mathfrak{P}^{52}$
$\mathfrak{P}^{87}$

free
$\mathfrak{P}^{9}$
$\mathfrak{P}^{13}$(?)
$\mathfrak{P}^{37}$
$\mathfrak{P}^{40}$
$\mathfrak{P}^{45}$
$\mathfrak{P}^{46}$
$\mathfrak{P}^{66}$
$\mathfrak{P}^{69}$
$\mathfrak{P}^{78}$

I do not agree with the Alands' categorizations of several of the papyri. First, some of the manuscripts belong to the same codex or—at least—were done by the same scribe. Therefore, they must be in the same category: $\mathfrak{P}^{4}$+$\mathfrak{P}^{64}$+$\mathfrak{P}^{67}$, $\mathfrak{P}^{15}$+$\mathfrak{P}^{16}$, $\mathfrak{P}^{49}$+$\mathfrak{P}^{65}$. Second, I would add more to the "strict" category, such as $\mathfrak{P}^{4}$+$\mathfrak{P}^{64}$+$\mathfrak{P}^{67}$, $\mathfrak{P}^{30}$, $\mathfrak{P}^{32}$, $\mathfrak{P}^{49}$+$\mathfrak{P}^{65}$, and $\mathfrak{P}^{87}$. Third, the following manuscripts are not "free": $\mathfrak{P}^{13}$, $\mathfrak{P}^{46}$, $\mathfrak{P}^{66}$ (in its corrected form); they are normal, even "at least normal." $\mathfrak{P}^{66}$ in its uncorrected form is free, but not in its corrected form. Finally, several other early papyri need to be categorized. These criticisms aside, the Alands' categorizations are a step in the right direction.

Using different terminology and with a different emphasis, I would call the "strict" manuscripts and the "at least normal" manuscripts, "reliable" texts. These manuscripts, produced with acumen, display a standard of excellence. The scribes' motivation for accuracy could have come from their respect for the sacredness of the text or from their scriptoral training, or both. In any event, they produced reliable copies that largely preserve the original wording of authorized published texts. In my estimation, these manuscripts are as follows: $\mathfrak{P}^{1}$, $\mathfrak{P}^{4}$+$\mathfrak{P}^{64}$+$\mathfrak{P}^{67}$, $\mathfrak{P}^{23}$, $\mathfrak{P}^{27}$, $\mathfrak{P}^{30}$, $\mathfrak{P}^{32}$, $\mathfrak{P}^{35}$, $\mathfrak{P}^{39}$, $\mathfrak{P}^{52}$, $\mathfrak{P}^{65}$, $\mathfrak{P}^{70}$, $\mathfrak{P}^{75}$, $\mathfrak{P}^{77}$, $\mathfrak{P}^{87}$, $\mathfrak{P}^{90}$, $\mathfrak{P}^{91}$, $\mathfrak{P}^{101}$, $\mathfrak{P}^{104}$, $\mathfrak{P}^{106}$, $\mathfrak{P}^{108}$, $\mathfrak{P}^{111}$, $\mathfrak{P}^{115}$, $\mathfrak{P}^{119}$, $\mathfrak{P}^{120}$, and $\mathfrak{P}^{125}$. It is to these manuscripts that we look for the preservation of the original wording of the various writings of the published New Testament. This is not to say that these manuscripts are perfect. Many of these manuscripts contain singular readings and some "Alexandrian" polishing, which needs to be sifted out. Once this is done, I think we can be quite confident that we usually have the original wording of the published New Testament text.

Some may argue that we can only be confident that we have good manuscripts of an "early" form of the text but not necessarily of the originally published text. This hypothesis cannot be disproved. However, I think it is highly doubtful for four reasons: (1) The intervening time between the publication date of various New Testament books (from AD 60–90) and the date of several of our extant manuscripts (from AD 110–200) is narrow, thereby giving us manuscripts that are probably only three to five "manuscript generations" removed from the originally published texts. (2) We have no knowledge that any of these manuscripts go back to an early "form" that post-dates the published form. (3) We are certain that there was no major Alexandrian recension in the second century. (4) Text critics have not been able to detect any other second-century textual aberrations, such as the D text, which was probably created near the end of the century, not the beginning. Thus, it stands to reason that these "reliable" manuscripts are excellent copies of the authorized published texts.

The Canons of Textual Criticism

Most modern textual critics use one rule-of-thumb or "canon" as they go about doing the task of recovering the original wording of the text. They try to abide by the rule that the reading that is most likely original is the one that best explains the variants. This canon is actually a development of Bengel's maxim, *proclivi scriptoni praestat ardua* ("the harder reading is to be preferred"),[6] a maxim he formulated in responding to his own question as to which variant reading is likely to have arisen out of the others.

This overarching canon for internal criticism involves several criteria, which one scholar or another has posited and/or implemented during the past three hundred years of New Testament textual criticism. Having made a thorough historical survey of the development of canons for internal criticism, Epp summarized all the criteria as follows:

1. A variant's status as the shorter or shortest reading.
2. A variant's status as the harder or hardest reading.
3. A variant's fitness to account for the origin, development, or presence of all other readings.
4. A variant's conformity to the author's style and vocabulary.
5. A variant's conformity to the author's theology or ideology.
6. A variant's conformity to Koine (rather than Attic) Greek.
7. A variant's conformity to Semitic forms of expression.
8. A variant's lack of conformity to parallel passages or to extraneous items in its context generally.
9. A variant's lack of conformity to Old Testament passages.
10. A variant's lack of conformity to liturgical forms and usages.
11. A variant's lack of conformity to extrinsic doctrinal views.[7]

It should be admitted that some of these criteria are problematic when implemented. Two textual critics, using the same principle to examine the same variant unit, will not agree. For example, with respect to the fourth canon, one critic will argue that one variant was produced by a copyist attempting to emulate the author's style; the other will claim the same variant has to be original because it accords with the author's style. And with respect to the fifth canon, one will argue that one variant was produced by an orthodox scribe attempting to rid the text of a reading that could be used to promote heterodoxy or heresy; another will claim that the same variant has to be original because it is orthodox and accords with Christian doctrine (thus a heterodoxical or heretical scribe must have changed it).

Furthermore, internal criticism allows for the possibility that the reading selected for the text can be taken from any manuscript of any date. This produces subjective eclecticism. Those who advocate "thoroughgoing eclecticism," such as Kilpatrick and Boismard, have argued for the legitimacy of certain variant readings on the basis of internal criticism alone. The readings they favor do have some manuscript support, but often it comes from one Latin version (versus all Greek witnesses), or a late minuscule, or the testimony of some church father. Modern textual scholars try to temper the subjectivism by employing a method called "reasoned eclecticism." According to Holmes, "Reasoned eclecticism applies a combination of internal and external considerations, evaluating the *character* of the variants in light of the MSS evidence and vice versa in order to obtain a balanced view of the matter and as a check upon purely subjective tendencies."[8]

In this volume, manuscript evidence is given priority of place inasmuch as the readings of the earliest manuscripts are always followed. In this sense, documentary evidence has priority of place.[9] When the testimony of the earliest manuscripts is divided, I apply the principles of textual criticism in accord with reasoned eclecticism. I must admit, however, that the original reading cannot always be determined. In some instances, two options are viable candidates for being the original wording. These are noted throughout.

The Nomina Sacra (Sacred Names) in the New Testament

There is one final feature in New Testament manuscripts that needs our attention—that is, the presence of the nomina sacra on nearly every page of the New Testament. Those who have read the New Testament in an English version have missed out on seeing a fascinating feature of the written word. Even those who have read it in Greek editions have not seen this because it is featured only in actual manuscripts. What I am speaking about is a phenomenon that occurred when the books of the New Testament were written, published, and distributed in the first century and thereafter. Either the writers themselves or the very earliest copyists used a special written form for the divine names. Instead of writing out in full (in *plene*) the Greek words *kurios* (Lord), *Iesous* (Jesus), *Christos* (Christ), *theos* (God), and *pneuma* (Spirit), the

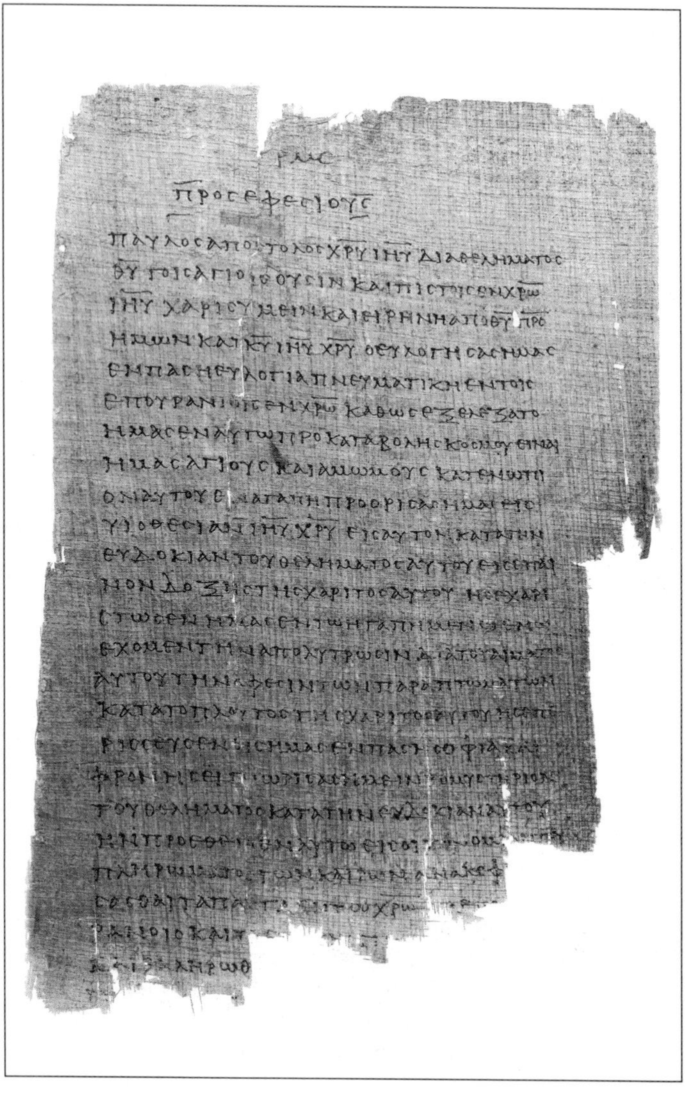

Lines 1–26 of Ephesians (1:1–11) from 𝔓[46] at the University of Michigan.

writers and/or earliest scribes wrote these words in special abbreviated (or contracted) forms. Very few know about this, even those who read the Greek New Testament, because the nomina sacra (sacred names) are not replicated in any fashion in printed editions of the Greek New Testament.

Anyone who reads the ancient manuscripts of the Greek New Testament is struck by this phenomenon: the names *kurios* (Lord), *Iesous* (Jesus), *Christos* (Christ), and *theos* (God) are written in this unique fashion. These four titles are the primary and most primitive divine names to be written in a special way; they can be seen in all the earliest Greek manuscripts.[10]

Another early divine name written in a special way is *pneuma* (Spirit); it may be as early as the other four or it could have been developed slightly later. These specially written names are called "nomina sacra," meaning sacred names (the singular is "nomen sacrum"). The inventor of the term "nomina sacra" was L. Traube. After his study on the nomina sacra, the most thorough study was done by A. H. R. E. Paap.[11]

In the manuscript on the previous page (namely, $\mathfrak{P}^{46}$, showing the first page of Ephesians) one can see the nomina sacra, as follows. Line 1: $\overline{\mathrm{XP}\Upsilon}$ (nomen sacrum for XPICTOΥ= of Christ), $\overline{\mathrm{IH}\Upsilon}$ (nomen sacrum for IHΥCOΥ = of Jesus), in the expression "an apostle of Christ Jesus." Line 2: $\overline{\Theta\Upsilon}$ (nomen sacrum for ΘEOΥ = of God), in the expression "will of God." Lines 2 and 3: $\overline{\mathrm{XP}}$ (nomen sacrum for XPICTΩ = in Christ), $\overline{\mathrm{IH}\Upsilon}$ (nomen sacrum for IHCOΥ = in Jesus) in the expression "faith in Christ Jesus." Line 4: $\overline{\mathrm{K}\Upsilon}$ (nomen sacrum for KΥPIOΥ = of the Lord), $\overline{\mathrm{IH}\Upsilon}$ (nomen sacrum for IHΥCOΥ = of Jesus), and $\overline{\mathrm{XP}\Upsilon}$(nomen sacrum for XPICTOΥ = of Christ) in the expression "and of the Lord Jesus Christ."

Scattered across the pages of nearly every extant Greek New Testament manuscript can be seen the following nomina sacra:

$\overline{\mathrm{KC}}$ for KΥPIOC (*Kurios*) = LORD

$\overline{\mathrm{IH}}$ or $\overline{\mathrm{IC}}$ or $\overline{\mathrm{IHC}}$ for IHCOΥC (*Iesous*) = JESUS

$\overline{\text{XP}}$ or $\overline{\text{XC}}$ or $\overline{\text{XPC}}$ for XPICTOC (*Christos*) = CHRIST

$\overline{\Theta\text{C}}$ for ΘEOC (*theos*) = GOD

$\overline{\Pi\text{NA}}$ for ΠNEΥMA (*pneuma*) = SPIRIT

The earliest Christian writers used three ways to write the nomina sacra. The first way is called "suspension"—that is, the first two letters of the name are written and the rest are suspended. This is illustrated by $\overline{\text{IH}}$, which are the first two letters of IHCOΥC (Jesus). The second way is called "contraction"—that is, the first and last letters are written, with the in-between letters omitted. This is illustrated by $\overline{\text{IC}}$, which are the first and last letters of IHCOΥC (*Iesous*). The third way is a longer form of contraction, as in $\overline{\text{IHC}}$, which has the first two letters and the last letter of IHCOΥC (*Iesous*).

After the scribe wrote the suspended or contracted form, he would place an overbar over the entire name, as in $\overline{\text{IC}}$. It is quite likely that the placing of the overbar was a carryover from the way scribes wrote documents; scribes everywhere had a habit of using the overbar to signal an abbreviation. This was especially common for the use of numerals, which would be written as $\overline{\text{IA}}$ or "eleven," $\overline{\text{IB}}$ for "twelve," etc. The overbar stroked above the word was a signal to the reader that the word could not be pronounced as written. The reader would have to know what the coded form signified in order to read it correctly.[12] It should also be mentioned that placing an overbar over the contracted or suspended nomen sacrum was a great help for the oral reader working his or her way through *scriptura continuum* (words run into each other, as was common in ancient Greek texts.)

The nomina sacra for "Lord," "Jesus," "Christ," "God," and "Spirit" are present in all of the extant, second-century New Testament manuscripts where one or more of these nomina sacra are extant. The second-century manuscripts that clearly show these nomina sacra are as follows:

$\mathfrak{P}^{4}$+$\mathfrak{P}^{64}$+$\mathfrak{P}^{67}$, Matthew, Luke
$\mathfrak{P}^{20}$, James

$\mathfrak{P}^{27}$, Romans
$\mathfrak{P}^{32}$, Titus
$\mathfrak{P}^{46}$, Paul's Epistles
$\mathfrak{P}^{66}$, John
$\mathfrak{P}^{75}$, Luke, John
$\mathfrak{P}^{90}$, John[13]
$\mathfrak{P}^{118}$, Romans

The nomina sacra for "Lord," "Jesus," "God," "Christ," and "Spirit" are also present in all the third-century New Testament manuscripts (including those dated c. 200), where one or more of these names is preserved in the extant text:

$\mathfrak{P}^{1}$, Matthew
$\mathfrak{P}^{5}$, John
$\mathfrak{P}^{9}$, 1 John
$\mathfrak{P}^{12}$, Hebrews
$\mathfrak{P}^{13}$, Hebrews
$\mathfrak{P}^{15}+\mathfrak{P}^{16}$, 1 Corinthians, Philippians
$\mathfrak{P}^{17}$, Hebrews
$\mathfrak{P}^{18}$, Revelation
$\mathfrak{P}^{21}$, Matthew
$\mathfrak{P}^{22}$, John
$\mathfrak{P}^{\text{23vid}}$, James
$\mathfrak{P}^{24}$, Revelation
$\mathfrak{P}^{28}$, John
$\mathfrak{P}^{29}$, Acts
$\mathfrak{P}^{30}$, 1 Thessalonians
$\mathfrak{P}^{35}$, Matthew
$\mathfrak{P}^{37}$, Matthew
$\mathfrak{P}^{38}$, Acts
$\mathfrak{P}^{39}$, John
$\mathfrak{P}^{40}$, Romans
$\mathfrak{P}^{45}$, Gospels, Acts
$\mathfrak{P}^{47}$, Revelation

$\mathfrak{P}^{48}$, Acts
$\mathfrak{P}^{49}$+$\mathfrak{P}^{65}$, Ephesians, 1 Thessalonians
$\mathfrak{P}^{50}$, Acts
$\mathfrak{P}^{53}$, Matthew
$\mathfrak{P}^{69}$, Luke
$\mathfrak{P}^{70vid}$, Matthew
$\mathfrak{P}^{78}$, Jude
$\mathfrak{P}^{80vid}$, John
$\mathfrak{P}^{86}$, Matthew
$\mathfrak{P}^{91}$, Acts
$\mathfrak{P}^{92}$, 1 and 2 Thessalonians
$\mathfrak{P}^{100}$, James
$\mathfrak{P}^{101}$, Matthew
$\mathfrak{P}^{106}$, John
$\mathfrak{P}^{108}$, John
$\mathfrak{P}^{110}$, Matthew
$\mathfrak{P}^{111}$, Luke
$\mathfrak{P}^{113}$, Romans
$\mathfrak{P}^{114}$, Hebrews
$\mathfrak{P}^{115}$, Revelation
$\mathfrak{P}^{120}$, John
$\mathfrak{P}^{121}$, John
$\mathfrak{P}^{125}$, 1 Peter
0162, John
0171, Matthew, Luke
0189, Acts
0220, Romans[14]
P. Oxyrhynchus 5073 (amulet, Mark 1:1–2)

The nomina sacra are also present in Greek Old Testament manuscripts and other Christian writings produced by Christians.[15] This includes several second-century manuscripts noted below:

Old Testament:
P. Chester Beatty VI, Numbers, Deuteronomy

P. Baden 4.56 (P. Heidelberg inv. 8), Exodus and Deuteronomy
P. Antinoopolis 7, Psalms
PSI 921, Psalms
P. Oxyrhynchus 1074, Exodus
P. Chester Beatty Papyrus VIII, Jeremiah
P. Chester Beatty Papyrus IX, Ezekiel, Daniel, Esther{s}6{xs}

Other Christian Writings:
P. Geneva 253, Christian homily
P. Egerton 2, Unknown Gospel
P. Oxyrhynchus 405, fragment of Irenaeus
P. Oxyrhynchus 406, Unknown Gospel?
P. Oxyrhynchus 5072, Uncanonical Gospel?

One of the main reasons we know that the Old Testament manuscripts are Christian manuscripts and not Jewish is the presence of nomina sacra in the text. Significantly, not one copy of the Greek Old Testament found at Qumran has these nomina sacra, because this was a Jewish, not a Christian community. Jews never wrote nomina sacra the way Christians did. The Jews did things differently for one divine name and one divine name only: Yahweh. Jewish scribes would frequently write this in its Hebrew contracted form (even in paleo-Hebrew letters) and then continue on with the Greek text. Christians used the word KΥPIOC (*kurios* = Lord) in place of Yahweh (YHWH), and wrote it in nomen sacrum form. Many Greek Old Testament manuscripts produced by Christians display this nomen sacrum. This can be seen in all six of the second-century Greek Old Testament manuscripts noted above.

The earliest copies of the New Testament writings (perhaps some of the autographs themselves) included these specially inscripted forms for the sacred names. These writings made the rounds from church to church and thereby influenced the scribes in each church to write certain divine titles as nomina sacra. Since there was no official rule book as to the exact form in which the nomina sacra were to be written, there were some slight variations in form. As noted above, some writers and/

or scribes used the first letter and last letter of the name; others used the first two letters and the last letter. Thus, for example, XPICTOC (Christ) was written either as $\overline{XP}$ (a very rare form), $\overline{XPC}$, or $\overline{XC}$ (the most common form). In whatever form, XPICTOC (Christ) was always written as a nomen sacrum.

The nomina sacra for "Lord," "Jesus," "Christ," "God," and "Spirit" must have been created in the first century. The earliest form seems to have been a contraction of "Lord" (KYPIOC, *kurios*), written as $\overline{KC}$. The next name to have been written as a nomen sacrum was "Jesus" (IHCOYC, *Iesous*), written as $\overline{IH}$ or $\overline{IC}$ or $\overline{IHC}$. The contracted form for "Christ" (XPICTOC) was early; it was maintained in most manuscripts in the form $\overline{XC}$. A longer form of contraction was also used: $\overline{XPC}$. Only two manuscripts display the suspended form, $\overline{XP}$—$\mathfrak{P}^{18}$ (Rev. 1:5) and $\mathfrak{P}^{45}$ (one time; Acts 16:18). The title "God" was contracted as $\overline{\Theta C}$ from earliest times and remained constant thereafter.

It is difficult to say whether the nomina sacra were first written with the suspended form and then later with the contracted form, or vice versa. In arguing for the suspended form, it could be said that several early manuscripts show the suspended form. However, one of the earliest Christian manuscripts, P. Chester Beatty VI, shows the contracted form, as do several other early Christian manuscripts. The suspended form of abbreviation was very common in both documentary and literary works from the first century BC on into the second century AD. McNamee wrote, "Methods of abbreviation throughout [this] period covered are the same in literary as in documentary papyri. The most common means was suspension, in which one or more letters were omitted from the end of a word."[16]

If the prevailing practice of suspended abbreviations in the papyri was a primary influence on the formation of the Christian nomina sacra, then the suspended forms came first. If so, it is possible that scribes found these to be impractical from a grammatical perspective inasmuch as the suspensed form could not denote grammatical function. As such, the suspended form $\overline{IH}$ may have been elongated to $\overline{IHC}$ (nominative), $\overline{IHY}$ (genitive), and $\overline{IHN}$ (accusative), thereby creating a contracted form. However, this phenomenon can be argued only for "Jesus." None of the other divine names went in this direction orthographically.

It could be argued that the contracted form (which allows for grammatical denotation from the onset) was primary—written either in short form (using the first letter and last) or longer form (using the first two letters and last). The contracted form was also used for abbreviations in the Hellenistic writings of the first century AD, though not as extensively as the suspended form. Certain Christian scribes could have emulated this practice from the contemporary literature. Or, more likely, the contracted form could have been modeled after the Hebrew tetragrammaton, YHWH. Since the contracted form is the prevailing form for all the primary nomina sacra (only "Jesus" and "Christ" appear in suspended form), it stands to reason that this form was primary and the suspended secondary. But I cannot be dogmatic about this.

A few other terms may have been written as nomina sacra in the original writings or, at least, in the very earliest copies: the Greek words for "cross" (*stauros*) and "crucify" (*stauromai*). I say this because these words were written as nomina sacra in the earliest New Testament manuscripts ($\mathfrak{P}^{45}$, $\mathfrak{P}^{46}$, $\mathfrak{P}^{47}$, $\mathfrak{P}^{66}$, $\mathfrak{P}^{75}$). In due course, two other divine names began to appear as nomina sacra: "Father" and "Son." "Father" was contracted by using the first letter and last letter of ΠΑΤΗΡ as $\overline{\Pi \mathrm{P}}$, and Son (ϒΙΟC) was contracted as $\overline{\Upsilon \mathrm{C}}$. These two divine names were sometimes written out in full (in *plene*) and sometimes written as nomina sacra in the early manuscripts. And sometimes there was discrepancy within the same manuscript. Thus, we can tell that these two titles were probably not written as nomina sacra in the original manuscripts but were a later development. Beginning in the second and third centuries some other titles were treated as nomina sacra—namely, "Son of Man," "Son of David," and "Christian."

As noted before, it is easy to spot any of the nomina sacra on the page of a Greek New Testament manuscript by looking for the overbars. The special written forms of the nomina sacra would not be enigmatic to Christian readers; they could easily decipher them. In fact, these forms would heighten their importance in the text and prompt the readers (lectors) to give them special attention when reading the text out loud to the congregation.

One of the primary results of making a name a nomen sacrum was that it desecularized the term; it uplifted the term to sacred status. For example, scribes could differentiate between "the Lord" and "lord" / "sir" / "master" by writing $\overline{\text{KC}}$ or *kurios* (in *plene*), and they could distinguish between "Spirit" (the divine Spirit) and "spirit" (the human spirit) by writing the first as a nomen sacrum ($\overline{\Pi\text{NA}}$ and any other kind of spirit as *pneuma* (in *plene*). The term *pneuma* in ordinary, secular Greek meant "wind," "breath," or "spirit." Writing it as a nomen sacrum signals that this is the divine Spirit.

When one studies the extant Christian manuscripts, a general chronological evolution of which names were written as nomina sacra and which were not emerges. First, the name *Kurios* (Lord) was chosen and/or *Iēsous* (Jesus). These two were soon followed by *Christos* (Christ), *theos* (God), and *pneuma* (Spirit). These five were primary nomina sacra by the beginning of the second century. The noun "cross" and the verb "crucify" were also dignified as a nomina sacra by the beginning of the second century. From the beginning of the second century and into the third, other names were experimented with: *anthrōpos* (man), *patēr* (Father), *huios* (Son), *Dauid* (David) *Ierousalem* (Jerusalem), *Israēl* (Israel), and *ouranos* (heaven). Some scribes treated them as a nomen sacrum; others did not. Some scribes in the same manuscript treated them both as nomina sacra and not as such. By the time we get to the fourth century, some experimentation was still going on (as in codex Sinaiticus), but for the most part there seems to have been a conscious effort to limit the nomina sacra to "Lord," "Jesus," "Christ," "God," and "Spirit."

In my estimation, the origination of the nomina sacra could have come from one of two sources: (1) a scribe or scribes (whether Jewish Christian or Gentile Christian) created a nomen sacrum form for *kurios* (Lord) that reflected knowledge of and purposeful distinction from the Hebrew tetragrammaton, YHWH, or (2) a scribe or scribes (whether Jewish Christian or Gentile Christian) created a nomen sacrum form for *kurios* (Lord) that reflected knowledge of and purposeful distinction from the presence of *kurios* in Hellenistic literature as describing a particular god or Ceasar. In the second option, the creation of the nomen sacrum could have also been for *theos* for the same reasons. (For a complete discourse on these two views, see Comfort, *Encountering the Manuscripts*, 206–215). For further discussion on the Nomina Sacra, see Appendix II.

Endnotes

1. Westcott and Hort, *New Testament in the Original Greek*, 17; Colwell "Hort Redivivus: A Plea and a Program," *Studies in Methodology in Textual Criticism of the New Testament*, 152.
2. This is illustrated in my doctoral dissertation, "The Scribe as Interpreter: A New Look at New Testament Textual Criticism according to the Reader Response Theory." This is summarized in an article, "Scribes as Readers: Looking at New Textual Variants according to Reader Reception Analysis," *Neotestamentica* (2004), 38.1:28–53.
3. Westcott and Hort, *New Testament in the Original Greek*, 250–251.
4. Fee, "$\mathfrak{P}^{75}$, $\mathfrak{P}^{66}$, and Origen: The Myth of the Early Textual Recension in Alexandria." *New Dimensions in New Testament Study*, 19–45.
5. Alands, *Text of the New Testament*, 93–95.
6. Bengel, *Gnomon Novi Testamenti.*
7. Epp, "The Eclectic Method in New Testament Textual Criticism: Solution or Symptom?" *Harvard Theological Review* 69 (1976), 243.
8. Holmes, "New Testament Textual Criticism." *Introducing New Testament Interpretation,* 53.
9. Comfort, *New Testament Text and Translation Commentary*, Appendix D, 881–884.
10. The earliest translations of the New Testament in Coptic and Latin also have their own form of nomina sacra for "Lord," "Jesus," "God," and "Christ."
11. The inventor of the term "nomina sacra" was L. Traube, in *Nomina Sacra* (Munich, 1906). After his study on the nomina sacra, the most thorough study was done by A. H. R. E. Paap, *Nomina Sacra in the Greek Papyri of the First Five Centuries A.D.* (Leiden: E. J Brill, 1959).

Endnotes

12. For a full explanation of these matters, see C. H. Roberts, *Manuscript, Society, and Belief in Early Christian Egypt*, chpt. 2.
13. Among the earliest manuscripts we see all the nomina sacra used. In the $\mathfrak{P}^{4}$+$\mathfrak{P}^{64}$+$\mathfrak{P}^{67}$, the scribe used nomina sacra for "Lord," "Jesus," "God," and "Spirit." In $\mathfrak{P}^{32}$, "God" is contracted. In $\mathfrak{P}^{46}$ we see contractions for "Lord," "Jesus," "God," "Christ," and "Spirit." In $\mathfrak{P}^{66}$, we see contractions for "Jesus," "Lord," "Christ," "God," and "Spirit." In $\mathfrak{P}^{90}$, the nomen sacrum abbreviation for "Jesus" appears in John 19:5, and it fits the lacunae for John 18:37 and 19:2. In $\mathfrak{P}^{107}$, the lacuna has to be filled with nomina sacra for "Son" and Father" due to the spacing. In $\mathfrak{P}^{77}$, $\mathfrak{P}^{87}$, $\mathfrak{P}^{98}$, $\mathfrak{P}^{103}$, and $\mathfrak{P}^{109}$ (all second-century manuscripts) there are no extant portions or even lacuna where nomina sacra occur. See *The Text of The Earliest New Testament Greek Manuscripts* (Comfort and Barrett) for a new transcription of each of these manuscripts.
14. See *The Text of The Earliest Greek New Testament Manuscripts* for a new transcription of each of these manuscripts.
15. Other second-century Old Testament manuscripts believed to be Christian (because they are codices and not scrolls) but lacking nomina sacra are as follows: P. Yale 1, Genesis; Bodleian Gr. Bib. g. 5, Psalms (note: I think the transcription should be reconstructed using a nomen sacrum for *theos*); P. Lips. inv. 170, Psalms. For a listing and bibliography of these second-century Christian Old Testament MSS (all codices), see C. H. Roberts, *Manuscript, Society, and Belief in Early Christian Egypt*, 13.
16. Kathleen McNamee, *Abbreviations in Greek Literary Papyric and Ostraca*, xi, xxx.

Chapter Two

An Annotated List of the Manuscripts of the New Testament

This chapter provides an annotated list of all the most significant manuscripts. The earliest manuscripts (second to fourth century) are, generally speaking, the most important because they provide the earliest testimony to the original wording of the New Testament text. As such, I provide a brief discussion about the dating of each early manuscript (prior to AD 300). According to the First Appendix of the Nestle Aland text, *Novum Testamentum Graece* (27th edition), there are only four New Testament papyri listed as being second century: $\mathfrak{P}^{52}$, $\mathfrak{P}^{90}$, $\mathfrak{P}^{98}$(?), and $\mathfrak{P}^{104}$. A few others are listed as "c. 200"—$\mathfrak{P}^{32}$, $\mathfrak{P}^{46}$, $\mathfrak{P}^{64+67}$, and $\mathfrak{P}^{66}$. This is far too conservative, in my opinion, as well as in the opinion of some other paleographers (whom I will cite throughout). There are 16 manuscripts that belong in the second century: $\mathfrak{P}^{4}$ (with $\mathfrak{P}^{64+67}$), $\mathfrak{P}^{20}$, $\mathfrak{P}^{27}$, $\mathfrak{P}^{32}$, $\mathfrak{P}^{46}$, $\mathfrak{P}^{52}$, $\mathfrak{P}^{66}$, $\mathfrak{P}^{75}$, $\mathfrak{P}^{77}$ (with $\mathfrak{P}^{103}$), $\mathfrak{P}^{87}$, $\mathfrak{P}^{98}$, $\mathfrak{P}^{104}$, $\mathfrak{P}^{109}$, $\mathfrak{P}^{115}$, and $\mathfrak{P}^{118}$. Furthermore, I list 14 manuscripts as "c. 200": $\mathfrak{P}^{1}$, $\mathfrak{P}^{13}$, $\mathfrak{P}^{23}$, $\mathfrak{P}^{29}$, $\mathfrak{P}^{38}$, $\mathfrak{P}^{45}$, $\mathfrak{P}^{95}$, $\mathfrak{P}^{106}$, $\mathfrak{P}^{107}$, $\mathfrak{P}^{108}$, $\mathfrak{P}^{109}$, $\mathfrak{P}^{113}$, $\mathfrak{P}^{121}$, and 0189. For the sake of brevity, I will get straight to the point about morphological comparisons, without always noting how each of these manuscripts (which I date c. 200) was originally dated in its *editio principes*.

Papyrologists date manuscripts according to comparative paleography. As a rule of thumb, a literary manuscript with a documentary text on the verso can be dated with a high degree of certainty to within 25–50 years—the time in which a literary text would have been surrendered to documentary use. As such, many literary texts with documentary texts on the verso have been dated with confidence. (Sometimes literary texts were written on the verso of documentary texts; these will be noted throughout.) If another manuscript has similar morphology to such a dated literary text, then the dating can be made with confidence. Several of the second century New Testament papyri have morphology comparable to these kinds of dated, second-century manuscripts. Other New Testament manuscripts are given dates based on morphological features prominent in certain time periods.

To date, there are 127 New Testament papyrus manuscripts, about 300 uncial manuscripts (listed with an 0 first, as in 0162 and 0171), and about 2,800 minuscule manuscripts (listed with numbers from 1 to 2818). The reader should see listings by the Alands in *The Text of the New Testament* (96–101, 105, 128) and see Appendix 1, "Codices Graeci et Latini" in *Novum Testamentum Graece* (27th edition). For more recent papyri, see *The Text of the Earliest New Testament Greek Manuscripts* (Comfort and Barrett, 2001). Metzger adds 2,209 Greek lectionaries to this list.[1]

Complete lists with short descriptions of all the manuscripts are provided by the Alands in *The Text of the New Testament* (section three, "The Manuscripts of the Greek New Testament"). Metzger, in *The Text of the New Testament* (1968; seventh printing, 1980), has also supplied lists and descriptions of the New Testament manuscripts. References to Aland and Metzger in the following descriptions come from these two sources. A fuller discussion of the early papyrus manuscripts (with bibliography) can be found in *The Text of the Earliest New Testament Greek Manuscripts* (editors, Comfort and Barrett), abbreviated as *Text of Earliest MSS.*

For each manuscript listed below, the siglum is listed first, followed by bibliography for the *editio principes* (publication of the first transcription), housing location of the manuscript, date of manuscript (the date for each manuscript prior to AD 300 is discussed below), and comments concerning the textual character of the manuscript.

The bibliography provided for each of the following manuscripts is usually the primary edition of the transcription (the *editio principes*) of the text and/or facsimile edition. A complete bibliography for these manuscripts (and many more) can be found in J. K. Elliott's work, *A Bibliography of Greek New Testament Manuscripts* (Cambridge University Press, 1989). The manuscripts listed below are among the most important witnesses to the text of the New Testament.

The Papyrus Manuscripts

𝔓[1] *(P. Oxy. 2)*

* Grenfell and Hunt, *Oxyrhynchus Papyri* I (1898), no. 2, 4–7.
* Matthew 1:1–9, 12, 14–20
* Philadelphia, Pennsylvania: University Museum, University of Pennsylvania (E 2746)
* c. 200. Morphological likeness to P. Marmarica strongly suggests a date for 𝔓[1] to be c. 200. P. Marmarica has a solid date because it is a literary text on whose verso are land registers dated between AD 191 and 215; this means the literary text must be c. 200. In a personal letter to me, Kim dated 𝔓[1] as c. 200
* The copyist of 𝔓[1] seems to have faithfully followed a very reliable exemplar. Where there are major variants, 𝔓[1] agrees with the best Alexandrian witnesses, especially B, from which it rarely varies. I have studied the actual manuscript.

𝔓[2] *(P. Firenze 7134)*

* E. Pistelli, "Papiri Evangelica" in *Revista di Studi religiosi* VI (1906), 129.
* John 12:12–15 (The Coptic on the other side contains Luke 7:22–26).
* Firenze: Museum Egizio (inv. 7134)
* Post 500
* This Greek-Coptic manuscript is too small to assess its textual affinities.

𝔓[3] *(P. Vienna 2323)*

* C. Wessley, *Wiener Studien* VII (1885), 69ff.

* Luke 7:36–45; 10:38–42
* Vienna, Osterreichischen Nationabibliothek (Pap. G. 2323)
* Sixth/seventh century
* The manuscript is strongly Alexandrian.

$\mathfrak{P}^{4+64+67}$ *(fragments of same codex)*

* $\mathfrak{P}^{4}$ (P. Paris Bibl. Nat. Suppl. Gr. 1120) contains portions of Luke 1–6. Parts of this were originally published by Vincent Scheil, "Archeologie, Varia," *Revue Biblique* 1 (1892), 113–115. A more complete transcription was provided by J. Merell, "Nouveaux fragments papyrus IV," in *Revue Biblique* 47 (1938), 5–22. $\mathfrak{P}^{64}$ (P. Magdalene 18) and $\mathfrak{P}^{67}$ (P. Barcelona Inv. 1) contain portions of Matthew 3, 5, and 26. $\mathfrak{P}^{64}$ was first published by Colin Roberts in "An Early Papyrus of the First Gospel" (*Harvard Theological Review*, 46 (1953), 233–237. $\mathfrak{P}^{67}$ was first published by P. Roca-Puig in a booklet called *Un Papiro Griego del Evangelio de San Mateo* (Barcelona, 1957). After Roberts realized that $\mathfrak{P}^{64}$ and $\mathfrak{P}^{67}$ were two parts of the same manuscript and then confirmed this with Roca-Puig, the latter published another article entitled, "Nueva publicacion del papiro numero uno de Barcelona" in *Helmantica* 37 (1961), 5–20, in which Roca-Puig gives a full presentation of the entire manuscript. Roberts appended a note to this article explaining how he had discovered that $\mathfrak{P}^{64}$ and $\mathfrak{P}^{67}$ were part of the same manuscript. I have presented a full argument for the common identity of $\mathfrak{P}^{4+64+67}$.[2] T. C. Skeat has also argued that these three manuscripts belong to the same codex.[3] As such, $\mathfrak{P}^{4+64+67}$, as part of the same codex, should be assigned the same date. (Fuller bibliography is found in *Text of Earliest NT Greek MSS*, 43–45.) Having examined $\mathfrak{P}^{4}$ and $\mathfrak{P}^{64}$ in person, I can attest to their common identification. One clue that ties the Matthew manuscript ($\mathfrak{P}^{64+67}$) to the Luke manuscript ($\mathfrak{P}^{4}$) is that a fragment with the reading "Gospel according to Matthew" is located with $\mathfrak{P}^{4}$ in Paris. This could be the title page to $\mathfrak{P}^{64+67}$. Whether $\mathfrak{P}^{4}$ and $\mathfrak{P}^{64+67}$ were part of the same codex or were produced by the same scribe for two different codices, they must be dated the same.

* $\mathfrak{P}^{64}$: Oxford, England: Oxford University, Magdalen College Library (Gr. 17)
* $\mathfrak{P}^{67}$: Barcelona, Spain: Fundacion San Lucas Evangelista (P. Barc. 1)
* $\mathfrak{P}^{4}$ contains Luke 1:58–59, 62–2:1, 6–7; 3:8–4:2, 29–32, 34–35; 5:3–8, 30–6:16.
* $\mathfrak{P}^{64+67}$ contains Matthew 3:9, 15; 5:20–22, 25–28; 26:7–8, 10, 14–15, 22–23, 31–33.
* $\mathfrak{P}^{4+64+67}$ is written in a "Biblical Uncial" hand dated to the late second century. The handwriting lines up remarkably well with P. Oxyrhnychus 2404 (2nd century), P. Oxyrhynchus 661 (c. 150), and P. Vindob. 29784 (late 2nd century) (for photo, see Cavallo, *Richerche sulla maiuscola biblica*, plate 12a). In a letter to me, Skeat said he thought the dating of P. Vindob. 29784 was "particularly valuable because the text of the fragment is not Christian and Cavallo was not under any pressure to date it as early as possible but could assess it on purely morphological and stylistic grounds." Another papyrologist I consulted, who wished to remain anonymous, dated $\mathfrak{P}^{4+64+67}$ to the reign of Marcus Aurelius (AD 161–180).
* The text of $\mathfrak{P}^{4+64+67}$ is extremely good, showing remarkable agreement with $\mathfrak{P}^{75}$ (in Luke), as well as with ℵ and B.

$\mathfrak{P}^{5}$ *(P. Oxy. 208)*

* Two separate portions were unearthed from Oxyrhynchus by Grenfell and Hunt, both from the same papyrus manuscript. The first portion contains John 1:23–31, 33–40 on one fragment and John 20:11–17 on another—probably on the first and last quires of a manuscript containing only the Gospel of John. This portion was published in volume II of *Oxyrhynchus Papyri* in 1899 (no. 208); the second portion—containing John 16:14–30—was not published until 1922 in volume XV of *Oxyrhynchus Papyri*.
* John 1:23–31, 33–40; 16:14–30; 20:11–17, 19–20, 22–25
* London, England: British Museum (Inv. nos. 782, 2484)
* First half of the third century
* After examining the first portion, Grenfell and Hunt said, "The text is a good one, and appears to have affinities with that of Codex Sinaiticus,

with which the papyrus agrees in several readings not found elsewhere." The agreement of 𝔓[5] with ℵ against B is evident in critical passages (John 1:34; 16:22, 27, 28). This impression, however, was slightly modified after their inspection of the second portion. The affinity between 𝔓[5] and ℵ is still there, but it is less pronounced. The papyrus, written in a documentary hand, is marked for its brevity.

𝔓[6] *(P. Coptic 379, 381, 382, 384)*

* C. M. Cobern, *New Archaeological Discoveries* (1928), 152.
* Strasbourg, University Library (P. Copt. 379, 381, 382, 384)
* John 10:1–2, 4–7, 9–10; 11:1–8, 45–52 (a bilingual Greek-Achmimic codex)
* Early fourth century
* The manuscript displays an independent text, having more Alexandrian readings than not.

𝔓[7] *(KDA 553)*

* C. R. Gregory, *Textkritik* III, 1086.
* Kiev: Centre Nauc. Bibl. (F. 301)
* Luke 4:1–2
* Third/fourth century
* The manuscript is too small to determine its textual character.

𝔓[8] *(P. Berlin 8683)*

* C. R. Gregory, *Textkritik* III, 1087–1090; P. L. Hedley, *Church Quarterly Review* (1934), 216.
* Berlin: Staatliche Museum (inv. 8683)
* Acts 4:31–37; 5:2–9; 6:1–6, 8–15
* Fourth century
* The manuscript is Alexandrian.

𝔓[9] *(P. Oxy. 402)*

* Grenfell and Hunt, *Oxyrhynchus Papyri* III (1903), no. 402, 2–3.
* 1 John 4:11–12, 15–17

* Cambridge, Massachusetts: Harvard University, Semitic Museum (no. 3736)
* Late third century
* The manuscript was written very carelessly in a common hand. The handwriting is crude and irregular, and the copy contains some unintelligible spellings.

$\mathfrak{P}^{10}$ *(P. Oxy. 209)*

* Grenfell and Hunt, *Oxyrhynchus Papyri* II (1899), 8–9.
* Romans 1:1–7
* Cambridge, Massachusetts: Harvard University, Semitic Museum (no. 2218)
* c. 316. The manuscript was tied up with a contract dated AD 316, and with other documents of the same period.
* The manuscript displays the hand of a student learning to write Greek.

$\mathfrak{P}^{11}$ *(P. Gr. 258 A)* + $\mathfrak{P}^{14}$ *(P. Harris 14)*

* Aland, *Neue Neutestamentliche Papyri*, 269–278 (for $\mathfrak{P}^{11}$); J. R. Harris, *Biblical Fragments from Mt. Sinai* (1896), 54–56 (for $\mathfrak{P}^{14}$). Both manuscripts came from St. Catherine's monastery and are parts of the same codex.
* 1 Corinthians 1:17–22, 25–27; 2:6–8, 9–12, 14; 3:1–3, 5–6, 8–10, 20; 4:3–5; 5:7–8; 6:5–9, 11–18; 7:3–6, 10–14
* St. Petersburg Ross. Nanc. Bibl. Gr 258 A ($\mathfrak{P}^{11}$); Sinai, Kathaerinen-Kl., P. Sinai II, Harris 14 ($\mathfrak{P}^{14}$)
* Sixth century
* The manuscript is Alexandrian.

$\mathfrak{P}^{12}$ *(Amherst Papyri 3b)*

* Grenfell and Hunt, *The Amherst Papyri* Vol. 1; London, 1900:28–31.
* Hebrews 1:1
* New York: Pierpon Morgan Library (no. Gr. 3)
* c. 285
* The manuscript may have been a writing exercise or an amulet.

$\mathfrak{P}^{13}$ *(P. Oxy. 657 and PSI 1292)*

* Grenfell and Hunt, *Oxyrhynchus Papyri* IV (1904), no. 657, 36–48; Vittorio Bartolletti and M. Norsi, *Papiri greci e latini della Societa Italiana* (1951), PSI 1292, 209–210.
* Hebrews 2:14–5:5; 10:8–22; 10:29–11:13; 11:28–12:7; it contains 12 columns from a roll—with pagination from 47–50, 61–65, 67–69; 23–27 lines per column. (The pagination reveals that other epistles may have preceded this one—perhaps Romans, as in $\mathfrak{P}^{46}$.)
* London, England: British Library (Inv. no. 1532v); Florence, Italy: Biblioteca Laurenziana (no. 1292)
* c. 200. This manuscript, displaying the "Severe style" (i.e., slanted letters), should be dated c. 200 because of its morphological likeness to P. Oxyrhynchus 852. The Oxyrhynchus manuscript (a portion of Euripides's *Hypsipyle*) has a solid date because there are accounts on the recto dated to the second half of the second century. $\mathfrak{P}^{13}$ is also similar to P. Oxyrhynchus 852 (late second ot early third century) in the formation of most letters, the ligature between letters, and overall appearance. And $\mathfrak{P}^{13}$ is like P. Oxyrhynchus 2635 (dated no later than c. 200)—note especially the long-tailed swooping upsilon. These manuscripts strongly suggest a date of c. 200 for $\mathfrak{P}^{13}$, which is also the date stated by Kim in a personal letter to me.
* The manuscript very often agrees with B, and it supplements B where it is lacking—namely, from Heb. 9:14 to the end of Hebrews. $\mathfrak{P}^{13}$ and $\mathfrak{P}^{46}$ display nearly the same text. Out of a total of eighty-eight variation-units, there are seventy-one agreements and only seventeen disagreements. (The copyists of $\mathfrak{P}^{13}$ and $\mathfrak{P}^{46}$ made similar use of double points for punctuation, and the pagination of both documents indicates that Romans preceded Hebrews in $\mathfrak{P}^{13}$ as well as in $\mathfrak{P}^{46}$.)

$\mathfrak{P}^{14}$

* See $\mathfrak{P}^{11}$.

$\mathfrak{P}^{15}$ *(P. Oxy. 1008)* + $\mathfrak{P}^{16}$ *(P. Oxy. 1009)*

* Grenfell and Hunt conjectured that $\mathfrak{P}^{15}$ and $\mathfrak{P}^{16}$ might have been

parts of the same manuscript, written in a documentary hand. Both manuscripts have the same formation of letters, line space, and punctuation (indicated by spacing). The only notable difference is the color of ink on both manuscripts. However, this distinction could indicate that the same scribe switched to a different ink sometime after making 1 Corinthians and before copying Philippians. $\mathfrak{P}^{15}$ displays a black ink (the more expensive type—a carbon-based ink), whereas $\mathfrak{P}^{16}$ displays a brownish ink (the less expensive type—blended with iron sulfate and gum arabic). Since these manuscripts are from the same codex, it only stands to reason that they were originally a part of a Pauline corpus. Furthermore, the two must have the same date (late third century), not third century for $\mathfrak{P}^{15}$ and third/fourth century for $\mathfrak{P}^{16}$ (as listed in Appendix 1 of NA^{27}).

$\mathfrak{P}^{15}$ *(P. Oxy. 1008)*

* Grenfell and Hunt, *Oxyrhynchus Papyri* VII (1910), no. 1008, 4–8.
* 1 Corinthians 7:18–8:4
* Cairo, Egypt: Egyptian Museum of Antiquities (JE 47423)
* Late third century
* This manuscript was part of the same codex to which $\mathfrak{P}^{16}$ belonged. The manuscript is proto-Alexandrian, showing the greatest agreement with B.

$\mathfrak{P}^{16}$ *(P. Oxy. 1009)*

* Grenfell and Hunt, *Oxyrhynchus Papyri* VII (1910), no. 1009, 8–11.
* Philippians 3:10–17; 4:2–8
* Cairo, Egypt: Egyptian Museum of Antiquities (JE 47424)
* Late third century
* This manuscript was part of the same codex to which $\mathfrak{P}^{15}$ belonged. The manuscript is proto-Alexandrian, showing the greatest agreement with א and then B.

$\mathfrak{P}^{17}$ *(P. Oxy. 1078)*

* Grenfell and Hunt, *Oxyrhynchus Papyri* VIII (1911), 11–13.
* Hebrews 9:12–19

* Cambridge: Cambridge University Library (Add. Mss. 5893)
* Fourth century
* The manuscript is too small to determine its textual character.

$\mathfrak{P}^{18}$ *(P. Oxy. 1079)*

* Grenfell and Hunt, *Oxyrhynchus Papyri* VIII (1911), 13–14.
* Revelation 1:4–7
* London, England: British Library (inv. no. 2053v)
* Second half of third century
* A miniature codex, this manuscript shows the greatest agreement with C.

$\mathfrak{P}^{19}$ *(P. Oxy. 1170)*

* Grenfell and Hunt, *Oxyrhynchus Papyri* IX (1912), 7–8.
* Matthew 10:32–11:5
* Oxford, England: Bodleian Library (bibl. d. 6)
* c. 400
* The manuscript is unusual in that it does not have sacred names written as nomina sacra. The text, not Alexandrian, displays independent readings.

$\mathfrak{P}^{20}$ *(P. Oxy. 1171)*

* Grenfell and Hunt, *Oxyrhynchus Papyri* IX (1912), no. 1171, 9–11.
* James 2:19–3:9
* Princeton, New Jersey: University Libraries (AM 4117)
* Second century. $\mathfrak{P}^{20}$ bears some paleographic resemblance to P. Oxyrhynchus 1230 and P. Oxyrhynchus 3830, both of the second century. It has more similarity to P. Oxyrhynchus 1075 and P. Geneva 253 (a Christian homily), both of the second century. A paleographic comparison of $\mathfrak{P}^{20}$ and $\mathfrak{P}^{27}$ suggests that the same scribe produced both manuscripts. The following letters are formed identically: *alpha, beta, delta, epsilon, kappa, iota, omicron, pi, rho, sigma, phi, upsilon, psi, omega*. However, the *eta, mu,* and *nu* are dissimilar enough to caution against 100 percent, positive identification. Nevertheless, $\mathfrak{P}^{27}$ should be dated the same as $\mathfrak{P}^{20}$, to the second century.

* The manuscript is a fairly reliable copy; the text is clearly proto-Alexandrian, showing the greatest agreement with א and B.

𝔓[21] *(P. Oxy. 1227)*

* Grenfell and Hunt, *Oxyrhynchus Papyri* X (1914), no. 1227, 12–14.
* Matthew 12:24–26, 32–33
* Allentown, Pennsylvania: Muhlenberg College (Theol. Pap. 2)
* Fourth century
* The manuscript displays an independent text.

𝔓[22] *(P. Oxy. 1228)*

* Grenfell and Hunt, *Oxyrhynchus Papyri* X (1914), no. 1228, 14–16.
* John 15:25–16:2, 21–32 (two consecutive columns of a roll; the reverse side is blank)
* Glasgow, Scotland: University Library (Ms. 2-X, 1)
* Middle of third century
* The manuscript displays an independent text.

𝔓[23] *(P. Oxy. 1229)*

* Grenfell and Hunt, *Oxyrhynchus Papyri* X, no. 1229, 16–18.
* James 1:10–12, 15–18
* Urbana, Illinois: University of Illinois (G. P. 1229)
* c. 200. A similar style can be seen in first hand of P. Chester Beatty IX (Ezekiel), which should be dated c. 200. The appearance of 𝔓[23] seems somewhat earlier in that it exhibits small serifs in many letters (*alpha*, *iota*, *lambda*, *mu*, *nu*) and no small omicrons—all characteristics of the second century.
* The manuscript is an accurate copy; the text is clearly proto-Alexandrian, showing the greatest agreement with א, A, and C (which represent the best text of the General Epistles).

𝔓[24] *(P. Oxy. 1230)*

* Grenfell and Hunt, *Oxyrhynchus Papyri* X (1914), no. 1230, 18–19.
* Revelation 5:5–8; 6:5–8

* Newton Centre, Massachusetts: Andover Newton Theological School, Franklin Trask Library (O.P. 1230).
* Second half of third century
* The manuscript shows textual agreement with A, but it is too small to determine its overall textual character.

𝔓[25] *(P. Berlin 16388)*
* O Stegmuller, *Ein Bruchstuck aus dem griechischen Diatessaron* (P. 16388), 224–225.
* Berlin, Staatliche Museem (Inv. 16388)
* Matthew 18:32–34; 19:1–3, 5–7, 9–10
* Fourth century
* The manuscript displays an independent text.

𝔓[26] *(P. Oxy. 1354)*
* Grenfell and Hunt, *Oxyrhynchus Papyri* XI, no. 1354, 6–9.
* Romans 1:1–16
* Dallas, Southern Methodist University, Bridwell Library
* c. 600
* The manuscript displays an independent text.

𝔓[27] *(P. Oxy. 1355)*
* Grenfell and Hunt, *Oxyrhynchus Papyri* XI, no. 1355, 9–12.
* Romans 8:12–22, 24–27; 8:33–9:3, 5–9
* Cambridge, England: Cambridge University Library (Add. Mss. 7211)
* Second century (see discussion on 𝔓[20])
* The scribe of 𝔓[27] may have also written 𝔓[20] (an early copy of James). His manuscript is reliable; it shows general agreement with ℵ, B, and other Alexandrian witnesses.

𝔓[28] *(P. Oxy. 1596)*
* Grenfell and Hunt, *Oxyrhynchus Papyri* XIII (1919), no. 1596, 8–10.
* John 6:8–12, 17–22

* Berkeley, California: Pacific School of Religion, Palestine Institute Museum (Pap. 2)
* Late third century
* The manuscript is proto-Alexandrian, showing more agreement with 𝔓[75] than any other manuscript.

𝔓[29] *(P. Oxy. 1597)*

* Grenfell and Hunt, *Oxyrhynchus Papyri* XIII (1919), 10–12.
* Acts 26:7–8, 20
* Oxford, England: Bodleian Library (Gr. bibl. g. 4 [P])
* c. 200. 𝔓[29] belongs to the same time period as 𝔓[45], namely c. 200. Both manuscripts manifest some unusual, nearly identically shaped letters: triangular *theta*, square *pi*, and squashed *epsilon* with lower inward hook. (See comments on 𝔓[45] below.)
* The manuscript might be related to the D-type text; but the fragment is too small to be certain of its textual character.

𝔓[30] *(P. Oxy. 1598)*

* Grenfell and Hunt, *Oxyrhynchus Papyri* XIII, no. 1598, 12–14. A new portion in 2 Thess. 2 was identified by Comfort and Barrett (*Text of Earliest NT Greek MSS*, 128–133).
* 1 Thessalonians 4:12–13, 16–17; 5:3, 8–10, 12–18, 25–28; 2 Thessalonians 1:1–2; 2:1, 9–11
* Ghent, Belgium: Rijksuninersiteit, Univ. Bibliotheek (inv. 61)
* First half of third century
* A carefully executed manuscript, 𝔓[30] exhibits the greatest agreement with א and then with B.

𝔓[31] *(P. Rylands 4)*

* A. S. Hunt, *Catalogue of the Greek Papyri in the John Rylands Library* I (Manchester, 1911), 10–11 (Papyrus Ryland 5).
* Romans 12:3–8
* Manchester, England: John Rylands University Library (Gr. P. 4)
* Late sixth/early seventh century.

* The manuscript is too small to determine its textual affinities, though it shows some agreement with codex Sinaiticus.

𝔓^{32} *(P. Rylands 5)*

* A. S. Hunt, *Catalogue of the Greek Papyri in the John Rylands Library* I (Manchester, 1911), 10–11 (Papyrus Ryland 5).
* Titus 1:11–15; 2:3–8
* Manchester, England: John Rylands University Library (Gr. P. 5)
* Middle to late second century. The manuscript displays an informal "Decorated Rounded" hand found in manuscripts of the second century, a date assigned to 𝔓^{32} by H. I. Bell,[4] as well as by C. H. Roberts and T. C. Skeat.[5] The handwriting is comparable to P. Oxyrhynchus 656 (second century), and especially P. London 130, which mentions a horoscope of AD April 1, 81 and can therefore safely be dated to the early second century. The likeness between 𝔓^{32} and P. London 130 can be seen in the formation of two kinds of *alpha*, the bell-shaped *delta*, *theta* (with ligature), the swooping *zeta*, *chi*, *rho*, *upsilon*, and *phi*.
* A reliable manuscript, 𝔓^{32} shows agreement with א and with F and G. Since F and G (nearly identical manuscripts) go back to the same archetype, it is quite possible that 𝔓^{32} could be traced to the same source.

𝔓^{33} + 𝔓^{58} *(Pap. G. 17973, 26133, 35831 [=*𝔓^{58}*], 39783)*

* J. H. Ropes, Beginnings of Christianity III (1926), xix, ccx; C. Wessely, *Studien zur Palaographie und Papyruskunde* 12 (1912), Theological Text 25.
* Acts 7:6–10, 13–18; 15:21–24, 26–32
* Vienna, Osterreichischen Nationalbibliothek (Pap. G. 17973, 26133, 35831 [=𝔓^{58}], 39783)
* Sixth century
* The manuscript displays an Alexandrian text.

𝔓^{34} *(Pap. Gr. 39784)*

* C. Wessely, *Studien zur Palaographie und Papyruskunde* 12 (1912), Theological Text 26.

* 1 Corinthians 16:4–7, 10; 2 Corinthians 5:18–21; 10:13–14; 11:2, 4, 6–7
* Vienna, Osterreichischen Nationalbibliothek (Pap. Gr. 39784)
* Seventh century
* The manuscript displays an essentially Alexandrian text.

$\mathfrak{P}^{35}$ *(PSI 1)*
* G. Vitelli, *Papiri greci e latine della Societa Italiana* vol 1 (1912), 1.
* Matthew 25:12–15, 20–23
* Florence, Biblioteca Medicea Laurenziana (PSI 1)
* Third century (the handwriting greatly resembles that found in $\mathfrak{P}^{40}$)
* The manuscript is proto-Alexandrian.

$\mathfrak{P}^{36}$ *(PSI 3)*
* G. Vitelli, *Papiri greci e latine della Societa Italiana* vol 1 (1912), 5.
* John 3:14–18, 31–32, 34–35
* Florence, Biblioteca Medicea Laurenziana (PSI 3)
* Early fifth century
* The manuscript displays an independent text.

$\mathfrak{P}^{37}$ *(Michigan Papyrus 1570)*
* Henry A. Sanders, "An Early Papyrus Fragment of the Gospel of Matthew in the Michigan Collection" in *Harvard Theological Review*, 19 (1926), 215–226.
* Matthew 26:19–52
* Ann Arbor, Michigan: University of Michigan (Inv. no. 1570)
* Second half of third century
* The manuscript has an independent text, showing some affinities with $\mathfrak{P}^{45}$.

$\mathfrak{P}^{38}$ *(Michigan Papyrus 1571)*
* Henry A. Sanders, "A Papyrus Fragment of Acts in the Michigan Collection" in *Harvard Theological Review* 20 (1927), 1–19.
* Acts 18:27–19:6, 12–16
* Ann Arbor, Michigan: University of Michigan Library (Inv. no. 1571)

* c. 200. This manuscript, written in a "Reformed Documentary" hand, should be dated c. 200 because of morphological likeness in several manuscripts of that time period. Sanders cites several manuscripts: P. Oxyrhynchus 843 (late second century), P. Oxyrhynchus 1607 (late second to early third century), and P. Oxyrhynchus 26 (second century, displaying an earlier form than in 𝔓[38]). To these, I would add P. Oxyrhynchus 37 (c. 200), P. Oxyrhynchus 405 (c. 200), and P. Oxyrhynchus 406 (early third century).
* The manuscript, having a D-text, is a representative of the "Western" form of the book of Acts.

𝔓[39] *(P. Oxy. 1780)*

* Grenfell and Hunt, *Oxyrhynchus Papyri* XV (1922), no. 1780, 7–8.
* John 8:14–22
* Rochester, New York: Ambrose Swabey Library (Inv. no. 8864)
* Early third century. This manuscript exhibits the work of a professional scribe who wrote in an early form of the "Biblical Uncial" script. The form is not as early as that found in 𝔓[4]+𝔓[64+67] (see comments above), but it lines up remarkably well with P. Rylands 16 (dated quite confidently to late second/early third century), and with P. Oxyrhynchus 25 (dated early third century).
* The manuscript is proto-Alexandrian, agreeing with 𝔓[75] and B.

𝔓[40] *(Papyrus Heidelberg 645)*

* Friedrich Bilabel, "Romerbrieffragmente" in *Veroffentilichungen aus den Badischen Papyrussammlungen* IV (1924), 28–31, 124–127 (P. Baden 57).
* Romans 1:24–27, 31–2:3; 3:21–4:8; 6:2–5, 15–16; 9:16–17, 27 [fragment a + d (Rom. 1:24–27, 31–2:3); fragment b (3:21–4:8); fragment c (Rom. 6:4b-5, 16); fragment e (Rom. 9:16–17, 27); with two previously unidentified fragments, one of which has been newly identified by Comfort and Barrett as Romans 6:2–4a and 6:15 (this could be called fragment f)—see Comfort and Barrett, *Text of Earliest NT Greek MSS*, 150–154).

* Heidelberg, Germany: Papyrussammlung der Universita¡t (Inv. no. 645)
* Third century
* Although the scribe was occasionally careless in his work, the text manifests a proto-Alexandrian exemplar, agreeing mostly with א and then A and B.

$\mathfrak{P}^{41}$ *(Pap. Gr. 7377, 7384, 7396, 7426, 7451–48, 7731, 7912, 7914)*

* C. Wessely, *Studien zur Palaographie und Papyruskunde* 15 (1914), Nr. 237; J. H. Ropes, *The Beginnings of Christianity* III, 271–275.
* Acts 17:28–18:2, 17–18, 22–25, 27; 19:1–4, 6–8, 13–16, 18–19; 20:9–13, 15–16, 22–24, 26–38; 21:1–4, 26–27; 22:11–14, 16–17
* Vienna, Osterreichischen Nationalbibliothek (Pap. Gr. 7377, 7384, 7396, 7426, 7451–48, 7731, 7912, 7914)
* Eighth century
* The manuscript displays a D-text or what some call "Western" text.

$\mathfrak{P}^{42}$ *(Pap. K. 8706)*

* C. Wessely, *Studien zur Palaographie und Papyruskunde* IX (1909), no. 3
* Luke 1:54–55; 2:29–32
* Vienna, Osterreichischen Nationalbibliothek (Pap. Gr. 8706)
* Seventh/eighth century
* The manuscript is too small to determine its textual character.

$\mathfrak{P}^{43}$ *(P. Brit. 2241)*

* Milne, *Catalogue of Literary Papyri*, 185.
* Revelation 2:12–13; 15:8–16:2
* London, British Library (Inv. 2241)
* Sixth/seventh century
* The manuscript is too small to determine its textual character.

$\mathfrak{P}^{44}$

* W. Crum and H. Evelyn-White, *The Monastery of Epiphanius at Thebes*, II, 120–121 (No. 583), 301.

* Matthew 17:1–3, 6–7; 18:15–17, 19; 25:8–10; John 9:3–4; 10:8–14; 12:6–8
* New York, Metropolitan Museum of Art, Department of Egyptian Art (Inv. 14.1.527)
* Sixth/seventh century
* The manuscript is essentially Alexandrian.

𝔓45 *(Chester Beatty Papyrus I)*

* Frederic G. Kenyon, *Chester Beatty Biblical Papyri* II/1: *The Gospels and Acts, Text* (London, 1933); II/2: *The Gospels and Acts, Plates* (London, 1934); Gunther Zuntz, "Reconstruction of one Leaf of the Chester Beatty Papyrus of the Gospels and Acts (Mt 25:41–26:39)," Chronique d'Egypte 26 (1951), 191–211; T. C. Skeat and B. C. McGing, "Notes on Chester Beatty Papyrus I (Gospels and Acts)." Pp. 21–25 in *Hermathena* 150 (1991). (This provides a reconstruction of John 4:51–5:2, 21–25.)
* Matthew 20:24–32; 21:13–19; 25:41–26:39; Mark 4:36–9:31; 11:27–12:28; Luke 6:31–7:7; 9:26–14:33; John 4:51–5:2, 21–25; 10:7–25; 10:30–11:10, 18–36, 42–57; Acts 4:27–17:17 (with many lacunae). According to Kenyon, the order of books in the original intact manuscript was probably as follows: Matthew, John, Luke, Mark, Acts (the so-called Western order).
* Dublin, Ireland: Chester Beatty Collection (I)
* c. 200. 𝔓45 should be dated c. 200 because there are several manuscripts in this time period displaying comparable calligraphy, manuscripts with certain dating. First is P. Michigan 3, dated to the second half of the second century inasmuch as a documentary text on the verso is dated AD 190. Second is P. Oxyrhynchus 232, which has a fairly firm date of the late second century or early third because the verso of the papyrus has two columns of cursive writing of the end of the second century or early third. Third is P. Rylands 57, which is dated c. 200. The dating of this literary manuscript is quite certain as it came from the Heroninos archives. As such it must be predated AD 260. Since it was a literary text (on the recto), which was eventually put to use as a letter (on the

verso), it is likely the literary text (p. Rylands 57) should be dated AD 200–225.

* The text of 𝔓⁴⁵ varies. According to a study done by Colwell, the scribe of 𝔓⁴⁵ worked "without any intention of exactly reproducing his source." He wrote with a great amount of freedom—"harmonizing, smoothing out, substituting almost whimsically." In short, "the scribe does not actually copy words. He sees through the language to its idea-content, and copies that—often in words of his own choosing, or in words rearranged as to order."[6]

It was apparent to Colwell that the scribe of 𝔓⁴⁵ copied his exemplar phrase by phrase and clause by clause (as opposed to more careful copyists who transcribe the text letter by letter, as in 𝔓⁷⁵). While copying phrases and clauses, he worked at reproducing what he imagined to be the thought of each phrase. Thus, he transposed and omitted many words and deleted several phrases. Colwell said, "The most striking aspect of his style is its conciseness. The dispensable word is dispensed with. He omits adverbs, adjectives, nouns, participles, verbs, personal pronouns—without any compensating habit of addition."[7]

Another study on 𝔓⁴⁵ done by Royse affirms Colwell's observations about the scribe's penchant for brevity. Royse comments, "the scribe has a marked tendency to omit portions of text, often (as it seems) accidentally but perhaps also by deliberate pruning."[8] The result of this pruning is that the scribe produced a very readable text, with very little need of correction.

Further study of the manuscript shows that the omissions were not simply the result of scribal excision for the sake of trimming. In Mark 6:40 the scribe of 𝔓⁴⁵ made a deletion to bring Mark's account into harmony with Matthew's (see 14:19) or John's (see 6:10). In John 11:25 the scribe of 𝔓⁴⁵ thought it tautological to add "and the life" to "I am the resurrection," because the latter is Jesus's poignant rejoinder to Martha who believed in the final resurrection as being nothing more than an event. And in John 11:49 the change reveals the scribe's knowledge of history and his sensitivity to the accurateness of the historicity of the text.[9]

The text of 𝔓[45] varies with each book. According to Kenyon, 𝔓[45] in Mark shows a strong affinity with those manuscripts which used to be called Caesarean (i.e., W, f^1, f^{13}, 565, and 700). In Matthew, Luke, and John, 𝔓[45] stands midway between the "Alexandrian" manuscripts and so-called "Western" manuscripts. In Acts, 𝔓[45] shows the greatest affinity with the Alexandrian uncials (א, A, B, and C)—as over against the manuscripts with a D-text.

𝔓[46] *(Chester Beatty Papyrus II)*

* Frederic G. Kenyon, *The Chester Beatty Biblical Papyri III/1: Pauline Epistles and Revelation, Text* (London, 1934); III/3 (Supplement): *Pauline Epistles, Text* (London, 1936); III/4: *Pauline Epistles, Plates* (London, 1937); Henry A. Sanders, *A Third-century Papyrus Codex of the Epistles of Paul* (Ann Arbor: University of Michigan Press, 1935)
* The papyrus has most of Paul's Epistles (excluding the pastorals) in this order: Romans 5:17–6:14; 8:15–15:9; 15:11–16:27; Hebrews 1:1–13:25; 1 Corinthians 1:1–16:22; 2 Corinthians 1:1–13:13; Ephesians 1:1–6:24; Galatians 1:1–6:18; Philippians 1:1–4:23; Colossians 1:1–4:18; 1 Thessalonians 1:1; 1:9–2:3; 5:5–9, 23–28 (with minor lacunae in each of the books). The University of Michigan library has thirty leaves containing the following portions: Romans 11:35–14:8; Romans 15:11—Hebrews 8:8; Hebrews 9:10–26; 1 Corinthians 2:3–3:5; 2 Corinthians 9:7–13:14; Ephesians; Galatians 1:1–6:10. The Chester Beatty Collection has fifty-six leaves containing Romans 5:17–6:14; 8:15–11:35; 14:19–15:11; Hebrews 8:9–9:10; Hebrews 9:26–1 Corinthians 2:3; 1 Corinthians 3:6–2 Corinthians 9:7; Galatians 6:10–18; Philippians; Colossians; 1 Thessalonians 1:1–2:3; 5:5–28.
* Middle second century. Kenyon, the editor of the *editio principes* of 𝔓[46], dated the manuscript to the third century without providing any specific paleographic comparisons. Kim redated it to the late first century.[10] I don't think either are correct. I would place 𝔓[46] in the second century based on its morphological likeness to the following manuscripts: (1) P. Oxyrhynchus 841, dated with certainty

to AD 125–150 (a document on the verso is dated 81–96); (2) P. Oxyrhynchus 1622, dated with certainty to AD 117–138 (a document on the verso is dated 148); (3) P. Oxyrhynchus 3721, assigned a date of the second half of the second century (I examined this manuscript at the Ashmolean and immediately noticed its likeness to $\mathfrak{P}^{46}$); (4) P. Greek Berolinses 9810, assigned a date of the first half of the second century; (5) P. Rylands III 550, assigned a date of early second century. $\mathfrak{P}^{46}$ belongs in the second century, probably 150–175.

* On the whole, the text of $\mathfrak{P}^{46}$ is fairly reliable. The scribe who produced this manuscript used an early, excellent exemplar. He was a professional scribe because there are stichoi notations at the end of several books (see the conclusion of Romans, 2 Corinthians, Ephesians, Philippians). The stichoi were used by professionals to note how many lines had been copied for commensurate pay. Most likely, an official of a scriptorium (perhaps connected with a church library) paginated the codex and indicated the stichoi. The scribe himself made a few corrections as he went, and then several other readers made corrections here and there. Thus, the manuscript was very well used—probably by various members of the church.

The text of $\mathfrak{P}^{46}$ shows a strong affinity with B (especially in Ephesians, Colossians, and Hebrews) and next with א. $\mathfrak{P}^{46}$ agrees much less with the later representatives of the Alexandrian text (namely, A C P 33). In short, $\mathfrak{P}^{46}$ is proto-Alexandrian. In Hebrews, $\mathfrak{P}^{46}$ and $\mathfrak{P}^{13}$ display nearly the same text. Out of a total of eighty-eight variation-units, there are seventy-one agreements and only seventeen disagreements.

$\mathfrak{P}^{47}$ *(Chester Beatty Papyrus III)*

* Frederic G. Kenyon, *Chester Biblical Papyri III/l: Pauline Epistles and Revelation, Text* (London: 1934); III/2: *Revelation, Plates* (London: 1936)
* Revelation 9:10–17:2
* Dublin, Ireland: Chester Beatty collection (III)
* Third century

* The manuscript is closest in its textual character to א. $\mathfrak{P}^{47}$ and א form one early textual alliance for Revelation; their testimony is generally considered to be somewhat inferior to that found in $\mathfrak{P}^{115}$, A, and C.

$\mathfrak{P}^{48}$ *(PSI 1165)*

* G. Vitelli and S. G. Mercati, *Pubblicazioni della Societa Italiana, Papiri Greci e Latini*, Vol. 10 (1932), 112–118.
* Acts 23:11–17, 23–29
* Florence, Italy: Biblioteca Laurenziana (no. 1165)
* Early third century
* The manuscript, displaying a D-text, is a representative of the "Western" form of the book of Acts.

$\mathfrak{P}^{49+65}$ *(Yale Papyrus 415 + PSI 1373)*

* W. H. P. Hatch and C. B. Wells, "A Hitherto Unpublished Fragment of the Epistle to the Ephesians" in *Harvard Theological Review*, 51 (1958), 33–37; John F. Oates, Alan E. Samuel, C. Bradford Welles, *Yale Papyri in the Beinecke Rare Book and Manuscript Library* (New Haven: American Society of Papyrologists, 1967), 9–13; Vittorio Bartoletti, *Pubblicazioni della Societa Italiana, Papiri Greci e Latini*, XIV (1957), 5–7. Two further publications of the Yale manuscript, $\mathfrak{P}^{49}$, offer further revisions: (1) Susan Stephens, *Yale Papyri in the Beinecke Rare Book and Manuscript Library* II, 1–2 (1985); (2) Stephen Emmel, "Biblical Papyri in the Beinecke Library" (*Zeitschrift für Papyrologie und Epigraphik* 112:1986), 291–294.
* $\mathfrak{P}^{49}$ is in New Haven, Connecticut: Yale University Library (inv. 415 + 531); $\mathfrak{P}^{65}$ is in Florence, Italy: Istituto di Papirologia G. Vitelli (PSI 1373).
* Ephesians 4:16–29; 4:31–5:13; 1 Thessalonians 1:3–10; 2:1, 6–13
* Middle of the third century
* $\mathfrak{P}^{49}$ (Ephesians) and $\mathfrak{P}^{65}$ (1 Thessalonians) are part of the same codex. $\mathfrak{P}^{49}$ was first published in 1948 by Hatch and Welles. $\mathfrak{P}^{65}$ was published by Bartoletti in 1957, who indicated that he thought $\mathfrak{P}^{49}$ and $\mathfrak{P}^{65}$ were produced by the same scribe. $\mathfrak{P}^{49}$ (which is Yale

Papyrus 415 + 531) was republished in a superior transcription by Oates and Welles in the Yale Papyri series. These editors then affirmed that the two manuscripts came from the same hand. Both manifest a very idiosyncratic formation of certain letters, such as the tilted *lambda*, tilted *sigma*, doubled curved and extended *iota*, and long-tailed *upsilon*. Welles remarked that "there is not a single case of difference in the letter shapes in the two papyri." And in both manuscripts the nomina sacra are written with a crossbar extending to the right (the width of one letter).

* The manuscript displays strong agreement with א and B.

𝔓[50] *(P. Yale 1543)*

* Oates, Samuel, Welles, *Yale Papyri in the Beinecke Rare Book and Manuscript Library* (New Haven, 1967), 15–21.
* Acts 8:26–32; 10:26–31
* New Haven, Connecticut: Yale University Library (P. 1543)
* Late third/early fourth century
* The manuscript generally concurs with B and א.

𝔓[51] *(P. Oxy. 2157)*

* Lobel, Roberts, Wegener, Oxyrhynchus Papyri XVIII (1941), no. 2157, 1–3, 8.
* Galatians 1:2–10, 13, 16–20
* Oxford, Ashmolean Museum (P. Oxy. 2157)
* Fourth century (bears resemblance to Chester Beatty, Ecclesiasticus)
* The manuscript displays an independent text.

𝔓[52] *(P. Rylands 457)*

* C. H. Roberts, *An Unpublished Fragment of the Fourth Gospel in the John Rylands Library* (Manchester: 1935). This was republished with a few alterations in the *Bulletin of the John Rylands Library* XX (1936), 45–55; and then again in the *Catalogue of the Greek and Latin Papyri in the John Rylands Library* iii (Manchester: 1938), 1–3. The last publication contains critical notes and bibliography of scholarly reviews.
* John 18:31–34, 37–38

* Manchester, England: John Rylands Library (Gr. P. 457)
* c. 110–125. Many paleographers (Kenyon, Bell, Deismann, Hatch, Wilcken) have concurred with C. H. Roberts's dating of 𝔓52 to the early second century on the basis of its morphological likeness to P. Fayum (AD 94), P. London 2078 (AD 81–96), P. Oslo 22 (AD 127), and P. Berolinses 6854 (dated pre AD 117). Another comparable manuscript with certain dating is P. Bremer 5 (AD 117–120). All of these manuscripts, in my opinion, bear resemblance to 𝔓52 in various letters. However, the one manuscript that has the most overall resemblance to 𝔓52 is P. Oxyrhynchus 2533, which I examined at the Ashmolean. The editors of P. Oxyrhynchus 2533 said the handwriting could be parallel with first century manuscripts but has the appearance of being second century (to which they dated it).
* Though the amount of text in 𝔓52 is hardly enough to make a positive judgment about its textual character, the text seems to be "Alexandrian." Its greatest value is its early date, for it testifies to the fact that the autograph of John's Gospel must have been written before the close of the first century.

𝔓53 *(Michigan Papyrus 6652)*
* Henry A. Sanders, "A Third Century Papyrus of Matthew and Acts" in *Quantulacumque: Studies Presented to Kirsopp Lake*, editors R. Casey, S. Lake, A. K. Lake (London: 1937), 151–161.
* Matthew 26:29–40; Acts 9:33–10:1 (Sanders said the two fragments are probably part of the same manuscript. This was confirmed by H. I. Bell. The two fragments were found together; they were part of a codex containing the four Gospels and Acts or just Matthew and Acts.)
* Ann Arbor, Michigan: University of Michigan Library (inv. no. 6652).
* Second half of third century
* The manuscript is proto-Alexandrian.

𝔓54 *(P. Princeton 15)*
* E. H. Kase, *Papyri in the Princeton University Collections* II, 1–3, no. 15; Schofield, *Papyrus Fragments*, 206–214.

* James 2:16–18, 22–26; 3:2–4
* Princeton, Princeton University Library, Papyrus Collection (7742)
* Early fifth century
* The manuscript displays an Alexandrian text.

𝔓[55] *(P. Gr. Vindob. 26214)*
* Peter Sanz, *Griechische Literarische Papyri Christlichen Inhaltes I*, 58–59.
* John 1:31–33, 35–38
* Vienna, Osterreichischen Nationalbibliothek (P. Gr. 26214)
* Sixth/seventh century
* The manuscript is too small to determine its textual character.

𝔓[56] *(P. Gr. Vindob. 19918)*
* Peter Sanz, *Griechische Literarische Papyri Christlichen Inhaltes I*, 65–66.
* Acts 1:1, 4–5, 7, 10–11
* Vienna, Osterreichischen Nationalbibliothek (P. Gr. 19918)
* Early fifth century
* The manuscript is too small to determine its textual character.

𝔓[57] *(P. Gr. Vindob. 26020)*
* Peter Sanz, *Griechische Literarische Papyri Christlichen Inhaltes II*, 11–12.
* Acts 4:36–5:2, 8–10
* Vienna, Osterreichischen Nationalbibliothek (P. Gr. 26020)
* c. 400
* The manuscript is too small to determine its textual character.

𝔓[58]
* Part of the same manuscript as 𝔓[33] (see above).

𝔓[59] *(P. Colt 3)*
* Colt, *Excavations at Nessana*, 79–92.
* John 1:26, 28, 48, 51; 2:15–16; 11:40–52; 12:25, 29, 31, 35; 17:24–26; 18:1–2, 16–17, 22; 21:7, 12–13, 15, 17–20, 23

* New York, Pierpont Morgan Library (P. Colt 3)
* Seventh century
* The manuscript is generally Alexandrian.

𝔓[60] *(P. Colt 4)*

* Colt, *Excavations at Nessana*, 94–111.
* John 16:29–30, 32–17:6, 8–9, 11–15, 18–25; 18:1–2, 4–5, 7–16, 18–20, 23–29, 31–37, 39–40; 19:2–3, 5–8, 10–18, 20, 23–26
* New York, Pierpont Morgan Library (P. Colt 4)
* Seventh century
* The manuscript is generally Alexandrian.

𝔓[61] *(P. Colt 5)*

* Colt, *Excavations at Nessana*, 112–120.
* Rom. 16:23–27; 1 Cor. 1:1–2, 4–6; 5:1–3, 5–6, 9–13; Phil. 3:5–9, 12–16; Colossians 1:3–7, 9–13; 4:15; 1 Thess. 1:2–3; Titus 3:1–5, 8–11, 14–15; Philem. 4–7
* New York, Pierpont Morgan Library (P. Colt 4)
* c. 700
* The manuscript is generally Alexandrian.

𝔓[62] *(P. Osloensis 1661)*

* Leiv Amundsen, *Christian Papyri from the Oslo Collection,* 121–125.
* Matthew 11:25–30
* Oslo University Bibl. (1661)
* Fourth century
* The manuscript is too small to determine its textual character.

𝔓[63] *(P. Berlin 11914)*

* O. Stegmuller, *Zu den Bibelorakein im Codex Bezae*, 15–19.
* John 3:14–18; 4:9–10
* Berlin, Staatliche Museum (P. 11914)
* c. 500
* The manuscript is too small to determine its textual character.

$\mathfrak{P}^{64+67}$

Part of the same manuscript as $\mathfrak{P}^{4}$ (see above).

$\mathfrak{P}^{65}$

Part of the same manuscript as $\mathfrak{P}^{49}$ (see above).

$\mathfrak{P}^{66}$ *(Papyrus Bodmer II)*

* Victor Martin, *Papyrus Bodmer II: Evangile de Jean, 1–14* (Cologny/Geneva, 1956); *Papyrus Bodmer II: Supplement, Evangile de Jean, 14–21* (Cologny/Geneva, 1958); Victor Martin and J. W. B. Barns, *Papyrus Bodmer II: Supplement, Evangile de Jean, 14–21* (Cologny/Geneva, 1962); Kurt Aland, "Neue neutestamentliche Papyri III," in *New Testament Studies* 20 (1974), 357–381 (a publication containing previously unidentified fragments belonging to the same manuscript); M. Gronewald, "Christliche Texts, 214 Johannes Evangelium: Kap 19:8–11, 13–15, 18–20, 23–24," pp.73–76 in *Kolner Papyri Band 5* (a publication containing previously unidentified fragments belonging to the same manuscript). New portions are also reconstructed in *Text of Earliest NT Greek MSS,* (see citation on p. 388; see also Comfort, "New Reconstructions and Identifications of New Testament Papyri." *Novum Testamentum* 41 (1999), 215–216).
* John 1:1–6:11; 6:35–14:26, 29–30; 15:2–26; 16:2–4, 6–7; 16:10–20:20, 22–23; 20:25–21:9.
* Geneva/Cologny, Switzerland: Bibliotheca Bodmeriana; one leaf in Institut für Altertumskunde Papyrologie/Epigraphik
* Middle second century. This manuscript displays a medium-sized "Rounded Decorated" hand, slowly written, which was dated by the editor of the *editio principes* (Martin) to "c. 200," comparing it to P. Oxyrhynchus 1074. Hunger, founder of the Vienna Institute of Papyrology, redated $\mathfrak{P}^{66}$ to the first half of the second century.[11] He notes some documentary manuscripts of the late first century bearing some morphological resemblance: P. Oxyrhynchus 286 (AD 82), P. Oxyrhynchus 270 (AD 94), and P. London II 141 (AD 88). But these are earlier than $\mathfrak{P}^{66}$ in overall appearance.

The manuscripts of the second century which Hunger notes have greater morphological likeness. These are P. Oxyrhynchus 1434 (AD 107/108), P. Oxyrhynchus 2436 (end of first century/ beginning of second), P. Oxyrhynchus 841 (c. 125–150), P. Oxyrhynchus 2161+2162 + PSI 1208–1210 (second century), P. Berolinses 9782 (second century), and P. Lit. London 132 (dated with certainty to the first half of the second century). These last two manuscripts have the closest resemblance to 𝔓[66], both in overall appearance and formation of individual letters. I would add the following manuscripts to those noted by Hunger: P. Oxyrhynchus 1241 (first half of the second century), P. Oxyrhynchus 2891 (early second century), Bodleian Gr. Bib. g. 5 (middle second century), P. Oxyrhynchus 656 (second century), and P. Antinoopolis 7 (middle of second century). In conclusion, comparative paleography places 𝔓[66] in the second century, probably in the middle of the century, which is a date for 𝔓[66] recognized by the paleographers Seider[12] and Cavallo.[13]

* A full description of the work of the scribe and the correctors is found in *Text of Earliest NT Greek MSS*, 381–388. The original scribe was quite free in his interaction with the text; he produced several singular readings which reveal his independent interpretation of the text. While the numerous scribal mistakes would seem to indicate that the scribe was inattentive, many of the singular readings—prior to correction—reveal that he was not detached from the narrative of the text. Rather, he became so absorbed in his reading that he often forgot the exact words he was copying. His task as a copyist was to duplicate the exemplar word for word, but this was frustrated by the fact that he was reading the text in logical semantic chunks and often became a coproducer of a new text. As a result, he continually had to stop his reading and make many in-process corrections. But he left several places uncorrected, which were later corrected by the *diorthotes*. A paleographic study of the second corrector's handwriting reveals that the first paginator is the same as the second corrector because the ligatures line up exactly. As noted by Fee, many of these corrections bring the manuscript

into line with an Alexandrian-type text.[14] This corrector could have been an official proofreader in the scriptorium who used a different exemplar to make his emendations.

* Fee's studies on $\mathfrak{P}^{66c}$ and $\mathfrak{P}^{75}$ in John 1–9 show that $\mathfrak{P}^{66c}$ demonstrates more agreement with $\mathfrak{P}^{75}$ than does $\mathfrak{P}^{66}$. This means that $\mathfrak{P}^{66}$ was often corrected in the direction of $\mathfrak{P}^{75}$ in John 1–9. When we add John 10–21 to the equation and track $\mathfrak{P}^{66}$ corrected relationship to $\mathfrak{P}^{75}$ in John 10:1–15:8 and then to B in 15:9–21:22, where $\mathfrak{P}^{75}$ is not extant (presuming B to be the closest textual extension of $\mathfrak{P}^{75}$), then the percentage of agreement goes up significantly. Of the 450 corrections in $\mathfrak{P}^{66}$, about 50 are of nonsense readings. Of the remaining 400, 284 made the text of $\mathfrak{P}^{66}$ normative (i.e., in agreement with a text supported by all witnesses). Of the remaining 116 corrections, 88 brought the text into conformity with $\mathfrak{P}^{75}$ in John 1:1–13:10; 14:8–15:10, and with B in the remaining sections of John. This means that 75% of the substantive changes conformed $\mathfrak{P}^{66}$ to a $\mathfrak{P}^{75}$/B-type text.

$\mathfrak{P}^{67}$

* Part of the same manuscript as $\mathfrak{P}^{4}$ and $\mathfrak{P}^{64}$ (see above under $\mathfrak{P}^{4}$).

$\mathfrak{P}^{68}$ *(P. Leningrad Gr. 258)*

* K. Aland, *Neue Neutestamentliche Papyri*, 266–268.
* 1 Corinthians 4:12–17, 19–5:3
* St. Petersburg, Ross. Nac. Bibl. (Gr 258 B)
* Seventh century
* The manuscript is too small to determine its textual character.

$\mathfrak{P}^{69}$ *(P. Oxy. 2383)*

* Lobel, Roberts, Turner, Barns, *Oxyrhynchus Papyri* XXIV (London, 1957), no. 2383, 1–4.
* Luke 22:41, 45–48, 58–61 The manuscript does not include Luke 22:41–44. The editors were fairly confident that the only reason to account for this large lacuna would be that the copyist's exemplar did not contain Luke 22:43–44.

* Oxford, England: Ashmolean Museum
* First half of third century
* The manuscript displays an independent text.

𝔓[70] *(P. Oxy. 2384)*

* Lobel, Roberts, Turner, Barns, *Oxyrhynchus Papyri* XXIV (London, 1957), no. 2384, 4–5. M. Naldini, "Nuovi frammenti del vangelo di Matteo," *Prometheus* 1 (1975), 195–200. (After the Istituto di Papirologia realized that they possessed another part of the same manuscript previously published in *Oxyrhynchus Papyri*, Naldini made this publication.)
* Matthew 2:13–16; 2:22–3:1; 11:26–27; 12:4–5; 24:3–6, 12–15
* Oxford, England: Ashmolean Museum—portion with Matt. 11 and 12; Florence, Italy: Istituto di Papirologia, G. Vitelli (CNR 419, 420)—portion with Matt. 2–3, 24.
* Late third century
* The manuscript has a fairly reliable text, though somewhat carelessly written.

𝔓[71] *(P. Oxy. 2385)*

* Lobel, Roberts, Turner, Barns, *Oxyrhynchus Papyri* XXIV (London, 1957), no. 2385, 5–6.
* Oxford, England: Ashmolean Museum
* Matthew 19:10–11, 17–18
* Fourth century
* The manuscript is too small to determine its textual character.

𝔓[72] *(Papyrus Bodmer VII-VIII)*

* Michael Testuz, *Papyrus Bodmer VII–IX: L'Epitre de Jude, Les deux Epitres de Pierre, Les Psaumes 33 et 34* (Cologny/Geneva, 1959); Carlo M. Martini, *Beati Petri Apostoloi Epistulae, Ex Papyro Bodmeriano VIII* (Milan, 1968); Sakae Kubo, "𝔓[72] and the Codex Vaticanus" in *Studies and Documents* 27 (1965), University of Utah Press.
* 1 Peter 1:1–5:14; 2 Peter 1:1–3:18; Jude 1–25 (which are in the

same document as the Nativity of Mary, the apocryphal correspondence of Paul to the Corinthians, the eleventh ode of Solomon, Melito's Homily on the Passover, a fragment of a hymn, the Apology of Phileas, and Psalms 33 and 34)
* Geneva/Cologny, Switzerland: Bibliotheca Bodmeriana (1 and 2 Peter now in Biblioteca Vaticana)
* Late third/early fourth century (c. 300)
* 𝔓72 is a small codex made for private use and not for church meetings. Scholars think that four scribes took part in producing the entire manuscript (for contents, see above). 1 Peter has clear Alexandrian affinities—especially with B and then with A. 2 Peter and (especially) Jude display more of an uncontrolled type text (usually associated with the "Western" text), with several independent readings.

𝔓73 *(P. Bodmer L)*
* C. Thiede, *Papyrus Bodmer L*, "Das neutestamentliche Papyrusfragment 𝔓73 = Mt 25, 43 / 26:2–3."
* Matthew 25:43; 26:2–3
* Geneva/Cologny, Switzerland: Bibliotheca Bodmeriana
* Seventh century
* The manuscript is too small to determine its textual character.

𝔓74 *(Papyrus Bodmer XVII)*
* Rudolf Kasser, *Papyrus Bodmer XV II: Actes de Apotres, Epitres de Jacques, Pierre, Jean et Jude* (Cologny/Geneva, 1961).
* Acts and General Epistles (with lacunae)
* Geneva/Cologny, Switzerland: Bibliotheca Bodmeriana
* Seventh century
* Despite the late date, this manuscript is important because it presents an Alexandrian text and is an excellent witness for the book of Acts.

𝔓75 *(Papyrus Bodmer XIV-XV)*
* Rudolf Kasser and Victor Martin, *Papyrus Bodmer XIV-XV, I: XIV:*

Luc chap 3–24; II:XV: Jean chap. 1–15 (Cologny/Geneva, 1961); Kurt Aland, "Neue neutestamentliche Papyri III," *New Testament Studies* 22 (1976), 375–396 (a publication containing previously unidentified fragments of the same manuscript).

* Luke 3:18–4:2; 4:34–5:10; 5:37–18:18; 22:4–24:53; John 1:1–11:45, 48–57; 12:3–13:1, 8–9; 14:8–30; 15:7–8.
* Geneva/Cologny, Switzerland: Bibliotheca Bodmeriana
* Late second century. Kasser and Martin, the editors of the *editio principes* of $\mathfrak{P}^{75}$ said the hand of $\mathfrak{P}^{75}$ is "a lovely vertical uncial, elegant and careful," which they dated to 175–225 on the basis of morphological comparability to P. Oxyrhynchus 2293, 2322, 2362, 2363, and 2370. It should be noted that P. Oxyrhynchus 2293, 2363, and 2370 are dated "late second century, possibly third." It is also significant that Kasser and Martin noted that the handwriting of $\mathfrak{P}^{75}$ is like that of P. Fuad. Univ. XIX papyrus, a documentary text dated AD 145–146. I would add that there are a number of Oxyrhynchus papyri, all belonging to the second half of the second century, that are morphologically comparable to $\mathfrak{P}^{75}$—namely, P. Oxyrhynchus 1174, 1175, 2077, 2180 and PSI 1302. And P. Oxyrhynchus 2452 is remarkably similar to $\mathfrak{P}^{75}$. In summary, then, $\mathfrak{P}^{75}$ belongs to the second half of the second century.
* The copyist of $\mathfrak{P}^{75}$ was a professional, Christian scribe. The professionalism shows through in his tight calligraphy and controlled copying. The large typeface indicates that the manuscript was composed to be read aloud to a Christian congregation. The scribe even added a system of sectional divisions to aid any would-be lector. As to the scribe's scriptoral acumen, he is probably the best of all the early Christian scribes. Concerning the scribe who made this excellent copy, Colwell said, "his impulse to improve style is for the most part defeated by the obligation to make an exact copy."[15] And concerning his work Colwell commented: "In $\mathfrak{P}^{75}$ the text that is produced can be explained in all its variants as the result of a single force, namely the disciplined scribe who writes with the intention of being careful and accurate. There is no evidence of revision of his work by anyone else, or in fact of any real

revision, or check. . . . The control had been drilled into the scribe before he started writing."[16] Calvin Porter clearly established the fact that $\mathfrak{P}^{75}$ displays the kind of text that was used in making Codex Vaticanus. Porter demonstrated 87% agreement between $\mathfrak{P}^{75}$ and B. In general, textual scholars have a high regard for $\mathfrak{P}^{75}$'s textual fidelity.[17]

$\mathfrak{P}^{76}$ *(Pap. G. 36102)*

* H. Hunger, "Zwei unbekannte neutestamentliche Papyrusfragmente der Osterreichischen Nationalbibliothek," *Biblos* 8 (1959), 7–12.
* John 4:9, 12
* Vienna, Osterreichischen Nationalbibliothek (Pap. G. 36102)
* Sixth century
* The manuscript is too small to determine its textual character.

$\mathfrak{P}^{77}$ *(P. Oxy. 2683 + P. Oxy. 4405) +* $\mathfrak{P}^{103}$ *(P. Oxy. 4403)?*

* The first portion of $\mathfrak{P}^{77}$ was edited by Ingrams, Kingston, Parsons, Rea in *Oxyrhynchus Papyri*, XXXIV (London: 1968), no. 2683, 1–3. The second portion was edited by J. David Thomas, *Oxyrhynchus Papyri*, LXIV (London: 1997), no. 4405, 8–9. $\mathfrak{P}^{103}$ probably belongs to the same codex (see discussion in *Text of Earliest NT Greek MSS*, 609).
* Matthew 23:30–39; with Matthew 13:55–56; 14:3–5 (from P. Oxy. 4403)
* Oxford, England: Ashmolean Museum
* Middle to late second century. $\mathfrak{P}^{77}$ displays the well-crafted hand of a professional scribe. The editor of the *editio principes* (Parsons) dated the first portion of $\mathfrak{P}^{77}$ (P. Oxyrhynchus 2683) late second century on the basis of its morphological comparability to P. Oxyrhynchus 1082, 2663, and 2683, as well as to P. Antinoopolis 26. Another portion of $\mathfrak{P}^{77}$ was published as P. Oxyrhynchus 4405, also dated as late second century. Yet another portion is likely P. Oxyrhynchus 4403 (= $\mathfrak{P}^{103}$), which, if not from the same codex, was probably produced by the same scribe as $\mathfrak{P}^{77}$. In any event, $\mathfrak{P}^{77}$ and $\mathfrak{P}^{103}$ both belong to the late second century.

* The manuscript is clearly a literary production. According to Roberts, 𝔓77 was written "in an elegant hand [and] has what was or became a standard system of chapter division, as well as punctuation and breathings."[18] 𝔓77 has the closest affinity with א.

𝔓78 *(P. Oxy. 2684)*
* Ingrams, Kingston, Parsons, Rea, *Oxyrhynchus Papyri* XXXIV (1968), 4–6.
* Jude 4–5, 7–8
* Oxford, England: Ashmolean Museum
* Third/fourth century (c. 300)
* The manuscript displays an independent text.

𝔓79 *(P. Berlin 6774)*
* K. Treu, Neutestamentliche Fragmente, 37–38.
* Hebrews 10:10–12, 28–30
* Berlin, Staatliche Museum (P. 6774)
* Seventh century
* The manuscript is too small to determine its textual character.

𝔓80 *(P. Barcelona 83)*
* R. Roca-Puig, "Papiro del evangelio de San Juan con 'Hermeneia,' in *Atti dell' XI Congresso Internazionale di Papirologia* (Milan, 1966), 226–236.
* John 3:34 (with *hermeneia*)
* Barcelona, Spain: Fundacion San Lucas Evangelista (inv. no. 83)
* Second half of third century (c. 260)
* The manuscript is too small to determine its textual character.

𝔓81 *(S. Daris, Inv. 20)*
* Sergio Daris, "Un Nuovo Frammento della Prima Lettera di Pietro," *Papyrologica Castroctaviana* (Barcelona, 1967), 11–37.
* 1 Peter 2:20–3:1, 4–12
* Trieste, Spain
* c. 300 (like P. Chester Beatty IV, Genesis)

* The manuscript has strong agreement with Alexandrian manuscripts, especially B.

𝔓[82] *(P. Gr. 2677)*
* J. Schwartz, "Fragment d'evangile sur Papyrus," *Zeitschrift für Papyrologie und Epigraphik* 3 (1968), 157–158.
* Luke 7:32–34, 37–38
* Strasbourg, Bibliotheque Nationale et Universitaire (P. Gr. 2677)
* Fourth century
* The manuscript is too small to determine its textual character.

𝔓[83]
* P. A. M. Khirbet Mird
* Matthew 20:23–25, 30–31; 23:39–24:1, 6
* Louvain, Bibl. De l'Univ. (P. Khirbet Mird 16, 29)
* Sixth century
* The manuscript is too small to determine its textual character.

𝔓[84]
* P. A. M. Khirbet Mird
* Mark 2:2–5, 8–9: 6:30–31, 33–34, 36–37, 39–41; John 5:5; 17:3, 7–8
* Louvain, Bibl. De l'Univ. (P. Khirbet Mird 4, 11, 26, 27)
* Sixth century
* The manuscript is too fragmentary to determine its textual character.

𝔓[85] *(P. Gr. 1028)*
* J. Schwartz, "Papyrus et Tradition Manuscrite," *Zeitschrift für Papyrologie und Epigraphik* 4 (1969), 178–182.
* Revelation 9:19–10:1, 5–9
* Strasbourg, Bibliotheque Nationale et Universitaire (P. Gr. 1028)
* Fourth century
* The manuscript is too small to determine its textual character.

𝔓[86] *(P. Colon. Inv 5516)*
* Charalambakis, Hagedorn, Kaimakis, Thungen, "Evangelium

nach Mattaus 5:13–16, 22–25," *Vier literarische Papyri der Kolner Sammlung*.

* Matthew 5:13–16, 22–25
* Cologne: Institut für Alterumskunde, Inv. Nr. 5516
* Early fourth century (c. 300)
* The manuscript is too small to determine its textual character.

𝔓^{87} *(Inv. Nr. 12)*

* Kramer, Romer, Hagedorn, *Kolner Papyri 4: Papyrologica Coloniensa* Vol. VII (1982), 28–31.
* Philemon 13–15, 24–25
* Cologne: Institut für Alterumskunde, P. Col. theol. 12.
* Late second century. The editors (Kramer, Romer, Hagedorn) of the *editio principes* of 𝔓^{87} say it displays a good Roman uncial hand like that found in 𝔓^{46}, and therefore (like 𝔓^{46}) belongs to the early third century. But since I have argued that 𝔓^{46} belongs to the second century (see above), so follows 𝔓^{87}. One should also note 𝔓^{87}'s likeness to P. Oxyrhynchus 841, second hand (dated AD 120–130).
* The manuscript is proto-Alexandrian.

𝔓^{88} *(P. Med. Inv. 69.24)*

* S. Daris, *Papiri Letterari dell'Universita Cattolica de Milano*, 80–91.
* Mark 2:1–26
* Milano, Universite Cattolica (P. Med. Inv. 69.24)
* Fourth century
* The manuscript is generally Alexandrian.

𝔓^{89} *(PL III/292)*

* R. Pintaudi, "N.T. Ad Hebreos VI, 7–9; 15–17 (PL III/292)," *Zeitschrift für Papyrologie und Epigraphik* 42 (1981), 42–44.
* Hebrews 6:7–9, 15–17
* Firenze, Bibl. Medecia Laurenziana (PL III/292)
* Third/fourth century
* The manuscript is too small to determine its textual character.

𝔓[90] *(P. Oxy. 3523)*

* Theodore A. Skeat, *Oxyrhynchus Papyri* L (London, 1983), no. 3523, 3–8.
* John 18:36–19:7
* Oxford, England: Ashmolean Museum
* Late second century. Displaying a "Decorated Rounded" hand, 𝔓[90] belongs to the late second century, according to T. C. Skeat, editor of the *editio principes*. Skeat notes 𝔓[90]'s morphological similarities with P. Egerton (the Egerton Gospel) dated c. 150 and with P. Oxyrhynchus 656 (later second century). While visiting the Ashmolean, I observed that 𝔓[90] is very similar to P. Oxyrhynchus 656. I would suggest other manuscripts of comparable morphology: P. Oxyrhynchus 4022 (second century), P. Yale 1273 (c. AD 100, whose lettering is similar to 𝔓[90] but earlier), and P. Geneva 253 (second century).
* The manuscript has more textual affinity with 𝔓[66] than with any other single manuscript, though it does not concur with 𝔓[66] in its entirety. Otherwise, it shows some affinity with ℵ.

𝔓[91] *(P. Macquarie Inv. 360 + P. Mil. Vogl. Inv. 1224)*

* Claudio Gallazzi, "P. Mil. Vogl. Inv. 1224: Novum Testamentum, Act. 2,30–37 E 2,46–3,2" in *Bulletin of American Society of Papyrologists* 19 (1982): 39–45; S. R. Pickering, "The Macquarie Papyrus of the Acts of the Apostles," a preliminary report (Aug. 30, 1984); S. R. Pickering, "P. Macquarie Inv. 360 (+ P. Mil. Vogl. Inv. 1224): Acta Apostolorum 2.30–37, 2.46–3.2," in *Zeitschrift für Papyrologie und Epigraphik* 65 (1986): 76–79. In this publication, the transcription for both portions of the manuscript is given.
* Acts 2:30–37, 46–3:2. One portion (the larger one): Milan, Italy: Istituto di Papirologia, Universita Degli Studi di Milano (P. Mil. Vogl. Inv. 1224); the other portion (the smaller one): North Ryde, Australia: Ancient History Documentary Research Centre at Macquarie University (P. Macquarie inv. 360)
* Second half of third century
* The manuscript is proto-Alexandrian, though the extant portion is too fragmentary to be sure.

$\mathfrak{P}^{92}$ *(P. Narmuthis inv. 69.39a and 69.229a)*

* Claudio Gallazzi, "Frammenti di un Codice con le Epistole di Paolo," in *Zeitschrift für Papyrologie und Epigraphik* 46 (1982): 117–122.
* Ephesians 1:11–13, 19–21; 2 Thessalonians 1:4–5, 11–12
* Cairo, Egypt: Museo Egizio del Cairo (P. Narmuthis inv. 69.39a and 69.229a)
* Late third/early fourth century (c. 300)
* The manuscript shows strong affinity with $\mathfrak{P}^{46}$, א, and B.

$\mathfrak{P}^{93}$ *(PSI inv. 108)*

* M. Manfredi, *Trenta Testi Greci da Papiri Letterari e Documentari*, 10–11.
* John 13:15–17
* Firenze, Istituto Papirologico, G. Vitelli (PSI inv. 108)
* End of fourth/early fifth century (c. 400)
* The manuscript is too small to determine its textual character.

$\mathfrak{P}^{94}$ *(P. Cairo 10730)*

* *Greek Papyri in the Cairo Museum*, 89.
* Romans 6:10–13, 19–22
* Cairo, Egyptian Museum (10730)
* Fifth/sixth century
* The manuscript is too small to determine its textual character.

$\mathfrak{P}^{95}$ *(Firenze PL II/31)*

* Jean Lenaerts, "Un papyrus l'Evangile de Jean: PL II/31," in *Chronique d'Egypte* 60 (1985): 117–120.
* John 5:26–29, 36–38
* Firenze: Biblioteca Medicea Laurenziana (PL II/31)
* c. 200. The editor of the *editio principes* (Laenarts), comparing $\mathfrak{P}^{95}$ to P. Rylands 542, dated $\mathfrak{P}^{95}$ to the early third century. But it should be noted that P. Rylands 542 comes from the same manuscript as PSI 1377, which was dated by Bartoletti as being anywhere from the second half of the second century to the beginning of the third. $\mathfrak{P}^{95}$ is also morphologically similar to P. Oxyrhynchus 224 + P. Rylands

547 of the later second century, as well as with P. Oxyrhynchus 406 (c. 200). All things considered, it is fair to date 𝔓[95] as c. 200.
* The manuscript is proto-Alexandrian, though it is too fragmentary to be certain.

𝔓[96] *(Pap. K 7244)*
* T. Orlandi, *Mitteilungon ans der Papirisammlung der Osterr. Nat. Bibl.;* (1974), 49–51.
* Matthew 3:13–15
* Vienna, Osterreichischen Nationalbibliothek (Pap. K 7244)
* Sixth century
* The manuscript is too small to determine its textual character.

𝔓[97] *(P. Chester Beatty XVII)*
* P. Chester Beatty XVII.
* Luke 14:7–14
* Dublin, Chester Beatty Library
* Sixth/seventh century
* The manuscript is too small to determine its textual character.

𝔓[98] *(P. IFAO inv. 237b +a)*
* G. Wagner, "Cette liste d'objects divers ne fait peut-etre pas partie d'une letter," P. IFAO II (1971), 31. D. Hagedorn "P.IFAO II 31: Johannesapokalypse 1,13–20" *Zeitschrift für Papyrologie und Epigraphik* 92 (1992), 243–247, pl. IX.
* Revelation 1:13–2:1
* Cairo, Egypt: Institut Francais d'Archéologie Orientale (P. IFAO inv. 237b [+a])
* Late second century. In the first publication of this manuscript, the editor (Wagner) thought the fragment was a list of objects; he dated the manuscript to the second century on the basis that the document on the recto was dated to late first or early second century. Later, it was discovered by Hagedorn that the list was actually text of Revelation 1. 𝔓[98], written in a common hand, bears some resemblance to P. Berolinses 6849, a documentary text dated to AD 148.

* The manuscript displays textual independence.

𝔓[99] *(P. Chester Beatty 1499)*
* not yet published
* An extensive table of conjugated verbs from the following verses: Romans 1:1; 2 Corinthians 1:3–17; 2:1–8:22; 9:2–11:23; 11:26–13:11; Galatians 1:4–11, 18–6:15; Ephesians 1:2–2:21; 3:8–6:24.
* Dublin, Chester Beatty Library (Ac. 1499, fol. 11–14)
* Mid-fourth century
* The manuscript is too fragmented to determine its textual character.

𝔓[100] *(P. Oxy. 4449)*
* R. Hubner, *Oxyrhynchus Papyri*, LXV (London: 1998), no. 4449, 24–29.
* James 3:13–4:4, 9–5:1
* Oxford, England: Ashmolean Museum
* Late third/early fourth century (c. 300)
* The manuscript generally concurs with the Alexandrian witnesses, 𝔓[74], **א**, A, and B.

𝔓[101] *(P. Oxy. 4401)*
* J. David Thomas, *Oxyrhynchus Papyri*, LXIV, 4401, 1–3.
* Matthew 3:10–12; 3:16–4:3
* Oxford, England: Ashmolean Museum
* Third century (handwriting is similar to that found in P. IFAO inv. 89 and P. Koln VII 282, both assigned to the third century).
* The manuscript is proto-Alexandrian, having more affinity with codex Sinaiticus than codex Vaticanus.

𝔓[102] *(P. Oxy. 4402)*
* J. David Thomas, *Oxyrhynchus Papyri*, LXIV, 4402, 4–5.
* Matthew 4:11–12, 22–23
* Oxford, England: Ashmolean Museum
* c. 300. The handwriting is similar to that found in P. Hermes 5, dated c. 325.

* The manuscript is too small to determine its textual character.

$\mathfrak{P}^{103}$

Same manuscript as $\mathfrak{P}^{77}$ (see above).

$\mathfrak{P}^{104}$ *(P. Oxy. 4404)*

* J. David Thomas, *Oxyrhynchus Papyri*, LXIV, 4404, 6–7.
* Matthew 21:34–37, 43, 45(?)
* Oxford, England: Ashmolean Museum
* Early second century. J. D. Thomas, the editor of the *editio principes* of $\mathfrak{P}^{104}$, dated $\mathfrak{P}^{104}$ to the second half of the second century. I would date it to the first half of the first century, with the possibility that it could be c. 100. The manuscript is written in a carefully executed "Decorated Rounded" style, a style that was prominent from 100 BC to AD 150, at the latest.[19] In this style there is a conscious effort to round letters and to finish every vertical stroke with a serif or decorated roundel. $\mathfrak{P}^{104}$, exemplifying this style almost to perfection, shows an early formation akin to what one sees in the Herculaneum papyri (dated pre-AD 79). One can especially see the similarities in P. Herculaneum 208, even more so with P. Herculaneum 697. $\mathfrak{P}^{104}$, however, is probably later. Another comparable manuscript to $\mathfrak{P}^{104}$ with firm dating is P. Oxyrhynchus 454 + PSI 119. The date of this manuscript (mid-second century) is quite solid because it was written on the verso of a documentary text with military accounts dated AD 111. Though similar, $\mathfrak{P}^{104}$ is more rigid and consistently decorated. Other manuscripts bearing some likeness to $\mathfrak{P}^{104}$ are P. Oxyrhynchus 2743 (second century) and P. Oxyrhynchus 3009 (second century). Even more likeness is seen in P. Oxyrhynchus 3010 (early second century); nearly every letter is shaped similarly (note the letter combinations *mu-epsilon-nu*, and *pi-rho-omicron-sigma*). And yet there are two more manuscripts whose likeness to $\mathfrak{P}^{104}$ is unmistakable. The first is PSI 1213 (which is likely from the same codex as P. Oxyrynchus 4301), dated late first/early second century, written in an elegant, decorated hand of the Roman Uncial type (note the formation of the *gamma, iota, lambda, mu, pi, rho,*

tau; the spacing between letters and the relationship of each letter to the binary lines). The second comparable manuscript is P. Berolinses 6845, which is dated "first/second century." The likeness to 𝔓^{104} is unmistakable (note the formation of *alpa, kappa, mu, pi, rho, upsilon*). All in all, 𝔓^{104} could be the earliest extant New Testament manuscript, dated as early as "c. 100," or at the latest, "early second century." I think it should share a place of prominence with 𝔓^{52}, long recognized as the earliest New Testament manuscript.

* Because it is a small fragment, its textual character cannot be determined. However, it should be noted that it does not include Matt. 21:44 (contra א, B, C, L, W, and Z).

𝔓^{105} *(P. Oxy. 4406)*

* J. David Thomas, *Oxyrhynchus Papyri*, LXIV, 4406, 10–11.
* Matthew 27:62–64; 28:2–5
* Oxford, England: Ashmolean Museum
* Fifth/sixth century
* The manuscript is too small to determine its textual character.

𝔓^{106} *(P. Oxy. 4445)*

* W. E. H. Cockle, *Oxyrhynchus Papyri* LXV, 4445, 13–17.
* John 1:29–35, 40–46
* Oxford, England: Ashmolean Museum
* c. 200. 𝔓^{106} bears notable resemblance to P. Rylands 463 (Gospel of Mary, early third century), P. Oxyrhynchus 1100 (a document dated AD 206), and P. Oxyrhynchus 2539 (assigned a date of second/third century). As such, 𝔓^{106} could be dated c. 200.
* The manuscript of 𝔓^{106} is proto-Alexandrian, aligning with 𝔓^{66}, 𝔓^{75}, א, and B.

𝔓^{107} *(P. Oxy. 4446)*

* W. E. H. Cockle, *Oxyrhynchus Papyri*, LXV (London: 1998), no. 4446, 17–19.
* John 17:1–2, 11
* Oxford, England: Ashmolean Museum

* Early third century. The manuscript bears notable resemblance to P. Oxyrhynchus 2659 (second century), but is slightly later (especially in the shape of the *epsilon* and *kappa*).
* The manuscript is too small to determine its textual character.

𝔓108 *(P. Oxy. 4447)*
* W. E. H. Cockle, *Oxyrhynchus Papyri*, LXV (London: 1999), no. 4447, 20–22.
* John 17:23–24; 18:1–5
* Oxford, England: Ashmolean Museum
* c. 200. The handwriting bears remarkable resemblance to P. Chester Beatty IX-X (Ezekiel), dated to the second century. 𝔓108 is probably slightly later because it was written with metallic ink.
* The manuscript, though small, concurs with א.

𝔓109 *(P. Oxy. 4448)*
* W. E. H. Cockle, *Oxyrhynchus Papyri* LXV, no. 4448, 22–24.
* John 21:18–20, 23–25
* Oxford, England: Ashmolean Museum
* c. 200. According to the editor (Cockle) of the *editio principes* (P. Oxyrhynchus 4448), the manuscript bears morphological resemblance to 𝔓66. The small size of 𝔓109, however, does not allow for a full-scale comparison to 𝔓66. Nonetheless, Cockle dated 𝔓109 to the early third century on the basis of its likeness to 𝔓66, which he says "is usually assigned to the first part of the third century." However, several paleographers (Hunger, Seider, Cavallo) date 𝔓66 to the second century, and that is where 𝔓109 should also be placed (see discussion above on 𝔓66).
* The manuscript is too small to determine its textual character.

𝔓110 *(P. Oxy. 4494)*
* W. E. H. Cockle, *Oxyrhynchus Papyri*, LXVI (London: 1999), no. 4494, 1–4.
* Matthew 10:13–15, 25–27
* Oxford, England: Ashmolean Museum

* Second half of third century, having similarites to 𝔓45 and P. Florence II 108 (dated c. 260)
* The manuscript displays an independent text.

𝔓111 *(P. Oxy. 4495)*

* W. E. H. Cockle, *Oxyrhynchus Papyri*, LXVI (London: 1999), no. 4495, 4–6.
* Luke 17:11–13, 22–23
* Oxford, England: Ashmolean Museum
* First half of the third century, bearing some similarities with P. Giss. 40 (dated 215)
* The manuscript concurs with 𝔓75 almost completely.

𝔓112 *(P. Oxy. 4496)*

* W. E. H. Cockle, *Oxyrhynchus Papyri*, LXVI (London: 1999), no. 4496, 6–7.
* Acts 26:31–32; 27:6–7
* Oxford, England: Ashmolean Museum
* Fifth century
* The manuscript is too small to determine its textual character, but there is an expansion in Acts 26:32, found in Old Latin MSS.

𝔓113 *(P. Oxy. 4497)*

* W. E. H. Cockle, *Oxyrhynchus Papyri*, LXVI (London: 1999), no. 4497, 8–9.
* Romans 2:12–13, 29
* Oxford, England: Ashmolean Museum
* c. 200. Though 𝔓113 is only a scrap (and therefore limits full analysis), it bears resemblance to P. Oxyrhynchus 2341 (dated AD 202) and P. Oxyrhynchus 223 (written on the back of a document dated AD 186 and therefore dated c. 200). 𝔓121, with more text than 𝔓113, has the same kind of "Severe" style and shows the same likeness to P. Oxyrhynchus 2341 and 223. Both 𝔓113 and 𝔓121 also show similarities with P. Oxyrhynchus 1604 and 1788 (both assigned to the late second century). 𝔓113 and 𝔓121 could safely be dated as c. 200.

* The manuscript is too small to determine its textual character.

𝔓114 *(P. Oxy. 4498)*

* W. E. H. Cockle, *Oxyrhynchus Papyri*, LXVI (London: 1999), no. 4498, 10–11.
* Hebrews 1:7–12
* Oxford, England: Ashmolean Museum
* Third century, having resemblance to P. Oxyrhynchus 23 (which predates 295) and P. Oxyrhynchus 2700 (which clearly belongs to the third century)
* The manuscript is too small to determine its textual character.

𝔓115 *(P. Oxy. 4499)*

* Juan Chapa, *Oxyrhynchus Papyri*, LXVI, 4499, 11–39.
* Revelation 2:1–3, 13–15, 27–29; 3:10–12; 5:8–9; 6:5–6; 8:3–8, 11–9:5, 7–16, 18–10:4, 8–11:5, 8–15, 18–12:5, 8–10, 12–17; 13:1–3, 6–16, 18–14:3, 5–7, 10–11, 14–15, 18–15:1, 4–7
* Oxford, England: Ashmolean Museum
* Middle third century. The handwriting resembles two manuscripts from the Heroninos Archive (which must predate 256, according to documentary texts in the collection, namely P. Flor. 108 and P. Flor. 259. 𝔓115 also resembles P. Oxyrhynchus 1016 (which predates 234).
* The manuscript aligns with A and C in its textual witness, which are generally regarded as providing the best testimony to the original text of Revelation. Thus, 𝔓115 has superior testimony to that of 𝔓47, which aligns with codex Sinaiticus and together form the second-best witness to the text of Revelation.

𝔓116 *(Pap. G. 42417)*

* Not yet published
* Hebrews 2:9–11; 3:3–6
* Vienna: Ostereichischen Nationalbibliothek (Pap. G. 42417)
* Sixth/seventh century
* The manuscript is too small to determine its textual character.

$\mathfrak{P}^{117}$

* P. Hamburg Inv. NS 1002
* 2 Cor. 7:7–11
* Hamburg: Staas-und Universitatsbibliothek
* Fourth/fifth century
* The manuscript is too small to determine its textual charcter.

$\mathfrak{P}^{118}$ *(P. Koln 10311)*

* G. Shenke, *Kolner Papyri* 10 (2003), 33–37.
* Romans 15:26–27, 32–33; 16:1, 4–7, 11–12. (Interestingly, the text of $\mathfrak{P}^{118}$ runs straight from Romans 15:33 to 16:1; so it differs from $\mathfrak{P}^{46}$ which has the doxology [usually printed at 16:25–27] immediately following 15:33.)
* Universitat zu Koln
* Middle to late second century. The editor (Schenke) dates the manuscript to the third century by likening it to $\mathfrak{P}^{66}$, which was dated by Turner to the early third century (see *Greek Manuscripts of the Ancient World*, 2nd edition, no. 63). The likeness to $\mathfrak{P}^{66}$ is unmistakable, but $\mathfrak{P}^{66}$ belongs in the second century, not the third. (See the discussion on the date of $\mathfrak{P}^{66}$ above.)
* The manuscript is too small to determine its textual character.

$\mathfrak{P}^{119}$ *(P. Oxy. 4803)*

* Juan Chapa, *Oxyrhynchus Papyri,* LXXI, 4803, 2–6.
* John 1:21–28, 38–44
* Oxford, England: Ashmolean Museum
* Third century. The handwriting (which is Reformed Documentary) is quite similar to that found in $\mathfrak{P}^{114}$ (P. Oxy. 4498), which belongs to the third century. $\mathfrak{P}^{119}$ can be dated with certainty to the third century because it is also like P. Oxy. 23, which is dated before 295 (according to a documentary text on the other side). The hand of $\mathfrak{P}^{119}$ is also like P. Oxyrhynchus 2098 (see C. H. Roberts, *Greek Literary Hands* 19b), a Herodotus passage written in the first half of the third century (on the verso of the Herodotus passage is a land survey written during the reign of Gallienus, 253–268).

* The manuscript has some textual affinities with $\mathfrak{P}^{5}$.

$\mathfrak{P}^{120}$ *(P. Oxy. 4804)*

* Juan Chapa, *Oxyrhynchus Papyri* 71:6–9, no. 4804
* John 1:25–28, 33–38, 42–44
* Oxford, England: Ashmolean Museum
* Third century. The handwriting is that of a professional scribe producing a Biblical Uncial. The editor of the *edito principes* (Chapa) likens the manuscript to Chester Beatty IV (Genesis), which is assigned with confidence to the first half of the fourth century (a line added in the upper margin folio 24 verso is written in a semi-cursive hand of a type well known in the first half of the fourth century). But $\mathfrak{P}^{120}$ has clearer affinities with the other two manuscripts noted by Chapa—namely, $\mathfrak{P}^{38}$ (early third century, see comments there) and P. Oxy. 4442 (Exodus), assigned a date of the third century. $\mathfrak{P}^{120}$ also has definite affinity with the hand displayed in P. Oxy. 405, a third century manuscript. For these reasons, I would date $\mathfrak{P}^{120}$ in the third century (perhaps middle to late third century).
* Though the extant text is small, the manuscript shows general agreement with $\mathfrak{P}^{66}$ and $\mathfrak{P}^{75}$ (especially in 1:34, where both these papyri read "Son of God" versus "chosen One of God" found in $\mathfrak{P}^{5}$ and $\mathfrak{P}^{106}$).

$\mathfrak{P}^{121}$ *(P. Oxy. 4805)*

* Juan Chapa, *Oxyrhynchus Papyri* LXXI, 4805, 9–11.
* John 19:17–18, 25–26
* Oxford, England: Ashmolean Museum
* c. 200. The handwriting, which is in the Severe style, is similar to P. Oxy. 1604 and P. Oxy. 1788 (both assigned to the late second century), as well as P. Oxy. 2341 (see C. H. Roberts' *Greek Literary Hands* 19c), a document dated to 202, and P. Oxy. 223 (see C. H. Roberts' *Greek Literary Hands* 21a), written on the verso of a document (P. Oxy. 237) dated 186. (The verso text of Homer [P. Oxy. 223] has a few cursive entries that are early third century). The hand of the manuscript $\mathfrak{P}^{121}$ is also like $\mathfrak{P}^{113}$ (P. Oxy. 4497) dated to the third century.
* The manuscript is too small to determine its textual character.

$\mathfrak{P}^{122}$ *(P. Oxy. 4806)*

- Juan Chapa, *Oxyrhynchus Papyri* LXXI, 4806, 11–14.
- John 21:11–14, 22–24
- Oxford, England: Ashmolean Museum
- Fourth century (like P. Chester Beatty IV, Genesis)
- The manuscript displays some textual resemblance to W.

$\mathfrak{P}^{123}$ *(P. Oxy. 4844)*

- D. Thompson, *Oxyrhynchus Papyri* LXXII, 4844, 1–3.
- 1 Corinthians 14:31–34; 15:3–4
- Oxford, England: Ashmolean Museum
- Late third/early fourth century. The editor (Thompson) dates it to the early fourth century, comparing the hand to P. Hermes 4 (c. 320). The handwriting of $\mathfrak{P}^{123}$ is a bilinear Reformed Documentary, slightly slopes to the right, is semi-cursive, with curved letters having noticeable hooks at the foot of the curve. This hand is somewhat like that found in P. Florentine II.259 (*Greek Literary Hands*, 22d), which is dated to c. 260 (as part of the Heroninos correspondence). It is more like P. Oxyrhynchus 2601, a letter by a Christian named Copres. This sloping semi-cursive manuscript was written during the time of the Diocletian persecution around AD 303.
- Though the manuscript is too small to determine its textual affinities, it does supply another early witness (with $\mathfrak{P}^{46}$, **א**, and B) to the placement of 1 Cor. 14:34–35 immediately following 1 Cor. 14:33, as opposed to following 1 Cor. 14:40 (as in D, F, and G).

$\mathfrak{P}^{124}$ *(P. Oxy. 4845)*

- D. Thompson, *Oxyrhynchus Papyri* LXXII, 4845, 4–6.
- 2 Corinthians 11:1–4, 6–9
- Oxford, England: Ashmolean Museum
- Sixth century
- The manuscript is too small to determine its textual character.

$\mathfrak{P}^{125}$ *(P. Oxy. 4934)*

- J. Chapa, *Oxyrhynchus Papyri* LXXIII, 4934, 17–22.

* 1 Peter 1:23–2:5, 7–12
* Oxford, England: Ashmolean Museum
* Mid-third century. The handwriting of $\mathfrak{P}^{125}$ is like that found in P. Florentine II.208 (*Greek Literary Hands*, 22a), a text of the *Iliad* that has a letter of the Heroninus archive on the verso. The *Iliad* text is dated with certainty to c. 260. The hand of $\mathfrak{P}^{125}$, which is bilinear and sloping slightly to the right, displays notable similarities with three third-century New Testament papyri: $\mathfrak{P}^{1}$, $\mathfrak{P}^{15}$, and especially $\mathfrak{P}^{101}$ (see discussions on each of these papyri). To date, $\mathfrak{P}^{125}$ is the earliest manuscript of 1 Peter. ($\mathfrak{P}^{72}$ is c. 300, and $\mathfrak{P}^{81}$ is fourth century.)
* The manuscript agrees, for the most part, with $\mathfrak{P}^{72}$, א, A, and B.

$\mathfrak{P}^{126}$ *(PSI inv. 1479)*
* *Papiri greci e latini della Societa Italiana,* no. 1479
* Hebrews 13:12–13, 19–20
* Florence, Italy: Istituto Papirologico "G. Vitelli"
* Fourth century
* The manuscript is too small to determine its textual character.

$\mathfrak{P}^{127}$ *(P. Oxy. 4968)*
* D. C. Parker and S. R. Pickering, *Oxyrhynchus Papyri* LXXIV, 4968, 2–45.
* Acts 10:32–35, 40–45; 11:2–5, 30; 12:1–3, 5, 7–9; 15:29–31, 34–36, 38–41; 16:1–4, 13–40; 17:1–10.
* Oxford, England: Ashmolean Museum
* Early fourth century. The handwriting of $\mathfrak{P}^{127}$ is like that found in $\mathfrak{P}^{81}$ (c. 300) and P. Chester Beatty IV, Genesis (early fourth century).
* The manuscript displays an independent text.

Other Papyrus Manuscripts

¦ *Egerton Gospel* (*P. Egerton 2* and *P. Koln 608*)
* *Fragments of An Unknown Gospel and Other Early Christian Papyri*, H. I. Bell and T. C. Skeat, 1–15.

* Section one parallels John 5:39–47; 10:31; section two parallels Matthew 8:1–4; section three parallels Matthew 22:16–17; 15:8–9; section four parallels no existing Gospel text.
* London: British Museum
* Early to middle second century. It bears unmistakable likeness to 𝔓52 (early second c.), P. Berolinensis 6854 (a document dated in the rein of Trajan, who died in AD 117), P. London 130 (early second c.), and P. Oxyrhynchus 656 (mid-to-late second century).
* The manuscript displays an independent text.

¦ *P. Antinoopolis 2.54*
* *Antinoopolis Papyrus*, J. W. B. Barns and H. Zilliacus, Part 2, 6–7.
* Matt. 6:10–12
* Oxford, England: Ashmolean Museum
* Third century
* The manuscript is too small to determine its textual character.

¦ *P. Oxyrhynchus 655*
* B. P. Grenfell, A. S. Hunt, *The Oxyrhynchus Papyri* IV, 655, 22–28.
* Fragment of a lost Gospel.
* Oxford, England: Ashmolean Museum
* Third century
* The manuscript displays an independent text.

¦ *P. Oxyrhynchus 5073*
* G. S. Smith and A. E. Bernhard, *Oxyrhynchus Papyri* LXXVI, 5073, 19–23.
* Mark 1:1–2 (amulet)
* Oxford, England: Ashmolean Museum
* Late third century. The handwriting is like that found in P. Oxy. 1015 (middle to late third c.) and P. Hermes Rees (with a firm date of c. 325).
* The manuscript is too small to determine its textual character, though it agrees with codex Sinaiticus in reading "the gospel of Jesus Christ" in Mark 1:1.

Significant Uncial Manuscripts

The manuscripts typically classified as "uncial" are so designated to differentiate them from papyrus manuscripts. In a sense, this is a misnomer because the real difference has to do with the material they are written on—vellum (treated animal hide) as compared to papyrus—not the kind of letters used. Indeed, the papyri are also written in uncials (capital letters), but the term "uncial" typically describes the majuscule lettering that was prominent in fourth-century biblical texts, such as in codex Sinaiticus (**א**) and codex Vaticanus (B).

א *(Codex Sinaiticus)*

* This codex was discovered by Constantin von Tischendorf in St. Catherine's Monastery (situated at the foot of Mount Sinai). Tischendorf greatly used the textual evidence of codex Sinaiticus in preparing his critical editions of the Greek New Testament. Tischendorf issued an edition of codex Sinaiticus printed in facsimile type in 1862: *Codex Sinaiticus Petropolitanus* (Leipzig). See also Kirsopp Lake's *Codex Sinaiticus Petropolitanus*. Oxford University Press: 1911 (a photographic reproduction), and two works by Milne and Skeat: *The Scribes and Correctors of the Codex Sinaiticus* (Oxford: Oxford University Press, 1938); *The Codex Sinaiticus and the Codex Alexandrinus*. (London, 1951 and 1963).
* Entire Old Testament, and New Testament in this order: Four Gospels, Pauline Epistles (including Hebrews), Acts, General Epistles, Revelation. It also includes the Epistle of Barnabas and the Shepherd of Hermes. (The manuscript contains 346 leaves of fine parchment, written in four columns.)
* London, British Museum
* c. 350–375. The codex cannot be earlier than 340 (the year Eusebius died) because the Eusebian sections of the text are indicated in the margins of the Gospels by a contemporary hand.
* Tischendorf thought four scribes had originally produced the codex, whom he named Scribes A, B, C, D. After reinvestigation, Milne and Skeat identified only three scribes: A (who wrote the historical and poetical books of the Old Testament, as well as most of

the New Testament), B (who wrote the Prophets and the Shepherd of Hermas), and D (who wrote some Psalms, Tobit, Judith, 4 Maccabees, and redid small sections of the New Testament). Milne and Skeat demonstrated that Scribe A of Codex Vaticanus was likely the same scribe as Scribe D of Codex Sinaiticus.[20] If this true, then א is contemporary with B—perhaps produced in the same scriptorium in Alexandria.

Some scholars have detected nine correctors at work on this manuscript. Only two are typically noted, as follows:

א[1] (designates the corrector who worked in the scriptorium on the manuscript before it left the scriptorium.)

א[2] (designates a group of correctors working in Caesarea in the sixth or seventh century who corrected the text by bringing it into general conformity with the Byzantine texts.)

Codex Sinaiticus provides a fairly reliable witness to the New Testament; however, the scribe was not as careful as the scribe of B. He was more prone to error and to creative emendation. Hort's comparison between B and א affirms this: "Turning from B to א, we find ourselves dealing with the handiwork of a scribe of a different character. The omissions and repetitions of small groups of letters are rarely to be seen; but on the other hand all the ordinary lapses due to rapid and careless transcription are more numerous, including substitutions of one word for another, . . . The singular readings are very numerous, especially in the Apocalypse, and scarcely ever commend themselves on internal grounds. It can hardly be doubted that many of them are individualisms of the scribe himself."[21] The scribe of א displayed his creativity not only in Revelation but also in John, especially in the first eight chapters. In an extensive study, Fee demonstrated that א is clearly a "Western" text in John 1:1–8:38.[22]

A (Codex Alexandrinus)

* *Facsimile of the Codex Alexandrinus*; ed. E. M. Thompson. London,

1879–1883; Milne, H. J. M. and T. C. Skeat, *The Codex Sinaiticus and the Codex Alexandrinus*. London, 1951 and 1963.

* Only 773 of the original 820 or so pages still exist. The rest were lost as the book was passed down through the centuries. The surviving parts of Alexandrinus contain a Greek translation of the whole Old Testament, the Apocrypha (including four books of Maccabees and Psalm 151), most of the New Testament, and some early Christian writings (of which the *First and Second Epistles of Clement to the Corinthians* are the most important). Missing sections of the New Testament are Matthew 1:1–25:6; John 6:50–8:52, and 1 Corinthians 4:13–12:6.
* London: British Museum
* Early fifth century
* Kenyon thought the codex was the work of five scribes, to each of whom he designated a Roman numeral. According to Kenyon, scribes I and II copied the Old Testament; scribe III did Matthew, Mark, 1 Corinthians 10:8—Philemon 25; scribe IV did Luke–Acts, General Epistles, Romans 1:1–1 Corinthians 10:8; and scribe V did Revelation.[23] Milne and Skeat, however, argued that the whole codex was the work of two copyists (I and II).[24]

Evidently, the scribes of this codex used exemplars of varying quality for various sections of the New Testament. Compared to the General Epistles and Revelation (where Alexandrinus presents a reliable witness), the exemplar used for the Gospels was of poor quality, reflecting a Byzantine text type. Furthermore, the scribe of A infused his own readings into the text. Hort said, "in the New Testament an appreciable number of the singular readings of A consist in the permutation of synonyms, and it can hardly be doubted that these readings are true individualisms."[25]

Codex Alexandrinus is a witness to the Byzantine text-type in the Gospels. Its testimony in the Epistles is much better, and in Revelation it provides the best witness to the original text.

B (Codex Vaticanus)

* A photographic edition was published by the Vatican Library

authorities: *Bibliorum SS. Graecorum Codex Vaticanus 1209*. Milan: Vatican Library, 1904–1907.

* Originally it must have had about 820 leaves (1640 pages), but now it has 759, 617 in the Old Testament and 142 in the New. The major gaps of the manuscript are Genesis 1:1–46:28; 2 Samuel 2:5–7, 10–13; Psalms 106:27–138:6, Hebrews 9:14–13:25; the Pastoral Epistles; and Revelation.
* Rome: Vatican Library
* c. 350
* This codex, generally recognized as one of the most trustworthy witnesses to the New Testament text, is the work of two scribes, who are known as A (for the Old Testament) and B (for the New Testament). According to the studies of Milne and Skeat, two correctors worked on the New Testament: designated B^1 (a corrector nearly contemporary with the scribe) and B^2 (a tenth or eleventh century corrector, who retouched the writing and added accents and marks of punctuation).[26]

Codex Vaticanus is generally recognized as an eminent witness—especially in the Gospels. (Its "Western" tendencies in the Epistles have lessened its value for those books.) The scribe of B did his task with rote fidelity. This is underscored by Hort's comments about this scribe's copying habits: "The final impression produced by a review of all the trustworthy signs is of patient and rather dull or mechanical type of transcription, subject now and then to the ordinary lapses which come from flagging watchfulness, but happily guiltless of ingenuity or other untimely activity of brain, and indeed unaffected by mental influences except of the most limited and unconscious kind."[27]

C (Codex Ephraemi Rescriptus)

* Constantin von Tischendorf, *Codex Ephraemi Syri rescriptus sive fragmenta Novi Testamenti*. Leipzig, 1843 (with plates); Robert W. Lyon, "A Re-examination of Codex Ephraemi Rescriptus" in *New Testament Studies* 5 (1958–1959), 260–272. This article provides a list of corrections to Tischendorf's work.

* The codex originally contained the entire Bible but now has only parts of six Old Testament books and portions of all New Testament books except 2 Thessalonians and 2 John. The single-column Bible text, written in the fifth century AD was erased in the twelfth century and replaced by a two-column text of a Greek translation of sermons or treatises by a certain Ephraem, a fourth-century Syrian church leader.
* Paris: Bibliotheque Nationale (Codex Gr. 9)
* Early fifth century
* According to Metzger, the text of C "seems to be compounded from all the major text types, agreeing frequently with the later Koine of Byzantine type, which most scholars regard as the least valuable type of New Testament text."[28] Scholars have been able to detect various correctors, designated as follows:

C^1

* This is the original corrector.

C^2

* This is the corrector of the sixth century (probably in Palestine).

C^3

* This is the corrector of the ninth century (probably in Constantinople) who added accents and breathing marks.

D (Codex Bezae)

* The first edited transcription was published by F. H. Scrivener: *Bezae Codex Cantabrigiensis*. Cambridge, 1864. The facsimile edition of *Codex Bezae Cantabrigiensis* was published by Cambridge University Press in 1899.
* Greek-Latin diglot containing Matthew–Acts, 3 John, with lacunae. According to the Alands, the codex was produced in either Egypt or North Africa by a scribe whose mother tongue was Latin.[29] Parker argues that it was copied in Beirut, a center of Latin legal studies during the fifth century, where both Latin and Greek were used.[30]
* Early fifth century

* According to Parker, it was produced by a scribe who knew Latin better than Greek, and then was corrected by several scribes.[31] According to the Alands, this codex is the most controversial of the New Testament uncials because of its marked independence. Its many additions, omissions, and alterations (especially in Luke and Acts) are the work of a significant theologian.[32] A few earlier manuscripts ($\mathfrak{P}^{29}$?, $\mathfrak{P}^{38}$, $\mathfrak{P}^{48}$, and 0171) appear to be precursors to the type of text found in D, which is considered the principal witness of the Western text-type. Thus, Codex Bezae could be a copy of an earlier revised edition. This reviser must have been a scholar who had a propensity for adding historical, biographical, and geographical details. More than anything, he was intent on filling in gaps in the narrative by adding circumstantial details.

D (Codex Claromontanus)—also designated Dp

* Constantin von Tischendorf, *Codex Claromontanus*. Leipzig, 1852.
* Greek-Latin diglot containing Pauline Epistles including Hebrews. Two of the pages had been used before, containing faintly visible lines from Euripides' *Phaethon*. The Pauline letters are complete except for a few verses from Romans missing from both the Greek and the Latin, and a few Latin verses from 1 Corinthians.
* Paris: Bibliotheque Nationale (Codex Gr. 107, 107AB)
* Sixth century
* The Latin text is not a translation of the Greek text it parallels but an independent text copied alongside, perhaps to serve a community where Latin was understood better than Greek. Between the sixth and ninth centuries corrections were made to the manuscript by about nine different people. The manuscript is usually described as being "Western" because its geographical origin seemed to be the western areas of the Mediterranean. However, it should be noted that the Western readings in the Epistles are not so striking as those in the Gospels and Acts.

E (Codex Laudianus 35)—also designated Ea

* Constantin von Tischendorf, *Codex Laudianus Mon sac IX*. Leipzig, 1870.

* Acts (in Latin and Greek)
* Oxford: Bodleian Library (Gr. 35)
* Sixth century
* The manuscript is mixed, sometimes agreeing with D, more often Byzantine. It is the earliest extant manuscript to have Acts 8:37, the Ethiopian's confession of faith.

F (Codex Augiensis)—also designated Fp

* F. H. A. Scrivener, *An Exact Transcript of Codex Augiensis [with] a Full Collation of Fifty Manuscripts*. Cambridge, 1859.
* Pauline Epistles (in Greek and Latin), with Hebrews in Latin only
* Cambridge: Trinity College (B.XVII.1)
* Ninth century
* The manuscript displays a text type that is "Western."

G (Codex Boernerianus)—also designated Gp

* A photographic reproduction with introduction was made by A. Reichardt: *Der Codex Boernerianus*. Leipzig, 1909.
* Pauline Epistles (Greek with Latin interlinear; contains superscript after Philemon for an Epistle to the Laodecians but no text follows)
* Dresden: Sachsische Landesbibliothek (A 145b)
* Ninth century
* The manuscript probably had the same archetype as F, both of which resemble the manuscript 037 from St. Gall.

H (Codex Coislinianus)—also designated Hp

* Kirsopp Lake, *Facsimiles of the Athos Fragments of the Codex H of the Pauline Epistles*. Oxford,1905.
* Pauline Epistles (parts of 1 and 2 Cor., Gal., Col., 1 Thess., Heb., 1 and 2 Tim., Titus—arranged according to the colometric edition of the Epistles prepared by Euthalius)
* Paris (22); Athos, Great Lavra (8); Kiev (3); Leneingrad (3); Moscow (3); Turin (2).
* Sixth century

* The manuscript is later Alexandrian.

I (Codex Freerianus or the Washington Codex)
* Henry A. Sanders, *The New Testament Manuscripts in the Freer Collection: Part IV*. New York: MacMillan, 1914.
* Pauline Epistles (1 Corinthians–Hebrews, Pastoral Epistles)
* Washington, D.C.: Freer Gallery of Art (06.275)
* Early fifth century (c. 400)
* According to Sanders, this manuscript has an Egyptian text, showing more agreement with א and A than with B.

K (Codex Cyprius)
* Collation by Scholz, *Curae criticae in historiam textus evangelorium* (Heidleburg, 1820), 80–90.
* Four Gospels
* Paris: Bibliotheque Nationale (Gr. 63)
* Ninth/tenth century
* The text is Byzantine.

K (Codex Mosquensis)
* J. Leroy, "Un temoin ancien des petis catecheses de Theodore Studite," *Scriptorium* 15 (1961), 36–40.
* Acts, Paul Epistles, General Epistles
* Moscow: History Museum (V, 93 S. 97)
* Ninth/tenth century
* The manuscript displays an independent text.

L (Codex Regius)
* Constantin von Tischendorf, *Codex Regius Mon sac*. Leipzig, 1846.
* Four Gospels (nearly complete)
* Paris: Bibliotheque Nationale (Gr. 62)
* Eighth century
* Though the manuscript contains several scribal errors, the basic text is still good, generally agreeing with B. It contains two endings to the Gospel of Mark (see comments on Mark 16:9–20).

M (Codex Campianus)
* B. Montfaucon, *Paleographia Graeca.* Paris, 1708.
* Four Gospels
* Paris: Bibliotheque Nationale
* Ninth century
* The text is Byzantine.

N (Codex Purpureas Petropolitanus)
* Scrivener, *Full and Exact Collation.*
* Four Gospels
* Leningrad: Imperial Library (several leaves)
* Sixth century
* The text is Caesarean.

O (Codex Sinopensis)
* H. Omont, *Notices et extraits des manuscrits de la bibliotheque nationale* (Paris, 1901).
* Matthew
* Paris: Bibliotheque Nationale
* Sixth century
* The text is Caesarean.

P (Codex Porphyrianus)
* Constantin von Tischendorf, *Codex Porphyrianus Mon sac VI.* Leipzig, 1860.
* Acts–Revelation, a palimpset with commentary of Euthalius on Acts and Pauline Epistles written (in 1301) over the biblical text
* Leningrad: Public Library (Gr. 225)
* Ninth century
* The manuscript has a text that is Byzantine and Alexandrian—related to the Andreas-type of text in Revelation.

Q (Codex Guelferbytanus B)
* Tischendorf, *Codex Guelferbytanus Mon sac III.* Leipzig.

* Luke–John, a palimpset with Latin text of Isidore of Seville's *Origins* and *Letters* written over biblical text
* Wolfenbuttel: Herzog August Biliothek. Weissenburg 64
* Fifth century
* The manuscript is Byzantine.

R (Codex Nitriensis)

* Tischendorf, *Monumenta sacra inedita* II. Leipzig, 1846.
* Luke
* London: British Museum
* Seventh century
* The text is Western.

S (Codex Vatican 354)

* Bianchini, *Evangelium quadra*.
* Four Gospels
* Rome: Vatican Library
* AD 949
* The text is Byzantine.

T (Codex Borgianus)

* A. A. Giorgi, *Fragmentum Evangelii S. Johannis Graecum Copto-Sahidicum*. Rome, 1789.
* Portions of Luke (6, 18–24) and John (1, 3, 4–8)—a Coptic Sahidic-Greek diglot
* Rome: Collegium de Propoganda Fide
* Fifth century
* Because it is a Coptic Sahidic-Greek diglot, there is no question that it was produced in Egypt. Codex T is one of the fifth-century manuscripts that perpetuated the kind of Alexandrian scholarship that produced Codex B. Indeed, the text of T "is very close to that represented by codex Vaticanus."[33]

W (Codex Washingtonianus or, The Freer Gospels—named after its owner, Charles Freer)

* Henry Sanders, *The New Testament Manuscripts in the Freer Collection: Part I, The Washington Manuscript of the Four Gospels.* New York: MacMillan, 1912; Henry Sanders, *Facsimile of the Washington Manuscript of the Four Gospels in the Freer Collection.* Ann Arbor, 1912.
* Matthew–Acts
* Washington, D.C.: Freer Gallery of Art (06.274)
* c. 400
* According to Sanders, Codex W was copied from a parent manuscript (exemplar) that had been pieced together from several different manuscripts. This is obvious because the textual presentation of W is noticeably variegated and even the stratification of the text is matched by similar variations in paragraphing. Sanders suggested that the parent manuscript was probably put together shortly after the Diocletian persecution, when manuscripts of the New Testament were scarce: "The patchwork character of the parent manuscript plainly indicates origin in a time when Biblical manuscripts came near extinction in certain regions at least. As the last great persecution, in which we are expressly told that the sacred books were ordered destroyed, was begun by Diocletian in 303, we are probably justified in dating the parent of W soon after that." The scribe who collated the parent manuscript drew upon various sources to put together his Gospel codex. Based on the textual evidence, Sanders conjectured that the scribe of the parent manuscript used a text that came from North Africa (the "Western" text) for first part of Mark, and the scribe of W used manuscripts from Antioch for Matthew and the second part of Luke "to fill the gaps in the more ancient manuscript, which he was copying" (139). Detailed textual analysis reveals the variegated textual stratifications of W, as follows: in Matthew the text is Byzantine; in Mark the text is first Western (1:1–5:30), then Caesarean in Mark 5:31–16:20 (akin to $\mathfrak{P}^{45}$); in Luke the text is first Alexandrian (1:1–8:12) then Byzantine. John is more complicated because the first part of John (1:1–5:11), which fills a quire, was the work of a seventh-century scribe who must have replaced a damaged quire. This first section has a mixture of Alexandrian and Western

readings, as does the rest of John. The siglum W^s designates the work of this seventh-century scribe.

The extreme textual variation in this manuscript reveals the tremendous liberties the scribes (of the parent manuscript of W and W itself) exerted in producing a codex. They not only selected various exemplars of various portions of each gospel (at least as many as seven different exemplars), they also harmonized, and filled textual gaps. Codex W is a prime example of what happened to many New Testament manuscripts after the major shift occurred. Each gospel as an individual literary work was utilized and thereby changed for the purpose of making a four-fold Gospel codex.

X (Codex Monacensis)

* Scrivener, *A Plain Introduction to the Textual Criticism of the New Testament*. London, 1894.,
* Four Gospels (in this order: Matthew, John, Luke, Mark)
* Munich: University Library
* Ninth century.
* The text is Byzantine.

Z (Codex Dublinensis)

* John Barrett, *Evangelium secundum Matthaeum ex codice rescripto in bibliotheca collegii sae Trinitatis iuxta Dublinum*. Dublin, 1801; Samuel P. Tregelles, *The Dublin Codex Rescriptus: a Supplement*. London, 1863.
* Matthew, a palimpset with patristic writings written over biblical text
* Dublin: Trinity College (K 3.4)
* Sixth century
* The manuscript is Alexandrian; it agrees with א.

Δ = *037 Codex Sangallensis*

* H. C. M. Rettig, *Antiquissimus quatuor evangeliorum canonicorum Codex Sangallensis Graeco-Latinus interlinearis*. Zurich, 1836.

* Four Gospels—Greek-Latin diglot, with Latin interlinear
* Gallen: Stiftbibliothek (48)
* Ninth century
* The manuscript is Byzantine generally; later Alexandrian in Mark (similar to L).

Θ = *038 Codex Koridethi*

* A transcription of the entire text was produced by Gustav Beermann and Caspar R. Gregory: *Die Koridethi Evangelien*. Leipzig, 1913.
* Four Gospels
* Tiflis, Georgia: Manuscript Institute (Gr. 28)
* Ninth century
* The scribe was probably a Georgian who did not know Greek. He drew his letters, rather than write them. In Matthew, Luke, and John the text is Byzantine. In Mark it is Caesarean in the sense that it agrees with the type of text that "Origen and Eusebius used in the third and fourth centuries at Caesarea."[34] This manuscript, often associated with 565 and 700, is considered by many to be the chief representative of the Caesarean text.

Λ = *039 Codex Tischendorfianus III*

* Tischendorf, *Notitia editionis codicis Bibliorum Sinaitici*. Leipzig, 1860.
* Luke, John
* Oxford: Bodleian Library
* Ninth century.
* The text is Byzantine.

Ξ = *040 Codex Zacynthius*

* Samuel P. Tregelles, *Codex Zacynthius*. London, 1861.
* Luke 1:1–11:33 (with lacunae)—a palimpset with a twelfth-century Gospel lectionary written over original text that is itself surrounded by commentary
* London: British and Foreign Bible Society (24)
* Sixth century

* The manuscript is later Alexandrian; it agrees with B and contains the same system of chapter divisions as B (as well as 579).

Π = *041 Codex Petropolitanus*
* Tischendorf, *Notitia editionis codicis Bibliorum Sinaitici*. Leipzig, 1860.
* Four Gospels
* St. Petersburg: National Library
* Ninth century
* The text is Byzantine.

Σ = *042 Codex Rossanensis*
* Gebhardt and Harnack, *Evangeliorum Codex Graecus Purpureus Rossanensis*. Leipzing, 1880.
* Matthew, Mark
* Rossano: Museum Diocessano
* Sixth century.
* The text is Byzantine, agreeing with N.

Φ = *043 Codex Beratinus*
* P. Batiffol, "Les Manuscrits grecs de Berat d'Albanie et le codex purpureus Φ" in *Archives des missions scientifiques et litteraires*, third series, vol. 13. Paris, 1887.
* Matthew and Mark—written with silver ink on purple parchment
* Tirane: National Archives (1)
* Sixth century
* The manuscript is Byzantine; it contains a noteworthy long addition after Matthew 20:28.

Ψ = *044 Codex Athous Laurae*
* Kirsopp Lake, "Texts from Mount Athos," in *Studia Biblica et Ecclesiastica* 5:89–185. Oxford, 1903.
* Mark 9—Acts, General Epistles, Pauline Epistles, Hebrews
* Monastery of the Laura, Mount Athos: Lavra (B' 52)
* Eighth or ninth century

* The manuscript is generally Byzantine, with Western and Alexandrian affinities in Mark, where it has two endings (as in L).

Ω = *045 Codex Athous Dionysiou*

* M.-J. Lagrange, *Critique textuelle*, II, *La Critique rationelle*. Paris, 1935.
* Four Gospels
* Mount Athos: Monastery of Dionysius
* Eighth/ninth century
* The text is Byzantine.

046 Codex Vaticanus 2066

* Tregelles, *An Account of the Printed Text*, 156ff. London, 1854.
* Revelation
* Rome: Vatican Library
* Eighth/ninth century
* The text is independent.

058

* Gregory, *Textkritik des Neuen Testamentes* I, 72–73. Leipzig, 1900–1909.
* Matthew 18:18–29
* Vienna: Osterreichischen Nationalbibliothek (G. 39782)
* Fourth century
* The manuscript is too small to determine its textual character.

0162 (P. Oxy. 847)

* Grenfell and Hunt, *Oxyrhynchus Papyri,* V (1909), 4–5.
* John 2:11–22
* New York: Metropolitan Museum of Art (09.182.43)
* Early fourth century
* The manuscript shows great affinity with $\mathfrak{P}^{66}$ and $\mathfrak{P}^{75}$, as well as with B.

0169 (P. Oxy. 1080)

* Grenfell and Hunt, *Oxyrhynchus Papyri* VIII (1911), 14–15.
* Revelation 3:19–4:3
* Princeton, New Jersey: Princeton Theological Seminary (Pap. 5)
* Fourth century
* The manuscript generally agrees with codex Sinaiticus.

0171 (PSI 2.124)

* *Pubblicazioni della Societa Italina, Papiri Greci e Latini.* Vol. 1 (1912): 2–4; Vol. 2 (1913): 22–25. A transcription of the text is printed in *New Documents Illustrating Early Christianity* vol. 2, editor G. H. R. Horsley (1982).
* J. Neville Birdsall, "A fresh examination of the fragments of the gospel of St. Luke in ms. 0171 and an attempted reconstruction with special reference to the recto." Pp. 212–227 in *Philologia Sacra*; editor Roger Gryson. Verlag Herder Freiburg, 1993.
* Matthew 10:17–23, 25–32; Luke 22:44–56, 61–64
* Florence: Bibliotheca Laurenziana (PSI 2.124)
* c. 300
* The manuscript is related to the D-text in Acts.

0188 (Papyrus Berlin 13416)

* Salonius, A. H. "Die griechischen Handschriftenfragmente des Neuen Testaments in den Staatlichen Museen zu Berlin." *Zeitschrift für die Neutestamentliche Wissenschaft* 26 (1927):100–102.
* Matthew 11:11–17
* Berlin, Germany: Staatliche Museen (P. 13416)
* Fourth century
* The manuscript is too small to determine its textual character.

0189 (Papyrus Berlin 11765)

* Salonius, A. H. "Die griechischen Handschriftenfragmente des Neuen Testaments in den Staatlichen Museen zu Berlin." *Zeitschrift für die Neutestamentliche Wissenschaft* 26 (1927):115–119.
* Acts 5:3–21

* Berlin, Germany: Staatliche Museen (P. 11765)
* c. 200. This is the earliest parchment manuscript of the New Testament. 0189 bears morphological resemblance to late second century manuscripts $\mathfrak{P}^{4+64+67}$ (see comments above), P. Oxyrhynchus 661, and P. Oxyrhynchus 2404. But 0189 is later in overall appearance, especially the small omicron. Thus, it is fair to date 0189 as c. 200.
* The manuscript nearly always agrees with the Alexandrian witnesses.

0212

* C. Kraeling, *A Greek Fragment of Tatian's Diatessaron from Dura, S & D*. London, 1935.
* Diatessaron: Matt. 27:56–57; Mark 15:40, 42; Luke 23:49–51, 54; John 19:38
* New Haven: Yale University Library (P. Dpg 24)
* Third century
* The manuscript, which is a fragment of Tatian's Diatessaron, has an independent text.

0206 (P. Oxy. 1353)

* Grenfell and Hunt, *The Oxyrhynchus Papyri* XI, 506.
* 1 Peter 5:5–13
* Dayton: Theological Seminary
* Early fourth century
* The manuscript displays an independent text.

0207 (PSI 1166)

* M.-J. Lagrange, *Critique textuelle*, II, *La Critique rationelle*, 585–586. Paris, 1935.
* Revelation 9:2–15
* Firenze: Bibl. Medecia Laurenziana (PSI 1166)
* Fourth century
* The manuscript has an independent text.

0220 (MS 113)

* W. H. P. Hatch, *Harvard Theological Review* 45 (1952): 81–85.

* Romans 4:23–5:3, 8–13
* Oslo/London: the Schoyen Collection
* Third century
* The manuscript agrees with B everywhere except in Rom. 5:1.

0230

* G. Mercati, *Papiri greci e latini della Societa Italiana* XIII, 87–102.
* Ephesians 6:11–12
* Firenze: Bibl. Medecia Laurenziana (PSI 1166)
* Fourth century
* The manuscript is too small to determine its textual character.

0231 (P. Antinoopolis 11)

* C. H. Roberts, *The Antinoopolis Papyri I* (London, 1950), 23–24.
* Matthew 26:75–27:1, 3–4
* Oxford: Ashmolean Museum
* Fourth century
* The manuscript is Alexandrian.

0232 (P. Antinoopolis 12)

* C. H. Roberts, *The Antinoopolis Papyri I* (London, 1950), 24–26, plate 1.
* 2 John 1–9
* Oxford: Ashmolean Museum
* Fourth century
* The manuscript is Alexandrian.

0242 (MS 71942)

* R. Roca-Puig, "Un pergamino greigo del Evangilio de San Mateo," *Emerita* 27 (1959), 59–73.
* Matthew 8:25–9:2, 13, 32–38, 40–46
* Cairo, Egypt: Cairo Egyptian Museum
* Fourth century
* The manuscript displays an independent text.

Uncial Manuscripts from St. Catherine's Monastery

A number of uncial New Testament manuscripts were discovered at St. Catherine's Monastery in the 1970s. None of these have been published as individual texts with transcriptions. However, the Alands were permitted access to the manuscripts and have incorporated their evidence into the textual apparatus of *Novum Testamentum Graece*. These are listed with the other uncial manuscripts in Appendix I in the 27th edition (pp. 702–703), as follows:

0278 (Paul's Epistles) ninth century
0279 (Luke 8, 22) eighth/ninth century
0281 (Matt. 6–21) seventh/eighth century
0282 (Phil. 2–3) sixth century
0285 (Rom.–2 Cor.; Eph.; 1 Tim.; Heb.; 1 Pet.) sixth century
0289 (Rom.; 1 Cor.) seventh/eighth century
0291 (Luke 8–9) seventh/eighth century
0292 (Mark 6–7) sixth century
0293 (Matt. 21, 26) sixth century
0294 (Acts 14–15) sixth/seventh century
0296 (2 Cor. 7; 1 John 5) sixth century

Minuscules

The minuscules are manuscripts written in cursive letter form rather than in separate-letter uncial form. The minuscules came later than the uncials—at a time when the Byzantines were mass-producing copies of the Bible via oral dictation. Since speed of copying was an issue, scribes used a cursive form rather than an uncial form.

f^1

* f^1 designates a family of manuscripts including 1, 118, 131, 209
* Kirsopp Lake, *Texts and Studies* 7. Cambridge, 1902.
* Four Gospels
* Minuscule 1 is at Basel: Universitatsbibliothek (A. N. IV, 2)
* Twelfth—fourteenth century
* The text type of f^1 has been traced to a third or fourth-century

"Caesarean" archetype; the text agrees with codex Koridethi in Mark.

f^{13}

- f^{13} designates a family of manuscripts including 13, 69, 124, 174, 230, 346, 543, 788, 826, 828, 983, 1689, 1709 (known as the Ferrar group)
- Kirsopp and Silva Lake, *Family 13 (The Ferrar Group)* in *Studies and Documents* 11 (London and Philadelphia, 1941).
- Four Gospels
- Minuscule 13 is at Paris: Bibliotheque Nationale (Gr. 50).
- Eleventh—fifteenth century
- The text type of f^{13}, which has affinities with the so-called Caesarean text type, has been traced to an archetype from Calabria in southern Italy or Sicily. In these manuscripts Luke 22:43–44 follows after Matt. 26:39, and the pericope concerning the adulteress (John 7:53–8:11) appears after Luke 21:38, not after John 7:52.

Codex 33

- This manuscript was collated by S. P. Tregelles and used in his edition of the *Greek New Testament* (1857–1879).
- All of New Testament except Revelation
- Paris: Bibliotheque Nationale (Gr. 14)
- Ninth century
- This manuscript, often called "the Queen of the Cursives," is a prime example of a late manuscript that retained (for the most part) the Alexandrian text type.

Codex 81

- F. H. Scrivener, *An Exact Transcript of Codex Augiensis with a Full Collation of Fifty Manuscripts*. Cambridge, 1859.
- Acts, Paul's Epistles, General Epistles
- Alexandria: Greek Patriarchate 59 (255 folios); London: British Library Add. 20003 (57 folios)
- 1044 (the manuscript has a specific date)

* The manuscript is Alexandrian.

Codex 565

* Johannes Belsheim, *Christiana Videnskabs-Selskabs Forhandlinger*, 1885 (No. 9)—text of Mark and collation of other three Gospels. Corrections were published by H. S. Cronin in *Texts and Studies* V (4); Cambridge, 1899.
* Gospels (gold letters on purple vellum)
* Leningrad: Public Library (Gr. 53)
* Ninth century
* In Mark, this manuscript is closely aligned to codex Koridethi, a Caesarean text.

Codex 700

* H. C. Hoskier, *A Full Account and Collation of the Greek Cursive Codex Evangelium 604*; London, 1890.
* Gospels
* London: British Library (Egerton 2610)
* Eleventh century
* This manuscript greatly differs from the Textus Receptus (nearly 2,750 times) and has many singular readings. One of its most striking readings includes a variation of the Lord's prayer (see comments on Luke 11:2).

Codex 1424 (or Family 1424)

* Gospels, Acts, General Epistles, Revelation, Paul's Epistles
* Maywood, Illinois: Jesuit-Krauss-McCormick Library (Gruber Ms. 152)
* Ninth or tenth century
* Several other manuscripts share essentially the same text as 1424 and therefore comprise a family of manuscripts: M, 7, 27, 71, 115, 160, 179, 185, 267, 349, 517, 659, 692, 827, 945, 954, 990, 1010, 1082, 1188, 1194, 1207, 1223, 1293, 1391, 1402, 1606, 1675, 2191.

Codex 1739

* A collation of the manuscript was made by Morton S. Enslin in *Six Collations of New Testament Manuscripts*, eds. Kirsopp Lake and Silva New, in *Harvard Theological Studies* 17; Cambridge, Mass., 1932.
* Acts and Epistles
* Athos: Lavra (B' 42)
* Tenth century
* For the Pauline Epistles, Zuntz demonstrated the textual affinities of $\mathfrak{P}^{46}$, B, 1739, Coptic Sahidic, Coptic Boharic, Clement, and Origen. The relationship between $\mathfrak{P}^{46}$, B, and 1739 is remarkable because 1739 is a tenth-century manuscript that was copied from a fourth-century manuscript of excellent quality. According to a colophon, the scribe of 1739 for the Pauline Epistles followed a manuscript which came from Caesarea in the library of Pamphilus and which contained an Origenian text. The three manuscripts, $\mathfrak{P}^{46}$, B, and 1739, form a clear textual line: from $\mathfrak{P}^{46}$ (early second century) to B (early fourth century) to 1739 (tenth century based on fourth century). Zuntz said, "Within the wider affinities of the 'Alexandrian' tradition, the Vaticanus is now seen to stand out as a member of a group with $\mathfrak{P}^{46}$ and the pre-ancestor of 1739. The early date of the text-form that this group preserves is fixed by its oldest member, and its high quality is borne out by many striking instances. B is in fact a witness for a text, not of c. AD 360, but of c. AD 200."[35]

Codex 2053

* Josef Schmid, *Studien zur Geschichte des griechischen Apokalypse-Textes*, vol. 2; Munich, 1955.
* Revelation (with Oecumenius's commentary on it)
* Messian: Biblioteca Universitario (99)
* Thirteenth century
* According to Schmid, this manuscript—with A and C 2344—is one of the best authorities for the book of Revelation.

Codex 2344

* Josef Schmid, *Studien zur Geschichte des griechischen Apokalypse-Textes*, vol. 2; Munich, 1955.
* Acts, General Epistles, Paul's Epistles, Revelation
* Paris: Bibliotheque Nationale (Coislin Gr. 18)
* Eleventh century
* According to Schmid, this manuscript—with A and C 2053—is one of the best authorities for the book of Revelation.

The majority of minuscules are noted in NA^{27} as M; in this volume as Maj. Quite often, but not always, the reading of Maj concurs with the Textus Receptus (TR). For the book of Revelation, M^{A} designates a number of manuscripts that follow the text of Andreas of Caesarea's commentary on Revelation, and M^{K} designates the great number of manuscripts that display a Koine (or Byzantine) text type.

Ancient Versions

As the gospel spread in the early centuries of the Christian era, Christians in various countries wanted to read the Bible in their own language. As a result, many translations were made in several different languages—as early as the second century. For example, there were translations done in Coptic for the Egyptians, in Syriac for those whose language was Aramaic, in Gothic for the Germanic people called the Goths, and in Old Latin for the Romans and Carthagenians.

Among the ancient versions that are used for establishing the original text are the following: Old Latin, Coptic, Syriac, Gothic, Ethiopic, Armenian, and Georgian. However, readers should be aware that ancient translators, as well as modern, took liberties in the interest of style when they rendered the Greek text. In other words, there is no such thing as a literal, word-for-word translation in any translation. Therefore, the witness of the various ancient versions is only significant when it pertains to significant verbal omissions and/or additions, as well as significant semantic differences. One should not look to the testimony of any ancient version for conclusive evidence concerning word transpositions, verb changes, articles, or other normal stylistic variations involving noun insertions, conjunction additions, and slight changes in prepositions. The citation of such versions for these kinds of variant readings in the apparatuses of critical editions of the Greek New Testament can be quite misleading. In the commentary that follows the versions will usually not be listed for these kinds of variants. Among the more important versions are the following:

Syriac (syr)

¦ *syrc (Syriac Curetonian)*

* William Cureton, *Remains of a Very Ancient Recension of the Four Gospels in Syriac.* London, 1858.
* Francis Crawford Burkitt, *Evangelion da-mepharreshe: The Curetonian Version of the Four Gospels, with the readings of the Sinai Palimpset* (vol. 1 *Text*; vol. 2 *Introduction and Notes.*) Cambridge, 1904.
* Gospels
* London: British Museum
* Fifth century
* Scholars had thought that the form of the text reflected in this manuscript and the Syriac Sinaiticus (see below) came from the late second century because of their perceived association with the Diatessaron. But this association has not been proven. Therefore, it is safer to say that Old Syriac translations began to be made in the early fourth century. The Syriac Sinaiticus represents an early stage in this process, and the Syriac Curetonian probably represents the next stage—i.e., it is a revision. Both manuscripts are generally regarded as "Western."

¦ *syrs (Syriac Sinaiticus)*

* Agnes S. Lewis, *The Old Syriac Gospels or Evangelion da-mepharreshe; being the Text of the Sinai or Syro-Antiochene Palimpset, including the latest additions and emendations, with the variants of the Curetonian Syriac.* London, 1910.

* Gospels (a palimpset)
* Fourth century
* This manuscript is the earliest extant document of the Old Syriac translation. Together with the Syriac Curetonian, it displays an independent text type (see discussion above).

Old Latin

Like the Aramaic targums of Jewish worshipers, the Old Latin Bible had an informal beginning. In the early days of the Roman Empire and of the church, Greek was the language of Christians. Even the first bishops of Rome wrote and preached in Greek. As empire and church aged, Latin began to win out, especially in the West. It was natural that priests and bishops began informally to translate the Greek New Testament and Septuagint into Latin. The initial Latin version is called the Old Latin Bible. No complete manuscript of it survives. Much of the Old Testament and most of the New, however, can be reconstructed from quotations in the early church fathers. Scholars believe that an Old Latin Bible was in circulation in Carthage in North Africa as early as AD 250. From the surviving fragments and quotations there seem to have been two types of Old Latin text, the African and the European. The European existed in an Italian revision also. In textual studies the major importance of the Old Latin is in comparative study of the Septuagint because the Old Latin was translated from the Septuagint before Origen made his *Hexapla*.

Among the many extant manuscripts of the Latin New Testament, five are worthy of mention:

¦ *it^{a} (Codex Vercellenis)*

* Gospels (in the Western order: Matthew, John, Luke, Mark)
* Vercelli: Biblioteca Capitolare
* Fourth century
* The manuscript displays a "Western" text.

¦ *it^{b} (Codex Veronensis)*

* Gospels (in the Western order: Matthew, John, Luke, Mark)

* Verona: Biblioteca Capitolare
* Fifth century
* This manuscript, which is "Western," represents the kind Jerome used in making the Latin Vulgate.

¦ *it^{d} (Codex Cantabrigiensis)*
* Gospels (Western order), Acts, 3 John—the Latin text of Codex Bezae (a Greek-Latin diglot)
* Cambridge: Cambridge University Library
* Fifth century
* The Latin translation, as with the Greek text of this manuscript, displays an independent text, quite unlike other early Latin versions.

¦ *it^{e} (Codex Palantinus)*
* Gospels (written with silver ink on purple parchment)
* Trent: Museo Nazionale
* Fifth century
* The text is of the North African variety (as opposed to the European in it^{a} and it^{b}), though it is less pure than it^{k}.

¦ *it^{k} (Codex Bobiensis)*
* Matthew 1–15; Mark 8–16 (with lacuna)
* Turin: Biblioteca Universitaria Nazionale (G. VII.15)
* c. 400
* This manuscript is the earliest and purest form of the North African variety. It is the only manuscript to display just the short ending after Mark 16:8.

Other Versions

These versions are occasionally cited in this volume.

¦ *Armenian* (arm)

Christians from Syria carried their faith to their Armenian neighbors in eastern Asia Minor. As early as the third century, with the conversion of Tiridates III (who reigned 259–314), Armenia became a

Christian kingdom—the first such in history. Sometime during the fifth century an Armenian alphabet was created so that the Bible could be translated into the language of these new believers. The Armenian translation is considered one of the most beautiful and accurate of the ancient versions of the Greek, even though textual evidence indicates it may have been done from the Syriac first and then modified according to the Greek. (The Armenian language is allied closely with the Greek in grammar, syntax, and idiom.) An old tradition says that the New Testament was the work of Mesrop (a bishop in Armenia, 390–439) who is credited with inventing both the Armenian and Georgian alphabets.

The first translations of the New Testament into Armenian were probably based on Old Syriac versions. Later translations, which have the reputation for being quite accurate, were based on Greek manuscripts of the Byzantine text type but also show affinity with Caesarean manuscripts.

¦ *Coptic* (cop)

Coptic was the last stage of the Egyptian language and thus the language of the native populations who lived along the length of the Nile River. It was never supplanted by the Greek of Alexander and his generals or even threatened by the Latin of the Caesars. Its script is composed of twenty-five Greek uncials and seven cursives taken over from Egyptian writing to express sounds not in the Greek.

Through the centuries it developed at least five main dialects: Achmimic, sub-Achmimic (Memphitic), Sahidic, Fayyumic, and Bohairic. Fragments of biblical material have been found in all five dialects. They gradually faded out of use until—by the eleventh century—only Bohairic, the language of the Delta, and Sahidic, the language of Upper Egypt, remained. They too, however, had become strictly religious languages used only in Coptic churches by the seventeenth century because of the long dominance of Arabic that began with the Islamic conquest of Egypt in 641.

The earliest translation was in Sahidic in Upper Egypt, where Greek was less universally understood. The Sahidic Old and New Testaments were probably completed by around AD 200. Greek was so much more dominant in the Delta that the translation of the Scriptures into Bohairic probably was not completed until somewhat later. Since Bohairic was the language of the Delta, however, it was also the language of the Coptic Patriarch in Alexandria. When the Patriarchate moved from Alexandria to Cairo in the eleventh century, the Bohairic texts went along. Bohairic gradually became the major religious language of the Coptic church. The Copts had separated from the Roman Catholic church over doctrinal issues after the Council of Chalcedon in 451 and had then been isolated from Western Christendom by centuries of Islamic rule.

There were several dialects of Coptic, the three most prominent being Boharic (designated cop^{bo}) in north Egypt, Fayyumic (cop^{fay}) in central Egypt, and Sahidic (designated cop^{sa}) in southern Egypt. We have several extant translations of the New Testament into Coptic, some dated as early as the fourth century.

Ethiopic (eth)

By the middle of the fifth century a Christian king ruled in Ethiopia (Abyssinia), and until the Islamic conquests close ties were maintained with Egyptian Christianity. The Old Testament was probably translated into Old Ethiopic (called Ge'ez) by the fourth century. The Old Ethiopic version of the Old Testament contains several books not in the Hebrew Apocrypha. Most interesting of these is the book of Enoch, which is quoted in Jude 14 and was unknown to Bible scholars until James Bruce brought a copy to Europe in 1773.

The New Testament was translated into Old Ethiopic somewhat later than the Old Testament and contains a collection of writings mentioned by Clement of Alexandria, including the Apocalypse of Peter. Both Testaments are extant in Ethiopic manuscripts. None, however, is earlier than the thirteenth century, and these manuscripts seem to rest rather heavily on the Coptic and the Arabic. Nothing survived the total chaos that reigned in Ethiopia from the seventh to the thirteenth centuries. In Paul's Epistles, the Ethiopic version frequently agrees with $\mathfrak{P}^{46}$ (and B), with little or no support from other manuscripts. In Paul's Epistles, this translation frequently agrees with $\mathfrak{P}^{46}$ (and B), with little or no other support.[36]

¦ *Frankish*
The New Testament was translated into the ancient language of the western-European Germanic Franks, about AD 500–800 Only fragments of the gospel of Matthew remain from an eighth-century manuscript.

¦ *Georgian* (geo)
The same tradition that credits Mesrop with translating the Bible into Armenian also credits an Armenian slave woman with being the missionary through whom Georgian-speaking people became Christian. The earliest manuscripts for the Georgian Scriptures go back only to the eighth century, but behind them is a Georgian translation with Syriac and Armenian traces. Evidently the Gospels first came in the form of the Diatessaron; therefore, Georgian fragments are important in the study of that text. There is a whole manuscript copy of the Georgian Bible in two volumes in the Iberian Monastery on Mount Athos. The earliest extant manuscript is called the Adysh manuscript of 897 (designated geo^1); two other manuscripts of the tenth century are designated geo^2.

¦ *Gothic* (goth)
In the middle of the fourth century, Ulfilas translated the Bible from Greek into Gothic (for which he created the Gothic alphabet). His translation, as reflected in later editions, appears to be quite literal and dependent on the early Byzantine text.

Ulfilas may have been captured by Gothic raiders as a youth. Yet his residence by early adulthood was Constantinople, the Roman Empire's eastern capital. Here undoubtedly he received his education and began his life of service to the church. In 341 Eusebius of Nicomedia, bishop of Constantinople, consecrated Ulfilas as bishop. Soon afterward the young bishop proceeded to Dacia (north of the Danube River), and for his remaining years he served as the church's principal missionary to the western Goths in this region. The many converts indicate that Ulfilas's efforts to spread the gospel had extensive results. After several years, persecution forced Ulfilas out of Dacia, and his work thereafter originated from a residence in Moesia (south of the Danube), an area within the empire's borders.

Ulfilas's removal to Moesia also saw the beginnings of the project for which he is best remembered. This was his translation of the Old and New Testaments into the Goths' vernacular language. Toward this end, Ulfilas first had to reduce Gothic speech to writing, a task involving the invention of an alphabet based on Greek. Surviving remnants of this translation, as copied in the early Middle Ages, represent the earliest extant examples of Gothic literature. Ulfilas appears to have translated the whole New Testament and also the Old Testament except for the books of Kings (1 and 2 Samuel, 1 and 2 Kings). It is supposed that the missing Old Testament sections were omitted purposely because of Ulfilas's fear that they would only encourage the aggressive Goths.

Among Ulfilas's known writings, the only modern survivals are the Bible translation and possibly a creedal statement. The sermons and interpretive writings are no longer extant. Portions of a beautiful copy of the Gothic Bible have been preserved at the University of Uppsala, Sweden. Early sources of information about Ulfilas exist mainly in works by fifth-century church historians, primarily Philostorgius, Socrates, and Sozomen. Scattered fragments of his Old Testament translation survive and only about half of the gospels are preserved in the Codex Argenteus, a manuscript of Bohemian origin of the fifth or sixth century now at Uppsala in Sweden.

Diatessaron

In the middle of the second century, Tatian, a Syrian from Mesopotamia, produced a harmony of the Gospels by weaving together the four narratives into one (hence the name Diatessaron, meaning "through the four"). This is not the same as harmonization of one gospel account to another, wherein each Gospel is left intact but emended to appear like the others. The Diatessaron is "a cut and paste job." Because of this, the citation of the Diatessaron in the critical apparatus of Greek New Testaments can be misleading because the entire text of the Diatessaron is an adaptation of the four Gospels into one new work. For example, to cite the Diatessaron as including the verse Matt. 17:21 (which is not present in codices Vaticanus and Sinaiticus) is misleading because Tatian could have simply been using Mark 9:29 at this point in his composition. The same is true for its presumed witness to the inclusion of Matt. 18:11 (which Tatian could have taken from Luke 19:10), and for the additions in Luke 11:2–4 (all of which could have been taken from Matt. 6:9–13).

In any event, the Diatessaron had a tremendous effect in Syria and in the East. Christians in Syria from the third to the fifth century generally read the Diatessaron as their Gospel text. (Ephraem's commentary in Syriac has been preserved, in part, in a fifth-century manuscript of the the Chester Beatty collection, 709.) As late as AD 423, Theodoret (a bishop in Syria) found that many copies of the Diatessaron were being used in his diocese. Because Tatian had become heretical later in life and because Theodoret believed his congregations were in danger of being corrupted by Tatian's work, he destroyed all the copies he could find (about 200 of them) and replaced them with copies of the four separate gospels. "As a result of the zeal of Bishop Theodoret, and doubtless of others like him, no complete copy of Tatian's Diatessaron is extant today."[37] Only one small fragment discovered from Dura-Europas has been unearthed—namely, 0220.

It is difficult to determine how much influence the Diatessaron had on the transmission of the text of the separate Gospels. The general scholarly consensus is that some "instances of harmonization of the text of the Gospels in certain witnesses (notably the Western witnesses) are to be ascribed to Tatian's influence."[38] These influences are not at all apparent in Egyptian manuscripts; thus, it is unlikely that the Diatessaron had much effect on Egyptian scribes either before the fourth century or thereafter.

Church Fathers

Several church fathers are cited in this volume as witnesses to various textual variants. They are as follows (the date given is that of their death):

Ambrose 397
Anastasius 700
Apostolic Constitutions 380

Athanasius 373
Augustine 430
Basil 379
Chrysostom 407
Clement 215
Cyprian 258
Cyril 444
Didymus 398
Dionysius 265
Epiphanius 403
Eusebius 339
Eusebian Canons fourth century
Eustathius 337
Gregory-Nazianus 390
Gregory-Nyssa 394
Hegesippus 180
Hesychius 450
Hilary 367
Hippolytus 235
Irenaeus 202
Jerome 420
Julian 454
Justin 165
Lucifer 375
Nestorius 451
Origen 254
Serapion 362
Severian 408
Tertullian 220
Valentinians second century

Endnotes

1. Metzger, *Manuscripts of the Greek Bible*, 54.
2. Comfort, "Exploring the Common Identification of Three New Testament Manuscripts: $\mathfrak{P}^{4}$, $\mathfrak{P}^{64}$, $\mathfrak{P}^{67}$." *Tyndale Bulletin* 46 (1995):43–54.

3. T. C. Skeat, "The Oldest Manuscript of the Four Gospels?" *New Testament Studies* 43 (1997):1–34.
4. H. I. Bell, *Evidences of Christianity in Egypt*, 201.
5. Roberts and Skeat, *Birth of the Codex*, 40–41.
6. Ernest Colwell, "Method in Evaluating Scribal Habits: A Study of $\mathfrak{P}^{45}$, $\mathfrak{P}^{66}$, $\mathfrak{P}^{75}$," 106–124.
7. Ibid., 118–119.
8. James Royse, "Scribal Habits in Early Greek New Testament Papyri," 156.
9. Comfort, "The Scribe as Interpreter: A New Look at New Testament Textual Criticism according to Reader Response Theory," 103–151.
10. Young-Kyu Kim, "Paleographic Dating of $\mathfrak{P}^{46}$ to the Later First Century." *Biblica* 69 (1988) 248–257.
11. Herbert Hunger, "Zur Datierung des Papyrus Bodmer II ($\mathfrak{P}^{66}$)," *Anzieger der osterreichischen Akademie der Wissenschaften*, phil.-hist., Kl. Nr. 4 (1960), 12–23.
12. R. Seider, *Paleographie der Griechischen Papyri*, 121.
13. Cavallo, *Richerche sulla maiuscola biblica*, 23.
14. G. Fee, *Papyrus Bodmer II ($\mathfrak{P}^{66}$): Its Textual Relationships and Scribal Characteristics*, 71–75.
15. Colwell, "Method in Evaluating Scribal Habits," 121.
16. Ibid.
17. Calvin Porter, "Papyrus Bodmer XV ($\mathfrak{P}^{75}$) and the Text of Codex Vaticanus," in the *Journal of Biblical Literature* 81 (1962):363–376.
18. C. H. Roberts, *Manuscript, Society, and Belief in Early Christian Egypt*, 23.
19. I have provided 25 examples of manuscripts displaying the "Decorated Rounded" style from the first century BC to the early second century in *Encountering the Manuscripts*, 113–117.
20. Milne and Skeat, *The Scribes and Correctors of the Codex Sinaiticus*, 89–90.
21. Westcott and Hort, *Introduction to the New Testament in the Original Greek*, 246–247.
22. Fee, "Codex Sinaiticus in the Gospel of John: A Contribution to Methodology in Establishing Textual Relationships," 23–44.
23. Kenyon, *The Codex Alexandrinus*, 9ff.
24. Milne and Skeat, *Scribes and Correctors*, 91ff.

25. Westcott and Hort, *Introduction to the New Testament*, 232–233.
26. Milne and Skeat, *Scribes and Correctors*, 87ff.
27. Westcott and Hort, *Introduction to the New Testament*, 237.
28. Metzger, *The Text of the New Testament* (third edition), 49.
29. Alands, *The Text of the New Testament*, 108.
30. D. C. Parker, *Codex Bezae. An Early Christian Manuscript and Its Text*, 261–278
31. Ibid., 279–286.
32. Alands, *The Text of the New Testament*, 108.
33. Metzger, *The Text of the New Testament* (third edition), 56.
34. Ibid., 58.
35. Zuntz, *The Pauline Epistles*, 83.
36. Metzger, *The Text of the New Testament* (third edition), 84.
37. Ibid., 89–90.
38. Ibid., 92.

Chapter Three

The Synoptic Gospels (Matthew, Mark, and Luke)

In this chapter and those that follow, I list what I think is the original wording in a verse in bold type; variant readings follow. Manuscript information is provided for each reading in the manuscripts (abbreviated as MSS), followed by an explanation. The names "God," "Lord," "Jesus," and "Christ" are almost *always* written as nomina sacra (sacred names) in all the MSS; so these are not noted throughout. There are notes for other nomina sacra (sacred names), and sometimes for "Lord" in certain contexts.

THE GOSPEL ACCORDING TO MATTHEW

Title: The Gospel according to Matthew
According to the earliest manuscript evidence, the first gospel should be titled, "The Gospel according to Matthew." This is the title found in a Paris papyrus fragment, stored with $\mathfrak{P}^{4}$ (at the Bibliotheque Nationale), which I have seen in person. I think it is the title page for the Matthew portion of $\mathfrak{P}^{4+64+67}$ (dated late 2nd c.), a codex originally containing Matthew and Luke (see discussion in previous chapter). $\mathfrak{P}^{1}$ (c. 200) is untitled in its extant form (the MS begins with the first page of Matthew, numbered as "a" = 1); however, it is possible the original papyrus had a title page. $\mathfrak{P}^{62}$ (fourth century) labels this book as a "Gospel" (*euangelion*). א and B title this "According to Matthew."

1:1 | A record of the genealogy of Jesus Christ, Son of David, son of Abraham.
"Jesus" and "Christ" are written as nomina sacra (sacred names) in all the early MSS. $\mathfrak{P}^{1}$, written around 200, writes "Son of David" as a sacred name; this is a royal, messianic title—the Jews expected the Messiah-King to be the Son of David (2 Sam. 7:13, 16; Jer. 23:5; Ezek. 37:24). א also writes "Son of David" as a sacred name. It should be capitalized in English translations. The expression "son of Abraham" is not a sacred name or messianic title, but a description of Jesus as being in the line of Abraham.

1:6 | David fathered Solomon.
The original wording "David" is found in the three earliest MSS ($\mathfrak{P}^{1}$ א B). This was expanded to "David the king" in later MSS (C L W 33 Maj; so KJV). This is scribal expansion influenced by the previous phrase.

1:7 | Abijah fathered Asaph.
The original wording "Asaph" is found in four early MSS ($\mathfrak{P}^{1}$ א B C). This was changed in L W 33 Maj (so KJV) to "Asa," by way of scribal conformity to 1 Chron. 3:10–11.

1:10 | Manasseh father Amos.
The original wording "Amos" is found in the three earliest MSS (א B C). This was changed to "Amon" in L W Maj (so KJV), by way of scribal conformity to 1 Chron. 3:14.

1:18 | she was found to be with child by the Holy Spirit.
The divine name "Spirit" is written as a nomen sacrum (sacred name) in the earliest MSS ($\mathfrak{P}^{1vid}$ א B L W).

1:20 | the child conceived in her is by the Holy Spirit.
The divine name "Spirit" is written as a nomen sacrum (sacred name) in the earliest MSS: $\mathfrak{P}^{1}$ א B W.

1:23 | the virgin will conceive and bear the Son.
This verse, in all the MSS, quotes Isaiah 7:14 from the Septuagint. The Greek word for "virgin" is *parthenos*, while the Hebrew word is *'almah*, which refers to a young woman who is old enough to be married. The reference in Isaiah is not to a virgin birth in its immediate historical setting, as the context makes clear. However, the Greek text of Isa. 7:14 uses the term *parthenos* (virgin) to translate the Hebrew word. Matthew followed this. There has never been any debate about what Matthew intended; his wording makes it absolutely clear that he was describing a female with no sexual experience. The debate has been over the term Isaiah used, as to whether it means "virgin" or "young woman." Isaiah 8:8, 10 speaks of this birth as bringing the presence of God to his people; hence the child is called "Immanuel." Matthew saw this fulfilled in Jesus, who is God's presence among humanity. "Son" is written as nomen sacrum (sacred name) in א and C to designate "the Son of God." Most English versions, however, write this as "a son."

1:25 | she had borne a son.
The original wording "son" is found in the earliest MSS (א B Z 071). This was expanded to "firstborn son" in C D L W 087 Maj (so KJV), by way of scribal conformity to Luke 2:7, a parallel verse. The word "son" was not written as a nomen sacrum in א and B, pointing to one who is "a son."

2:15 | Out of Egypt I called my Son.

This verse quotes Hosea 11:1. In the context of Hosea, the reference is to the people of Israel as a son that was called out of Egypt. Matthew saw a second meaning and shows that the prophecy was also fulfilled when the infant Jesus fled with his parents to Egypt. The word for "Son" in 𝔓[70] (the earliest MS) ℵ C is written as a nomen sacrum (sacred name), indicating these scribes saw this prophecy as fulfilled in the Son of God. Most modern English versions are reluctant to capitalize "son" in this quote (see, for example, RSV NIV NRSV). A few versions do capitalize it so as to demonstrate that the prophecy was fulfilled in God's Son (see TEV, NLT).

2:18 | there was wailing and great mourning.

The original wording "wailing and great mourning" is found in the earliest MSS (ℵ B) and Z. This was expanded to "wailing and weeping and great mourning" in C D L W 0233 Maj (so KJV), by way of scribal conformity to Jer. 31:15 LXX.

2:23a | he settled in a town called Nazareth.

The Greek for "Nazareth" is *Nazara* (in 𝔓[70vid] Eusebius), *Nazaret* (in ℵ B D L 33), and *Nazareth* (in C K N W G 0233). "Nazara" has the earliest testimony (𝔓[70]); see Matt. 4:13, where it is spelled the same.

2:23b | He will be called a Nazarene.

Though there is no such exact wording in the OT prophets, the idea might be that Jesus is likened to the *Netzer*, the Hebrew word for "Branch," a metaphor for the Messiah (see Isa. 11:1; Jer. 23:5). This depiction is similar to the image of Jesus being the *Anatole* (2:1, 9), which means both "sunrising" and "sprout" (see Luke 1:78 and note).

3:11a | I baptize you with water for repentance, but the coming One is more potent than me.

The earliest MS (𝔓[101]) reads, "the coming One is more potent than me." The reading "the One coming after me is more potent than me" is found in א C D L W 0233. The words "after me" may have been added from parallel accounts (Mark 1:7; John 1:15).

3:11b | He will baptize you with the Holy Spirit and fire.
The divine name "Spirit" is written as a nomen sacrum (sacred name) in the earliest MSS: א B D W.

3:16–17
The earliest extant manuscript that preserves Matthew's record of Jesus's baptism is P. Oxyrhynchus 405, which preserves a portion of Irenaeus's *Against Heresies* (3.9) in which Matt. 3:16–17 is quoted. (The editors of P. Oxy. 405 dated the MS to the late second century. As such, this MS represents a very early copy of Irenaeus's original work, which was produced around AD 150–175.) The account of Jesus's baptism, as recorded in Matt. 3:16–17, is repeated in the course of Irenaeus's argument. A careful transcriptional reconstruction reveals that this manuscript most likely concurs with א and B. (See following comments.)

3:16a | the heavens were opened.
The original wording "were opened" is found in the earliest MSS, א* B (and Irenaeus, according to a citation of Matt. 3:16–17 in P. Oxy. 405). The wording "were opened to him" is found in later MSS ($א^1$ D^s L W 0233 Maj; so KJV). Since the documentary support for the omission of "to him" is strong (the three earliest MSS), it is likely that a later scribe added "to him" in an attempt to harmonize this part of the verse to 16b, which states that Jesus (not the crowd gathered there) saw God's Spirit descending upon him. It is also possible that scribes harmonized Matthew to Mark, who portrays the baptism as Jesus's private experience (Jesus sees the heavens opened and hears the heavenly voice). But the whole tenor of Matthew's account implies a public unveiling.

3:16b | he saw the Spirit of God descending like a dove.
The divine "Spirit" is written as a nomen sacrum (sacred name) in the earliest MSS: א B D W.

3:17 | This is my beloved Son.
"Son" is written as a nomen sacrum (sacred name) in an early MS, א (also L).

4:1 | Jesus was led by the Spirit into the wilderness.
The divine "Spirit" is written as a nomen sacrum (sacred name) in the earliest MSS (א B D W), showing it was the divine Spirit (not an inner compunction of the human spirit) that led Jesus into the wilderness.

4:3 | If you are the Son of God, command these stones to become bread.
"Son of God" is written as a nomen sacrum (sacred name) in the earliest MSS (א B D W).

4:6a | If you are the Son of God, throw yourself down.
"Son of God" is written as a nomen sacrum (sacred name) in the earliest MSS (א B D W).

4:10a | Jesus said to him, "Go away, Satan."
The original wording is "go away" in the earliest MSS (א B W). The wording "get behind me" is found in later MSS (C^2 [sixth century] D L 33 Maj; so KJV), by way of scribal conformity to Matt. 16:23.

4:13 | He left Nazareth and settled in Capernaum.
Nazara (the spelling in all MSS) is better known as "Nazareth" (see note on 2:23a).

4:21–22
The verses are present in $\mathfrak{P}^{102}$ (only part of 4:22 is extant in this early MS) א B D. These verses are not present in W and 33, most likely due to homoeoteleuton (both 4:20 and 4:22 end with the same two words in Greek; translated as "they followed him").

4:24 | they brought to him those suffering the torments of being demon-possessed.
The wording "those suffering the torments of being demon-possessed"

is found in B C*. The reading "those suffering torments and those being demon-possessed" is found in ℵ C^2 [sixth century] D W Maj. The textual evidence is divided; either reading could possibly be the original.

5:3 | blessed are the poor in spirit.

The scribe of B did not write *pneuma* (spirit) as a nomen sacrum (sacred name). Jesus was probably speaking of the human spirit. The scribes of ℵ D W write it as a nomen sacrum (sacred name), suggesting the idea of being poor with respect to God's Spirit.

5:16 | they may give glory to your Father in heaven.

The divine "Father" is written as a nomen sacrum (sacred name) in two early MSS (ℵ W), as well as L.

5:19 | but whoever practices and teaches them will be called great in the kingdom of heaven.

This wording is found in some early MSS ($ℵ^1$ B C). The words are omitted in other early MSS (ℵ* D W). Though the textual evidence is divided, the omission was most likely due to homoeoteleuton (the previous sentence ends with the same last six words).

5:20

The verse is included in early MSS ($\mathfrak{P}^{64+67}$ ℵ B C W). The verse is omitted in D. The scribe of D continued the omission begun in 5:19 to the end of 5:20, which ends with the same last three words.

5:22a | if you are angry with a brother you will be liable to judgment.

The original wording "angry with a brother" is found in the earliest MSS ($\mathfrak{P}^{64+67}$ ℵ* B). This is expanded to "angry with a brother without cause" in later MSS ($ℵ^2$ [seventh century] D L W Maj; so KJV). The addition of "without cause" was a scribal attempt to soften Jesus's bold assertion and to thereby justify anger if it is for a good reason. But this insertion must be rejected on internal grounds (had it originally been in the text why would it have been deleted?) and on documentary grounds. The second-century manuscript, 𝔓64+67, does not include this word, nor do א and B.

5:25 | lest your accuser hand you over to the judge and the judge to the guard.

The original wording "and the judge to the guard" is found in the three earliest MSS (𝔓64+67 א B). This is expanded to "and the judge hand you over to the guard" in (D) L W 33 Maj, by way of scribal gap-filling.

5:44a | I say to you, "love your enemies."

The original wording "love your enemies" is found in the two earliest MSS (א B). This is expanded to "love your enemies, bless those who curse you, do good to those who hate you" in later MSS (D L W 33 Maj; so KJV), by way of scribal harmonization to Luke 6:27–28, parallel verses.

5:44b | pray for the ones persecuting you

This original wording is found in the two earliest MSS (א B). This is expanded to "pray for the ones despitefully using you and persecuting you" in later MSS (D L W 33 Maj; so KJV), by way of scribal harmonization to Luke 6:27–28, parallel verses.

5:45, 48 | your Father.

The divine "Father" is written as a nomen sacrum (sacred name) in two early MSS (א W), as well as L.

6:1a | beware of practicing your righteous deeds before others.

The original wording "righteous deeds" (lit. "righteousnesses") is found in early MSS (א*,2 B D). The word was changed to "alms" in L W Z (so KJV) and to "gifts" in א1. The first variant was probably a harmonization to 6:2 or an early gloss on "righteousness" since "righteousness" in Hebrew was often rendered as "alms" in the Septuagint. The second variant was also an attempt to explain what it means "to do righteousness before people" by indicating that it was a matter of giving gifts in the sight of others.

6:1b | your Father in heaven.

The divine "Father" is written as a nomen sacrum (sacred name) in two early MSS (ℵ W).

6:4 | your Father who sees in secret will reward you.

The original wording "reward you" is found in early MSS (ℵ B D W). The wording "reward you openly" is found in L W Maj (so KJV). The addition of "openly" was created by scribes to give symmetrical, antithetical balance to the expression, "in secret."

6:4, 6 | your Father.

The divine "Father" is written as a nomen sacrum (sacred name) in two early MSS (ℵ W).

6:8 | your Father knows what you need.

The original wording "your Father" is found in several MSS (ℵ* D L W Z 0170^{vid} 33 Maj). The wording "God your Father" is found in $ℵ^1$ B. Since Matthew never elsewhere uses the expression "God your Father," it was probably adapted from Pauline usage. The divine "Father" is written as a nomen sacrum (sacred name) in two early MSS (ℵ W).

6:9 | our Father in heaven.

The divine "Father" is written as a nomen sacrum (sacred name) in two early MSS (ℵ W). In the Gospels, we often hear Jesus referring to God as "Father." This means he is the source of life and the head of the spiritual Christian family. He is Jesus's Father and the Father of all who believe in Jesus. That is why Jesus prayed, "our Father."

6:10–12

The earliest extant wording of the prayer is found in P. Antinoopolis 2.54 (third century), which was probably an amulet (for Greek text, see Comfort and Barrett, *Text of Earliest NT Greek MSS*, 678–679). The extant text shows "[let your will] be done on earth as it is in heaven. Give us our daily [*epiousion*] bread, and forgive us our trespasses."

The Greek word *epiousion* gave ancient translators difficulty because it occurs only here and in Luke 11:3 in the New Testament and because it doesn't appear in other Hellenistic literature. Origen thought the word was "coined by the evangelist" (BAGD). The meaning of the word has been sought from its derivation: (1) *epi* + *ousia*, translated as "necessary for existence" (so Origen Chrysostom Jerome); (2) *epi thn ousa* translated as "for this day"; (3) *he epiousa*, rendered as "for the following day." The word, found in all Greek MSS (the earliest being P. Antinoopolis 2.54 of the third century) either speaks of what is necessary for existence or of what supplies our day by day need.

Most modern translators opt for a translation that addresses the daily need. Some ancient translators did the same, while others focused on the issue of sustaining existence: (1) *cottidianum* in Old Latin MSS; (2) *supersubstantialem* (that which substantiates) in the Vulgate (3) "neccesary" in $syr^{h,(p)}$; (4) "of tomorrow" in cop^{sa}; (5) *crastinum* (of tomorrow) in cop^{bo}; (6) *mahar* (tomorrow) in Gospel according to the Hebrews.

In Jerome's *Commentary on Matthew* (6:11) he wrote, "In the Gospel according to Hebrews, for 'substantial bread' I found '*mahar*,' which means 'belonging to tomorrow'; so the sense is: our bread of the morrow, that is, of the future, give us this day." This means that "the disciples are to pray for tomorrow's bread today, since tomorrow would be the day of the Messiah (cf. Exod. 26:22ff.). This interpretation coincides nicely with the emphasis in the first part of the prayer on the coming of the kingdom. However, the other translations mentioned above also provide for solid exegesis because the Lord's Prayer does address our need to depend on God for our every day existence.

6:13 | rescue us from the evil one.

The original prayer ends with the wording "rescue us from the evil one" in the earliest MSS (א B D Z 0170). Among other MSS, there are six different additions to the short form of the Lord's Prayer, as follows: (1) add "amen" in 17 (one Vulgate manuscript); (2) add "because yours is the power and the glory forever. Amen." in $cop^{sa,fay}$ (Didache omits amen); (3) add "because yours is the kingdom and the glory forever. Amen." in syr^{c}; (4) "because yours is the kingdom and the power and the glory forever" in it[k] syr[p]; (5) add "because yours is the kingdom and the power and the glory forever. Amen"—so L W Θ 0233 33 Maj. (6) "because yours is the kingdom of the Father and of the Son of and of the sacred Spirit, forever and ever. Amen." in 1253 Chrysostom.

These represent the six basic variations of the doxology that were added to the Lord's Prayer. The testimony of the earliest extant witnesses reveals that the prayer must have concluded with a petition for deliverance from evil. The variety among the variants speaks against the genuineness of any of the additions. What is presented above shows the continual expansion of the addition—from the simple "amen" in variant 1 to the elaborate Trinitarian doxology in variant 6. In the first stage of additions, it appears that scribes used "power and glory" (probably adapted from verses such as 1 Chron. 29:11; Ps. 62:3 LXX; Dan. 2:37; 1 Peter 4:11; Jude 25). This is the reading in the Didache, and this same ending (in transposed order—glory and power) appears at the end of the late-third century Christian prayer in P. Oxyrhynchus 407. In the next stage, "kingdom" was added, and "amen" was appended. The longer form probably came from the Didache (otherwise known as "The Teaching of the Twelve"), which was written in Syria or Palestine during the early second century. This was elongated still further by the addition of "kingdom" to the wording found in the Didache: "power and glory." This particular form—"kingdom, power, and glory"—became popular by its inclusion in the Textus Receptus and in the KJV.

6:14, 15b, 18a | your Father.

The divine "Father" is written as a nomen sacrum (sacred name) in two early MSS (א W).

6:15a | if you do not forgive people.

The original wording "forgive people" is found in א D. This is expanded to "forgive people their trespasses" in B L D W 33 Maj (so KJV).

6:18b | your Father who sees in secret will reward you.

The original wording "will reward you" is found in early MSS (א B D). This is expanded to "will reward you openly" in L W 33 Maj (so KJV).

The addition of "openly" was created to give symmetrical, antithetical balance to the expression, "in secret."

6:25 | do not be anxious about your life | what you will eat.
The wording "what we will eat" is found in א. The wording is "what we will drink" in L 0233 Maj, and "what we will eat or drink" in B W 33 (so KJV).

6:26 | your heavenly Father.
The divine "Father" is written as a nomen sacrum (sacred name) in two early MSS (א W).

6:28 | the lilies of the field; they do not card or spin or labor.
This wording is found in two early MSS (א* P. Oxyrhynchus 655). The wording is "the lilies of the field grow; they do not spin or labor" in א[1] (B), and "the lily of the field grows; it does not spin or labor" in L W 0233 0281 Maj (so KJV). The second-century Gospel of Thomas preserved in P. Oxy. 655 I a, b (third century) reads as follows: "[Take no thought] from morning until evening or from evening until morning, either for your food, what you will eat, or for your clothes, what you will put on. You are far better than the lilies which do not card or spin . . . . Having one garment, what do you [lack]? . . . Who could add to your span of life?"

T. C. Skeat (in the "Lilies of the Field," *Zeitschrift für die neutestamentliche Wissenschaft* 37:211–214 [1938]) was given a clue to understanding a correction in codex Sinaiticus [א] after he examined P. Oxy. 655 and determined that the reading was *ou xainousin* (do not card), not *auxanousin* (they grow), as originally transcribed by Grenfell and Hunt. This led Skeat to reexamine this verse in codex Sinaiticus under ultraviolet light and determine the reading underneath the corrected reading. The presence of *xenousin* in codex Sinaiticus and P. Oxy. 655 is significant; it could very well reflect the original text—how easy it would be for *ou xenousin* (they do not card) to become *auxanousin* (they grow) in the copying process—especially since there was no space between letters. The statement indicates that there are three things lilies do not do: they don't card (i.e., comb wool), spin, or labor (with no mention of growth per se). This pattern mirrors the triple verbal description about the birds: "they neither sow nor reap nor gather into barns" (6:26). (See note on Luke 12:27 concerning a similar variant.)

6:32 | your heavenly Father.
The divine name "Father" is written as a nomen sacrum (sacred name) in two early MSS (א W).

6:33 | seek first the kingdom.
The original wording "the kingdom" is found in the earliest MSS (א B). This was expanded to "the kingdom of God" in L W 0233 33 Maj (so KJV).

7:11 | your Father.
The divine name "Father" is written as a nomen sacrum (sacred name) in two early MSS (א W).

7:13 | the road to destruction is wide open.
This wording is found in two early witnesses (א* Clement). The wording "the gate is wide and the road to destruction is open" is found in several other MSS ($א^2$ [seventh century] B C L W; so KJV). The words "the gate" were probably added by scribes to complete the parallelism with 7:14. However, it is also possible that the words may have been deleted so as to make the adjectives "wide and spacious" describe only "the road."

7:22 | Lord, Lord.
The original wording "Lord, Lord" is written as nomina sacra (sacred names) in the earliest MSS (א B C W). The duplication of the divine name provides oral effect.

7:21 | the will of my Father in heaven.
The divine "Father" is written as a nomen sacrum (sacred name) in two early MSS (א W).

8:2 | Lord, if you are willing, you can cleanse me.
"Lord" is written as a nomen sacrum (sacred name) in all the MSS. Some English versions (NEB, REB, Moffatt) render this as "sir." But the ancient MSS present this as a divine name (א B L W). This shows that the leper considered Jesus to be more than an ordinary man—rather, he considered Jesus divine.

8:6, 8 | Lord.
"Lord" is written as a nomen sacrum (sacred name) in all the MSS. Some English versions (NEB, REB, NJB, Moffatt) render this as "sir." But the ancient MSS present this as a divine name (א B L W). This shows that the centurion considered Jesus to be more than an ordinary man—rather, he considered Jesus divine.

8:10 | with no one in Israel have I found such faith.
The original wording "with no one in Israel" is found in two early MSS (B W). The wording "not even in Israel" is found in א C L Maj (so KJV), by way of scribal conformity to the words in Luke 7:9, a parallel verse.

8:13 | the servant was healed in that hour.
This original wording is found in two early MSS (א^{1} B). Other wording, "the servant was healed in that hour, and the centurion returned to his house that same hour and found his servant healed," is found in א$^{*, 2}$ C Θ f^{1} (33), by way of scribal expansion probably influenced by John 4:52–53.

8:15 | she got up and was serving him.
The original wording "serving him" is found in two early MSS (B C). The wording "serving them" is found in א^{1} L 33, by way of scribal conformity to Mark 1:31, a parallel verse.

8:20 | the Son of Man has nowhere to lay his head.
"Son of Man," a messianic title (Dan. 7:13–14), is written as a nomen sacrum (sacred name) in an early MS (א), as well as L.

8:21 | another disciple spoke to him.
The original wording "another disciple" is found in the two earliest MSS (א B). The wording "another of his disciples" in C L W Θ 0250 $f^{1,13}$ Maj (so KJV) is scribal clarification.

8:28 | he came to the country of the Gadarenes.
The original wording is "Gadarenes," according to the earliest MSS (א* B C). The wording is "Gergesenes" in $א^2$ [seventh century] L W Maj (so KJV). Some ancient versions (Syriac Coptic) read "Gerasenes." In every instance in the synoptic Gospels where the writer records Jesus's visit to the region on the eastern side of the Galilee (where he healed the demoniac), there is textual variation as to what this region is named. In this verse, Mark 5:1, and Luke 8:26 all three readings occur: "Gerasenes," "Gergesenes," and "Gadarenes." Origen (*Commentary on John* 5.41.24) spoke of the textual problem while commenting on John 1:28. Origen objected to Gadara (a reading he saw in a few MSS), which is about five miles southeast of the Sea of Galilee, and he rejected Gerasa, which is thirty miles southeast of the Sea of Galilee. Origen suggested the name Gergesa on the basis of local tradition and because its name was supposed to mean "dwelling of those that have driven away." Fond of finding etymological significance in names, Origen said the name suited the place because there the citizens asked Jesus to leave their territory. "Gadarenes" has the best testimony in Matthew, and adequately suits the context for the story. Josephus (*Life* 42.9) said Gadara had territory and villages on the border of the lake; one of these villages must have been called "Gerasa," which is the name found in the best MSS in Mark 5:1 and Luke 8:26. The first variant, "Gergesenes," probably shows the influence Origen had on later traditions; and the second variant, "Gerasenes," is scribal harmonization to Mark 5:1 and Luke 8:26.

8:29 | "What do you, God's Son, have to do with us?"
The original wording "God's Son" is found in the early MSS (א B C*), as well as L 33, which all write it as a nomen sacrum (sacred name). The wording "Jesus, God's Son" is found in C^3 [ninth century] W Maj (so KJV), and is a scribal expansion of a divine name.

9:6 | the Son of Man has authority to forgive sins.
"Son of Man," a messianic title (Dan. 7:13–14), is written as a nomen sacrum (sacred name) in two early MSS (א W).

9:8 | the crowds were afraid.
The original wording is "were afraid" according to excellent manuscript evidence (א B D W 0281 33). The wording was changed to "marveled" in C L 0233 Maj (so KJV). The original reading is the more difficult reading because the expected response to witnessing a miracle is awe and praise, not fear and praise ("they were afraid and glorified God"). The crowds were afraid because they saw something entirely new: a man forgiving the sins of another man and healing him to prove it. They sensed that Jesus was no mere mortal, no normal Rabbi, but a supernatural human being endowed with authority from God.

9:14 | why do the Pharisees fast?
The original wording is "fast" according to the earliest MSS (א* B). This was changed to "fast frequently" (א¹) and "fast often" (א² [seventh century] C D L W 0233 Maj; so KJV). Both variants appear to be scribal additions intended to make a more effective contrast between the fasting of the Pharisees and John's disciples with the lack thereof on the part of Jesus's disciples. Indeed, many copyists would not want readers thinking that Jesus condemned fasting completely.

9:27 | Son of David, have mercy on us.
"Son of David" is written as a nomen sacrum (sacred name) in one early MS (א). It is a royal, messianic title—the Jews expected the Messiah-King to be the Son of David (2 Sam. 7:13, 16; Jer. 23:5; Ezek. 37:24).

9:28 | They said to him, "Yes, Lord."
"Lord" is written as a nomen sacrum (sacred name) in ancient MSS. Some English versions (NEB, Moffatt) render this as "sir." But the ancient MSS present this as a nomen sacrum (sacred name): א B C W. This shows that the two blind men considered Jesus to be more than an ordinary man—rather, they considered Jesus divine.

9:34

The original text includes this verse, according to the earliest MSS (א B C W). It is omitted in D Old Latin MSS and Syriac MSS. Several scholars affirm the omission of this verse, arguing that it is an assimilation to Matt. 12:24 and its parallel in Luke 11:15. Other scholars argue that 10:25 presupposes this statement because in 10:25 Jesus mentions that the Jewish leaders had already maligned him by associating him with Beelzebul. The cause for omission in the "Western" witnesses noted above cannot be ascribed to transcriptional error; perhaps it was excised because the previous verse provides a more positive ending to the pericope. But when all is said about internal evidence, the verdict for its inclusion in the text is determined by its strong documentary attestation.

10:3 | Thaddaeus.

According to the original text, the disciple's name is "Thaddaeus" (so א B). This was changed to "Lebbaeus" (D), "Lebbaeus, the one called Thaddaeus" (C L W 33 Maj, so KJV), "Thaddeaus, the one called Lebbaeus" (13), and "Judas Zelotes" (some Old Latin MSS), and "Judas the son of James" (one Syriac MS). By comparing the listings of apostles (see Matt. 10:2–4; Mark 3:16–19; Luke 6:13–16), Thaddaeus must be Judas son of James or Judas brother of James (possibly the author of Jude). The textual variations in this verse (as in Mark 2:18, see comments there) are the result of scribes attempting to harmonize the Gospel accounts. Either "Lebbaeus" or "Thaddaeus" is original (most likely the latter).

10:4 | Simon the Cananean.

According to the original text, the disciple's name is "Simon the Cananean (= Simon the zealot)—so B C (D) L 33. This was changed to "Simon the Canaanite" in א Maj (so KJV). The variant reading is not just an alternate spelling of the same name; the difference is significant. The name *Kananaios* (Cananaean) is the Aramaic form of "Zealot"; the name *Kananith* describes a pagan Gentile, "a Canaanite." If the text is correct, then it is possible that this disciple of Jesus was zealous for the law, or he was "a zealous nationalist prior to his call to follow Jesus . . . Later, the term zealot was used to designate the religiously motivated Jewish revolutionaries who were active in guerilla-type warfare in the period leading up to AD 70 and the destruction of Jerusalem" (DJG, 1812).

10:12 | As you enter the house, greet it.

This is probably the original wording according to two early MSS (B C). Several MSS (א*,2 D L W 0281vid) add, "saying, 'peace to this house.'" The addition, though found in a number of witnesses, was probably taken from Luke 10:5 by scribes who considered Matthew's wording too terse.

10:20a | the Spirit of your Father will be speaking in you.

"Spirit of your Father" is written as nomen sacrum (sacred name) in two early MSS (א W), as well as L.

10:23 | until the Son of Man comes.

"Son of Man," a messianic title (Dan. 7:13–14), is written as a nomen sacrum (sacred name) in two early MSS (א W), as well as L

10:25 | if they have called the master of the house "Beelzeboul."

The name is "Beelzeboul" in 𝔓110 C (D L) W 33 Maj, "Beezebul" in א B, and "Beelzebub" in Old Latin and Syriac MSS. The first reading has the support of the earliest MS, 𝔓110 (dated c. 300). The religious leaders may have invented this term by combining two Hebrew words: *ba'al* ("lord," from Hos. 2:18), which stood for the local Caananite fertility god; and *zebul* ("exalted dwelling," from 1 Kings 8:13). The variant in א and B is a spelling change that avoids the "lz" combination, which is most unusual in Greek. The second variant in the Old Latin and Syriac versions is an attempt to identify this one with the god of Ekron (see 2 Kings 1:2–3, 6, 16), an idol worshiped by pagans. As all idolatry was regarded as devil worship (Lev. 17:7; Deut. 32:17; Ps. 106:37; 1 Cor. 10:20), there seems to have been something peculiarly satanic about the worship of this hateful god, which caused his name to be a synonym of Satan. Here it is used to denote the most opprobrious language that could be applied by one to another.

10:29 | your Father.

The divine "Father" is written as a nomen sacrum (sacred name) in two early MSS (א W), as well as L.

10:32 | I will also confess him before my Father.

The divine "Father" is written as a nomen sacrum (sacred name) in early MSS, א B (a rare occurrence in B) W.

10:33 | I will also deny him before my Father.

The divine "Father" is written as a nomen sacrum (sacred name) in two early MSS (א W), as well as L.

10:37 | whoever loves father or mother more than me is not worthy of me.

Two early MSS ($\mathfrak{P}^{19}$ B*) and D end the verse here. Other MSS (א B^{mg} C L W Maj, so KJV) add: "whoever loves son or daughter more than me is not worthy of me." $\mathfrak{P}^{19}$ alone also omits all of 10:38, probably due to homoeoteleuton (10:37a and 10:38 both end with *axios* = worthy). However, it is possible that $\mathfrak{P}^{19}$'s exemplar did not include 10:37b and that homoeoteleuton accounts only for the omission of 10:38. The scribe of B originally wrote 10:37, lacking this clause, which was then added in the lower margin. This tells us that this clause may not have appeared in the original text.

11:9

There are two options for this verse: "What did you go out to see? A prophet?" (in $א^c$ $B^{*,2}$ C D L 0233 Maj), or, "Why did you go out? To see a prophet?" (in א* B^1 W Z 0281^{vid}). Either reading could be original; the textual evidence is equally divided.

11:12 | the kingdom suffers violence because violent people seize it.

The image is that the kingdom has been under attack by violent men trying to seize control of it. A marginal note in MS 1424 says that the Gospel of the Nazarenes (a second-century Hebrew translation of Matthew's Gospel) reads, "the kingdom of heaven is ravished."

11:19a | the Son of Man came eating and drinking.
"Son of Man," a messianic title (Dan. 7:13–14), is written as a nomen sacrum (sacred name) in two early MSS (א W), as well as L.

11:19b | wisdom is vindicated by her deeds.
The original wording "by her deeds" is found in the early MSS (א B* W). This was changed to "by her children" in B² [10th or 11th century] C D L 33 Maj, by way of scribal conformity to Luke 7:35, a parallel verse. Wisdom, though momentarily jeered, is always proven correct by her future deeds. The emphasis in Luke is on Wisdom's future generations. "Wisdom" (*sophia*) is a divine name presented in the feminine gender.

11:25 | I praise you, Father, Lord of heaven and earth.
The divine "Father" is written as a nomen sacrum (sacred name) in the early MSS (𝔓⁶² א), as well as L. God the Father is called "Lord of heaven and earth," thereby indicating his universal lordship. "Lord" is written as a nomen sacrum (sacred name) in all the early MSS.

11:27a | Father.
The divine "Father" is written (all three times) as a nomen sacrum (sacred name) in the early MSS (𝔓⁶² א W), as well as L.

11:27b | Son.
"Son" is written (all three times) as a nomen sacrum (sacred name) in the early MSS (𝔓⁶² א), as well as L.

12:4 | he ate the bread of the Presence.
The original wording is probably "he ate," according to 𝔓⁷⁰ C D L W 33 Maj. The wording is "they ate" in א B. Although the first reading could be the result of scribal harmonization to parallel passages (Mark 2:26; Luke 6:4), it has the earliest (𝔓⁷⁰) and most diverse testimony,

and is the more difficult reading because the OT passage alluded to here (1 Sam. 21:1–6) implies that David and his men—not just David—ate the bread. And so does the previous verse, which speaks of "the ones with him" (i.e., David's companions). Thus, the variant could represent conformity to the immediate context and/or to the OT passage.

12:8 | The Son of Man is Lord of the Sabbath.

Both titles, "Son of Man," a messianic title (Dan. 7:13–14), and "Lord," are written as nomina sacra (sacred names) in some early MSS (א W). Jesus, as the Son of Man, is Lord of the Sabbath. This means that he exerts his divine prerogatives over what happens on that day—quite specifically, he can heal on that day.

12:18 | I will put my Spirit upon him.

The divine "Spirit" is written as a nomen sacrum (sacred name) in three early MSS (א D W), as well as L, indicating the divine Spirit was put on Jesus.

12:23 | Can this be the Son of David?

"Son of David" is written as a nomen sacrum (sacred name) in two early MSS (א C) because it is a royal, messianic title—the Jews expected the Messiah-King to be the Son of David (2 Sam. 7:13, 16; Jer. 23:5; Ezek. 37:24).

12:24, 27 | Beelzeboul

The original wording is "Beelzeboul" in $\mathfrak{P}^{21}$ (12:24 only) C D L W 0281 33 Maj. The reading is "Beezeboul" in א B; "Beelzebub" in Old Latin and Syriac MSS. See comments on 10:25.

12:28 | If I cast out demons by the Spirit of God.

"Spirit of God" is written as a nomen sacrum (sacred name) in the earliest MSS (א B D W).

12:30

The literal reading is "whoever does not gather with me is scattering me," as is found in 33 ℵ cop syr (also Origen Athanasius). Other MSS do not have the final "me" (B C D L W Maj). To modern sensibilities, the literal may sound strange. (Not one English version has followed this reading or even noted it.) But this must not have been so for some ancient scribes, exegetes, and translators who retained the reading "scatters me." The whole metaphor speaks of gathering and scattering sheep. We might not think of scattering sheep as including the shepherd (Jesus), but he is so identified with his flock that to scatter Jesus's sheep is to scatter/divide Jesus himself inasmuch as he is united to those who are his own. The same textual variation occurs in Luke 11:23, with better documentary support for the shorter text than the variant (see note).

12:31, 32b | Spirit, Holy Spirit.
The divine "Spirit" is written as a nomen sacrum (sacred name) in the early MSS (ℵ D W), as well as L.

12:32a | whoever speaks against the Son of Man will be forgiven.
"Son of Man," a messianic title (Dan. 7:13–14), is written as a nomen sacrum (sacred name) in early MSS (ℵ W), as well as L.

12:40 | the Son of Man will be in the heart of the earth three days and three nights.
"Son of Man," a messianic title (Dan. 7:13–14), is written as a nomen sacrum (sacred name) in one early MS (ℵ), as well as L.

12:47 | omit verse.
Verse 47 is not present in the earliest MSS (ℵ* B), as well as L G and some Old Latin, Syriac, and Coptic MSS. This verse reads, "Someone told him, 'Look, your mother and your brothers are standing outside, wanting to speak to you.'" It is present in ℵ[(1), 2 [seventh century]] C (D) W Z 33 Maj (so KJV) some Syriac MSS and Coptic MSS. The arguments in favor of its inclusion are twofold: (1) the verse was omitted due to homoeoteleuton (both 12:46 and 12:47 end with the same word, *lalesai*); (2) Jesus's response in 12:48 requires a response to someone's

statement. If 12:47 were missing, Jesus wouldn't be answering anyone. The arguments for the omission are twofold: (1) The array of witnesses supporting the omission is substantial, calling into question whether homoeoteleuton could have occurred in so many witnesses. (2) Scribes would have been prompted by the context to fill in the gap between 12:46 and 12:48, whereas Matthew may have expected readers to do this gap-filling on their own. All things being equal, the text (lacking this verse) has the better support and is the reading that was most likely changed.

12:50 | whoever does the will of my Father.

The divine "Father" is written as a nomen sacrum (sacred name) in one early MS [א].

13:14–15

This text comes from Isaiah 6:9–10, Septuagint. This is the most often cited OT passage in the NT; it appears here, Mark 4:12; Luke 8:10; John 12:40; Acts 28:26–27; Rom. 11:8. It is also quoted in P. Oxyrhynchus 406, an early Christian document (c. 200) in which the writer is appealing to this Scripture to explain why certain people [the Jews?] did not realize that Jesus was the Christ. Paul took the same approach in Acts 28:26–27. Indeed, this passage is an apt description of why the religious establishment of Jesus's day rejected him as the Messiah. The rest of the poem expands the same theme as the citation by using terms of sight and hearing (each of which appears five times in the poem) to show that only with open hearts and receptive spirits can people really see and hear God's truths.

13:35a | what had been spoken through the prophet.

The original wording is "through the prophet," according to א^{1} B C D L W 0233 0242 Maj. Another reading is "through Isaiah the prophet" in א* 33 MSS$^{\text{according to Eusebius and Jerome}}$; yet another is "Asaph the prophet" in MSS$^{\text{according to Jerome}}$. This textual problem hinges on the fact that Asaph, not Isaiah, was the prophet Matthew quoted. This problem was discussed as early as the third century. Eusebius said that some copyists must not have understood that "the prophet" meant by Matthew was Asaph, and therefore added in the Gospel "through Isaiah the prophet," but in the accurate copies it stands without the addition. Thus, Eusebius was arguing for the reading of the text, declaring that it was in the accurate copies (see Tregelles 1.47). Jerome conjectured that "Asaph was the original reading, for it was found in all the old MSS, but then was removed by ignorant men and replaced with Isaiah." However, not one extant manuscript reads "Asaph." What is interesting, though, is that Jerome was responding to Porphyry (a third-century critic of Christianity) who used this verse to show that Matthew was ignorant. Thus, we know that in the third century some MSS must have read "Isaiah." In defense of the text, it could be said that "Isaiah" was inserted because it was typical for Matthew to name "Isaiah" in prophetic quotations (3:3; 4:14; 8:17; 12:17) and where he didn't, for scribes to add his name (see 1:22; 2:5 and comments).

13:35b | I will proclaim what has been hidden from the beginning.

The original wording is "hidden from the beginning" according to early MSS ($\aleph^1$ B). The wording "hidden from the beginning of the world" is found in $\aleph^{*,2}$ C D L W 0233 Maj. (The Greek word for "beginning" [*katabole*] can also be rendered as "foundation.") According to the longer reading, this verse says that the prophet spoke "things that were hidden from the world's foundation." This is a quotation taken from Ps. 78:2. The Hebrew text says these things were hidden "from of old," which in the context of the Psalm probably refers to the beginning of the nation of Israel. The Septuagint says these things were hidden "from the beginning," which could convey "the beginning of creation." On the basis of internal evidence, either reading can be argued for. Therefore, we must turn to the external evidence, which slightly favors the first reading.

13:36 | fully explain the parable to us.

The original reading is "fully explain" (Greek *diasapheson*), according to the earliest MSS ($\aleph^*$ B 0242^{vid}). The wording is "explain" (Greek *phrason*) in $\aleph^2$ C D L W 0106 0233 0250 33 Maj.

13:37, 41 | the Son of Man.

"Son of Man," a messianic title (Dan. 7:13–14), is written as a nomen sacrum (sacred name) in one early MS (א), as well as L. Jesus's favorite self-description was "Son of Man." It was a lesser known messianic title, derived from Dan. 7:13–14.

13:43 | the kingdom of their Father.

The divine "Father" is written as a nomen sacrum (sacred name) in early MSS (א D W), as well as L.

13:55 | his brothers, James and Joses and Simon and Judas.

The name of one of Jesus's brothers is "Joses" according to the earliest MS ($\mathfrak{P}^{103}$); it is "Joseph" in א B. The names of Jesus's four brothers are James, Joses, Simon, and Judas. "Joses" is the Galilean pronunciation (*yose*) of the Hebrew *yosep* ("Joseph").

14:3a | For Herod had arrested John, bound him, and put him in prison.

This is the original wording according to the testimony of א C D L W. A few MSS (B f^{13}) have the word *tote* (= previously) before the verb *kratetas* (had arrested) to help the reader understand that 14:3 chronologically occurs before 14:1–2.

14:3b | Herodias, his brother Philip's wife.

This is the original wording according to excellent testimony (א B C L W Θ 33). Another reading is "Herodias, his brother's wife" in D and some Old Latin MSS. Herod's first wife was the daughter of Aretas; he divorced her to marry Herodias. According to Matthew, Herodias had been married to Herod Philip, son of Herod the Great, and therefore Herod Antipas's half-brother. But according to Josephus (*Antiquities* 18.5.4), Herodias's first husband was named Herod, son of Herod the Great, whereas Herod Philip married Salome, the daughter of Herodias. Either Herodias had been the wife of Philip (Herod's son) or Herod (also Herod's son). (In either case, Herodias was Herod's niece, and their marriage was incestuous.) The simplest solution to the name problem was for scribes to drop the name "Philip" from the text, as was done by D and some Old Latin MSS in this verse, and probably by Luke himself in 3:19.

14:24 | the boat was in the middle of the sea.

This wording is found in many MSS (א C L W 0106 f[1] Maj). But this is "the boat was many stadia away from the land" in B f[13]; and "the boat was considerable stadia away from the land" in Syriac; and "the boat was [went] into the middle of the sea" in D. On the basis of documentary support alone, the first reading is probably the best reading, even though its concordance with Mark 6:47 makes it somewhat suspect as a case of scribal conformity. To be in the middle of the Sea of Galilee means to be about three or four miles from shore; to be many stadia from land could mean they were just a half mile from shore or four miles from shore. John 6:19 tells us specifically that they were 25 to 30 stadia (one stadion was about 600 feet or 185 meters) away from shore, which is about four miles out. This puts the boat in the middle of the Sea of Galilee, which is about seven miles across. To be in the middle of the Sea (which was about 200 feet deep at this point) during a violent storm was cause for great consternation; it increases the drama of Jesus's rescue.

14:30 | seeing the wind.

The original wording is likely "the wind" (found in א B* 073 33). Another wording is "the strong wind" (in B[1] C D L [W adds "very"] 0106 f[1,13] Maj). It is possible that *ischuron* (strong) was accidentally dropped due to homoeoteleuton—the two previous words both end with the same last two letters. But it is more likely that the adjective was added to intensify the description of the wind.

14:33 | Truly you are the Son of God.

"Son of God" is written as a nomen sacrum (sacred name) in the earliest MSS (א B D W). The disciples recognized Jesus as *the* divine Son of God, not just a son of God.

15:6 | you nullify the law of God.

The wording "the law of God" is found in א[*,2] [seventh century] C 073

f^{13} Ptolemy, while the wording "the word of God" is found in $\aleph^1$ B D. Another wording is "the commandment of God" (L W 0106 f^1 33 Maj, so KJV). According to the text, Jesus said, "You nullify the law of God by your tradition." The third variant can easily be dismissed because it has inferior documentary attestation and it is the expected word inasmuch as the previous verses speak about "the commandment" of God. The true reading has to be one of the other two variants, both of which have fairly good support. Since the first variant ("word of God") may have been harmonized to Mark 7:13, it is likely that Jesus was contrasting "the law of God," the Torah, with the traditions of the Jews—which were their applicational interpretations of the law for Jews to practice. This reading has good documentary support, including ℵ* (which was changed to *logon* [word] then back to *nomon* [law]) and the early witness of Ptolemy (c. AD 180).

15:13 | my heavenly Father.

The divine "Father" is written as a nomen sacrum (sacred name) in early MSS (ℵ W), as well as L.

15:22 | have mercy on me, Lord, Son of David.

"Lord" is written as a nomen sacrum (sacred name) in ℵ B D L W. "Son of David" is written as a nomen sacrum in one early MS (ℵ), as well as L. "Son of David" is a royal, messianic title—the Jews expected the Messiah-King to be the Son of David (2 Sam. 7:13, 16; Jer. 23:5; Ezek. 37:24).

15:39 | he went to the region of Magadan.

The original wording is "Magadan," according to ℵ* (*Magedan* $\aleph^2$) B D. Other readings are "Magdala" (L $f^{1,13}$ Maj) and "Magdalan" (C W 33). The original wording has a place-name (Magadan) which is unknown. Arguing for the second variant (Magdala), some scholars have suggested that it would be easy for scribes to accidentally mistake MAGDALA for MAGADAN because the *delta*, *alpha*, and *lambda* look similar in the unicial letters of ancient MSS. But this does not account for the Greek letter *nu* at the end of MAGADAN, which is distinctly different from *delta*, *alpha*, and *lambda*. Thus, most other scholars are inclined to adopt the more difficult reading because it has the best external support. (See comments on Mark 8:10.)

16:2–4 | He answered them, "An evil and adulterous generation seeks a sign. And no sign will be given to it except the sign of Jonah." And he left them.

The short text (lacking 16:2b–3) is supported by the earliest MSS (א B) and by X 1424mg MSSaccording to Jerome Origen syr cop. Later MSS (C D L W 33 Maj) add, "When it is evening, you say, 'It will be fair weather, for the sky is red.' And in the morning, 'It will be stormy today, for the sky is red and threatening.' You know how to interpret the appearance of the sky, but you cannot interpret the signs of the times." Had the additional words been original, there is no good reason to explain why the scribes of א B, et al., would have deleted the words on purpose, and there is no way to explain the omission as a transcriptional accident. Thus, it if far more likely and even probable that this portion was not written by Matthew, but inserted later by a scribe who either borrowed the concept from Luke 12:54–56 as a metaphor for "the signs of the times" or inserted these words from an oral or other written tradition to provide an actual example of what it meant for the ancients to interpret the appearance of the sky. Among the added words, there are several that are never used by Matthew or (in two instances) by any other writer in the NT: (1) *eudia* = "fair weather" (appears only here in the NT), (2) *purrazei* = "is fiery red" (appears only here in the NT and was used only by Byzantine writers; see BAGD, 731), (3) *stugnazō* = "being overcast" (appears only here and in Mark 10:22). This strongly suggests that a scribe added the text.

But the question remains: why was this addition made? A close look at the context supplies the answer. According to Matthew's account, the Jewish leaders came to Jesus twice, each time asking him to give them a sign that he was truly the Messiah sent from God. In Matt. 12:38, the leaders simply asked for a sign. In response, Jesus said that no sign would be given them but the sign of Jonah, who depicted Christ's death, burial, and resurrection (12:39–40). Later, the Jewish leaders asked Jesus for a sign "from heaven" (Matt. 16:1). Again, Jesus told them that no sign would be given them except the sign of Jonah (16:4), according to the reading of the shorter version. But the query for "a sign from heaven" does not seem to be answered by Jesus pointing to Jonah. This created a disappointment for various readers—a gap in the text that called for some kind of filling. Therefore, some scribe decided to fill the gap and did so by borrowing from the thought of Luke 12:54–56 and some other unknown source (perhaps the scribe's own knowledge). He added words about signs in the "sky" as complementing a request about a sign from "heaven."

Whoever filled the gap in Matthew must have done so by the middle of the fourth century because we know that around 380 Jerome saw MSS with and without the extra words. In fact, Jerome indicated that the extra words were not present in most of the MSS known to him. Nonetheless, he included them in his Latin translation. (The scribe of 1424 noted in the margin of the manuscript that many MSS did not contain these words.) Nearly all English translators have done exactly what Jerome and the scribe of 1424 did: they included the words in the text, knowing there is some doubt about their authenticity.

16:13 | Who do people say the Son of Man is?

"Son of Man," a messianic title (Dan. 7:13–14), is written as a nomen sacrum (sacred name) in two early MSS (א W), as well as L.

16:16 | You are the Christ, the Son of God.

"Christ" is written as a nomen sacrum (sacred name) in all the MSS. "Son of God" is written as a nomen sacrum (sacred name) in the earliest MSS (א B), as well as L. Peter used both divine names with respect to Jesus.

16:17 | my Father in heaven.

The divine "Father" is written as a nomen sacrum (sacred name) in early MSS (א W), as well as L.

16:21 | Jesus Christ began to explain.

The original wording is "Jesus Christ" according to the earliest MSS (א* B* cop). Other MSS read "Jesus" ($א^2$ [seventh century] [B^2] C [D] L W $f^{1,13}$). ($א^1$ omits the name, and should read "he.") This is a difficult textual variant because the external and internal evidence are in conflict. It should be noted that ℵ displays all three variants. The scribe of ℵ first wrote "Jesus Christ," which was then corrected by deleting "Jesus Christ," which was much later (7th or 8th century) corrected to "Jesus." Usually a reading supported by ℵ* and B* is accepted as original, but the absence of "Christ" in so many other MSS has led scholars to think that the second variant is a scribal addition prompted by Jesus having just been called "the Christ" in 16:18, 20. But it could have been the work of Matthew himself who begins the book (1:1) with the same title, "Jesus Christ," repeats it in 1:18, and uses it again here—each at a critical point in the Gospel. The change from "Jesus Christ" to "Jesus" can be explained as a change from the more unusual to the usual—in the Gospels the reader usually encounters the reading "Jesus" at the beginning of new episodes, not "Jesus Christ." It appears that in Matt. 16:18, Peter calls Jesus "the Christ." Jesus then tells them not to tell anyone he is "the Christ." In 16:21, which marks a major turning point in the ministry of Jesus as he faces his destiny of suffering and death in Jerusalem, Matthew says "Jesus Christ began to explain to his disciples that he had to go to Jerusalem and suffer many things."

16:27a, 28 | the Son of Man.

"Son of Man," a messianic title (Dan. 7:13–14), is written as a nomen sacrum (sacred name) in early MSS (ℵ W), as well as L.

16:27b | the glory of his Father.

The divine "Father" is written as a nomen sacrum (sacred name) in early MSS (ℵ W), as well as L.

17:4 | I will make three tabernacles.

The original wording is "I will make" according to early evidence (ℵ B C*). This was changed to "we will make" in C^3 [ninth century] D L W Θ 0281 $f^{1,13}$ 33 Maj (so KJV). According to the three earliest MSS, Peter was speaking for himself.

17:9a | until after the Son of Man has been raised from the dead.

"Son of Man," a messianic title (Dan. 7:13–14), is written as a nomen sacrum (sacred name) in early MSS (ℵ W), as well as L.

17:15a | Lord, have mercy on my son.

"Lord" is written as a nomen sacrum (sacred name) in B D L W. Some English versions (NEB, REB, Moffatt) render this as "sir," but the ancient MSS present this as a sacred name. This shows that the father considered Jesus to be more than an ordinary man—rather, he considered Jesus divine.

17:15b | he is an epileptic and is ill.

The original wording is "is ill" (Greek *kakōs echei*), according to early testimony (א B Z^{vid}), as well as L. The variant wording is "suffers terribly" (Greek *kakōs paschei*) in other MSS (C D W $f^{1,13}$ 33 Maj). Even though the variant is a rarer expression in the Greek, the documentary evidence favors the first reading.

17:21 | omit verse.

The earliest MSS (א* B) and 0281 33 it^{e} $syr^{c,s}$ $cop^{sa,bo}$ do not include verse 21, which reads, "but this kind does not come out except by prayer and fasting." This added verse is found in $א^{2}$ [seventh century] C D L W $f^{1,13}$ Maj. The evidence against including this verse is substantial, including א* B (the two earliest MSS), 0281 (a seventh-century MS discovered at St. Catherine's Monastery in the late 20th century), and early witnesses of Old Latin, Coptic, and Syriac. If the verse was originally part of Matthew's Gospel, there is no good reason to explain why it was dropped from so many early and diverse witnesses. Thus, it is far more likely that this added verse was assimilated from Mark 9:29 in its long form, which has the additional words "and fasting." In fact, the same MSS ($א^{2}$ [seventh century] C D L W $f^{1,13}$ Maj) that have the long form in Mark 9:29 have the additional verse here. Thus, some scribe took the full verse of Mark 9:29 as presented in his manuscript and inserted it here.

17:22 | they were gathering in Galilee.

The original wording "were gathering" (Greek *sustrephomenōn*) is found in the two earliest MSS (א B), as well as 0281^{vid} f^{1}. The variant reading is "were living" (Greek *anastrephomenōn*) in C (D) L W f^{13} 33 Maj. The first reading has the earliest documentary support. The rare word *sustrephomenōn*, appearing only twice in the NT, was changed to the more common one, *anastrephomenōn*, in later MSS.

17:22 | the Son of Man is going to be betrayed.

"Son of Man," a messianic title (Dan. 7:13–14), is written as a nomen sacrum (sacred name) in early MSS (א W), as well as L.

18:11 | omit verse.

The earliest MSS (א B) do not include 18:11, so also L* $f^{1,13}$ 33 it^{e} syr^{s} cop^{sa} Origen. Several later MSS (D L^{c} W 078^{vid} Maj $syr^{c,p}$; so KJV) add verse 11 as follows: "For the Son of Man came to save the lost." Still other MSS (L^{mg} it^{c} syr^{h}) expand it as: "For the Son of Man came to seek and to save the lost." The absence of this verse in several important and diverse witnesses attests to the fact that it was not part of the original text of Matthew. It was borrowed from Luke 19:10, a passage not at all parallel to this one. Most likely the addition first appeared in the shorter form (variant 1), and was later expanded to the longer form (variant 2), which concurs exactly with Luke 19:10. The MS L demonstrates all three phases: L* omits the verse; L^{c} has the shorter form of the addition; and L^{mg} has the longer form.

Very likely this verse was inserted in Matt. 18 to provide some sort of bridge between verses 10 and 12. In other words, a scribe perceived there was a semantic gap that needed filling. Luke 19:10 was used to introduce the illustration of a shepherd seeking out its lost sheep (the longer form also speaks of "seeking out," which makes the connection even clearer). However, the text must be read without the bridge 18:11 provides. Verse 12 follows verse 10 in the original in that it provides yet another reason why the "little ones who believe in Jesus" should not be despised: The shepherd is concerned for all sheep in the flock. In a flock of 100 sheep, if even one leaves, he will seek it out and find it.

18:14 | the will of your Father.

The divine "Father" is written as a nomen sacrum (sacred name) in early MSS (א W), as well as L.

18:15 | if your brother sins.

The original wording is "sins," according to the two earliest MSS (ℵ B), as well as 0281 f[1] cop[sa] Origen. Other wording is "sins against you" (D L W 073 f[13] 33 Maj, so KJV). The earliest testimony supports the text (note the witness of Origen). Futhermore, there is no adequate explanation, on transcriptional grounds, to explain why the words *eis se* (against you) would have been omitted from MSS such as ℵ B 0281. The expanded reading is a scribal expansion influenced by 18:21.

18:19, 35 | my Father.

The divine "Father" is written as a nomen sacrum (sacred name) in early MSS (ℵ W), as well as L.

19:4 | he created them male and female.

The original verb is probably "created" according to B f[1] it[e] cop Origen. The other wording is "made" in ℵ C D (L) W Z f[13] Maj syr. The variant is the result of scribal conformity to the following predicate ("he made") and/or to the Septuagint passage therein quoted (Gen. 1:27).

19:9 | and the one marrying the divorced woman commits adultery.

This original wording is found in early MSS (𝔓[25] B C* W Z), as well as 078 Maj, but omitted in ℵ L. The textual evidence favors the inclusion of the clause, even though it is suspect as having been borrowed from Matt. 5:32.

19:20 | I have kept all these things.

This is the original wording according to early testimony (ℵ* B), as well as L f[1]. The other wording is "I have kept all these things from my youth" (ℵ[2] [seventh century] C [D] W f[13] 33 Maj; so KJV). The variant reading, providing an expansion, is a harmonization to Mark 10:19 and Luke 18:21.

19:28 | when the Son of Man is seated on his throne.

"Son of Man," a messianic title (Dan. 7:13–14), is written as a nomen

sacrum (sacred name) in two early MSS (א W). When Jesus referred to himself as "the Son of Man" seated on the throne, he was clearly pointing to the vision in Dan. 7:13–14, where the Son of Man is pictured as being given authority over all the nations.

19:29a | leave houses or brothers or sisters or father or mother.
Several MSS add "or wife" to the list (א C L W f^{13} 33), but it is omitted in B D it[a]. The inclusion, which has the best documentary support, could be the result of harmonization to Luke 18:29, but the same can be argued against the variant—that it is the result of harmonization to Mark 10:29. Either way, an interpreter cannot say that Jesus never spoke of a male disciple leaving his wife to follow him, because this is made explicit in Luke 18:29 (where the word "wives" appears in all MSS).

19:29b | will receive a hundredfold.
The wording "hundredfold" is found in א C D W $f^{1,13}$ 33 Maj (so KJV); the wording "manifold" is found in B L Origen. The first reading may be the result of harmonization to Mark 10:30; the second, to Luke 18:30. Either way, the meaning is not significantly altered.

20:16 | the last will be first and the first last.
This is the original wording according to early and excellent documentary support: א B L Z 085. Other MSS (C D W $f^{1,13}$ 33 Maj; so KJV) add "for many are called but few are chosen." The addition came from 22:14. But whereas the statement perfectly suits the conclusion to the parable of the wedding feast in Matt. 22:1–14 (where several are invited but only a few attend), it is an odd addendum to the parable here. Exegetes who use the inferior text will have a difficult time explaining how the statement "many are called but few are chosen" has anything to do with a parable in which all were called and chosen to work in the vineyard. The point of this parable is captured by the shorter, superior text: "the last will be first and the first, last" because this cancels human endeavor to outdo others and exalts God's sovereignty to give grace as he pleases.

20:18 | the Son of Man will be handed over.
"Son of Man," a messianic title (Dan. 7:13–14), is written as a nomen sacrum (sacred name) in early MSS (א W), as well as L.

20:22 | Are you able to drink the cup that I am about to drink?
The original text ends here according to early and excellent documentary support: א B D L Z 085 $f^{1,13}$ $syr^{c,s}$ cop^{sa}. Other MSS (C W 33 Maj syr^{h}; so KJV) add "or to be baptized with the baptism that I am baptized with?" The variant reading is a scribal expansion borrowed verbatim from Mark 10:38–39. The MSS C and W are notorious for scribal harmonization of the Synoptic Gospels; the majority of MSS (Maj) followed suit.

20:23 | prepared by my Father.
The divine "Father" is written as a nomen sacrum (sacred name) in early MSS (א W), as well as L.

20:28 | the Son of Man did not come to be served but to serve.
"Son of Man," a messianic title (Dan. 7:13–14), is written as a nomen sacrum (sacred name) in one early MS (א), as well as L.

20:30 | Lord, Son of David.
Several early MSS ($\mathfrak{P}^{45vid}$ B C W Z) have the wording, "Lord, Son of David" whether before or after the expression "have mercy on us." A few MSS (א L Θ f^{13}) add "Jesus" after "Lord," the result of harmonization to Mark 10:47 and Luke 18:38 (parallel verses that have the word "Jesus"). "Son of David" is written as a nomen sacrum (sacred name) in $\mathfrak{P}^{45}$ א L, revealing that these scribes considered it a divine, royal-messianic title. The Jews expected the Messiah-King to be the Son of David (2 Sam. 7:13, 16; Jer. 23:5; Ezek. 37:24).

20:31 | Lord, Son of David.
"Lord, Son of David" is written as a nomen sacrum (sacred name) in one early MS (א), as well as L, revealing that these scribes considered it a divine, royal-messianic title. ($\mathfrak{P}^{45}$ is not extant in this part of the verse, but

given the scribes customary way of writing nomina sacra, "Son" would have appeared as a nomen sacrum.) The Jews expected the Messiah-King to be the Son of David (2 Sam. 7:13, 16; Jer. 23:5; Ezek. 37:24).

21:3 | the Lord needs them.

"Lord" is written as a nomen sacrum (sacred name) in early MSS (א B D W), as well as L, showing these scribes thought this was referring to the Lord Jesus, not the owner (master) of the colt.

21:9a | Hosanna to the Son of David.

"Son of David" is written as a nomen sacrum (sacred name) in one early MS (א), as well as L, because it is a royal, messianic title. The Jews expected the Messiah-King to be the Son of David (2 Sam. 7:13, 16; Jer. 23:5; Ezek. 37:24).

21:12 | Jesus entered the temple.

The original wording is probably "temple" according to early and good testimony (א B L 0281^{vid} f^{13} 33). This was expanded to "temple of God" in C D W f^{1} Maj. It is possible that scribes added "of God" when they realized the close connection between this verse and Mal. 3:1ff., which predicts that the Messiah would suddenly come to God's temple and purge it. Or it is possible that other scribes deleted it because "of God" does not appear in the parallel passages (Mark 11:15; Luke 19:45). But on the basis of documentary support, it must be judged that the variant is a scribal expansion, which happens to give good effect in that the expression "God's temple" stands in strong contrast to the temple profaned with men's merchandising.

21:15 | Hosanna to the Son of David.

"Son of David," a royal-messianic title, is written as a nomen sacrum (sacred name) in one early MS (א), as well as L 33. The Jews expected the Messiah-King to be the Son of David (2 Sam. 7:13, 16; Jer. 23:5; Ezek. 37:24).

21:28–31

The text underlying this story follows א B f^{13}. Other MSS (C* W it^{c} syr) invert the two sons in the story. Both versions, however, have the same message: the son who says he won't go to work but later changes his mind is the one who does the will of his father, according to the opinion of the religious leaders. But in D and some Old Latin MSS (as well as MSS known to Jerome), the religious leaders say that the son who says he will go but then doesn't go is the one who did the father's will.

According to the conclusion of the parable (21:31–32), it would seem that "the father" typifies John the Baptist, the "first son" symbolizes the Jewish leaders who appeared to listen to John but didn't really obey the message in getting ready for Jesus the Messiah, while "the second son" represents the tax collectors and prostitutes who didn't appear to have listened to John but eventually did because they accepted Jesus as the Messiah. But how do we account for the third reading? Is this just another aberration of D and its allied Western witnesses, or does it—as the most difficult reading of the three—represent the original text? Many scholars dismiss it as nonsensical; others (notably Jerome) perceive it as portraying the Jewish leaders' perverse thinking: Instead of giving Jesus the expected answer, the Jewish leaders intentionally tried to spoil the point of Jesus's parable by giving the wrong answer. In response, Jesus reproves them by saying, "the tax collectors and prostitutes will enter the kingdom of heaven before you do." But was this Matthew's literary ingenuity or the scribe of Codex Bezae (D)? Most likely it is the latter, for this scribe (or his predecessor) is known for the liberties he took with the text in the interest of making it more interesting literature.

21:37–38 | the Son.

"Son" is written as a nomen sacrum (sacred name) in one early MS (א), as well as L, thereby showing that the scribes of these MSS interpreted the son in the parable to be the divine Son of God.

21:40 | the Lord of the vineyard.

"Lord" (Greek, *kurios*) is written as a nomen sacrum (sacred name) in early MSS (א B D W), thereby showing that the scribes of these MSS interpreted the vineyard owner to be the Lord God.

21:44 | omit verse.

The earliest MS ($\mathfrak{P}^{104}$, dated early second century or even c. 100) and other witnesses (D 33 it syr^{s} Origen Eusebius) do not include 21:44. Other MSS (א B C L W Z 0102 f^{1,13} Maj syr^{c,h,p} cop) add verse 44: "The one who falls on this stone will be broken to pieces; and it will crush anyone on whom it falls." The inclusion has good documentary support, the kind that would usually affirm legitimacy for most textual variants. However, this is challenged by the earliest manuscript, $\mathfrak{P}^{104}$, as well as Origen, D, and other witnesses. The testimony of $\mathfrak{P}^{104}$ heightens the suspicion that this verse may be an interpolation taken from Luke 20:18. One caution against this view is that one would have expected that the interpolation would have been inserted (quite naturally) after Matthew 21:42 (in order to get the two OT citations together, as in Luke 20:17–18), not after 21:43. Nonetheless, its position after 21:43 is not awkward and could have been intentional.

The first quote, in Matt. 21:42, is taken from Ps. 118:22–23; it is quoted in all the Gospels to underscore the reality that Jesus, though rejected by the Jews, would become the cornerstone of the church. The next verse affirms this truth when it says, "the kingdom of God will be taken away from you [the Jews] and given to a people who will produce its fruit." Then follows 21:44: "he who falls on this stone will be broken to pieces, but he on whom it falls will be crushed" (taken from Isa. 8:14–15 and Dan. 2:34–35, 44–45). This prophecy depicts Christ as both the stone over which the Jews stumbled and were broken (cf. Rom. 9:30–33; 1 Cor. 1:23) and the stone that will smash all kingdoms in the process of establishing God's kingdom. Whether or not Matthew wrote this verse, it accords with Matthean theology.

22:30 | they are like angels in heaven.

The original wording "angels" is found in B D. Other wording is "the angels" (Θ f^{1}) or "angels of God" (א W f^{13} 33 Maj; so KJV). "Angels" (without a definite article) emphasizes the nature of being, not the personal identity of the being. Resurrected believers will not be the same as *the* angels of God in personality or classification of "being" (humans will always be humans and angels will always be angels); resurrected believers will, like angels, share in the condition of being unmarried.

22:32 | I am the God of Abraham, the God of Isaac, and the God of Jacob.
This comes from Exod. 3:6 LXX. Jesus's citation came from the LXX where the wording *ego eimi* (I am) is emphatic. The "presentness" of God forms the basis of Jesus's argument. Abraham, Isaac, and Jacob had already died by the time God spoke to Moses at the burning bush, yet God considered himself to be their God in the *present*, not just in their past lives.

22:43 | David by the Spirit calls him "Lord."
The divine "Spirit" is written as a nomen sacrum (sacred name) in early MSS (א B D W), as well as L; therefore, these scribes regarded this utterance as being prompted by the divine Spirit. "Lord" is written as a nomen sacrum (sacred name) in all MSS.

22:44 | The Lord said to my Lord, "Sit at my right hand until I put your enemies under your feet."
This comes from Ps. 110:1. In Hebrew, the first line is "Yahweh said to my Adonai." In the Greek text, it reads "Kurios said to my Kurios." Either way, deity is addressing deity. Thus, David (who wrote this psalm) called him who was to sit on the kingly throne, "my Adonai" (my Lord), not "my son." The OT predicted that the son of David would have an everlasting kingship through his descendants (2 Sam. 7:12–16; Ps. 89:1–4; 132:11–12; Jer. 23:5–8; Ezek. 37:21–24; Zech. 6:12–15). The teachers saw the Messiah as the son of David (see Psalms of Solomon 17–18, written 50 BC) as being the one to fulfill the role of being a military conqueror, liberator of kingdom rule, inaugurator of an everlasting dynasty in Jerusalem that would affect all nations of the world. They expected him to be an entirely earthly figure, a mortal man, while Jesus shows here that he was divine (cf. Jer. 23:6)—David's "Lord," not merely his son.

23:4 | heavy, unbearable burdens.

The word "unbearable" is found in B D W f^{13} Maj, but omitted in ℵ L. Though the extra verbiage may have been borrowed from Luke 11:46, the inclusion of the wording has the best textual support.

23:9 | your Father.

The divine "Father" (both times) is written as nomina sacra (sacred names) in early MSS (ℵ W), as well as L. No human on earth should be called "Father" because the true Father is God in heaven.

23:14 | omit verse.

Verse 14 is not part of the original text of Matthew according to excellent documentary evidence: ℵ B D L Z f^1 33 $it^{a,e}$ syr^s cop^{sa}. Other MSS (W 0102 0107 f^{13} Maj; so KJV) add here (or after verse 12) verse 14: "What miseries await you hypocritical scribes and Pharisees! For you devour widows' houses and for the sake of appearance you make long prayers; therefore you will receive the greater condemnation." This verse, not present in the earliest MSS and several other witnesses, was taken from Mark 12:40 or Luke 20:47 and inserted in later MSS either before or after 23:13.

23:35 | from righteous Abel to the blood of Zechariah son of Barachiah.

Most scholars think Jesus was summarizing the OT history of martyrdom. Gen. 4:8 records the murder of Abel, and 2 Chron. 24:20–22 records the murder of a priest named Zechariah. Since the Hebrew OT canon began with Genesis and ended with 2 Chronicles, this was Jesus's way of saying "from the beginning to the end of Scripture." The Zechariah who was murdered in 2 Chron. 24:20–22, however, was not the son of Barachiah but the son of Jehoiada. For this reason some MSS (13 6 *ℵ) omit "son of Barachiah" after "Zechariah" (see ESV mg), and the Gospel of the Nazarenes (according to Jerome's *Commentary on Matthew*) reads "son of Jehoiada." But all the other witnesses read "son of Barachia"—the earliest witness being provided by the second-century MS, $\mathfrak{P}^{77}$. Thus, it must be judged that this is what Matthew wrote.

Did Matthew confuse two names or was Matthew thinking of the prophet Zechariah, son of Barachiah (Zech. 1:1)? The patronym supports the latter, so does the context, which speaks of how Jerusalem rejected all the prophets (23:34, 37). Jesus's saying, therefore, refers to the martyrdoms of the first to the last prophet. (Abel was considered a prophet because his death had prophetic implications—see Heb. 11:4.) Most scholars reject this view because there is no record of Zechariah the prophet having been murdered and because Jesus's description of where the murder occurred seems to concur with what was described in 2 Chron. 24:20–22 (but see below). Thus, scholars have conjectured that Zechariah was the grandson of one called Barachiah, or even that Barachiah was also called Jehoiada.

23:38 | your house is left to you desolate.

The original word "desolate" (Greek, *eremos*) is included in many of the best MSS (𝔓[77] א C D W); it is absent in B L. The only argument against this reading is that scribes could have added the word *eremos* to make it conform to Jer. 12:7 or 22:5, the OT passages behind this verse. But it is more likely that the word was dropped because scribes thought the word was superfluous after "is left." In either case, Jesus was predicting God's abandonment of Jerusalem and the temple as the result of the Jews rejecting their Messiah. Ultimately, this abandonment and desolation would be realized in the destruction of Jerusalem and the temple in AD 70 (see note on Luke 13:35).

24:7 | there will be famines and earthquakes.

The original wording is "famines and earthquakes," according to א B D. Other wording, "famines and pestilences and earthquakes," is found in C L W 33 $f^{1,13}$ Maj (so KJV). It is possible that *loimoi* (pestilences) was accidentally dropped from the text because it looks so similar to *limoi* (famines), but it is more likely that *loimoi* was added to make this verse harmonize with a parallel passage, Luke 21:11. The two earliest MSS (א B) support the text.

24:27, 30 | the coming of the Son of Man

"Son of Man," a messianic title (Dan. 7:13–14), is written as a nomen sacrum (sacred name) in one early MS (א), as well as L.

24:36a | no one knows the day or hour, neither the angels of heaven nor the Son.

The original wording includes "nor the Son" according to the good testimony of א*,2 [seventh century] B D f^{13} it MSS[according to Jerome]. The phrase is omitted in א[1] L W f^1 33 Maj syr cop MSS[according to Jerome]. (The original scribe of codex Sinaiticus, working in the middle of the fourth century, wrote "nor the Son." This was deleted by a corrector also working in the fourth century, then it was added back into the text by another corrector in the seventh century.) The same omission of "nor the Son" occurs in the parallel passage, Mark 13:32, but in very few MSS. The documentary support in favor of its inclusion is impressive in both Gospels. Some have argued that the words were added in order to harmonize Matthew with Mark, but it is far more likely that the words were omitted because scribes found it difficult to conceive of Jesus not knowing something his Father knew—specifically, the time of the second coming (parousia). How could Jesus not know the time of his return when he had just predicted all the events that would lead up to it? This is hard to answer. What can be said is that the Son, after his incarnation, took a position of dependence on his Father. The Son, who was one with the Father, acted and spoke in dependence on the Father. If the Father did not reveal something to him, it was not revealed. The timing of the second coming was the Father's prerogative (see Acts 1:7).

24:37, 39 | the coming of the Son of Man.

"Son of Man," a messianic title (Dan. 7:13–14), is written as a nomen sacrum (sacred name) in one early MS (א), as well as L.

24:42 | you do not know what day your Lord is coming

The original wording is "day" according to early manuscript evidence (א B D W). The variant wording "hour" (in L 0281 Maj; so KJV), shows scribal conformity to Matt. 24:44, a parallel verse.

24:45, 46, 48, 50 | Lord.

"Lord" is written as a nomen sacrum (sacred name) in several early MSS

(א B D W), thereby revealing that these scribes considered the "master" of the story to be the divine Lord.

25:1 | they went out to meet the bridegroom.

The original wording is "bridegroom" according to excellent testimony (א B C L W Z f[13]); Other wording is "bridegroom and the bride" (in D Θ f[1] it syr). In a parable about Jesus coming as the bridegroom, many readers would expect that the one who is waiting for him is the bride. This expectation is heightened by the fact that the NT speaks of Christ and the church as bridegroom and bride (John 3:29; 2 Cor. 11:2; Eph. 5:25–32; Rev. 21:2). But for the sake of emphasizing individual readiness for the day of his coming, Jesus used ten bridesmaids, not one bride, to illustrate the importance of being ready. According to custom, on the evening of the wedding the bridegroom would go to the bride's house and take her to his home for the wedding festivities. Along the way, a procession of family and friends would follow the bridegroom and the bride, lighting up the way with their torches. In this parable we see ten bridesmaids who evidently would accompany the bridegroom back to the bride's home; five sensible bridesmaids took enough oil to keep their torches burning, while the other five did not. There is no mention of the bride because this would distract from the lesson of the parable: a call to individual readiness. The scribes and ancient translators (mainly of a "Western" tradition) who added "and the bride" did so (1) to get every character in the scene (according to the historical custom) and/or (2) to reflect the NT theme of Christ, the bridegroom, coming for the church, his bride.

25:13 | you do not know the day nor the hour.

The original wording is "the day nor the hour" according to the earliest MSS (𝔓[35] א B) and C* D L W f[1] syr cop. The wording is "the day or the hour in which the Son of Man is coming" (in C[3] [ninth century] f[13] Maj; so KJV), by way of scribal expansion.

25:18–24, 26 | Lord.

"Lord" is written as a nomen sacrum (sacred name) in several early MSS

(𝔓[35] A B D W), thereby revealing that these scribes considered the "master" of the story to be the divine Lord.

25:31 | all the angels.

The original wording is "angels" (so ℵ B D L f^1 33). The wording is "sacred angels" in A W f^{13} Maj, a scribal addition influenced by Mark 8:38 and/or Luke 9:26.

25:34 | blessed by my Father.

The divine "Father" is written as a nomen sacrum (sacred name) in early MSS (ℵ W), as well as L.

26:2 | the Son of Man will be handed over to be crucified.

"Son of Man," a messianic title (Dan. 7:13–14), is written as a nomen sacrum (sacred name) in early MSS (ℵ A W), as well as L.

26:3 | the leading priests and the elders of the people gathered.

The original wording is "the leading priests and the elders of the people" according to the earliest MSS (𝔓[45] ℵ A B) and D L 0293 $f^{1,13}$. Other wording is "the leading priests and the scribes and the elders" (Maj it; so KJV); and "the leading priests and the Pharisees" (W). According to the best MSS in Matthew, two groups of people were responsible for plotting Jesus's death: the leading priests and the elders of the people, who were the leading members of the Jewish religion and Jewish society. These men are identified by Matthew as the prime movers behind Jesus's murder (26:14; 27:1; 28:12). Along with them, Matthew mentions "the scribes" (26:57; 27:41) and "the Pharisees" (27:62), each of which were added here by various scribes.

26:24 | The Son of Man goes as it was written of him.

"Son of Man," a messianic title (Dan. 7:13–14), is written as a nomen sacrum (sacred name) in early MSS (ℵ W), as well as L.

26:28 | this is my blood of the covenant.

The original wording is "my blood of the covenant" according to early and diverse testimony: $\mathfrak{P}^{37}$ $\mathfrak{P}^{45vid}$ א B L Z Θ 0298^{vid} 33. The wording is "my blood of the new covenant" in A C (D) W $f^{1,13}$ Maj it syr cop. The original reading has excellent documentation—the four earliest Greek MSS attesting to the reading "covenant." (According to spacing, $\mathfrak{P}^{45}$ could not have contained the word *kaine* = new; see Comfort and Barrett, *Text of Earliest NT Greek MSS*, 164.) Influenced by Luke 22:20, which contains the word "new" before "covenant," later scribes harmonized the Matthean account to Luke's (see note on Luke 22:20). Of course, Jesus was instituting a new covenant, even "the new covenant" God promised through Jeremiah (31:31–34). So, it is not wrong to call this the new covenant, but it is not what Matthew wrote.

26:29 | the kingdom of my Father.

The divine "Father" is written as a nomen sacrum (sacred name) in early MSS ($\mathfrak{P}^{53}$ א D W), as well as L.

26:39a | my Father.

The divine "Father" is written as a nomen sacrum (sacred name) in one early MS (א), as well as L.

26:39b

At the end of this verse some late MSS (C^{3mg} [ninth century] f^{13}) and lectionaries (124 230 348 543 713 788 826 828 983) add Luke 22:43–44 (in the MSS) or Luke 22:43–45a (in the lectionaries). (For further discussion, see note on Luke 22:43–44.) The earliest witness to the inclusion of this pericope in Matthew 26 is a marginal gloss written by the third corrector of C, who lived in Constantinople in the ninth century. The pericope fits as well in the garden scene in Matthew as it does in Luke, but it is a spurious addition in both books. Its placement in Matthew shows that it was very likely a piece of floating oral tradition. The same kind of multiple placement occurred with the pericope of the adulteress (see comments on John 7:53–8:11).

26:41 | the Spirit is willing.

The divine "Spirit" is written as a nomen sacrum (sacred name) in early

MSS (𝔓[37] ℵ D W). B writes *pneuma* in full (in *plene*; i.e., not written as a sacred name), suggesting this refers to the human spirit, which is the way most translations understand it.

26:42 | my Father.
The divine "Father" is written as a nomen sacrum (sacred name) in early MSS (ℵ C), as well as L.

26:44 | he went away and prayed.
This is the original wording according to 𝔓[37] (the earliest MS) A D f[1]. This is expanded to "prayed for the third time" in ℵ B C L Maj (so KJV).

26:45 | the Son of Man is betrayed.
The "Son of Man," a messianic title (Dan. 7:13–14), is written as a nomen sacrum (sacred name) in early MSS (ℵ W), as well as L.

26:49 | he approached Jesus who said to him, "Friend."
This is the reading in the earliest MS (𝔓[37]). The wording is expanded in all other MSS to "he approached Jesus and said, 'Greetings, Rabbi,' and he kissed him. And Jesus said to him, 'Friend.'" If the reading in 𝔓[37] is not a scribal mistake, the longer text in the other MSS could be the result of harmonization to the parallel Gospel accounts.

26:53 | call upon my Father.
The divine "Father" is written as a nomen sacrum (sacred name) in early MSS (ℵ W), as well as L.

26:63 | Tell us if you are the Christ, the Son of God.
"Christ" is written as a nomen sacrum (sacred name) in all MSS. "Son of God" is written as a nomen sacrum (sacred name) in early MSS (ℵ B D W). The Jewish leaders were asking Jesus if he was *the* divine Son of God, not just a son of God.

26:64 | you will see the Son of Man.
"Son of Man," a messianic title (Dan. 7:13–14), is written as a nomen

sacrum (sacred name) in early MSS (א W), as well as L. The title "Son of Man" is the one messianic title Jesus used of himself throughout the Gospels. Jesus's exclamation to the Jewish leaders encapsulates his understanding of this title, which comes from Dan. 7:9–14, a passage that shows "the Son of Man" sharing dominion over all the nations with "the Ancient One," whom Matthew calls "the Powerful One" (or "the Potentate"). Thus, whenever Jesus called himself "the Son of Man" he had this picture in mind.

27:9a | the prophet Jeremiah.

The original wording is "the prophet Jeremiah," according to early and diverse testimony: א A B C L W. Other MSS read "Zechariah the prophet" (22 syr^{hmg}); "Isaiah the prophet" (21 it^{l}); "the prophet" (33 $it^{a,b}$ $syr^{p,s}$ cop^{bo} $MSS^{\text{according to Augustine}}$). The ascription of this prophecy to Jeremiah is difficult because the passage seems to come from Zechariah 11:12–13. Because of the difficulty of assigning this prophecy to Jeremiah, some scribes changed "Jeremiah" to "Zechariah" (variant 1), and others dropped the name before the prophet (variant 3). Still others changed the name to "Isaiah," probably because he is the most quoted prophet in the NT. But Matthew's ascription of the prophecy to Jeremiah is not wrong, because although the quotation comes mainly from Zech. 11:12–13 it also comes from Jer. 19:1–11; 32:6–9. Zechariah's words do not mention the purchase of a field, but Jeremiah's words do. In fact, it is Jeremiah who speaks of innocent blood (Jer. 19:4) and of changing the name of a potter's field (Jer. 19:6). And it is Jeremiah who purchased a potter's field (Jer. 32:6–9). Thus, Jeremiah received the credit because he was the more prominent prophet.

27:16–17 | Barabbas

The name of the prisoner is "Barabbas" according to early and diverse testimony: א A B D L W 064 0250 f^{13} 33. The name is "Jesus Barabbas" according to S^{mg} f^{1} 1 118 579 700 1582 $syr^{p,s}$ $MSS^{\text{according to Origen}}$. The variant reading is supported only by some so-called "Caesarean" witnesses. Some scholars, however, think that "Jesus" was in the archetype of B because the article *ton* was left before *Barraban* (in 27:17), presupposing that the name "Jesus" appeared before "Barabbas" in the scribe's exemplar. Several later MSS have glosses that indicate "Jesus" appeared in earlier MSS. In a marginal note to codex S (from the tenth century) a certain scribe says, "In many ancient copies which I have met with I found Barabbas himself likewise called 'Jesus.'" According to Metzger, "about twenty minuscules contain a marginal note stating that in very ancient MSS Barabbas is called Jesus; in one of these the note is attributed to Origen. Since Origen himself calls attention to this in his *Commentary on Matthew*, the reading must be of great antiquity" (TCGNT). Another argument that has been posited in favor of the reading "Jesus Barabbas" is that it is offset with the wording "Jesus, the one called Christ"—as if the second title serves to distinguish the two men called Jesus (see note in NET). However, this argument is weakened by the fact that Pilate uses the exact same designation a few verses later ("Jesus who is called Christ," 27: 22)—as a way of identifying Jesus per his messianic claims, not by way of distinguishing him from another Jesus called Barabbas.

If the reading "Jesus Barabbas" is ancient, why does it not appear in the most ancient MSS (namely, א A B D W)? Was it suppressed in most MSS, only to show up later, in ninth to twelfth century witnesses? Or was it added by some scribe early in the history of the transmission of the text because he considered "Barabbas" to not really be a name (it means "son of a father") or because he wanted to add some drama to Matthew's narrative? Perhaps the crowd outside Pilate's palace had been shouting, "give us Jesus, give us Jesus." To which Pilate responded, "Do you want Jesus the one called Barabbas or do you want Jesus the one called Christ?" Instead of asking for Jesus the Christ, they get Jesus the murderer. The irony is blatant: The murdering Jesus is set free, while the freeing Jesus is murdered.

27:24 | I am innocent of this man's blood.

This is the original wording according to the earliest MS (B) and D. The other wording is "I am innocent of this righteous man's blood" (א A L W $f^{1,13}$ Maj). The second reading is probably a scribal interpolation adapted from Pilate's wife's comment about Jesus being a just man (27:19; cf. Luke 23:14 and John 19:6). This bit of gap filling is important for the narrative of Jesus's trial because it tells us that Pilate thought Jesus was innocent of the crimes charged against him and even more so that Jesus was a just man. But as the text reads, it must be inferred that Pilate thought Jesus was innocent or he would not have washed his hands of Jesus's blood.

27:35 | they divided his garments by casting lots.

This is a quote from Ps. 22:18. The verse ends here according to early and diverse testimony (א A B D L W 33); other MSS (Θ 0250 $f^{1,13}$) add: "that it might be fulfilled what was spoken through the prophet, 'they parted my garments among them, and for my vesture they cast lots.'" Because of the excellent support for the shorter text, it must be judged that the long addition came from John 19:24, coupled with a typical Matthean introduction to a prophetic citation (see 4:14). It was natural for scribes, wanting to emulate Matthew's style, to make this addition because Matthew had a penchant for showing how various events in Jesus's life and ministry fulfilled the OT Scriptures (in this case, Ps. 22:18, the most quoted Psalm in the NT concerning the crucifixion). Some of the same scribes (Θ 0250 $f^{1,13}$) also made this addition in Mark 15:27.

27:40 | if you are the Son of God, come down from the cross.

"Son of God" is written as a nomen sacrum (sacred name) in early MSS (א B D W). This shows that those who were passing by were challenging his claim that he was *the* Son of God, not just a son of God.

27:43b | He said, "I am the Son of God."

"The Son of God" is written as a nomen sacrum (sacred name) in early MSS (א A B D W). This shows that those who were passing by were challenging his claim that he was *the* Son of God, not just a son of God.

27:46a | Eloi, Eloi, lema sabachthani

This is the original wording according to the two earliest MSS (א B), as well as 33. Other wording is "*Ēli, Ēli, lema sabachthani*" in A D (L) W 090 $f^{1,13}$ Maj. The second reading comes from the Hebrew word *eli* (my God), whereas the text comes from the Aramaic word *elahi* (my God). Although it could be argued that the first reading is the result of scribal conformity to Mark 15:34 (a parallel verse), this reading reflects the actual language Jesus spoke and has excellent documentary support. The remaining words of Jesus's cry, "*lema sabachthani*" are clearly Aramaic. Furthermore, it would be easier for the bystanders to mistake the three-syllable Aramaic word for the three-syllable word "Elijah" than to confuse *ēli* for "Elijah." Jesus was crying out to God, and in the words of Ps. 22:2 was asking God why he had forsaken him. The crowds thought he was crying to Elijah, who, according to some Jewish traditions, would come to the rescue of those in distress.

27:49 | Another took his spear and pierced his side, and out came water and blood.

This sentence is included in three early MSS (א B C), as well as L, but is excluded in A D W $f^{1,13}$ Maj it syr cop. The general consensus among scholars about the inclusion is that it was interpolated from John 19:34. However, the inclusion cannot be easily dismissed, for the following reasons: (1) The documentary evidence for its inclusion is strong; indeed, the testimony of א B C has far more often refuted that of A D W than vice versa in the NU text—why not here? The scribes of B (especially) and א usually refrained from being Gospel harmonists. (2) If it was taken from John 19:34, why wasn't it taken verbatim? As is, the order of the last words in Matthew is "water and blood," whereas in John it is "blood and water," and there are four other words used in Matthew that do not appear in John (*allos de labōn* and *exēlthen*). (3) The reason scribes would want to delete it from the text is because the spearing (according to John) happened after Jesus's death, whereas here it occurs just before his death (see 27:50). Thus, the deletion was made in the interest of avoiding a discrepancy among the Gospels. Such harmonization was done full-scale in MSS like A D W. (4) Another reason for scribes to delete it is that it appears to present a jarring contradiction to what was just described: While many of the bystanders were waiting to see if Elijah would come and save Jesus, a Roman soldier (in complete opposition to this sentiment) lances Jesus with his spear. Therefore, the longer text should not be easily dismissed because, in fact, it is the harder reading and has excellent documentary support.

27:50 | he gave up the Spirit.

The divine "Spirit" is written as a nomen sacrum (sacred name) in early MSS (א B D W), as well as L. (The occurrence of a nomen sacrum for *pneuma* in B is rare.) The idea is that Jesus released the divine Spirit at his death—perhaps symbolizing divine life coming out of death (cf. John 19:30, which has similar wording). The divine "Spirit" here could also be Jesus's spirit/Spirit, which scribes recognized as being divine and therefore wrote as a nomen sacrum (sacred name).

27:56 | Joses

Jesus's second brother is "Joses," according to early and diverse testimony: A B C D^c $f^{1,13}$ Maj. He is called "Joseph" in א D* L W. See note on 13:55 for the same textual variant concerning the name of one of Jesus's brothers.

28:6 | come see the place where he was lying.

This is the original wording according to א B 33. This was altered in three ways: "where the Lord was lying" (A C D L W 0148); "where Jesus was lying" (F); "where the body of Jesus was lying" (1424).

28:19 | the Name of the Father, and the Son, and the Holy Spirit.

In the Greek, the word for "Name" is singular (*to onoma*) followed by three titles. This emphasizes the unity of the Trinity. The Triune God has one Name, with three titles: Father, Son, and sacred Spirit. The divine "Father" is written as nomen sacrum (sacred name) in א A W; "Son" is written as a nomen sacrum (sacred name) in A Maj; the divine "Spirit" is written as a nomen sacrum (sacred name) in א A D W.

THE GOSPEL ACCORDING TO MARK

Title: The Gospel according to Mark
P. Oxyrhynchus 5073 (an amulet of the late third century) titles this book as "the gospel" (*euangelion*). Fourth-century MSS (א B) call it simply "According to Mark."

1:1 | Jesus Christ.
This is the original wording in P. Oxy. 5073 א* 28 cop^{saMS} Origen. This is expanded to "Jesus Christ, God's Son" in א^2 [seventh century] A B D L W Maj (followed many English translations). The documentary evidence favors the shorter title, "Jesus Christ." It is supported by the earliest manuscript (P. Oxy. 5073, an amulet from the late third century), as well as א* and Origen. "God's Son" is an expansion on the title. The same kind of expansion occurred in Peter's proclamation of Jesus's identity (see note on 8:29).

1:2 | Isaiah the prophet.
This is the original wording in P. Oxy. 5073 א B L 33. Other wording is "the prophets" in A W f^{13} Maj. Various scribes, aware that Mark was citing more than one prophet in the following verses (1:2–3), changed "Isaiah the prophet" to "the prophets" (so TR and KJV). (The first quote comes from Mal. 3:1; the second comes from Isa. 40:3 LXX.) The text has the support of the earliest MSS: P. Oxy. 5073 (later third c.); א and B (mid-fourth century).

1:8 | he will baptize you in the Holy Spirit.
The divine "Spirit" is written as nomen sacrum (sacred name) in early MSS (א B D W), as well as L. The occurrence of a nomen sacrum for *pneuma* (Spirit) in B is rare.

1:10a | the Spirit like a dove.
The divine "Spirit" is written as nomen sacrum (sacred name) in early MSS (א D W), as well as L.

1:10b | descended into him.

This is the original wording according to the earliest MS (B), as well as D f^{13}. Two other readings are "descended on him" (A L f^{1} Maj) and "descended and remained on him" (א W 33). The two variant readings are the result of scribal conformity to the other Gospels—the first variant to Matt. 3:16 and Luke 3:22, the second to John 1:33. In these Gospels (followed by the variant readings), the Spirit is said to descend upon Jesus after his baptism. But in the reading of B, the Spirit is said to enter into Jesus after his baptism. This is a significant difference because whereas "upon" suggests that Jesus was anointed and empowered with the Spirit, "into" suggests that Jesus was penetrated and inhabited by the Spirit. This reading could be readily used by Adoptionists to proof-text the baptismal regeneration of Jesus. In fact, the Ebionites (who were basically adoptionistic) held such a view about Jesus. According to Epiphanius (*Against Heresies* 30.13.7–8), the Gospel of the Ebionites reads, "After the people were baptized, Jesus also came and was baptized by John. And as he came up from the water, the heavens were opened, and he saw the Holy Spirit descending in the form of a dove and *entering into him*." All English translations follow the first variant reading and thereby obscure the idea that the Spirit came to dwell inside Jesus.

1:11 | You are my beloved Son.

"Son" is written as a nomen sacrum (sacred name) in one early MS (א), as well as L. God hereby indicated that Jesus was *the* divine Son of God, not just a son of God.

1:12 | the Spirit drove him out into the wilderness.

The divine "Spirit" is written as a nomen sacrum (sacred name) in early MSS (א D W), as well as L.

1:14 | gospel of God.

This is the original wording, according to the two earliest MSS (א B), as well as L $f^{1,13}$. A variant reading is "gospel of God's kingdom" (A D W Maj; so KJV). The variant is the result of scribal harmonization either to the immediate context (the next verse speaks of Jesus proclaiming the imminence of the kingdom) or to another Gospel (Matt. 4:17).

1:29 | as soon as they left the synagogue.

The original wording is "they," according to א A C L 33 Maj. The variant reading is "he" (B D W $f^{1,13}$). The variant arose as an attempt to smooth out the awkwardness of the text and/or to conform it to Matt. 8:14 and Luke 4:38.

1:34 | he would not permit the demons to speak because they knew him.

The original wording, "they knew him," is found in א A 0130 Maj. Other MSS (B L W f^1 33^{vid}) read "they knew him to be Christ," and other MSS ($א^2$ [seventh century] C f^{13}) read, "they knew him to be the Christ." The expansions in the variant readings are probably the result of scribal conformity to Luke 4:41, a parallel verse.

1:40 | a leper came to him begging.

This is the original wording according to the earliest MS (B), as well as D W. A variant reading is "begging and kneeling" (א A L Maj; so KJV), by way of scribal conformity to Matt. 8:12; Luke 5:12, parallel verses.

1:41 | moved with compassion.

This is the original wording, according to early and diverse testimony: א A B C L W $f^{1,13}$ 33 syr cop. A variant reading is "being angry" (D $it^{a,d}$). The documentary evidence strongly affirms the reading of the text. The scribe (or a predecessor) of D (codex Bezae) was a literary editor who had a propensity for making significant changes in the text. At this point, he decided to make Jesus angry with the leper for wanting a miracle—in keeping with the tone of voice Jesus used in 1:43 when he sternly warned the leper. But this wasn't a warning about seeking a miracle; it was a warning about keeping the miracle a secret so as to protect Jesus's identity.

2:8 | Jesus perceived in his Spirit.

The "Spirit" is written as a nomen sacrum (sacred name) in early MSS

(𝔓⁸⁸ ℵ D W), thereby showing his spirit (or, Spirit) to be divine. Scribes wrote Jesus's spirit/Spirit as a nomen sacrum throughout the Gospels. In codex B, *pneuma* is not written as a nomen sacrum and therefore can be understood to be Jesus's human spirit.

2:10 | the Son of Man has authority on earth to forgive sins.
"Son of Man," a messianic title (Dan. 7:13–14), is written as a nomen sacrum (sacred name) in one early MS (ℵ), as well as L.

2:16a | the scribes who were Pharisees
This is the original wording according to the three earliest MSS (𝔓⁸⁸ ℵ B), as well as L W 33. A variant reading is "the scribes and Pharisees" (A C D Maj; so KJV). P. Oxyrhynchus 1224, a fourth-century fragment of an unidentified Gospel, reads "scribes and Pharisees" in a strikingly similar passage (folio 2 verso, col. 2). The first reading is the more difficult of the two and the one with better attestation among the MSS. Mark was speaking of certain scribes who were also Pharisees. Quite interestingly, the punctuation in ℵ and B indicates that the scribes of the Pharisees (i.e., the scribes who were Pharisees) were following Jesus. This doesn't mean that they were his disciples, but simply that they were among the crowd that followed Jesus to Matthew's house.

2:22 | new wine is poured into fresh wineskins.
This is the original wording according to several early MSS (𝔓⁸⁸ ℵ A B C). The statement is omitted in D it. The omission was made by the scribe of D (and Old Latin translators) by way of stylization.

2:28 | The Son of Man is Lord even of the Sabbath.
"Son of Man," a messianic title (Dan. 7:13–14), is written as a nomen sacrum (sacred name) in one early MS (ℵ), as well as L. "Lord" is written as a nomen sacrum (sacred name) in all MSS.

3:8 | Idumea.
This region is found in four early MSS (ℵᶜ B C D), as well as Maj; it is omitted in ℵ* W f¹. The textual evidence favors its inclusion.

3:11 | You are the Son of God.
"Son of God" is written as a nomen sacrum (sacred name) in four early MSS (א B D W), as well as L. This shows that those who were demon-possessed recognized Jesus's divine identity—he was *the* Son of God, not just a son of God.

3:14 | he appointed twelve whom he designated apostles.
This is the original wording according to the earliest MSS (א B C*), as well as f^{13}. The phrase "whom he designated apostles" is omitted in A C^2 [sixth century] (D) L f^1 33 Maj. Scholars have been suspicious that the longer reading may have been taken from Luke 6:13. Indeed, many translators have followed the shorter text (note the change in TNIV from NIV). However, the longer text cannot be easily dismissed, because it has excellent documentary support and because Mark elsewhere used the term "apostles" to describe the Twelve (6:30).

3:15 | they had authority to exorcise demons.
This is the original wording according to the two earliest MSS (א B), as well as L. Two variants on this are "they had authority to proclaim [the good message] and exorcise demons" (D W), and they had authority to heal diseases and exorcise demons (A C^2 [sixth century] D W $f^{1,13}$ 33 Maj). The variants are scribal expansions influenced by Matt. 10:1.

3:16 | the twelve he appointed.
This is the original wording according to three early MSS (א B C*). The phrase is omitted in A C^2 [sixth century] (D) L f^1 33 Maj it syr cop^{bo} (so KJV). Although it could be argued that these words were repeated accidentally from 3:14 due to dittography, it is just as likely that Mark wrote them to pick up where he left off in 3:14 (3:14b–15 being parenthetical).

3:19 | Judas Iscariot.
This is the original wording according to three early MSS (א B C), as well as L 33 565. Another reading is "Judas of Kerioth" (A W $f^{1,13}$ Maj cop); and another is "Judas Scarioth" (D it). See note on Matt. 10:4.

3:22 | Beelzebul.

This is the original word according to early and diverse testimony: א A C D L W $f^{1,13}$ 33 Maj. Two variants are "Beezebul" (B) and "Belzebub" (Vulgate $syr^{p,s}$). See note on Matt. 10:25.

3:29 | whoever blasphemes against the Holy Spirit.

The divine "Spirit" is written as a nomen sacrum (sacred name) in three early MSS (א D W), as well as L.

3:32 | your mother and your brothers are outside.

The original wording "brothers" is found in א B C L W $f^{1,13}$ 33 syr. The variant reading is "brothers and sisters" (A D). Although it could be argued that the text is the result of scribal harmonization to Matt. 12:47 and Luke 8:20 or that the phrase "and sisters" was accidentally dropped, the shorter reading has, by far, superior documentary support. Disagreeing with the decision of the majority of NU editors (who included "and sisters"), Metzger (TCGNT) wrote: "The shorter text preserved in the Alexandrian and Caesarean text-types should be adopted; the longer reading, perhaps of Western origin, crept into the text through mechanical expansion. From a historical point of view, it is extremely unlikely that Jesus's sisters would have joined in publicly seeking to check him in his ministry. Thus, it is more likely that the longer text is the result of scribal harmonization to the immediate context (3:35)." In all of this, it should be pointed out that the omission of "and his sisters" does not indicate that the Bible says that Jesus did not have sisters; he did (see Matt. 13:56; Mark 6:3).

4:12

Isa. 6:9–10 (Septuagint) is the most frequent OT passage cited in the NT (Matt. 13:14; Mark 4:12; Luke 8:10; John 12:40; Acts 28:26; Rom. 11:8) as an apt explanation for why that generation rejected Jesus. (See note on Matt. 13:13–15 for its occurrence in P. Oxy. 406.)

5:1 | Gerasenes.

This is the original wording in the two earliest MSS (א* B), as well as D. Two other variants are "Gergesenes" ($א^2$ [seventh century] L W f^1

28 33 565) and "Gadarenes" (A C f^{13} Maj; so KJV). This place name appears in a variety of forms in the Synoptic Gospels. For Mark, the reading "Gerasenes" has the best witnesses (see note on Matt. 8:28).

5:21 | Jesus crossed again to the other side.

This is the original wording according to the earliest MS ($\mathfrak{P}^{45vid}$), as well as D f^{1} 28 565 700 it syr^{s}. Another reading is "Jesus crossed again in the boat to the other side" (א A B C L 0132 f^{13} 33 Maj; so KJV). The addition is most likely a case of scribal gap-filling.

5:42 | they were amazed.

This is the original wording according to the earliest MS ($\mathfrak{P}^{45}$), as well as A W $f^{1,13}$ Maj. Two variant readings are "they were immediately amazed" (א B C L), and "they all were amazed" (D it), both scribal expansions.

6:3a | the carpenter's son, the Son of Mary.

This is the reading (lit. "the one of the carpenter, the Son of Mary") of $\mathfrak{P}^{45vid}$, the earliest MS. But the original reading is just as likely "the carpenter, the son of Mary" as found in many MSS (א A B C D L W Θ f^{1} $syr^{h,p}$ cop^{sa} $Celsus^{according\ to\ Origen}$). A few other MSS ($f^{13}$ 33^{vid} 565 700 Origen) read, "the son of the carpenter and Mary." It is possible that both the readings which have "son of the carpenter" were created by scribes to harmonize Mark 6:3 with Matt. 13:55 or to obfuscate what some might consider an offensive statement—i.e., Jesus was said to be not just the son of a carpenter but a carpenter himself! For example, Origen countered Celsus, a second-century antagonist of Christianity who attacked its founder as being nothing but "a carpenter by trade." Origen argued that "in none of the Gospels current in the churches is Jesus himself ever described as a carpenter" (*Contra Celsus* 6.34, 36). But there is nothing demeaning about Jesus being a carpenter. The Greek term describes a person who works in wood or stone. According to a second-century tradition (Justin *Dialogue* 88), Jesus constructed farm implements such as plows and yokes (cf. Jesus's statement in Matt. 11:29). But he could have been a stone mason or house builder. Prior to beginning his ministry at the age of thirty, he supported himself and his family by the trade he had learned from his father (see Matt. 13:55). Finally, it should be noted that "Son" (in the expression "Son of Mary") is written as a nomen sacrum (sacred name) in 𝔓[45] א L, but written out in full (in *plene*; i.e., not written as a sacred name) in W f[1,13]. (In B and D "son" is almost always written in *plene* in the NT, so their testimony is not weighty here.) The phrase in the mouths of Jesus's hometown folks would not have been divine; by contrast, the pen of Christian scribes would want to highlight Jesus as "the divine Son" born of Mary.

6:14b | they were saying he was John the Baptist raised from the dead.
The original phrase "they were saying" is found in B (D) W. A variant reading is "he was saying" (א A C L Θ f[1,13] 33 Maj). The variant was created to achieve continuity with the previous singular verb "he heard"—i.e., Herod heard. But this clause and on to the end of 6:15 is a detached segment providing three samplings of what the people (i.e., "they") were saying about Jesus.

6:22 | his daughter Herodias.
This is the original wording according to the two earliest MSS (א B), as well as D L. A variant reading is "the daughter of Herodias herself" (A C Θ f[13] 33 Maj). The girl who danced before Herod had the same name as her mother, Herodias, and she is described as being the daughter of Herod. But 6:24 says that she is the daughter of Herodias (so also Matt. 14:6), and her name was Salome, according to Josephus (*Antiquities* 18.136). Therefore, many commentators and translators consider the variant reading to be more accurate, both historically and contextually. However, the documentary evidence favors the reading of the text. If this is what Mark wrote, then his designation "daughter" of Herod must be equivalent to "step-daughter."

6:44 | those who had eaten.
This is the original wording according to two early MSS (𝔓[45] א), as well as D W Θ f[1,13]. A variant reading is "those who had eaten the loaves" (A B L 33 Maj; so KJV) by way of scribal expansion.

6:45 | go on ahead.
This is the original wording according to the earliest MS ($\mathfrak{P}^{45vid}$) and W. It is expanded to "go on ahead to the other side" in א A B C D Maj.

7:3 | unless they wash their hands with a fist.
This is the original wording according to some early MSS (A B D), as well as L Θ 0131 0274 $f^{1,13}$ Maj it syr^{hmg} Origen. Another reading is "unless they wash their hands often" (א W it^{f} $syr^{h,p}$ cop^{bo}), and yet another is "unless they wash their hands" (syr^{s} cop^{sa} Diatessaron). It is difficult to explain what it meant for the Jewish people to wash "with a fist." The expression, known to the people of Jesus's time, refers to a Jewish cleansing ritual—perhaps pouring water over cupped hands (i.e., "fists"—see NLT). Scribes, unable to make sense of *pugmē* (with fist), changed it to *pukna* (often) or omitted it altogether.

7:4a | unless they sprinkle themselves.
This is the original wording according to the two earliest MSS (א B). Two variant readings are "unless they wash themselves" (A D W Θ $f^{1,13}$ 33 Maj) and "unless it is immersed" (L D). The first variant (*baptisontai*) is in the middle voice; this usage indicates that the Pharisees washed/immersed themselves. The second variant indicates that the food was immersed. The text is in the middle voice (*rantisontai*); it suggests that they sprinkled themselves before eating. This reading could be the result of Alexandrian scribal adjustment attempting to avoid the use of "baptize" in any context beside that of Christian baptism. But this verb was commonly used to describe normal washing (see Luke 11:38; 16:24; John 13:26; Rev. 19:13 for the use of the cognate verb *baptein*); so it does not follow that the scribes of א and B would have necessarily changed it to preserve it as a descriptor of the Christian rite. Rather, it is just as likely that *rantisontai* was the more unusual word that was changed to *baptisontai*.

7:4b | kettles.
This is the original wording according to the three earliest MSS ($\mathfrak{P}^{45vid}$ א B), as well as L. A variant reading is "kettles and dining couches" in A D W Θ $f^{1,13}$ 33 Maj, by way of scribal expansion.

7:16 | omit verse.

The earliest MSS ($\mathfrak{P}^{45vid}$ ℵ B) and L 0274 do not include 7:16. Other MSS (A D W Θ $f^{1,13}$ Maj; so KJV) add verse 16: "Let anyone with ears to hear listen." A line and letter count of $\mathfrak{P}^{45}$ (which averages 37 lines per page) between one extant page (which ends with 7:15) and the next extant page (which begins at 7:25b), shows that the missing text would be filled with 650 letters in 14 lines (averaging 47 letters per line). This factoring does not leave room for 7:16, thereby showing that $\mathfrak{P}^{45}$ very likely did not include the verse. The extra verse was added by scribes, borrowing it directly from 4:23 (see also 4:9) to provide an ending to an otherwise very short pericope, 7:14–15.

7:24 | Tyre and Sidon.

This is the original reading according to three early MSS (ℵ A B), as well as $f^{1,13}$ 33 Maj $syr^{h,p}$ cop. Another reading is "Tyre" in D L W D Θ 28 565 it syr^{s}. The shorter reading is most likely the result of harmonization to 7:31, which says that Jesus left the region of Tyre and went through Sidon (according to ℵ B $f^{1,13}$ Maj syr). Scribes surmised: "How, then, could Jesus have come into Tyre and Sidon, if, when he left Tyre, he entered into Sidon?" The easiest fix was to drop "and Sidon" from 7:24. The verse, however, doesn't need fixing because the one district had two major cities—Tyre and Sidon (see note on 7:31).

7:28 | She said to him, "Lord."

This is the reading in $\mathfrak{P}^{45}$, the earliest MS. A longer reading is "yes, Lord" (ℵ B D L). It is significant to note that all these MSS write the word "Lord" (*kurie*) as a nomen sacrum (sacred name), thereby showing the woman's attitude about Jesus's divine status.

7:31 | he returned from the region of Tyre and Sidon.

This is the wording in the earliest MS ($\mathfrak{P}^{45}$), as well as A W 0131 $f^{1,13}$ Maj syr. The variant reading is "he returned from the region of Tyre, passed through Sidon" (in ℵ B D L Δ Θ 33 565 700). Either reading could be original because the documentary support is evenly divided and because Tyre and Sidon were essentially the same region.

7:35 | his ears were opened immediately.
This is the original wording according to the earliest MS ($\mathfrak{P}^{45}$), as well as A W Θ f^{13} 33 Maj. The word "immediately" is omitted in א B D L, but it should be included.

8:10 | Dalmanutha.
This is probably the original word according to א A (B) C L 0274 Maj (*Dalmounia* W). Other readings are "Magedan" in $\mathfrak{P}^{45vid}$; "Magada" in D^c $it^{c,k}$ syr^s; and "Magdala" in $f^{1,13}$. The uncertainty of the location led to a number of textual variants. The best testimony supports "Dalmanutha," but the earliest manuscript ($\mathfrak{P}^{45}$) reads "Magedan." (See note on Matt. 15:39.)

8:12 | he sighed deeply in his Spirit.
The "Spirit" is written as a nomen sacrum (sacred name) in three early MSS (א D W), as well as L, thereby showing that these scribes considered Jesus's spirit (or, Spirit) to be divine. Codex B does not write *pneuma* as a nomen sacrum and therefore can be understood to be Jesus's human spirit.

8:15 | Herod.
This is probably the original word according to several early MSS (א A B C D), as well as L 0131 33. But a variant reading is "the Herodians" in the earliest MS ($\mathfrak{P}^{45}$), as well as W Θ $f^{1,13}$ 28 565. Several Caesarean witnesses changed "Herod" to "the Herodians" to align this verse with 3:6 and 12:13. The Herodians, mentioned only in Matthew (22:16) and Mark (here and in 12:13), were an influential group of men who had political affiliations with the Herodian household and religious affiliations with the Sadducees.

8:29 | Peter said to him, "You are the Christ."
"The Christ" is the original wording according to the early testimony of A B C D Origen. This is expanded in two ways: "the Christ, the Son of God" (א L), and "the Christ, the Son of the living God" (W f^{13} it^b syr^p). The second variant presents scribal conformity of Mark to Matthew's

account verbatim; in Matt. 16:18 Peter tells Jesus, "You are the Christ, the son of the living God." The first variant is not an exact harmonization from any of the other parallel accounts, because in Luke 9:20 it is "the Christ of God" and in John 6:69, "the holy One of God." The short reading, "the Christ," accords with the beginning of the Gospel of Mark where the best manuscript evidence reads, "the beginning of the gospel of Jesus Christ" (see note on 1:1).

8:31 | the Son of Man must suffer many things.
"Son of Man," a messianic title (Dan. 7:13–14), is written as a nomen sacrum (sacred name) in two early MSS (א W), as well as L.

8:38a | whoever is ashamed of me and my words.
This is the original reading according to early testimony (א A B C D), as well as L 33 Maj. Other witnesses substitute "mine" for "my words" (W it^{k} cop^{sa} Tertullian). $\mathfrak{P}^{45vid}$ is cited by NA^{27} as supporting the variant, but this is unfounded, given the fact that at this point in the manuscript, the left and right margins are uncertain and therefore defy reconstruction of the lacunae (see Comfort and Barrett, *Text of the Earliest NT Greek MSS*, 170). The variant reading is attractive because it is the shorter and more difficult of the two readings. In the parallel passage, Luke 9:26, "words" is also lacking in some witnesses (see note). Perhaps "words" was a later addition made by scribes attempting to make the text more applicable to contemporary needs—for it is more relevant in later centuries to speak of being ashamed of Jesus's words than of Jesus's disciples. However, the textual evidence supports the longer reading, and the shorter reading does not have the support of $\mathfrak{P}^{45}$.

8:38b | the Son of Man will be ashamed of him.
"Son of Man," a messianic title (Dan. 7:13–14), is written as a nomen sacrum (sacred name) in two early MSS (א W), as well as L.

8:38c | when he comes in the glory of his Father.
The divine "Father" is written as a nomen sacrum (sacred name) in two early MSS (א W), as well as L.

8:38d | and the holy angels.
This is the reading in the earliest MS ($\mathfrak{P}^{45}$) and W. The variant reading is "with the holy angels" (in ℵ A B C D L W). The meaning of the passage is different in each reading. The reading of the variant indicates that when Jesus comes, the angels come with him. The first reading indicates that the glory belongs to both the Father and the angels. The former is easier to understand because elsewhere the NT speaks of the angels coming with Jesus in the parousia (Matt. 25:31; 2 Thess. 1:7; cf. Mark 13:26–27). The first text is more difficult to understand because it indicates that the angels, Jesus, and the Father share the same glory.

9:2 | while he was praying, he was transfigured.
This is the reading in the earliest MS ($\mathfrak{P}^{45}$) and W Θ f^{13}. The phrase "while he was praying" is not included in ℵ A B C D Maj. These words may have been added under the influence of Luke 9:29, a parallel passage.

9:7 | This is my beloved Son.
"Son" is written as a nomen sacrum (sacred name) in one early MS (ℵ), as well as L, pointing to the One who is *the* divine Son of God.

9:9, 12 | Son of Man.
"Son of Man," a messianic title (Dan. 7:13–14), is written as a nomen sacrum (sacred name) in early MSS (ℵ W), as well as L.

9:19 | a faithless generation.
This is the original reading in several early MSS (ℵ A B C D). $\mathfrak{P}^{45vid}$ and W read, "a faithless and perverse generation," influenced by Matt. 17:17, a parallel verse.

9:24 | the father of the child cried out.
This is the original reading according to several early MSS ($\mathfrak{P}^{45}$ ℵ A* B C* W). This was expanded to "cried out with tears" in A^2 C^3 [ninth century] D Θ $f^{1,13}$ Maj (so KJV), by way of scribal expansion.

9:25 | he commanded the spirit.
This is the reading according to the earliest MS (𝔓[45]) and W f[1] syr[s]. All other MSS call it a "defiling spirit."

9:29 | this is exorcised by prayer.
This is the original wording according to the two earliest MSS (א* B), as well as 0274 it[k]. This is expanded to "prayer and fasting" in א[2] [seventh century] A C D L W Θ Ψ f[1,13] 33 Maj. The words "and fasting" were probably added by scribes who were influenced by the early church's strong emphasis on fasting. (See also notes on Matt. 17:21; Acts 10:30; 1 Cor. 7:5 for the same kind of addition.) NA[27] lists 𝔓[45vid] in support of the longer text but the lacunae in the manuscript doesn't allow for this supposition.

9:31 | the Son of Man is betrayed into the hands of men.
"Son of Man," a messianic title (Dan. 7:13–14), is written as a nomen sacrum (sacred name) in two early MSS (א W), as well as L.

9:44, 46 | omit verses.
The earliest and best MSS (א B C L W 0274) do not include verses 44 and 46, which have the same wording as in verse 48. A scribe added these verses, which appears in other MSS (A D Maj; so KJV) as a kind of poetic refrain: "where the devouring worm never dies and the fire is never quenched."

9:49 | everyone is salted with fire.
This is the original wording according to the two earliest MSS (א B), as well as L (W) Δ 0274 f[1,13] syr[s]. There are two other readings: "every sacrifice will be salted with salt" (D it), and "everyone will be salted with fire, even as every sacrifice will be salted with salt" (A C Θ Ψ Maj; so KJV).

The difficulty of this verse led to the textual variants. Among the many interpretations of this text, one of the most acceptable proceeds from the assumption that the "everyone" refers to everyone who follows Jesus. The "fire" can then be understood as a trial or test that a Christian must endure in order to be refined and perfected (see Isa. 33:14; Mal. 3:2; 1 Cor. 3:13, 15; 1 Pet. 1:7).

It is the expression "salted with fire" that has created the most difficulty. The best explanation of the origin of this image lies in the Jewish practice of salting a sacrifice. The meal offering was roasted first and then sprinkled with salt to symbolize the perfection of the offering (Lev. 2:13). Since salt made the grain good to eat, this act indicated, in a figurative way, that the sacrifice was acceptable to God. Jesus may have had this ritual in mind when he said that every one of his followers would have to be "salted with fire" in order to be made acceptable before God. With this understanding of the passage, one scribe (perhaps the scribe of D was the originator), borrowing from Lev. 2:13, changed the verse to read, "for every sacrifice will be salted with salt." Other scribes (as in the second variant) simply appended the gloss with a *kai*. Yet in order for this addition to be a helpful gloss, the *kai* must be understood as functioning epexegetically: "for everyone will be salted with fire, even as every sacrifice will be salted with salt."

10:7 | will part from his father and mother.

This is the original reading according to the two earliest MSS (א B), as well as Ψ syr^{s}. A variant reading is, "will part from his father and mother and be joined to his wife" (A C D L W Maj; so KJV). It is likely that the extra clause was added by scribes to conform Mark to either Matt. 19:5 or Gen. 2:24 (or both).

10:19 | you shall not defraud.

This reading has early and diverse testimony: א A B^{2} [tenth century] C D Θ Maj. Other MSS (B* W Δ Ψ f^{1,13}) omit the clause. The full quotation in this verse, which comes from Exod. 20:12–16, Deut. 5:16–20, and Lev. 19:18, has superior attestation.

10:24 | how difficult it is to enter into the kingdom of God.

This is the original reading according to early MSS (א B W it^{k}). This is expanded to "how difficult it is for those who trust their wealth" in A C D Θ f^{1,13} Maj syr. The variant reading is a scribal addition intended to clarify that it is those who trust wealth—not just everybody—who would have a difficult time entering the kingdom of God.

10:33 | the Son of Man will be betrayed.

"Son of Man," a messianic title (Dan. 7:13–14), is written as a nomen sacrum (sacred name) in two early MSS (א W), as well as L.

10:34 | after three days he will rise again.

This is the original reading according to early and diverse testimony: א B C D L it cop. This was changed to "on the third day he will rise again" in A (W) Θ $f^{1,13}$ Maj. The documentary evidence strongly supports the reading of the text; the variant is the result of certain scribes attempting to synchronize the timing of Jesus's resurrection which occurred on the third day.

10:40 | it is for those for whom it has been prepared.

This is the original reading according to early and diverse testimony: $א^{1}$ B C D L W Maj. Some MSS ($א^{*,2}$ [seventh century] f^{1}), add "by my Father" by way of scribal expansion.

10:45 | The Son of Man did not come to be served.

"Son of Man," a messianic title (Dan. 7:13–14), is written as a nomen sacrum (sacred name) in two early MSS (א W), as well as L.

10:47–48 | Son of David

"Son of David," a royal-messianic title, is written as a nomen sacrum (sacred name) in two early MSS (א W), as well as L. The Jews expected the Messiah-King to be the Son of David (2 Sam. 7:13, 16; Jer. 23:5; Ezek. 37:24).

11:3 | the Lord needs it.

"Lord" is written as a nomen sacrum (sacred name) in two early MSS (א B). The term in context could also be understood as "the owner" of the colt, but the scribes of א B designated the person as the Lord Jesus.

11:22 | have faith in God.

This is the original wording according to several early MSS (A B C W), as well as L. A variant reading is " if you have faith in God" (so א D Θ). The original wording has excellent testimony, and the variant is likely the result of scribal conformity to a parallel passage, Matt. 21:21 (see also Luke 17:6).

11:26 | omit verse.

The earliest MSS (א B) and L W Δ Ψ syr^{s} cop^{sa} do not include 11:26; A (C D) Θ (f^{1,13} 33) Maj add "but if you do not forgive, neither will your Father in heaven forgive your trespasses." Though it could be argued that verse 26 dropped out by a scribal mistake (both 11:25 and 11:26 end with the same three words), the reading of the text has much better documentation than the variant. Thus, it is more likely that verse 26 is a natural scribal expansion of verse 25, borrowed from Matt. 6:15, a parallel verse.

12:6 | he still had one beloved son.

"Son" is written as a nomen sacrum (sacred name) in two early MSS (𝔓^{45} א), as well as L, thereby showing that the scribes of these MSS interpreted "the Son" in the parable to be the divine Son of God.

12:9 | What then will the Lord of the vineyard do?

"Lord" (Greek, *kurios*) is written as a nomen sacrum in three early MSS (א B D), thereby showing that the scribes of these MSS interpreted the vineyard owner to be the Lord God.

12:35 | How can the scribes say that the Christ is the Son of David?

"Christ" is written as a nomen sacrum (sacred name) in all MSS. "Son of David," a royal-messianic title, is written as a nomen sacrum (sacred name) in two early MSS (א W), as well as L. The Jews expected the Messiah-King to be the Son of David (2 Sam., 7:13, 16).

12:36a | David declared by the Holy Spirit, "the Lord said to my Lord."

The divine "Spirit" is written as a nomen sacrum (sacred name) in four early

MSS (א B D W), as well as L; it is rare for B to have *pneuma* (Spirit) written as a nomen sacrum. "Lord" (both times) is written as a nomen sacrum (sacred name) in all MSS. In the Hebrew text of Ps. 110:1 (the verse quoted here), this reads "Yahweh said to my Adonai." In the Greek text it reads "*Kurios* said to my *Kurios*." Either way, deity is addressing deity. Thus, David (who wrote this psalm) called him who was to sit on the kingly throne, "my Adonai" (my Lord), not "my son." The OT predicted that the son of David would have an everlasting kingship through his descendants (2 Sam. 7:12–14; Ps. 89:1–4; 132:11–12; Jer. 23:5–8; Ezek. 37:21–24; Zech. 6:12–15). The teachers saw the Messiah as the son of David (see Psalms of Solomon 17–18, written 50 BC) as being the one to fulfill the role of a military conqueror, liberator of kingdom rule, inaugurator of an everlasting dynasty in Jerusalem that would affect all nations of the world. They expected him to be an entirely earthly figure, a mortal man, while Jesus shows here that he was divine (cf. Jer. 23:6)—David's "Lord," not merely his son.

14:21 | the Son of Man is betrayed.

"Son of Man," a messianic title (Dan. 7:13–14), is written as a nomen sacrum (sacred name) in two early MSS (א W), as well as L.

14:24 | this is my blood of the covenant.

The original wording is "covenant" according to the two earliest MSS (א B), as well as C D^{c} L it^{k}. This was altered to "new covenant in A f^{1,13} Maj syr (so KJV). The addition of "new" to "covenant" is a late expansion, borrowed from the liturgical texts, Luke 22:20 and 1 Cor. 11:25.

14:38 | the Spirit is willing but the flesh is weak.

The "Spirit" is written as a nomen sacrum (sacred name) in three early MSS (א D W), as well as L; whereas B writes the word *pneuma* in full (in *plene*; i.e., not written as a sacred name), thereby suggesting the human spirit, which is the way some translations interpret it.

14:41 | the Son of Man is betrayed into the hands of sinners.

"Son of Man," a messianic title (Dan. 7:13–14), is written as a nomen sacrum (sacred name) in two early MSS (א W), as well as L.

14:61 | the Son of the blessed One
"Son" is written as a nomen sacrum (sacred name) in one early MS (א), as well as L, pointing to the One who is *the* Son of God.

14:68 | he went out into the entryway.
This is the original wording according to the two earliest MSS (א B), as well as L W Ψ* it^{c} syr^{s} cop^{bo}. This is expanded to "he went out into the entryway and the rooster crowed" in A C D Θ $Ψ^{c}$ 067 $f^{1,13}$ Maj (so KJV). The documentary evidence strongly supports the shorter reading. Scribes added "and the rooster crowed" because they wanted to emphasize the literal fulfillment of Jesus's prediction in 14:30 and/or because they wanted to account for a first rooster-crowing because a second one is mentioned in 14:72 (see next note).

14:72 | a rooster crowed a second time.
This is the wording in A B D W Maj. The wording is "a rooster crowed" in א C^{*vid} L it^{c}. The manuscript evidence is divided; either reading could be original.

15:28 | omit verse.
The earliest and best MSS (א A B C) and D Ψ it^{k} syr^{s} cop^{sa} do not include 15:28. L Θ 083 0250 $f^{1,13}$ Maj $syr^{h,p}$ add verse 28: "And the scripture was fulfilled that says, 'and he was counted among the lawless.'" The documentary evidence decisively shows that this verse was not present in any Greek MS prior to the late sixth century (namely, 083—a MS discovered in the 1970s at St. Catherine's Monastery). Borrowing from a parallel passage, Luke 22:37 (which is a quotation of Isa. 53:12), later scribes inserted this verse as a prophetic prooftext for the phenomenon that Jesus died with the lawless.

15:34 | why have you forsaken me?
This is the original wording according to early MSS (א A B C). This was changed to "why have you reproached me?" in D $it^{c,i,k}$. The variant shows the creative editorialization of the scribe of the D-text, who thought it too much for Jesus to have been forsaken by God. Some scholars think

the word "reproached" was introduced to avoid an implication that Jesus had become separated from divinity and therefore could not himself be divine. Thus, the change would combat a Gnostic separationist Christology which posited that "the Christ" left Jesus to die on his own. In making the change, the D-reviser may have been thinking of the prophetic word, "The reproaches of those who reproached you have fallen on me," taken from Ps. 69:9 (also cited by Paul in Rom. 15:3).

15:39 | This man was the Son of God.

"Son of God" is written as a nomen sacrum (sacred name) in three early MSS (א B W), as well as L. Thus, the centurion recognized Jesus as *the* divine Son of God, not just a son of God.

16:3

One Old Latin manuscript, codex Bobiensis (it^{k}), dated c. 400, has an extended gloss at the end of this verse: "Suddenly, at the third hour of the day, there was darkness over the whole earth, and angels descended from heaven, and rising in the splendor of the living God they ascended with him [i.e., Jesus], and immediately it was light." This variant, which bears some resemblance to the Gospel according to Peter (35–44), is noteworthy because it is the only attempt to describe the actual resurrection of Jesus. None of the Gospels provide such a description; the reader is simply told that Jesus arose and then the reader (in the other Gospels) is given glimpses of Jesus's resurrection appearances. This variant is also significant in that it is found in one of the few MSS that conclude with the shorter ending after 16:8; thus, it is possible that the scribe of it^{k} provided his own resolution to the Gospel by including a description of the resurrection in 16:3.

16:8

The Gospel of Mark ends in 5 ways in various MSS:

1. The earliest MSS (א B) stop at verse 8. This is also evident in 304 syr^{s} cop^{saMS} arm geo^{MSS} Hesychius Eusebius's Canons $MSS^{\text{according to Eusebius}}$ $MSS^{\text{according to Jerome}}$ $MSS^{\text{according to Severus}}$.

2. One MS, codex Bobiensis (it^{K}), dated c. 400, supplies a shorter ending, as follows:

And all that had been commanded them they told briefly to those with Peter. And afterward Jesus himself sent out through them, from the east and as far as the west, the holy and imperishable proclamation of eternal salvation. Amen.

3. Other witnesses (A C D Θ f^{13} 33 Maj MSS$^{\text{according to Eusebius}}$ MSS$^{\text{according to Jerome}}$ MSS$^{\text{according to Severus}}$ Irenaeus, Apostolic Constitutions, Epiphanius, Severian, Nestorius, Ambrose, Augustine) supply a longer ending:

9 Now after he rose early on the first day of the week, he appeared first to Mary Magdalene, from whom he had cast out seven demons. 10 She went out and told those who had been with him, while they were mourning and weeping. 11 But when they heard that he was alive and had been seen by her, they would not believe it. 12 After this he appeared in another form to two of them, as they were walking into the country. 13 And they went back and told the rest, but they did not believe them. 14 Later he appeared to the eleven themselves as they were sitting at the table; and he upbraided them for their lack of faith and stubbornness, because they had not believed those who saw him after he had risen. 15 And he said to them, "Go into all the world and proclaim the good news to the whole creation. 16 He who believes and is baptized will be saved; but the one who does not believe will be condemned. 17 And these signs will accompany those who believe: by using my Name they will cast out demons; they will speak in new tongues; 18 they will pick up snakes in their hands, and if they drink any deadly thing, it will not hurt them; they will lay their hands on the sick, and they will recover."

19 So then the Lord Jesus, after he had spoken to them, was taken up into heaven and sat down at the right hand of God. 20 And they went out and proclaimed the good news everywhere, while the Lord worked with them and confirmed the message by the signs that accompanied it."

4. Some MSS (W MSS$^{\text{according to Jerome}}$) have this longer ending with an addition after 16:14, which reads as follows:

And they excused themselves, saying, "This age of lawlessness and unbelief is under Satan, who does not allow the truth and power of God to prevail over the unclean things of the spirits. Therefore reveal your righteousness now"—thus they spoke to Christ. And Christ replied to them, "The term of years of Satan's power has been fulfilled, but other terrible things draw near. And for those who have sinned I was handed over to death, that they may return to the truth and sin no more, that they may inherit the spiritual and imperishable glory of righteousness that is in heaven."

5. Some MSS (L Ψ 083 099 274^{mg} 579 syr^{hmg} cop^{sa,boMSS}) have the shorter ending (listed as #2) and the longer ending (listed as #3).

The ending to Mark's Gospel presents an intriguing dilemma for textual scholars: Which of the five endings, as presented above, did Mark write? Or is it possible that the original ending to Mark's Gospel was lost forever and that none of the above endings is the way the book originally ended. But before we come to a conclusion, let's look at the evidence.

The textual evidence for the first reading (stopping at verse 8) is the best. This reading is attested to by א and B (the two earliest extant MSS that preserve this portion of Mark), and some early versions (Syriac, Coptic, Armenian, Georgian). Of the church fathers, Clement, Origen, Cyprian, and Cyril of Jerusalem show no knowledge of any verses beyond 16:8. Eusebius, Jerome, and Severus knew MSS that concluded with 16:8. Eusebius said that the accurate copies of Mark ended with verse 8, adding that 16:9–20 were missing from almost all MSS (*Quaestiones ad Marinum* 1—MPG 22, 937). The pericope is also absent from the Eusebian canons. Jerome affirmed the same by saying that almost all the Greek codices did not have 16:9–20 (*Epistle* 120.3 *ad Hedibiam*). Several minuscule MSS (1, 20, 22, 137, 138, 1110, 1215, 1216, 1217, 1221, 1582) that include 16:9–20 have scholia (marginal notes) indicating that the more ancient MSS do not include this section.

Other MSS mark off the longer reading with obeli to indicate its questionable status. The textual evidence, therefore, shows that Mark's Gospel circulated in many ancient copies with an ending at verse 8. But this ending seemed to be too abrupt for many readers—both ancient and modern! As a result, various endings were appended. One short ending was appended to round off verse 8 and to indicate that the women had followed the angels' orders in bringing the report to Peter and the disciples. But in order to make this addition, it is necessary to delete the words "and said nothing to no one" from verse 8—which is exactly what was done in it[k].

The most well-known ending is the longer, traditional ending of 16:9–20. The earliest witnesses to this ending come from Irenaeus (via a Latin translation). The other patristic witnesses cited above are no earlier than the the fourth century (MSS[according to Eusebius] MSS[according to Jerome] MSS[according to Severus] Apostolic Constitutions [Epiphanius] Severian Nestorius Ambrose Augustine). Thus, we know that this ending was probably in circulation in the third century. It became the most popular of the endings after the fourth century, and was copied again and again in many uncial MSS. Eventually, it was accepted as canonical by the Council of Trent.

But the longer ending is stylistically incongruous with 16:1–8. Any fair-minded reader can detect the non-Markan flavor of the style, tone, and vocabulary of 16:9–20. This is apparent in the very first word in 16:9. The Greek verb *anastas* ("having risen") is an active aorist participle; it conveys the thought that Jesus himself rose from the dead. But almost everywhere else in the Gospels, the passive verb is used with respect to Jesus's resurrection. Furthermore, the additions are all narratively noncontiguous. This is especially apparent in the connection between verses 8 and 9. The subject of verse 8 is the women, whereas the presumed subject of verse 9 is Jesus. And Mary Magdalene is introduced as if she was not mentioned before or was not among the women of 15:47–16:8.

This longer ending was made even longer in codex W (the Freer Gospel) with an addition after 16:14. Prior to the discovery of W, we had the record from Jerome that there was another similar ending: "In certain exemplars and especially in the Greek MSS [of the Gospel] according to Mark, at the end of his Gospel, there is written, 'Afterward, when the Eleven reclined at meal, Jesus appeared to them and upbraided them for their unbelief and hardness of heart because they had not believed those who had seen him after his resurrection. And they made excuse, saying, "This age of iniquity and unbelief is under Satan who, through unclean spirits, does not permit the true power of God to be apprehended. Therefore, reveal your righteousness now.'"

The Freer text is an expansion of what was known to Jerome inasmuch as Jesus gives a response to their excuse concerning unbelief. The disciples, blaming Satan for the unbelief, made an appeal to Jesus for his parousia, which brings the full revelation of his vindictive righteousness. In response, Jesus declares that Satan's time has already come to its end, but before he (Jesus) can reveal his righteous kingdom, there will be a time "of terrible things." This terrible time—of apostacy and judgment—would be the prelude to the second coming.

Finally, some MSS include both the shorter reading and the traditional longer reading. The earliest evidence for these is in two eighth-century MSS, L and Ψ. Some ancient versions (syr^{hmg} cop^{sa,boMSS}) also have both endings. This is clearly the result of scribal ambiguity—the same kind that is manifest in several modern English versions that print both endings in the text.

What then do we make of the evidence? Scholarly consensus is that Mark did not write any of the endings (2–5 above); all are the work of other hands. Farmer's (*The Last Twelve Verses of Mark*) attempt to defend the view that Mark 16:9–20 was originally part of Mark's Gospel, which was later deleted by Alexandrian scribes, is not convincing. Farmer argues that Alexandrian scribes were troubled by the references to picking up snakes and drinking poison and therefore deleted the passage. If they had been troubled by these references, they would have deleted only those verses, not the entire passage! No one else has made a good case for the originality of any of the various additions. The historical fact appears to be that various readers, bothered that Mark ended so abruptly, completed the Gospel with a variety of additions. According to Aland ("Bemerkungen zum Schluss des Markusevangeliums," *Neotestamentica et Semitica* [1969], 157–180), the shorter and longer endings were composed independently in different geographical locations, and both were probably circulating in the second century. Metzger says that the longer ending displays some vocabulary (particulary *anisthmi* for *egeirō*) which "suggests that the composition of the ending is appropriately located at the end of the first century or in the middle of the second century" (*Text of the New Testament*, 297).

The reason the shorter ending was created has already been explained. The longer ending was composed afresh or taken verbatim from some other source so as to fill up what was perceived to be a gap in the text of Mark. This writer provided an extended conclusion derived from various sources, including the other Gospels and Acts, inserting his own theological peculiarities. The reason the longer ending has become so popular is that it is a collage of events found in the other Gospels and the book of Acts.

Jesus's appearance to Mary Magdalene (16:9) was adapted from John 20:11–17. Her report to the disciples (16:10) was taken from Luke 24:10 and John 20:18. However, the writer of the longer ending has this report concerning Jesus's appearance, whereas Mary's report in John comes after she has seen the empty tomb. John's account is affirmed by the account in Luke 24:11. In both John and Luke the disciples do not believe the report concerning the angelic appearance and the empty tomb; there was no mention yet of any appearance made by Jesus. The change of story in the longer ending to Mark was contrived because Mark 16:8 says that the women said nothing to anybody after seeing the empty tomb and the angelic messenger. The writer couldn't controvert this blatantly (by saying that Mary and/or any of the other women then went to the disciples and told them about the empty tomb), so the writer has Jesus appearing to Mary Magdalene, then Mary telling the disciples, who don't believe. Since this particular account contradicts the authentic Gospels, it should be dismissed.

After this, the writer of the longer ending relates Jesus's appearance to two disciples as they were walking from Jerusalem into the country (16:12); this clearly was taken from Luke 24:13–35. The report of further unbelief (16:13) was the interpretation of the composer; Luke does not tell us that the report of the two disciples was disbelieved. Jesus's first resurrection appearance to the disciples (16:14) was borrowed from Luke 24:36–49—with an added emphasis on their unbelief (perhaps adapted from Matt. 28:16–20). Jesus's great commission (16:15–16) is loosely based on Matt. 28:19–20—with an emphasis on baptism as a prerequisite to salvation. The promise of signs accompanying the believers (16:17–18) comes from the record of what happened in Acts—including the speaking in tongues (2:4; 10:46) and protection against snakes (28:3–6). The ascension (16:19) is adapted from Luke 24:50–53, and the final verse (16:20) seems to be a summary of the book of Acts, which seems to be preemptively out of place for inclusion in a Gospel and is another indication of its spuriousness. (None of the other Gospels tell us anything about the disciples' work after Jesus's resurrection and ascension.)

Even though much of this longer ending was drawn from other Gospels and Acts, the composer had an unusual emphasis on the disciples' unbelief in the resurrection of Christ. In this regard, the composer may have been following through on the Markan theme of identifying the unbelief and stubbornness of the disciples. Indeed, this Gospel, more than any other, focuses on the disciples' repeated failures to believe Jesus and follow him. The composer of the longer ending also had a preference for belief and baptism as a requisite for salvation, as well as an exalted view of signs. Christians need to be warned against using this text for Christian doctrine because it is not on the same par as verifiable New Testament Scripture. Nothing in it should be used to establish Christian doctrine or practice. Unfortunately, certain churches have used Mark 16:16 to affirm dogmatically that one must believe and be baptized in order to be saved, and other churches have used Mark 16:18 to promote the practice of snake-handling. (Even some boxes that keep the rattlesnakes are marked with "Mark 16:18" written on them.) Those who are bitten by rattlesnakes, they believe, will not be harmed if they are true followers of Christ. The writer of the longer ending also emphasized what we would call charismatic experiences—speaking in tongues, performing healings, protection from snakes and poison. Although the book of Acts affirms these experiences for certain believers, they are not necessarily the norm for all.

The longer ending of W (noted also by Jerome) was probably a marginal gloss written in the third century that found its way into the text of some MSS prior to the fourth century. This gloss was likely created by a scribe who wanted to provide a reason for the unbelief that is prevalent in the longer ending. Satan is blamed for the faithlessness, and an appeal is made for Jesus to reveal his righteousness immediately. But this revelation would be postponed until after a time of terrible things. This interpolation may have been drawn from several sources, including Acts 1:6–7; 3:19–21; and the Epistle of Barnabas 4:9; 15:7. In any case, it is quite clear that Mark did not write it. The style is blatantly non-Markan.

Having concluded that Mark did not write any of the endings, we are still left with the question: Did Mark originally conclude his Gospel with verse 8 or was an original extended ending lost?

In defense of the view that Mark originally ended his Gospel at verse 8, four arguments can be posited: (1) As is, the Gospel ends with an announcement of Christ's resurrection. Jesus doesn't need to actually appear in resurrection to validate the announcement. Our demand that the Gospel must record this appearance comes from our knowledge of the other Gospels. Mark did not have to end his Gospel the way the others did. (2) Mark, as a creative writer, may have purposely ended abruptly in order to force his readers to fill in the gap with their own imaginations. Perhaps Mark did not want to describe—or think himself capable of describing—the resurrection of Christ and/or the risen Christ; thus, he left it to the readers to imagine how the risen Christ appeared to Peter and the other disciples. (3) Throughout this Gospel, Mark presented a secrecy motif concerning Jesus being the Messiah (see note on 8:26). The final verse is the culmination of this motif: The women "said nothing to anyone." Of course, the reader knows that this silence would not last; indeed, the very opposite will happen—the word of Christ's resurrection will be announced to the disciples, and the disciples will proclaim this to the world. Thus, the ending was calculated by Mark to be the irony of ironies; perhaps he thought it would bring a smile to the face of the Christians reading or hearing this Gospel for the first time, for they knew how the word had gone out! (4) It ends on a note of failure—the women's failure to go to Peter and the other disciples—because this is consistent with another major theme in Mark's

Gospel: discipleship failure. All these four reasons could account for Mark purposely concluding the Gospel at 16:8.

However, many readers are not satisfied with these reasons—primarily because they, having read the other Gospels, have a different horizon of expectation for the conclusion of Mark. Thus, many readers have questioned whether it was Mark's original design to conclude with verse 8. Why conclude with merely an announcement of Jesus's resurrection and a description of the women's fear and bewilderment? In the Gospel of Mark, a pattern is set in which every one of Jesus's predictions is actually fulfilled in narrative form. According to Gundry (*Mark: A Commentary on His Apology for the Cross*, 1009), the predictions that were fulfilled were as follows: God's kingdom having come with power at the Transfiguration, the finding of a colt, the disciples' being met by a man carrying a jar of water, the showing of the Upper Room, the betrayal of Jesus by one of the Twelve, the scattering of the rest of the Twelve, the denials of Jesus by Peter, the Passion, and the Resurrection. Thus, since Jesus announced that he would see his disciples in Galilee (14:28), the narrative should have depicted an actual appearance of the risen Christ to his disciples in Galilee.

Since there isn't such a record (even in the additions), some readers have thought that an original extended ending got lost in the early transmission of Mark's Gospel—probably because it was written on the last leaf of a papyrus codex and was torn away from the rest of the manuscript. (Though Mark may have originally been written on a scroll, which would have preserved the last section rolled up inside, copies of Mark in codex form would have been in use as early as the end of the first century; see Comfort, *Encountering the Manuscripts*, 27–40). This codex could have contained just the Gospel of Mark or all four Gospels set in the typical Western order: Matthew, John, Luke, Mark (which was likely the case for $\mathfrak{P}^{45}$). In both scenarios, Mark 16 would have been the last sheet. However, it seems very odd and most unusual that this ending would not have survived in some MS somewhere. The history of textual transmission is characterized by tenacity; once a reading enters the textual stream, it will usually be preserved in some MS and show up somewhere down the line. Thus, this imagined ending to Mark must have been lost very soon after the composition of the Gospel, if there was such an ending.

It is possible that 16:7 was intended to be the concluding verse of the first paragraph of Mark's original last chapter (inasmuch as it concludes with the glorious angelic announcement of Christ's resurrection) and that 16:8 was the first sentence of the next paragraph. It seems that the last two words of 16:8, *ephobounto gar* ("for they were afraid"), could have been the first two words of a new sentence. Indeed, it is highly unusual for a sentence, let alone an entire Gospel, to end with the conjunctive *gar*; so it is likely that some word or words followed, such as *ephobounto gar lalein* ("for they were afraid to speak . . . "). After this, Mark's narrative would have continued to relate, most likely, that Jesus appeared to the women (as in Matthew and John), and that the women, no longer afraid, then went and told the disciples what they saw. This would have probably been followed by Jesus appearing to his disciples in Jerusalem and in Galilee. This is the basic pattern found in the other Gospels. And since Mark was probably used by the other Gospel writers, it stands to reason that their narrative pattern reflects Mark's original work.

THE GOSPEL ACCORDING TO LUKE

Title: The Gospel according to Luke
This is the title in the subscription in 𝔓[75] (late second century); had the inscription been extant in this manuscript, we would expect to see the same (see title to the Gospel of John). Later MSS, of the fourth century (א B), title it "According to Luke."

1:15 | he will be filled with the Holy Spirit.
The divine "Spirit" is written as a nomen sacrum (sacred name) in two early MSS (א W), as well as L. John the Baptist would be filled with the divine Spirit.

1:17 | in the spirit and power of Elijah.
The word "spirit" is written in full (in *plene*; i.e., not a sacred name) in B L. John the Baptist would come in the spirit and power of Elijah.

1:28 | the Lord is with you.
This is the original wording according to three early MSS (א B W), as well as L. Other MSS (A C D Θ f[1,13] Maj) add, "blessed are you among women." The variant reading is an expansion borrowed from 1:42, where it is Elizabeth who says that Mary is "blessed among women."

1:35a | the Holy Spirit will come upon you.
The divine "Spirit" is written as a nomen sacrum (sacred name) in two early MSS (א W), as well as L.

1:35b | He will be called the Son of God.
"Son of God" is written as a nomen sacrum (sacred name) in several early MSS (א B D W), indicating *the* divine Son of God, not just a son of God.

1:37 | no message from God will fail.
This is the original wording according to early MSS (א* B D W), as well as L. Another reading is "nothing is impossible for God," according to

ℵ[2] [seventh century] A C Maj (so KJV and some other English versions). The reading of the text has better manuscript support; the variant may be the result of scribal harmonization to Gen. 18:14 LXX.

1:41 | Elizabeth was filled with the Holy Spirit.
The divine "Spirit" is written as a nomen sacrum (sacred name) in three early MSS (ℵ D W), as well as L.

1:67 | Zechariah was filled with the Holy Spirit.
The divine "Spirit" is written as a nomen sacrum (sacred name) in early MSS (𝔓[4] ℵ W), as well as L.

1:68 | Blessed be the God of Israel.
"God" is the reading in 𝔓[4] (the earliest MS) W it. All other MSS read, "Lord God."

1:78 | the dawn will break upon us from on high.
This literally reads, "the Anatole [the eastern sun] will visit us from on high." The verb "will visit" is future tense in the Greek (*episkepsetai*) according to the best manuscript evidence (𝔓[4] ℵ* B L W). It is past tense in ℵ[2] [seventh century] A C D, a change scribes made in conformity to Luke 1:78 (the second line of the first poetic stanza). Even though the verb is future, the expression in context points to Christ's first advent—his visitation as the sunrising or dayspring from the heavens to the earth. The word Anatole has a secondary meaning: branch or shoot (see BAGD, 62), which was used in the LXX to translate the Hebrew word for "Branch" (Isa. 11:1; Jer. 23:5; 33:15; Zech. 3:8; 6:12). The dual image celebrates Christ's coming as the dayspring and Branch. In fact, this is the only NT reference to the OT messianic title, "Branch." The translation catches the dual idea of the dawning light and the branch with the expression "the eastern dawn springs."

1:80 | he was becoming strong in the Spirit.
The word "Spirit" is written as a nomen sacrum (sacred name) in the

earliest MS ($\mathfrak{P}^4$), as well as L W, denoting the divine Spirit. The word is written out in full (in *plene*; i.e., not a sacred name) in א B, signifying the human spirit (viz. "John was becoming strong in his spirit").

2:14 | peace on earth to those he favors.

The text literally reads, "peace on earth among men of [God's] pleasure," according to five early MSS (א* A B* D W), as well as cop[sa]. Other MSS (א[2] [seventh century] B[2] [tenth century] L Θ Ξ Ψ f[1,13] Maj) read "peace on earth, good pleasure [= will] among [= toward] men." The orthographic difference between the two readings is simply one letter: *eudokias/eudokia*. The first is genitive for "good pleasure/ good will"; the second is nominative. The genitive expression reflects a Semitic expression meaning "good pleasure of God." The entire clause means that peace is given on earth to those whom God takes pleasure in. Another way to say this is that God's peace rests on those whom he has chosen—i.e., it was God's good pleasure to select certain people to be the recipients of his peace that came with the coming of the Savior, Jesus Christ. Various documents among the Dead Sea Scrolls affirm this Semitic expression, such as "the sons of God's good pleasure" (1ΘH 4:32–33), "the elect of God's good pleasure" (1ΘH 11:9), and "among men of his good pleasure" (4ΘH[c] 18). The Coptic Sahidic translation of Luke 2:14 also affirms this reading: "peace among men of his pleasure."

2:25 | the Holy Spirit was upon him.

The divine "Spirit" is written as a nomen sacrum (sacred name) in three early MSS (א D W), as well as L.

2:26 | revealed by the Holy Spirit

The divine "Spirit" is written as a nomen sacrum (sacred name) in three early MSS (א D W), as well as L.

2:27 | directed by the Spirit

The divine "Spirit" is written as a nomen sacrum (sacred name) in three early MSS (א D W), as well as L.

2:40 | the child grew and became strong.
This is the original wording according to the two earliest MSS (א B), as well as D L N W. This is expanded to "became strong in spirit" in A Θ Ψ $f^{1,13}$ 33 Maj, by way of scribal conformity to Luke 1:80.

3:9 | every tree that does not produce fruit.
This is the wording in the earliest MS ($\mathfrak{P}^{4}$) and Origen. All other MSS read "good fruit."

3:16 | he will baptize you with the Holy Spirit.
The divine "Spirit" is written as a nomen sacrum (sacred name) in two early MSS (א W), as well as L.

3:22a | the Holy Spirit descended on him.
The divine "Spirit" is written as a nomen sacrum (sacred name) in four early MSS ($\mathfrak{P}^{4}$ $\mathfrak{P}^{75}$ א W), as well as L. Most MSS read *to pneuma to agion sōmatikō* ("the holy Spirit in bodily form [descended]"). $\mathfrak{P}^{75}$ lacks the article before *pneuma*, and $\mathfrak{P}^{4}$ reads *to pneuma to agion pneumati*. The editor for the *editio princeps* of $\mathfrak{P}^{4}$ (Merell 1938) explained *pneumati* as a simple case of dittography. But if that had been so, why didn't the scribe write *pneuma* again? Rather, he wrote the dative form (*pneumati*) as a nomen sacrum. As such, $\mathfrak{P}^{4}$ has this interesting variation that can be rendered as "the Holy Spirit descended as Spirit."

3:22b | you are my beloved Son, in whom I am well pleased.
This is the original wording according to $\mathfrak{P}^{4}$ א A B L W 0124 33 MSS$^{\text{according to Augustine}}$. A variant reading is "you are my Son; this day I have begotten you" in D it Justin Hillary MSS$^{\text{according to Augustine}}$. The original reading has the earliest and most diverse documentary support. (א and L write "Son" as a nomen sacrum [sacred name].) The variant reading is later and more localized (in the West)—a true "Western" reading. Augustine knew of both readings, although he made it clear that the variant reading was "not found in the more ancient manuscripts" (*De Cons. Evang* 2.14).

In spite of the documentary evidence, many scholars have

defended the variant reading as being the more difficult reading and therefore more likely original. They argue that the reading was originally a full quotation of Ps. 2:7, which (in the words of the NJB translators) shows Jesus to be "the King-Messiah of the Ps. [2:7] enthroned at the Baptism to establish the rule of God in the world." This reading was then harmonized to the baptism accounts in Matt. 3:17 and Mark 1:11 by orthodox scribes trying to avoid having the text say that Jesus was "begotten" on the day of his baptism—an erroneous view held by the Adoptionists. However, it can be argued the scribe of D (known for his creative editorialization) changed the text to replicate Ps. 2:7 or was himself influenced by Adoptionistic views. Indeed, the variant reading was included in the second-century Gospel of the Ebionites, who were chief among the adoptionists. They regarded Jesus as the son of Joseph and Mary, but elected Son of God at his baptism when he was united with the eternal Christ.

In any case, Ps. 2:7 appears to have been used exclusively by NT writers with reference to Jesus's resurrection from the dead (Acts 13:33; Heb. 1:5; 5:5). Since in Luke's book of Acts it is explicitly used to affirm the prophetic word about Jesus's resurrection, it would seem odd that he would use it to affirm Jesus's baptism. Given the reading of the text, it seems more likely that Luke was thinking of Ps. 2:7 for the first part of the statement ("this is my beloved Son") and Isa. 42:1 for the second part ("in whom I am well-pleased"). The Isaiah passage is especially fitting given its connection with the Messiah's reception of the Spirit.

3:23b–38

Luke's genealogy of Jesus is omitted in W, and D conformed Luke 3:23–31 to Matt. 1:6–16 and inverted the order. The genealogy as presented is affirmed by the earliest MSS ($\mathfrak{P}^{4}$ א B) with only a few orthographic variations. The word "son" occurs in 3:23 and then is implied through the rest of the genealogy.

4:1a | full of the Holy Spirit.

The divine "Spirit" is written as a nomen sacrum (sacred name) in several early MSS ($\mathfrak{P}^{4}$ $\mathfrak{P}^{7}$ $\mathfrak{P}^{75vid}$ א D W), as well as L.

4:1b | led by the Spirit.
The divine "Spirit" is written as a nomen sacrum (sacred name) in three early MSS ($\mathfrak{P}^7$ ℵ W), as well as L.

4:1c | in the wilderness.
This is the original wording in several early MSS ($\mathfrak{P}^4$ $\mathfrak{P}^7$ $\mathfrak{P}^{75}$ ℵ B D W), as well as L. Another wording is "into the wilderness" in A Θ Ξ Ψ 0102 $f^{1,13}$ 33 Maj, by way of scribal conformity to the parallel Matt. 4:1 and Mark 1:12, parallel verses.

4:3 | If you are the Son of God.
"Son of God" is written as a nomen sacrum (sacred name) in several early MSS (ℵ B D W), as well as L, identifying Jesus as *the* Son of God, not just *a* son of God.

4:4 | man does not live by bread alone.
This is the original wording according to the two earliest MSS (ℵ B), as well as L W syr^s cop^{sa}. A variant reading is "man does not live by bread alone but by every word of God" in A (D) Θ Ψ (0102) $f^{1,13}$ 33 Maj (so KJV), by way of scribal conformity to Matt. 4:4, a parallel verse. The OT quotation comes from Deut. 8:3.

4:5 | the devil led him up.
This is the original wording according to the two earliest MSS (ℵ* B) and L. A variant wording is "the devil led him up a high mountain" in $ℵ^2$ [seventh century] A D W 0102 33 Maj (so KJV), by way of scribal conformity to Matt. 4:8, a parallel verse.

4:8a | Jesus answered him.
This is the original wording according to the two earliest MSS (ℵ B) and D L W f^1. A variant reading is "Jesus answered him, 'Get behind me, Satan'" in A Θ Ψ 0102 f^{13} Maj (so KJV), by way of scribal conformity to Matt. 4:10, a parallel verse.

4:9 | If you are the Son of God.
"Son of God" is written as a nomen sacrum (sacred name) in early MSS (א B D), as well as L, designating Jesus as *the* Son of God, not just a son of God.

4:14 | in the power of the Spirit
The divine "Spirit" is written as a nomen sacrum (sacred name) in three early MSS (א D W), as well as L.

4:18 | the Spirit of the Lord is upon me.
"Spirit of the Lord" is written as a nomen sacrum (sacred name) in four early MSS (א B D W), as well as L.

4:18–19
The citation basically comes from Isa. 61:1–2 LXX. The poem is carried by the four infinitive phrases. Some MSS (A Θ Ψ 0102 Maj) add another infinitive phrase: "to heal the broken-hearted." But there is strong testimony against it (א B D L W), coupled with the likelihood that scribes added the phrase to make it conform to Isa. 61:1–2.

4:41 | you are the Son of God.
This is the original wording according to early and excellent testimony ($\mathfrak{P}^{75}$ א B C D L W). This is expanded to "you are the Christ, the Son of God" in A Q Θ 0102 $f^{1,13}$ Maj. $\mathfrak{P}^{75}$ is not listed in NA^{27}, but it supports the text (see Comfort and Barrett, *Text of Earliest NT Greek MSS*, 508). The variant is a scribal expansion that occurred in almost every Gospel text where Jesus is identified by others as "the Son of God." ("Son of God" is written as a nomen sacrum [sacred name] in $\mathfrak{P}^{75vid}$ א A B C D L Θ W.)

4:44 | he continued to preach in synagogues of Judea.
This is the original wording according to early and excellent testimony ($\mathfrak{P}^{75}$ א B C L). The place is changed to "synagogues of Galilee" in A D Θ Ψ f^{13} 33 Maj (so KJV), and to "synagogues of the Jews" in W. Scribes harmonized Luke's account to Matt. 4:23 and Mark 1:39, or they fixed

what they believed to be a contradiction of facts in Luke's account (Luke 4:14 and 5:1 indicate that Jesus was in Galilee). However, Luke probably used "Judea" to cover all of Palestine, which includes Galilee (see Luke 1:5; 6:17; 7:17; 23:5; Acts 10:37).

5:8 | "Go away from me, Lord."

"Lord" is written as a nomen sacrum (sacred name) in early MSS ($\mathfrak{P}^{75}$ B D W), showing that Peter recognized Jesus as "Lord" from the onset.

5:17 | the Lord's healing power was present with him.

This is the original wording according to the testimony of the two earliest MSS (א B), as well as L W syr^{s} cop^{sa}. Another reading is "the Lord's power was present to heal them" in A C D Θ Ψ f^{1,13} 33 Maj cop^{bo} (so KJV). The original wording, which has superior testimony, does not emphasize who Jesus was healing (that comes in the next verse), but it tells us that he had the Lord God's power to heal.

5:24 | the Son of Man has authority on earth.

"Son of Man," a messianic title (Dan. 7:13–14), is written as a nomen sacrum (sacred name) in one early MS (א), as well as L.

5:38 | new wine is poured into fresh wineskins.

This is the original wording according to early and excellent testimony ($\mathfrak{P}^{4}$ $\mathfrak{P}^{75vid}$ א B L W). A variant reading is "new wine is poured into fresh wineskins so that both can be preserved" in A C (D) Θ Ψ Maj (so KJV), by way of scribal conformity to Matt. 9:17, a parallel verse.

5:39

The documentary evidence supporting the inclusion of this verse is impressive: $\mathfrak{P}^{4}$ $\mathfrak{P}^{75vid}$ א A B C W Maj. The verse is excluded in the following witnesses: D it Marcion Eusebius Irenaeus. Marcion may have deleted it because he thought it validated the authority of the OT. It is also possible that it was deleted to conform the pericope to the parallel passages in Matthew and Mark, which have no such verse. Or it is possible that it was deleted by scribes who took offense at Jesus speaking about wine-drinking with such candor and knowledgeable detail. Westcott and Hort bracketed this verse perhaps thinking it might be a "Western non-interpolation" (though they left no note on this). The documentation favoring the text is so impressive that all doubt should be removed.

6:1 | one Sabbath.

This is the original reading according to early and excellent testimony ($\mathfrak{P}^{4}$ $\mathfrak{P}^{75vid}$ א B L W f^{1} 33). Another reading is "the second first Sabbath" in A C D Θ Ψ Maj, a scribal error. Westcott and Hort (*The New Testament in the Original Greek: Introduction and Appendix*, 58) suggest that a copyist added *prōtō* (first) as a correlative to the "other Sabbath" mentioned in 6:5, which was then changed to *deuterō* (second) by another scribe in light of 4:31. Both words were retained and combined in subsequent copies.

6:5 | The Son of Man is Lord of the Sabbath.

"Son of Man," a messianic title (Dan. 7:13–14), is written as a nomen sacrum (sacred name) in two early MSS ($\mathfrak{P}^{75vid}$ א), as well as L. "Lord" is written as a nomen sacrum (sacred name) in all MSS.

6:22 | the Son of Man.

"Son of Man," a messianic title (Dan. 7:13–14), is written as a nomen sacrum (sacred name) in two early MSS ($\mathfrak{P}^{75}$ א), as well as L.

6:35 | expecting nothing back.

This is the original wording in four early MSS ($\mathfrak{P}^{75}$ A B D), as well as L $f^{1,13}$ it cop. A variant reading is "despairing of no one" in א W $syr^{p,s}$. The textual variant (*mēdena* [no one] instead of *mēden* [nothing]) is the result of scribal perplexity concerning the verb *apelpizontes*, which usually means "despair." However, we know that from as early as the fourth century it was used with the meaning "to hope for some return." Luke must have employed it in the same way: a person should lend to others without expecting anything in return.

6:36 | your Father is merciful.
The divine "Father" is written as a nomen sacrum (sacred name) in one early MS ($\mathfrak{P}^{75vid}$).

6:48 | because it had been well built.
This is the original wording according to three early MSS ($\mathfrak{P}^{75vid}$ ℵ B), as well as L W 33. A variant reading is "because it had been founded upon the rock" in A C D Θ Ψ $f^{1,13}$ Maj (so KJV). The phrase is omitted by a few MSS ($\mathfrak{P}^{45vid}$ 700* syr^{s}). This variant, although the shorter reading, is probably not original because the scribe of $\mathfrak{P}^{45}$ is known for concision and brevity. The first variant is the result of scribal harmonization to Matt. 7:25, a parallel passage. The text has excellent documentation.

6:49 | because it collapsed.
The Greek verb is *sunepesen*, having the excellent support of $\mathfrak{P}^{45}$ $\mathfrak{P}^{75}$ ℵ B D L. This was changed to the more common verb, *epesen* (fell) in A C W Maj (so KJV).

7:7 | let my servant be healed.
This the original reading according to the two earliest MSS ($\mathfrak{P}^{75vid}$ B), as well as L. A variant reading is "my servant will be healed" in ℵ A C D W Θ Ψ $f^{1,13}$ 33 Maj (so KJV), by way of scribal conformity to Matt. 8:8, a parallel verse.

7:10 | found the servant healed.
This is the original wording according to four early MSS ($\mathfrak{P}^{75}$ ℵ B W), as well as f^{1} it cop. A variant reading is "found the servant, who had been sick, healed" in A C (D) Θ Ψ f^{13} 33 Maj, by way of scribal expansion.

7:34 | The Son of Man has come eating and drinking.
"Son of Man," a messianic title (Dan. 7:13–14), is written as a nomen sacrum (sacred name) in two early MSS, $\mathfrak{P}^{75vid}$ ℵ, as well as L.

7:39 | If this man were a prophet.
Two MSS (B* X) prefix a definite article before *prophētēs* (prophet)

thereby creating the reading, "the Prophet." As happened elsewhere in the NT text (see note on John 7:52), such an addition was intended to show that Jesus was "the Prophet" like Moses (Deut. 18:15; Acts 3:22–23; 7:37).

8:3 | many others provided for them out of their own resources.

The original wording is "them" according to early and excellent testimony (𝔓^{75vid} B D W f^{13}). The pronoun is "him" in ℵ A L Ψ f^{1} 33 it cop. It seems more likely that "them" was changed to "him" than vice versa because the variant is probably the result of harmonization to Matt. 27:55 and Mark 15:41. According to Luke, the women in Jesus's company (Mary Magdalene, Joanna, and Suzanna) financially supported Jesus and the Twelve—not just Jesus. This was no small undertaking; it would require the financial means that Joanna (wife of Chuza, Herod's steward) probably had access to.

8:25 | he commands even the winds and the water.

This is the original wording according to the two earliest MSS (𝔓^{75} B). All other MSS read "he commands even the winds and the water, and they obey him," by way of scribal conformity to Matt. 8:27, a parallel verse.

8:26 | Gerasenes.

This is the original word according to three early MSS (𝔓^{75} B D). Two other readings are "Gergesenes" (ℵ L Θ X f^{1} 33) and "Gadarenes" (A W Ψ f^{13} Maj). The two earliest MSS (𝔓^{75} B) support "Gerasenes" (see note on Matt. 8:28).

8:28 | Son of the Most High God.

This is written as a nomen sacrum (sacred name) in four early MSS (𝔓^{75} ℵ B W), as well as L.

8:37 | Gerasenes.

This is the original word according to the two earliest MSS (𝔓^{75} B), as well as C* D 0279. Two other readings are "Gergesenes" (ℵ^{*,c} C^{2}

[sixth century] L P f^{1,13} 33) and "Gadarenes" (ℵ^2 [seventh century] A W Maj). The two earliest MSS (𝔓^{75} B) support "Gerasenes" (see note on Matt. 8:28).

8:43 | she could not get anyone to cure her.

This is the original wording according to 𝔓^{75} B (D) 0279 syr^s cop^{sa} Origen. An expanded reading is "though she had spent all she had on physicians, she could not get anyone to cure her" (ℵ A C L W Θ Ξ Ψ f^{1,13} 33 Maj). The earliest MSS (𝔓^{75} B), plus 0279 (discovered in the 1970s at St. Catherine's Monastery) affirm the shorter text. The longer text was borrowed from Mark 5:26, a parallel verse.

8:45 | Peter said, "Master, the crowds are surrounding you and pressing against you."

The original wording is "Peter" according to the two earliest MSS (𝔓^{75} B), as well as syr cop. This is expanded to "Peter and those who were with him" in ℵ A C^3 [ninth century] D L W Θ Ξ Ψ f^{1,13} 33, by way of scribal conformity to Mark 5:31, a parallel verse.

9:22 | The Son of Man must suffer many things.

"Son of Man," a messianic title (Dan. 7:13–14), is written as a nomen sacrum (sacred name) in two early MSS (𝔓^{75} ℵ), as well as L.

9:23 | he must take up his Cross daily.

"Cross" is written as a nomen sacrum (sacred word) in one early MS (𝔓^{75}).

9:26a | whoever is ashamed of me and my message.

This is the original wording according to several early MSS (𝔓^{45} 𝔓^{75vid} A B C W), as well as L. This is worded as "whoever is ashamed of me and mine" in D it^{a,e} syr^c. As in Mark 8:38a (see note), so here the variant indicates that Jesus was speaking of himself and his disciples. If this is what Luke wrote, then the reading of the text, which has *logous* ("words" or "message"), is a scribal expansion attempting to make the text more contemporary—inasmuch as it is more relevant in later centuries to speak of being ashamed of Jesus's words than of Jesus's disciples. However, the textual evidence strongly favors the reading of the text, which would have been pertinent in Jesus's time, as well as in later generations. Furthermore, it can be argued that *logous* was accidentally dropped due to homeoteleuton—the two previous words end with *ous*.

9:26b | the Son of Man will be ashamed of him.

"Son of Man," a messianic title (Dan. 7:13–14), is written as a nomen sacrum (sacred name) in two early MSS (𝔓^{75} ℵ), as well as L.

9:26c | the glory of the Father.

The divine "Father" is written as a nomen sacrum (sacred name) in three early MSS (𝔓^{75} D W), as well as L.

9:35a | This is my Son.

"Son" is written as a nomen sacrum (sacred name) in two early MSS (𝔓^{45} ℵ), as well as L, denoting *the* divine Son of God.

9:35b | the chosen One.

This is the original wording according to early and excellent testimony (𝔓^{45} 𝔓^{75} ℵ B it^{a} syr^{s} cop). Two variant readings are "my beloved" (A C* W f^{13} 33 Maj) and "my beloved in whom I am well pleased" (C^{3} [ninth century] D Ψ). As often happened in the textual transmission of the Gospels, divine proclamations about Jesus were harmonized. At Jesus's transfiguration, each of the Synoptic Gospels has different wording. Matt. 17:5 reads, "this is my beloved Son, in whom I am well pleased"; Mark 9:7 reads, "this is my beloved Son"; and Luke 9:35 reads, "this is the Son, the chosen One." The first variant is a harmonization to Mark, and the second to Matthew (or perhaps Luke 3:22). The reading of the texts, supported by the four earliest MSS (𝔓^{45} 𝔓^{75} ℵ B), is without question the one Luke wrote. The wording in Luke reveals the twofold position of Jesus as both God's Son and the chosen One—that is, the Father chose his Son to be the Messiah. Luke's wording is reminiscent of Ps. 2:7 and especially Isa. 42:1 (LXX), which speaks of the messianic

Servant. This chosen Servant was destined to carry out God's will by suffering death on the cross. This entirely suits the context which speaks of Jesus's "exodus from Jerusalem" (9:31).

9:44 | The Son of Man is going to be betrayed.
"Son of Man," a messianic title (Dan. 7:13–14), is written as a nomen sacrum (sacred named) in two early MSS ($\mathfrak{P}^{75}$ ℵ), as well as L.

9:54 | command fire to come down and consume them.
This is the original wording according to early and excellent testimony ($\mathfrak{P}^{45}$ $\mathfrak{P}^{75}$ ℵ B L). This is expanded to "command fire to come down and consume them, as Elijah did" in A C D W Θ Ψ $f^{1,13}$ 33 Maj (so KJV), influenced by 2 Kgs 1:10.

9:55–56 | he rebuked them.
This is the original wording according to early and excellent testimony ($\mathfrak{P}^{45}$ $\mathfrak{P}^{75}$ ℵ A B C L W). This is expanded to "rebuked them, and said, "You do not know what spirit you belong to. [56] For the Son of Man has not come to destroy human lives but to save them," according to D (for the first sentence only) K Γ Θ $f^{1,13}$ it syr. The original wording says only that Jesus rebuked them; the actual words of the rebuke are not recorded. Dissatisfied with this gap in the narrative, scribes provided two additions—a short one (in D) and a longer one (perhaps built on the other). Most likely, the longer addition was adapted from Luke 19:10. There is a similar addition to Matt. 18:10, which suggests that this was a popular gloss.

9:58 | the Son of Man has no place to lay his head.
"Son of Man," a messianic title (Dan. 7:13–14), is written as a nomen sacrum (sacred name) in four early MSS ($\mathfrak{P}^{45}$ $\mathfrak{P}^{75}$ ℵ W), as well as L.

10:1 | the Lord appointed seventy-two.
This is the original wording according to early and excellent testimony ($\mathfrak{P}^{45vid}$ $\mathfrak{P}^{75}$ B D 0181 $syr^{c,s}$ cop^{sa}). Other MSS read "seventy" (ℵ A C L W Θ Ξ Ψ $f^{1,13}$ Maj; so KJV). See next note.

10:17 | the seventy-two returned with joy.

This is the original wording according to early and excellent testimony ($\mathfrak{P}^{45}$ $\mathfrak{P}^{75}$ B D 0181 $syr^{c,s}$ cop^{sa}). Other MSS have the number of disciples as "seventy" (א A C L W Θ Ξ Ψ 0115 $f^{1,13}$ Maj; so KJV). The same variant reading occurs in 10:1 and 10:17, because the former describes Jesus's selection and sending-out of these disciples, and the latter describes their return. Some MSS (including $\mathfrak{P}^{75}$ B D) read "seventy two," while others (including א A C L W) read "seventy." Thus, the pattern is the same for Luke 10:1 and 10:17—with one exception, $\mathfrak{P}^{45}$ has a lacuna at Luke 10:1. But it could easily be conjectured that it also read "seventy-two." Of the two readings, "seventy-two" has the earliest and most diverse support (Alexandrian, Western, Syriac). Furthermore, it is more difficult to imagine a scribe changing "seventy" to "seventy-two" than vice versa inasmuch as "seventy" was a familiar numeral in expressions such as "the seventy elders" (Exod. 24:1; Num. 11:16, 24), "the seventy descendants of Jacob" (Exod. 1:5; Deut. 10:22), and the seventy members of the Sanhedrin.

10:21a | he rejoiced in the Holy Spirit.

This is the wording in three early MSS ($\mathfrak{P}^{75}$ א B), as well as C D L 33. Another reading is "he rejoiced in the Spirit" ($\mathfrak{P}^{45vid}$ A W 0115 f^{13} Maj; so KJV). The strangeness of the expression "he rejoiced in the Holy Spirit" (for which there is no parallel in the Scriptures) may have led to the omission of *tō agiō* ("the holy") from $\mathfrak{P}^{45}$ A W etc. Indeed, this is a strange expression. The Gospel writers did not use the term "Holy Spirit" when speaking of an action that Jesus himself performed *en tō pneumati* ("in the spirit/Spirit") or of an emotion that emanated from his spirit. Jesus is said to have "perceived in his spirit/Spirit" (Mark 2:8), "sighed deeply in his spirit/Spirit" (Mark 8:12), "grown strong in spirit/Spirit" (Luke 2:40 in some MSS), "groaned in the [or his] spirit/Spirit" (John 11:33), and "was troubled in spirit/Spirit" (John 13:21). (In grammatical terms, any mention of the word *pneuma* in the dative case preceded by any verb in the active voice never appears elsewhere in the Gospels—with respect to Jesus—as "the Holy Spirit," with the exception of the statement about Jesus baptizing "with [or, in] the Holy Spirit"). Whenever the Gospel writers spoke about Jesus's mental or emotional activity related to the spirit/Spirit, they viewed it as an activity happening within his spirit. Thus, it would be unusual for Luke to say that Jesus "rejoiced in the Holy Spirit." But it is this unusualness, coupled with such good textual support, which seems to favor the reading of the text. As does the fact that "Spirit" is written as a nomen sacrum (sacred name) in several early MSS (𝔓45 𝔓75 א A C W).

However, in defense of the variant reading, it can be said that *to agio* ("the sacred") was added because (1) scribes had a propensity to add *agiō tō pneumati* and (2) some scribes may have felt that they wanted to clearly distinguish the divine "Spirit" (*pneuma*) mentioned in Luke 10:21 from the "spirits" (*pneumata*) mentioned in the previous verse (Luke 10:20, which says "do not rejoice in this, that the spirits are subject to you, but rejoice that your names are recorded in heaven"—NASB). If the second reading is original, the text could be read as Jesus rejoicing in the divine Spirit or in his spirit—the Greek can be taken either way. But it should be noted that the scribes of the early centuries wrote *pneuma* as a nomen sacrum even when referring to what most exegetes would consider Jesus's human spirit. They could have written it in *plene*, but chose not to. As a point of fact, the scribe of 𝔓45 wrote the nomen sacrum (sacred name) in Luke 10:21.

10:21b | Father, Lord of heaven and earth.

The divine "Father" is written as a nomen sacrum (sacred name) in an early MS (𝔓45), as well as L. "Lord" is written as a nomen sacrum (sacred name) in all MSS.

10:22 | Father . . . Son.

The divine "Father" is written (in both occurences) as a nomen sacrum (sacred name) in an early MS (𝔓75), as well as L. "Son" is written (in both occurences) as a nomen sacrum (sacred name) in two early MSS (𝔓75 א), as well as L.

10:42 | there is only one thing needed.

This is the original wording according to 𝔓45 𝔓75 (A) C* W f13 Maj. A variant reading is "a few things are necessary, or only one" in 𝔓3 א B

C^{2} [sixth century] L 33. The two earliest MSS (𝔓^{45} 𝔓^{75}), with others, support the shorter reading. The idea of the longer reading could be rendered as follows: "Martha, Martha, you are distracted and fretting about many things. However, few things are really needed, or, if you will, only one; for that indeed is what Mary has chosen."

11:2 | Father.

This is the original wording according to 𝔓^{45vid} 𝔓^{75} ℵ B syr^{s}. This is expanded to "Father in heaven" in A C W Θ Ψ 070 f^{13} 33^{vid} Maj it syr^{c,h,p} cop (so KJV) by way of scribal conformity to Matt. 6:9, a parallel verse. 𝔓^{45} typically writes the divine "Father" as a nomen sacrum (sacred name).

11:3 | may your kingdom come.

This is the original wording according to early and excellent testimony: 𝔓^{75} ℵ A B C L W f^{1,13} 33 it^{a,b,c,e} syr cop. There are two variant readings: "may your kingdom come upon us" (D it^{d}), and "may your Holy Spirit come upon us and cleanse us" (700). The MSS 𝔓^{75} B L syr^{c,s} include only the words "may your kingdom come"; other MSS (ℵ A C D W f^{13} 33^{vid} Maj it syr^{h,p} cop^{bo}) add "and let your will be done on earth as it is in heaven" by way of scribal conformity to Matt. 6:10, a parallel verse.

11:4 | don't lead us into temptation.

This is the original wording according to the three earliest MSS (𝔓^{75} ℵ^{*,2} B), as well as L syr^{s} cop$^{sa.}$ Other MSS (ℵ^{1} A C D W Θ Ψ 070 f^{13} 33 Maj it syr^{c,h,p}) add "but rescue us from evil" by way of scribal conformity to Matt. 6:13, a parallel verse.

11:12 | if he asks for an egg.

The original word is "egg" according to early and excellent testimony: 𝔓^{75} ℵ A B C D L W Maj. 𝔓^{45} reads "bread."

11:13a | the heavenly Father.

The divine "Father" is written as a nomen sacrum (sacred name) in the two earliest MSS (𝔓^{45} 𝔓^{75}), as well as L.

11:13b | the Holy Spirit.

This is the original wording according to early MSS ($\mathfrak{P}^{75}$ ℵ A B C W), as well as $f^{1,13}$ Maj. Variant readings are "good Spirit" ($\mathfrak{P}^{45}$ L syr^{hmg}), "good gift" (D it), and "good gifts" (Θ). (The divine "Spirit" is written as a nomen sacrum [sacred name] in $\mathfrak{P}^{45}$ $\mathfrak{P}^{75}$ ℵ B L W.) The text has excellent documentary support. The third variant is clearly the result of harmonization to Matt. 7:11 or a conflation derived from Luke 11:12; the second is a slight modification. The first variant is either the result of scribal inadvertence (confusing *agion* for *agathon*) or an interesting combination of "good [gifts]" with "Spirit."

11:15 | Beelzeboul.

This is the original word according to the two earliest MSS ($\mathfrak{P}^{45}$ $\mathfrak{P}^{75}$), as well as A C D (L) W Θ Ψ $f^{1,13}$ 33 Maj. The variant is "Beezeboul" in ℵ B. (See note on Matt. 10:25.)

11:25 | it finds the house swept.

The original wording is "swept" according to the testimony of two early MSS ($\mathfrak{P}^{75}$ ℵ*), as well as A D W 070 Maj. This is "empty, swept" in ℵ^{2} [seventh century] B C L $f^{1,13}$ 33, by way of scribal conformity to Matt. 12:44, a parallel verse.

11:30 | the Son of Man will be a sign to this generation.

"Son of Man," a messianic title (Dan. 7:13–14), is written as a nomen sacrum (sacred name) in two early MSS ($\mathfrak{P}^{75}$ ℵ), as well as L.

11:31 | the queen of the South will rise up at the judgment.

This is the original wording according to several early MSS ($\mathfrak{P}^{75}$ ℵ A B C), as well as L Maj. $\mathfrak{P}^{45}$ (known for brevity) and D omit "at the judgment."

11:33 | no one, after lighting a lamp, hides it.

This is the original wording according to the two earliest MSS ($\mathfrak{P}^{45}$ $\mathfrak{P}^{75}$), as well as L 070 f^{1} syr^{s} cop^{sa}. This is expanded to "hides it or puts it under a basket" in ℵ A B C D W f^{13} Maj (so KJV), by way of scribal conformity to Matt. 5:15 and Mark 4:21, parallel verses.

12:8 | the Son of Man.

"Son of Man," a messianic title (Dan. 7:13–14), is written as a nomen sacrum (sacred name) in three early MSS ($\mathfrak{P}^{45}$ $\mathfrak{P}^{75}$ א), as well as L.

12:10a | the Son of Man

"Son of Man," a messianic title (Dan. 7:13–14), is written as a nomen sacrum (sacred name) in two early MSS ($\mathfrak{P}^{45}$ $\mathfrak{P}^{75}$), as well as L.

12:10b | whoever blasphemes the Holy Spirit.

The divine "Spirit" is written as a nomen sacrum (sacred name) in four early MSS ($\mathfrak{P}^{75}$ א D W), as well as L.

12:12 | the Holy Spirit will teach you.

The divine "Spirit" is written as a nomen sacrum (sacred name) in four early MSS ($\mathfrak{P}^{75}$ א D W), as well as L.

12:24 | consider the ravens.

This is the original wording according to early and excellent testimony: $\mathfrak{P}^{75}$ א A B C D W Maj. This is expanded to "the birds of the sky and the ravens" in $\mathfrak{P}^{45}$, by way of scribal conformity to Matt. 6:26, a parallel verse.

12:27 | how a lily grows; it does not labor or spin.

This is the original wording according to five early MSS ($\mathfrak{P}^{45}$ $\mathfrak{P}^{75}$ א B W). A variant reading is "how a lily does not spin or weave" in D (it^{a}) syr^{c,s}. A similar variation occurred in Matt. 6:23 (see note). In this verse, the variant reading, which has Western support, conjoins two verbs that pertain to the making of clothing (spinning and weaving)—probably in anticipation of the following comparison to Solomon's clothing.

12:30 | your Father knows.

The divine "Father" is written as a nomen sacrum (sacred name) in three early MSS ($\mathfrak{P}^{45}$ Θ W), as well as L.

12:31 | pursue his kingdom.

This is the original reading in three early MSS ($\mathfrak{P}^{75}$ א B), as well as D*

L Ψ. This is expanded to "pursue the kingdom of God" in 𝔓[45] A D[1] Θ W Θ 070 f[1,13] 33 Maj (so KJV).

12:32 | your Father is pleased to give you the kingdom.
The divine "Father" is written as a nomen sacrum (sacred name) in four early MSS (𝔓[45] 𝔓[75] Θ W), as well as L.

12:36 | waiting for their Lord to come back.
"Lord" is written as a nomen sacrum (sacred name) in several early MSS (𝔓[45] 𝔓[75] ℵ B D W), as well as L, thereby showing these scribes considered the master in the story to be the Lord Jesus.

12:37 | their Lord finds them alert.
"Lord" is written as a nomen sacrum (sactred name) in several early MSS (𝔓[75] ℵ B D W), as well as L, thereby showing these scribes considered the master in the story to be the Lord Jesus.

12:39 | he would not have let his house be broken into.
This is the original wording according to two early MSS (𝔓[75] ℵ*), as well as (D) it[e,i] syr[c,s]. This was expanded to "he would have watched and he would have not let his house been broken into" in ℵ[1] (A) B L Θ W Θ Ψ 070 f[1,13] 33 Maj, by way of scribal conformity to Matt. 24:43, a parallel verse.

12:40 | the Son of Man will come.
"Son of Man," a messianic title (Dan. 7:13–14), is written as a nomen sacrum (sacred name) in two early MSS (𝔓[75] ℵ), as well as L.

12:42b–43, 45–46 | Lord.
"Lord" is written as a nomen sacrum (sacred name) in several early MSS (𝔓[75] ℵ B D W), as well as L, thereby showing these scribes considered the master in the story to be the Lord Jesus.

13:8 | Lord, leave it alone this year also.
"Lord" is written as a nomen sacrum (sacred name) in several early MSS

($\mathfrak{P}^{75}$ ℵ B D W), as well as L, thereby showing these scribes considered the master in the story to be the Lord Jesus.

13:19 | it grew and became a tree.

This is the original wording according to early and excellent testimony: $\mathfrak{P}^{75}$ ℵ B D L 070. This was expanded to "great tree" in $\mathfrak{P}^{45}$ A W Θ Ψ 0303 f^{13} 33 Maj. Although it could be argued that "great" was deleted by scribes in order to conform this text to Matt. 13:32 (a parallel verse), it is just as likely that the word was added to heighten the sense. Besides, the MSS with the shorter text (especially $\mathfrak{P}^{75}$ ℵ B) generally show far less harmonization in the Gospels than those that have the addition.

13:35 | your house is left to you.

This is the original wording according to early and excellent testimony: $\mathfrak{P}^{45vid}$ $\mathfrak{P}^{75}$ ℵ A B L W syr^{s} cop^{sa}. A variant reading is "your house is left to you desolate" in D N Δ Θ Ψ f^{13} 33 Maj it syr^{c}. Whereas in Matt. 23:38 the best documentation supports the inclusion of the word "desolate," in Luke it is just the opposite. It is quite likely that D, et al., added *erēmos* (desolate) to Luke from their text of Matt. 23:38, so that in these MSS Matt. 23:38 and Luke 13:35 perfectly harmonize.

14:5 | if you have a son or ox.

This is the original wording according to five early MSS ($\mathfrak{P}^{45}$ $\mathfrak{P}^{75}$ A B W). Three variants are "donkey or ox" (ℵ K L $f^{1,13}$ 33), "sheep or ox" (D it^{d}), and "foal of a donkey or an ox" (Θ). The reading of the text is preferred because it has the best documentary support. The variants are scribal attempts to have a pair of animals rather than a human paired with an animal.

14:8 | when you are invited by someone to a wedding feast.

This is possibly the original wording, according to $\mathfrak{P}^{45}$ A B D W Maj, but $\mathfrak{P}^{75}$ it^{b} cop^{sa} do not include "to a wedding feast."

14:21 | the servant reported to his Lord.

"Lord" is written as a nomen sacrum (sacred name) in several early MSS

($\mathfrak{P}^{45\text{vid}}$ $\mathfrak{P}^{75}$ ℵ B D), as well as L, thereby showing these scribes considered the master in the story to be the Lord Jesus or Lord God.

14:22 | "Lord, what you instructed has been done."
"Lord" is written as a nomen sacrum (sacred name) in several early MSS ($\mathfrak{P}^{45\text{vid}}$ $\mathfrak{P}^{75}$ ℵ B W), as well as L, thereby showing these scribes considered the master in the story to be the Lord Jesus or Lord God.

14:23 | the Lord said to his servant.
"Lord" is written as a nomen sacrum (sacred name) in several early MSS ($\mathfrak{P}^{45}$ $\mathfrak{P}^{75}$ ℵ B D W), as well as L, thereby showing these scribes considered the master in the story to be the Lord Jesus or Lord God.

14:27 | carry his own Cross.
"Cross" is written as a nomen sacrum (sacred word) in two early MSS ($\mathfrak{P}^{45}$ $\mathfrak{P}^{75}$), as well as L.

15:16 | wanted to satisfy himself.
This is the original wording according to $\mathfrak{P}^{75}$ ℵ B D L $f^{1,13}$. A variant reading is "he wanted to fill his stomach" in A (W) Θ Ψ Maj (so KJV). The three earliest MSS ($\mathfrak{P}^{75}$ ℵ B) support the text.

15:21 | I am no longer worthy to be called your son.
This is the original wording according to the earliest MS ($\mathfrak{P}^{75}$) and A L W Θ Ψ $f^{1,13}$ Maj $syr^{c,s}$ cop. This was expanded to "I am no longer worthy to be called your son; treat me as one of your hired servants" in ℵ B D 33 syr^{h}. There are two factors that favor the reading of the text: (1) it has earlier and more diverse testimony, and (2) the words in the variant were carried over from Luke 15:19 so that the son's actual speech would replicate the one he had planned.

16:3–8 | Lord.
The Greek word for "Lord" is *kurios*; it is written in full (in *plene*) in $\mathfrak{P}^{75}$ L; it is written as a nomen sacrum (sacred name) in ℵ A B D W $f^{1,13}$. In this verse and 16:5 (twice) and 16:8, the *kurios* of the story appears to be

a human master. However, the *kurios* in parables invariably represents the divine *kurios*, the Lord Jesus or Lord God. In this parable, various scribes vacillated between writing out *kurios* in full (in *plene*)—thereby signifying a human master—and writing it as a nomen sacrum—thereby designating the divine Lord. This vacillation appears in 16:3 ($\mathfrak{P}^{75}$ L written in full), 16:5a (B D written in full), and 16:5b (f^1 written in full). Since the scribes of $\mathfrak{P}^{75}$ B D L f^1 wrote out the word *kurios* (in *plene*) at least one time, it is possible that their exemplars had *kurios* written out in full in all these verses—but then the scribes reverted to their usual practice of making *kurios* a nomen sacrum (irrespective of context). In 16:8 all the primary MSS write the name *kurios* as a nomen sacrum (sacred name).

16:19b–20

This is the only parable told by Jesus in which one of the characters is given a name; the blind beggar is called Lazarus. Some witnesses provide testimony of scribal attempts (beginning as early as the second century) to also give the rich man a name. The scribe of $\mathfrak{P}^{75}$ provided him a name, *Neues*; and one Coptic Sahidic manuscript reads *Nineue*. Both of these names may be synonyms for Nineveh, the wealthy city that came under God's judgment. According to a pseudo-Cyprianic text (third century), the rich man is called "Finaeus." Priscillian also gave him the name "Finees," which is probably an alternate to Phinehas, Elezar's companion (Exod. 6:25; Num. 25:7, 11). Peter of Riga called him Amonofis, which is a form of "Amenophis," a name held by many Pharaohs (see TCGNT). These namings all exemplify the scribal desire to fill perceived gaps in the narrative text.

17:22 | the days of the Son of Man.

"Son of Man," a messianic title (Dan. 7:13–14), is written as a nomen sacrum (sacred name) in two early MSS ($\mathfrak{P}^{75}$ W), as well as L.

17:24 | so it will be with the Son of Man.

This is the original wording according to the two earliest MSS ($\mathfrak{P}^{75}$ B) and D it cop^{sa}. This is expanded to "so it will be with the Son of Man in his day" in ℵ A L W Θ Ψ $f^{1,13}$ Maj syr cop^{bo}. Scribes may have added "in his day" to make a parallel statement with 17:22 ("you will desire to see one of the days of the Son of Man"), or scribes could have dropped the phrase to make it conform to the Matthean parallel (Matt. 24:47). However, since the scribes of $\mathfrak{P}^{75}$ and B were rarely given to harmonization, it seems more likely that "in his day" was added later. ("Son of Man," a messianic title (Dan. 7:13–14), is written as a nomen sacrum [sacred name] in $\mathfrak{P}^{75}$ א L W.)

17:26, 30 | the Son of Man.
"Son of Man," a messianic title (Dan. 7:13–14), is written as a nomen sacrum (sacred name) in two early MSS ($\mathfrak{P}^{75}$ W), as well as L.

17:36 | omit verse.
The earliest MSS ($\mathfrak{P}^{75}$ א B) do not include 17:36. This verse, found in later MSS (D f^{13} 700) and versions (it syr) reads, "Two will be in the field; one will be taken and the other left." It is quite likely that the verse is a scribal interpolation borrowed from Matt. 24:40, with harmonization to the style of Luke 17:35.

18:8 | when the Son of Man comes.
"Son of Man," a messianic title (Dan. 7:13–14), is written as a nomen sacrum (sacred name) in some early MSS (א A W), as well as L.

18:11 | the Pharisee stood and prayed these things about himself.
This is the original wording according to $\mathfrak{P}^{75}$ $א^{2}$ B L T Θ Ψ f^{1}. Three variant readings are "stood by himself praying these things" (A W f^{13} Maj), "stood and prayed these things" (א* it cop^{sa}), and "stood and prayed these things privately" (D). The text has the earliest manuscript support; the variants are scribal attempts at clarifying the text.

18:24 | seeing this.
This is the original wording according to the two earliest MSS (א B), as well as L f^{1} cop. A variant reading is "seeing him become very sad" in A (D) W 078 f^{13} Maj syr. The shorter text has better support than the variant, which appears to be a carryover from 18:23.

18:41 | "Lord, let me see."
"Lord" is written as a nomen sacrum (sacred name) in early MSS (א B D T), as well as L, indicating these scribes considered the blind man to be addressing Jesus as the divine Lord.

19:8 | Lord.
"Lord" is written (both times) as a nomen sacrum (sacred name) in early MSS (א B D W), as well as L, indicating these scribes considered Zacchaeus to be addressing Jesus as the divine Lord.

19:16, 18, 20, 25 | Lord.
"Lord" is written as a nomen sacrum (sacred name) in early MSS (א B D W), as well as L, indicating these scribes considered the king in the parable to be the divine Lord.

19:25
This verse should be included on the basis of early and excellent testimony: א A (B) L Θ Ψ 0233 $f^{1,13}$ it^{a} cop^{sa}. The verse is omitted in D W $it^{b,d,e}$ $syr^{c,s}$, probably because the verse seems obtrusive and perhaps unnecessary. Furthermore, it might have been deleted because (1) the verse is not found in Matthew's parallel account (Matt. 25:28–29) and because (2) it is difficult to identify who is speaking here: some of the ten servants or those listening to Jesus's parable? In either case, the objection posed by these people all the more heightens the account in which the Lord gives one more mina to him who already had ten.

20:13 | I will send my own dear son (or, Son).
"Son" is written in full (in *plene*; i.e., not as a sacred name) in B D W, but written as a nomen sacrum (sacred name) in א, suggesting this scribe thought this "son" signified the Son of God.

20:21–25
The story in Luke 20:21–25 appeared in at least three different forms in the second century. An ancient version of this appears in

the second-century Egerton Papyrus, which is translated as follows: "Coming to him, they began to tempt him with a question, saying, 'Master, Jesus, we know you are come from God, for what you are doing bears testimony beyond that of all the prophets. Tell us, then, is it lawful to pay kings what pertains to their rule? Shall we give it to them or not?' But Jesus, knowing their thoughts, said, 'Why do you call me with your mouth Master, when you hear not what I say. Well did Isaiah prophesy of you, saying, 'This people honors me with their lips, but their hearts are from me. In vain they worship me; their precepts . . . .'"

This text is a type of "Diatessaron" in that it weaves together a Gospel narrative from preexisting Gospel accounts—in this case, probably from John 3:2; 10:25; Matt. 22:17–18; Mark 12:14–15; Luke 20:22–23; 6:46; 18:19; Mark 15:7–9; 7:6–7. Another version of Luke 20:21–25 is preserved in the writings of the second-century apologist, Justin Martyr (*Apology* 1.17.2): "For about that time some people came up to him and asked him whether one ought to pay taxes to Caesar. And he answered, 'Tell me, whose image does the coin bear?' And they said, 'Caesar's.' And he replied, 'Pay, then, to Caesar what is Caesar's and to God what is God's.'" This account more closely follows the Gospels, especially Luke 20:24 and Matt. 22:21.

The apocryphal Gospel of Thomas (section 100), composed in the second century, has its own rendition: "They showed Jesus a gold coin and said to him, 'Caesar's agents demand of us taxes.' He said to them, 'Give Caesar the things of Caesar, give God the things of God, and give me what is mine.'"

20:41 | How is it that they say that Christ is the Son of David?
"Christ" is written as a nomen sacrum (sacred name) in all MSS. "Son of David," a royal-messianic title, is written as a nomen sacrum (sacred name) in one early MS (א), as well as L. The Jews expected the Messiah-King to be the Son of David (2 Sam. 7:13, 16; Jer. 23:5; Ezek. 37:24).

20:42–43 | The LORD said to my LORD.
In the Hebrew text of Ps. 110:1 (the verse quoted here), this reads

"Yahweh said to my *Adonai*." In the Greek text it reads "*Kurios* said to my *Kurios*." Clearly, deity is addressing deity. Thus, David (who wrote this psalm) called him who was to sit on the kingly throne, "my *Adonai*" (my Lord), not "my son." The OT predicted that the son of David would have an everlasting kingship through his descendants (2 Sam. 7:12–14; Ps. 89:1–4; 132:11–12; Jer. 23:5–8; Ezek. 37:21–24; Zech. 6:12–15). The teachers saw the Messiah as the son of David (see Psalms of Solomon 17–18, written 50 BC) as being the one to fulfill the role of being a military conqueror, liberator, and inaugurator of an everlasting dynasty in Jerusalem that would affect all nations of the world. They expected him to be an entirely earthly figure, a mortal man, while Jesus shows here that he was divine (cf. Jer. 23:6)—David's "Lord," not merely his son.

21:27 | they will see the Son of Man.

"Son of Man," a messianic title (Dan. 7:13–14), is written as a nomen sacrum (sacred name) in two early MSS (א W), as well as L.

21:36 | stand before the Son of Man.

"Son of Man," a messianic title (Dan. 7:13–14), is written as a nomen sacrum (sacred name) in one early MS (א), as well as L.

21:38

It is interesting to note that eight of the MSS belonging to f^{13} (13 69 124 346 543 788 826 983) include the pericope of the adulteress after this verse. The insertion of this story (probably taken from an oral tradition) at this place in Luke's narrative is a much better fit than where it is typically placed in John's narrative (between 7:52 and 8:12). In John, it interrupts the connection between the Sanhedrin's rejection of Jesus (on the basis that he was a Galilean) and Jesus's following rejoinder. Chronologically, the story belongs in Jesus's last week in Jerusalem, at a time when he was going back and forth between the Temple (to teach in the day time) and the Garden of Gethsemane (to sleep at night). Thematically, the story belongs with the others that show the religious leaders trying to trap Jesus into some kind of lawlessness and thereby have grounds to arrest him. These encounters, according to the Synoptic Gospels, also appear in Jesus's last days in Jerusalem.

The group of MSS, f^{13}, could represent the earliest positioning of the pericope of the adulteress, which was then transferred to the end of John 7, or it could represent an independent positioning. Westcott and Hort (*The New Testament in the Original Greek, Introduction and Appendix*, 63) said this passage was probably known to a scribe "exclusively as a church lesson, recently come into use, and placed by him here on account of the close resemblance between Luke 21:37–38 and John 7:53–8:2. Had he known it as part of a continuous text of St John's Gospel, he was not likely to transpose it." It is also possible that the earliest scribe of a manuscript in the group of f^{13} (either the composer of the archetype in Calabria or the scribes of 124 and/or 788) made the editorial decision to move it from its usual spot at the end of John 7, to follow Luke 21. This transposition, which was a good editorial decision, affirms the transitory nature of the pericope of the adulteress—which is to say, it was not treated on the same par as fixed, inviolable Scripture. (See comments on John 7:53–8:11.)

22:17–20

These verses are found in early and diverse MSS: $\mathfrak{P}^{75}$ ℵ A B C L T^{vid} W. Codex D, some Latin MSS ($it^{a,d,i,l}$), and the Didache shorten this passage by omitting 22:19b–20. Other Latin MSS ($it^{b,e}$) have the shorter text with a transposed order of bread/cup, which is the traditional order of the Lord's Supper. The variants show attempts to resolve the apparent problem of cup/bread/cup in the longer text. The Bezaen editor (D) and Latin translators must not have realized that the cup mentioned in 22:17 was the cup of the Passover celebration, occupying 22:15–18. Going back to 22:16, it seems clear that the food of the Passover is implied when Jesus speaks of never again eating it until the kingdom of God is realized. Then, according to 22:17–18, Jesus passed around a cup of wine, again saying that he would not drink of it until the kingdom of God came. Thus, 22:16–18 has its own bread/cup sequence as part of the Passover meal. Following this, 22:19–20 has the bread/cup sequence of the new covenant.

22:22 | the Son of Man is to go as it has been determined.

"Son of Man," a messianic title (Dan. 7:13–14), is written as a nomen sacrum (sacred name) in several early MSS (ℵ A T W), as well as L.

22:30 | you will sit on thrones.

This is the original wording according to early and excellent testimony: $\mathfrak{P}^{75}$ ℵ* A B W Maj. A variant on this is "twelve thrones" (ℵ^{2} D) by way of scribal expansion.

22:43–44 | omit verses.

Nearly all the most ancient MSS ($\mathfrak{P}^{69vid}$ $\mathfrak{P}^{75}$ ℵ^{1} A B T W) do not include 22:43–44. These verses, found in ℵ^{*,2} [seventh century] D L Θ Ψ 0171^{vid} 0233 Maj, read, "Then an angel from heaven appeared to him and strengthened him. In anguish he prayed more earnestly, and his sweat became like great drops of blood falling down on the ground." Several other witnesses could be cited for exclusion and inclusion of the verses. Church fathers (Jerome, Hilary) knew of MSS both with and without these verses, several MSS that include the verses (D^{c} P^{c} 892^{c} 1079 1195 1216 cop^{boMSS}) are marked with obeli to signal suspicion about their right to be in the text, and f^{13} places the verses after Matt. 26:39.

The editors of $\mathfrak{P}^{69}$ (see P. Oxyrhynchus 2383), were fairly confident that the only way to account for the size of the lacuna in $\mathfrak{P}^{69}$ (from Luke 22:41 to Luke 22:45) is that the copyist's exemplar did not contain Luke 22:43–44 and that the scribe's eye moved from *prosēucheto* in 22:41 to *proseuchēs* in 22:45. The editors calculated that these two words would have been on the end of lines, four lines apart. The manuscript 0171 should be listed as "vid" (as in UBS^{4}) inasmuch as it shows only a portion of 22:44; however, there are no obeli or asterisks as noted in UBS^{4}. (For the reconstructions of $\mathfrak{P}^{69}$ and 0171 respectively, see Comfort and Barrett, *Text of Earliest NT Greek MSS*, 471–472, 687–691.)

The manuscript evidence is decidedly in favor of the exclusion of 22:43–44. The Greek MSS (dating from the second to fifth century) favoring the exclusion of these verses forms an impressive list: $\mathfrak{P}^{69vid}$ $\mathfrak{P}^{75}$

ℵ[1] B T W. (The first corrector of ℵ was a contemporary of the scribe who produced the manuscript of Luke; indeed, he was the diorthotes who worked on this manuscript before it left the scriptorium.) Other signs of its doubtfulness appear in MSS marking the passage with obeli or crossing out the passage (as was done by the first corrector of ℵ). Its transposition to Matt. 26 in some MSS and lectionaries indicates that it was a free-floating passage that could be interjected into any of the passion narratives (see note on Matt. 26:39).

The manuscript support for including the verses involves several witnesses, the earliest of which is 0171^{vid} (c. 300). None of the other MSS are earlier than the fifth century. However, several early fathers (Justin, Irenaeus, Hippolytus, Dionysius, Eusebius) acknowledged this portion as part of Luke's Gospel. When we turn to the writings of other early church fathers, we discover that many noted both the presence and absence of the "bloody sweat" passage in the MSS known to them. We have notes on this from Jerome, Hilary, Anastasius, and Epiphanius. For example, Epiphanius (*Ancoratus* 31.4–5) indicated that the verses were found in some "uncorrected copies" of Luke. This tells us that in the early course of textual transmission, the Gospel of Luke (in this chapter) was being copied in two forms—one that lacked the "bloody sweat" passage and one that included it.

The question, then, is: Did Luke write these verses, which were later deleted, or did someone else add them later? Metzger's view of this is true: "On grounds of transcriptional probability it is less likely that the verses were deleted in several different areas of the church by those who felt that the account of Jesus overwhelmed with human weakness was incompatible with his sharing the divine omnipotence of the Father, than that they were added from an early source" (TCGNT, 151). Westcott and Hort also considered the "bloody sweat" passage to be an early (second century) interpolation, added from an oral tradition concerning the life of Jesus (see Westcott and Hort, *The New Testament in the Original Greek: Introduction and Appendix*, 64–67).

22:48, 69 | the Son of Man.

"Son of Man," a messianic title (Dan. 7:13–14), is written as a nomen

sacrum (sacred name) in three early MSS (𝔓^{75} ℵ T), as well as L. The title "Son of Man" is the one messianic title Jesus used of himself throughout the Gospels. Jesus's exclamation to the Jewish leaders encapsulates his understanding of this title, which comes from Dan. 7:9–14, a passage that shows "the Son of Man" sharing dominion over all the nations with "the Ancient One."

22:70 | Are you the Son of God?

"Son of God" is written as a nomen sacrum (sacred name) in several early MSS (𝔓^{75} ℵ B D T), as well as L. It signifies that the religious leaders were asking Jesus if he was *the* divine Son of God, not just a son of God.

23:17 | omit verse.

Several early MSS (𝔓^{75} A B T), as well as L 070 892^{txt} it^{a} cop^{sa} , do not include 23:17. This verse ("it was necessary for him to release one [prisoner] for them at the festival") is included in ℵ W (Θ Ψ) f^{1,13} 892^{mg} Maj (D syr^{c,s} after 23:19). Since this verse is absent from several significant MSS and is transposed in D and syr^{c,s}, its presence in the other MSS is most likely the result of scribal interpolation—borrowing primarily from Mark 15:6, as well as Matt. 27:15. The verse was probably added to provide a reason for the crowd's request that Pilate release Barabbas instead of Jesus (23:18). But the text reads contiguously from 23:16 to 23:18, joining Pilate's statement about releasing Jesus to an immediate plea from the crowd to release Barabbas instead.

23:34 | omit verse.

Several early MSS (𝔓^{75} ℵ^{1} B D* W), as well as Θ 070 it^{a} syr^{s} cop^{sa} , do not include 23:34a. This verse ("And Jesus said, 'Father, forgive them, for they do not know what they are doing'") is included in ℵ^{*,2} [seventh century] (A) C D^{2} E (with obeli) L 0250 f$^{1,(13)}$ Maj syr^{c,h,p} Diatessaron Hegesippus. The omission of these words in early and diverse MSS (the earliest being 𝔓^{75}) cannot be explained as a scribal blunder. But were the words purposely excised? Westcott and Hort (*The Original Greek New Testament: Introduction and Appendix*, 68) considered willful excision to be absolutely unthinkable. But Marshall (*The Gospel of Luke*, 867–868) can think of several reasons why scribes might have deleted the words—the most convincing of which is that scribes might have been influenced by an anti-Judaic polemic and therefore did not want the text saying that Jesus forgave the Jews who killed him. This would be especially true for codex Bezae (D), whose scribe has been charged with having anti-Judaic tendencies (see Epp, *The Theological Tendency of Codex Cantabrigiensis in Acts*). However, there are four MSS—of diverse traditions—earlier than D (namely, $\mathfrak{P}^{75}$ B W it^{a}), which do not include these words. Thus, D could not have been responsible for being the first to eliminate the words. The primary argument against excision (on the basis of an anti-Judaic polemic) is that Jesus was forgiving his Roman executioners, not the Jewish leaders. The grammar affirms this; in 23:33 it says *estaurōsan auton* ("they [the Roman execution squad] crucified him"), then in 23:34 Jesus says, *aphes autois* ("forgive them")—i.e., the Roman execution squad. Furthermore, Jesus had already pronounced judgment on the Jewish leaders who would not believe in him and even worse who proclaimed that his works were empowered by Beelzebul, the prince of demons (Matt. 12:24–32).

It is easier to explain that the words were not written by Luke but were added later (as early as the second century—for it is attested to by Hegesippus and the Diatessaron). If the words came from an oral tradition, many scholars are of the opinion that they are authentic. Indeed, Westcott and Hort (*The New Testament in the Original Greek: Introduction and Appendix*, 67) considered these words and 22:43–44 to be "the most precious among the remains of the evangelic tradition which were rescued from oblivion by the scribes of the second century."

But what if the words did not come from an oral tradition about Jesus's life and sayings? What would have inspired their inclusion? My guess is that the words were added to make Jesus the model for Christian martyrs—of offering forgiveness to one's executioners. Whoever first added the words may have drawn from Acts 7:60, where Stephen forgives his executioners. Since Stephen's final words parallel Jesus's final utterances (cf. Acts 7:56 to Luke 22:69; Acts 7:59 to Luke 23:46), it seemed appropriate to have Luke 23:34 emulate Acts 7:60.

Or the words could have come from martyrdom stories, such as the account of the execution of James the Just, who is said to have forgiven his executioners (Eusebius' *Ecclesiastical History* 2.23, 16). Thus, it can be imagined that church leaders told would-be martyrs to forgive their executors because Jesus had done the same.

23:35 | He is the Christ, the Son of God.

This is likely the original reading according to $\mathfrak{P}^{75}$ (B) D (070) f^{13} syr^{h} cop. The phrase "Son of God" is not included in ℵ L W f^{1} A C^{3} Maj. The textual evidence for the inclusion of "Son of God" is solid, having the dual support of the two earliest MSS, $\mathfrak{P}^{75}$ B (which usually preserve the original wording in Luke and in this verse write "Son of God" as a nomen sacrum [sacred name]), as well as D 070 f^{13} syr^{h} Coptic MSS. This testimony is both early and diverse. With respect to internal considerations, it is noteworthy that according to Luke's account the Jewish leaders at Jesus's trial wanted to know if he was both "the Christ" and "the Son of God" (Luke 22:67–70). Thus, it is fitting for Luke to have both titles coming from the mouths of the same Jewish leaders who were taunting Jesus during his crucifixion. Furthermore, the inclusion of "Son of God" puts an emphasis on Jesus's divinity; as such, the Jewish leaders were asking Jesus to display his divine power by saving himself from death on the cross.

The argument in favor of the exclusion of "Son of God" is that scribes, in general, had a tendency to expand divine titles. However, the problem with adopting this position here is that the scribes of $\mathfrak{P}^{75}$ and B are not known as those who expanded titles. Therefore, we must ask if somewhere in the textual tradition other scribes deleted "the Son of God"—and, if so, what would have been the motivation? It is possible that scribes altered Luke to conform to Mark's account where the Jewish leaders taunt Jesus with this statement: "If you are the Christ, the King of Israel, come down from the cross" (Mark 15:32). Given this alteration, the account in Luke would be more fitting with Mark in that both would have taunts against Jesus as "the Christ" and "the King of Israel/the Jews" (Mark 15:32; Luke 23:35). However, there is a counter argument to this supposition of harmonization. In Matthew's Gospel, the taunt of the Jewish leaders includes two titles: "the Son of God" and "the King of Israel." Thus, it can always be argued that the scribes of $\mathfrak{P}^{75}$ B D, et al., added "Son of God" to harmonize Luke with Matthew. In the end, both external and internal arguments offset each other. In such cases, translators have no choice but to decide on one reading and then note the other in the margin. All things being equal, I would tend to follow a reading supported by $\mathfrak{P}^{75}$ and B.

23:38 | there was an inscription over him.

This is the original wording according to several early MSS ($\mathfrak{P}^{75}$ $\aleph^{1}$ B C*), as well as L 070 cop^{sa} $syr^{c,s}$. This is expanded to "there was an inscription over him in Greek, Latin, and Hebrew" in $\aleph^{*,c}$ A C^{3} D W Θ (Ψ) 0250 $f^{1,13}$ Maj. Borrowing from John 19:20, several scribes added an expression naming the three languages written on the placard nailed to Jesus's cross. This addition doesn't follow John 19:20 exactly, because John's order is Hebrew, Latin, Greek.

23:46 | into your hands I commit my Spirit.

The divine "Spirit" is written as a nomen sacrum (sacred name) in four early MSS ($\mathfrak{P}^{75}$ ℵ W Θ Ψ), as well as L. Codex B writes out the word in full (in *plene*), suggesting the human spirit. Most scribes saw Jesus's *pneuma* as being divine and worthy of being written as a nomen sacrum.

24:3 | the body of the Lord Jesus.

This is the original wording according to early and diverse testimony: $\mathfrak{P}^{75}$ ℵ A B C L W Θ Ψ 070 cop. This is shortened to "the body" in D it. Westcott and Hort (*The New Testament in the Original Greek: Introduction and Appendix*, 71–73) thought Codex Bezae (D) contained the original wording of Luke's Gospel in 24:3, 6, 12, 36, 40, 51, and 52. (All these portions are double-bracketed in WH to show the editors' strong doubts about their inclusion in the text.) Calling the omissions in D "Western non-interpolations," they posited the theory that all the other MSS contain interpolations in these verses. This theory affected the Nestle text until its twenty-sixth edition, at which point this theory was abandoned—note the changes in Luke 24:3, 6, 12, 36, 40, 51, 52, where none of the portions are double-bracketed.

This theory also affected several modern English versions—especially the RSV and NEB, which in nearly every one of these Luke 24 passages followed the testimony of D. The NASB was also affected by this theory, but not as much as the RSV and NEB. After all three of these translations were published, 𝔓[75] was discovered. And in every instance, 𝔓[75] attests to the longer reading. 𝔓[75] impacted the Nestle text, which now in every verse noted above follows the testimony of 𝔓[75], et al.

One wonders why Westcott and Hort were so taken with the evidence of D only in the latter part of Luke, when all throughout Luke D displays many omissions. In Luke, D displays at least 75 omissions that are two words or more—and frequently the excision is of a phrase, a clause, or an entire sentence. In chapter 24 alone, D has 13 such omissions. With respect to these omissions, D often stands alone among the witnesses, or has slim support from an Old Latin or Syriac manuscript. In nearly every case, the omission cannot be explained away as a transcriptional error; rather, the deletions are the careful work of an editor having a penchant for pruning (in the critical apparatus of NA[27] see Luke 1:26; 5:9, 12, 26, 30, 39; 6:12, 21, 34; 7:3, 7, 18, 27, 28, 30, 47; 8:5, 15, 24, 28a, 28b, 43, 44; 9:12, 15, 16, 23, 48; 10:19, 23, 24; 11:8, 31, 32, 46, 49;12:19, 41; 13:25; 16:6, 18; 17:24; 18:9, 40; 19:4, 25, 31, 36, 43, 44; 20:31, 36; 21:10, 24, 37; 22:19–20, 22, 54, 61; 23:39, 45, 56; 24:9, 12, 19, 20, 22, 25, 30, 36, 40, 46, 49, 51, 52). The reviser usually displayed an opposite penchant in the book of Acts—that of expanding but not always (see D-text subtractions in the textual commentary on Acts). The main point to realize about the D-reviser is that he was a redactor who both excised and enhanced. In this verse, the longer text accords with Luke's style (see Acts 1:21; 4:33; 8:16). The shorter text is a Western excision, perhaps influenced by 24:23.

24:6 | He is not here, but has risen.

This is the original wording according to early and diverse testimony: 𝔓[75] ℵ A B C[3] [ninth century] L (W) D Θ Ψ 070 f[1,13] syr[c,s] cop. The phrase is omitted in D it. In favor of the variant is the argument that the longer text could be the result of harmonization to parallel passages, Matt. 28:6 and Mark 16:6. But the wording in Luke does not exactly replicate Matthew or Mark and appears completely Lukan. Furthermore, textual support for the omission comes only from the Western witnesses, D and Old Latin MSS, which hardly outweigh the diverse and early testimony for the longer reading.

24:7 | a the Son of Man must be betrayed.
"Son of Man," a messianic title (Dan. 7:13–14), is written as a nomen sacrum (sacred name) in several early MSS ($\mathfrak{P}^{75}$ ℵ A C W), as well as L.

24:7b | be Crucified and rise again on the third day.
"Crucified" is written as a nomen sacrum (sacred word) in one early MS ($\mathfrak{P}^{75}$).

24:12
This verse is included in early and diverse MSS: $\mathfrak{P}^{75}$ ℵ B W D 070 079 $syr^{c,s}$ cop (A L Θ Ψ $f^{1,13}$) Maj. It is omitted in D it. Westcott and Hort (*The New Testament in the Original Greek: Introduction and Appendix*, 71) argued that the verse is a consolidated interpolation from John 20:3–10. However, the scribe of $\mathfrak{P}^{75}$ rarely interpolated from remote parallels, and the scribe of B did so only occasionally.

24:32 | Didn't our hearts burn?
This is the original wording according to the two earliest MSS ($\mathfrak{P}^{75}$ B), as well as D $syr^{c,s}$. A variant reading is "didn't our hearts burn within us" (ℵ A L W 33 Maj), by way of scribal exapansion.

24:36 | and he said to them, "Peace be with you."
This is the original wording according to four early MSS ($\mathfrak{P}^{75}$ ℵ A B), as well as L cop $syr^{c,s}$. This was expanded to "and he said to them, 'Peace to you. I am [here]; do not be afraid'" in P (W) $syr^{h,p}$ cop^{boMSS}. The phrase is omitted in D it. The first variant is a scribal addition borrowed from John 6:20. The statement *egō eimi* (I am) adds a theophanic element to this Christophany. The second variant was considered original by Westcott and Hort (see note above on Luke 24:3), who believed that the longer text was a scribal interpolation borrowed from John 20:19.

(WH included the words, though in double brackets.) But Luke and John probably derived their accounts about the resurrection from many of the same sources; thus, this verbal equivalence is not unusual.

24:40

This verse is included in early and diverse MSS: 𝔓⁷⁵ ℵ A B L W Δ Θ Ψ cop. It is omitted in D it syr[c,s]. Again, Westcott and Hort (see note above on Luke 24:3) considered the longer text to be a scribal interpolation borrowed from John 20:20. But Luke and John seemed to have used many of the same sources for their resurrection narratives; thus, this verbal equivalence is not unusual.

24:48 | I am sending you what my Father promised.

The divine "Father" is written as a nomen sacrum (sacred name) in two early MSS (𝔓⁷⁵ W), as well as L.

24:51 | and he was taken up into heaven.

This is the original wording according to early and diverse MSS: 𝔓⁷⁵ ℵ[c] A B C L W Δ Θ Ψ cop. The clause is omitted in ℵ* D it syr[s]. Westcott and Hort considered the variant to be a Western non-interpolation (see note on 24:3). They argued that the longer reading "was evidently inserted from an assumption that a separation from the disciples at the close of a Gospel must be the ascension. The ascension apparently did not lie within the proper scope of the Gospels, as seen in their genuine texts; its true place was at the head of the Acts of the Apostles, as the preparation for the Day of Pentecost, and thus the beginning of the history of the Church." Indeed, Jesus's separation from the disciples need not mean that he ascended, because after his resurrection Jesus intermittently appeared to his disciples in visible form, then disappeared. In this regard, the shorter text is exegetically defensible. But Westcott and Hort's next argument is weak because, in effect, they say that the longer text is the result of scribes attempting to harmonize Luke 24 with Acts 1 by adding a reference to the ascension.

It is far more likely that other scribes deleted the reference to the ascension in Luke so that it would not conflict with the chronology of the ascension recorded in Acts 1:3, 9–11. This is all the more apparent when we understand that the editor of Codex Bezae (perhaps followed by other Western scribes) was determined to eliminate any mention of Jesus's bodily ascension in both Luke and Acts (see Epp, "The Ascension in the Textual Tradition of Luke–Acts," *New Testament Textual Criticism: Its Significance for Exegesis*, 131–145). In Acts 1:2 and 1:9 (see notes), MSS belonging to the Western text omit the words about Jesus's ascension. In Acts 1:11 the ascension is kept but it is modified in the Western text from "taken up into heaven" to simply "taken up" (see note); and in Acts 1:22 the Western text (with all other witnesses) refers to Jesus being "taken up." Never does the Western text portray an actual physical ascension.

In conclusion, let us consider one more point: If one were to accept the shorter reading as original, does this mean that there is no mention of the ascension in the Gospels, as posited by Westcott and Hort? For Matthew this is true. For Mark this is also true, if we accept that the original text ended with 16:8. For John this is not true, because Jesus clearly speaks of an ascension to the Father on the morning of the resurrection (John 20:17). Since this ascension occurred before the one recorded in Acts 1:3, 9–11, why is it not possible for Luke to speak of yet another ascension—or, better still, to be speaking of the same ascension as Acts but in general terms (lacking specific chronology)? Indeed, in Acts 1:2 Luke clearly indicates that his Gospel covered the entire scope of Jesus's ministry up until the ascension. Thus, it is very likely that Luke spoke of Jesus's ascension in his Gospel and then again in Acts. (See comments on Luke 24:3.)

24:52 | and they worshiped him.

This is the original wording according to early and diverse MSS: $\mathfrak{P}^{75}$ ℵ A B C L W D Θ Ψ cop. The clause is omitted in D it syr^{s}. Again, Westcott and Hort considered the shorter text to represent the original wording of Luke (see note on 24:3), but the textual evidence speaks against this. Luke waited until the very end of his Gospel to speak of Jesus being worshiped, for his resurrection proved to the disciples that he was indeed God worthy of their worship.

24:53 | praising God.

This is the original wording according to early MSS ($\mathfrak{P}^{75}$ ℵ C* D W), as well as 33 it syr^s cop. Other MSS (A B C^2 [sixth century] Θ Ψ f^{13} Maj; so KJV) add "amen." Because the NT books were read orally in church meetings, it became customary to end the reading with an "amen." Gradually, this spoken word was added to the printed page of many late MSS. This addition took place in all four Gospels and Acts.

Chapter Four

The Gospel according to John

THE GOSPEL ACCORDING TO JOHN

Title: The Gospel according to John
This is the reading of the two earliest MSS ($\mathfrak{P}^{66}$ $\mathfrak{P}^{75}$). $\mathfrak{P}^{2}$ also calls this book a "gospel" (*euangelion*). ℵ and B read "according to John."

1:14 | the One and Only who came from the Father.
The divine "Father" is written as a nomen sacrum (sacred name) in two early MSS ($\mathfrak{P}^{66}$ W), as well as L.

1:18a | the One and Only, who is God.
This is a translation of *monogenēs theos,* supported by the earliest and best MSS ($\mathfrak{P}^{66}$ $\mathfrak{P}^{75}$ ℵ B C*), as well as L 33. Later MSS read *monogenēs huios* (one and only Son): A C^{3} [ninth century] W^{s} [seventh century] Θ Ψ f^{1,13} Maj. The two early papyri ($\mathfrak{P}^{66}$ and $\mathfrak{P}^{75}$), the earliest uncials (ℵ B C*) and some early versions (Coptic and Syriac) support the word *theos* (God), and many church fathers (Irenaeus, Clement, Origen, Eusebius, Serapion, Basil, Didymus, Gregory-Nyssa, Epiphanius, Valentinians) knew of this reading. The variant reading *huios* (Son) was known by many early church fathers (Irenaeus, Clement, Hippolytus, Alexander, Eusebius, Eustathius, Serapion, Julian, Basil, and Gregory-Nazianzus) and translated in some early versions (Old Latin and Syriac). However, the discovery of two second-century papyri, $\mathfrak{P}^{66}$ and $\mathfrak{P}^{75}$, both of which read *theos,* tipped the balance. It is now clear that *monogenēs theos* is the earlier reading—and the preferred reading. This was changed, as early as the beginning of the third century—if not earlier, to the more ordinary reading, *monogenēs huios* (the one and only Son). The phrase "one and only God" is very suitable for the closing verse of the prologue, in which Christ has been called "God" (1:1) and "an only One" (1:14), and finally, "one and only God," which combines the two titles into one. This is a masterful way of concluding the prologue, for 1:18 then mirrors 1:1. Both verses have the following three corresponding phrases: (1) Christ as God's expression (the "Word" and "he has explained him"), (2) Christ as God ("the Word was God" and "the one and only God"), and (3) as the one close to God ("the Word was with God" and "is near to the Father's heart").

1:18b | in the bosom of the Father

The divine "Father" is written as a nomen sacrum (sacred name) in two early MSS ($\mathfrak{P}^{66}$ W), as well as L.

1:27 | I am not worthy to untie his sandals.

This is the original wording according to early and diverse MSS: $\mathfrak{P}^{119vid}$ $\mathfrak{P}^{120}$ ℵ B C D L T Maj. $\mathfrak{P}^{66}$ and $\mathfrak{P}^{75}$ read "qualified" instead of "worthy" by way of scribal conformity to Matt. 3:12 and Mark 1:7, parallel verses.

1:32 | I saw the Spirit descending like a dove.

The divine "Spirit" is written as a nomen sacrum (sacred name) in early MSS ($\mathfrak{P}^{66}$ $\mathfrak{P}^{75}$ ℵ W), as well as $\mathfrak{P}^{55}$ L.

1:33 | Spirit . . . the Holy Spirit.

The divine "Spirit" is written as a nomen sacrum (sacred name) in early and diverse MSS: $\mathfrak{P}^{5}$ $\mathfrak{P}^{55vid}$ (both in second occurrences) $\mathfrak{P}^{66}$ $\mathfrak{P}^{75}$ ℵ L W.

1:34 | the chosen One of God.

This is probably the original wording according to early and diverse testimony: $\mathfrak{P}^{5vid}$ $\mathfrak{P}^{106vid}$ ℵ* it^{e} syr^{c,s}. A variant reading is "the Son of God," also in early and diverse MSS: $\mathfrak{P}^{66}$ $\mathfrak{P}^{75}$ $\mathfrak{P}^{120}$ ℵ^{2} [seventh century] A B C W Δ 083. Both readings have early and diverse manuscript support, and either could be original. (See Comfort and Barrett, *Text of Earliest NT Greek MSS*, 75 and 646, for transcriptions of $\mathfrak{P}^{5}$ and $\mathfrak{P}^{109}$ respectively.) The title "chosen One of God" is more unusual and therefore could be the one John originally wrote, which was then changed to the more usual title "Son of God"; but we cannot be certain in light of the documentary evidence. Therefore, this is a case where either reading could be original.

1:49 | you are the Son of God.

"Son of God" is written as a nomen sacrum (sacred name) in several early MSS ($\mathfrak{P}^{66}$ $\mathfrak{P}^{75}$ ℵ B W), as well as L. Nathanael was calling Jesus *the* divine Son of God, not just a son of God.

1:51 | the Son of Man.
"Son of Man," a messianic title (Dan. 7:13–14), is written as a nomen sacrum (sacred name) in four early MSS ($\mathfrak{P}^{66}$ $\mathfrak{P}^{75}$ ℵ W), as well as L. See Gen. 28:10–17.

2:15 | a kind of whip of cords.
This is the original reading according to the two earliest MSS ($\mathfrak{P}^{66}$ $\mathfrak{P}^{75}$). A variant reading is "a whip of cords" in ℵ A B Θ Ψ Maj.

2:16 | my Father's house.
The divine "Father" is written as a nomen sacrum (sacred name) in two early MSS ($\mathfrak{P}^{75}$ W), as well as L.

3:5 | born of water and Spirit.
The divine "Spirit" is written as nomen sacrum (sacred name) in four early MSS ($\mathfrak{P}^{66}$ $\mathfrak{P}^{75}$ ℵ W). Jesus was speaking of a spiritual rebirth enacted by the divine Spirit.

3:6 | that which is born of the Spirit is spirit.
The word *pneuma* appears twice—once referring to the divine Spirit and the other referring to the human spirit. In English, translators can distinguish between the divine Spirit and the human spirit (or any other kind of spirit) by capitalizing the former. Seemingly, there was no way this could be done in Greek MSS because all the words were written in capital letters. However, scribes could take advantage of a system known to early scribes of using special contractions for nomina sacra to display their own interpretation. Normally, they wrote the nomen sacrum form for *pneuma.* However, they could choose to write out the word *pneuma* in full (in *plene*) to indicate the human spirit. For example, in this verse the copyist of $\mathfrak{P}^{66}$ distinguished the divine Spirit from the human spirit by making the first word a nomen sacrum (sacred name) and by writing out (in *plene*) the second—thereby indicating that the divine Spirit is that which generates and the human spirit is that which is generated.

3:8 | The wind blows wherever it wills, and you hear the sound of it, but do not know where it comes from or where it is going. So it is with everyone born of the Spirit.

The poetic quality of this verse is found in the use of the Greek word *pneuma* (and the verbal form *pnei*) to connote several ideas in one: wind, breath, human spirit, and the divine Spirit. The person's spirit who is quickened by God's Spirit takes on the quality of being like the wind—thus, "those born of the Spirit are wind." An invisible presence, *pneuma*, like wind, is no less real; it can be seen in its influence. The first occurrence of *pneuma* (wind) is written in full (in *plene*; i.e., not written as a sacred name) in 𝔓^{66*} (for details, see Comfort and Barrett, *Text of Earliest NT Greek MSS*, 395); the second occurrence of *pneuma* is written as a nomen sacrum (a sacred name, "Spirit") in 𝔓^{66} 𝔓^{75} ℵ W.

3:13 | No one has ascended into heaven except the one who descended from heaven—the Son of Man.

"The Son of Man" is the original wording according to 𝔓^{66} 𝔓^{75} ℵ B L W^{s} [seventh century] 083 086 cop Diatessaron. This is expanded to "the Son of Man who lives in heaven" in (A*) Θ Ψ 050 f^{1,13} Maj. The shorter reading was also known to many church fathers, such as Origen, Didymus, and Jerome. The longer reading appears in some later Greek MSS, was known to many early church fathers (Hippolytus, Origen, Dionysius, Hesychius, Hilary, Lucifer, Jerome, Augustine), and was translated in some early versions (primarily Old Latin and Syriac). From a documentary perspective, the shorter reading is more trustworthy. "Son of Man," a messianic title (Dan. 7:13–14), is written as a nomen sacrum (sacred name) in several early MSS (𝔓^{66} 𝔓^{75} ℵ W), as well as L.

3:14 | the Son of Man must be lifted up.

"Son of Man," a messianic title (Dan. 7:13–14), is written as a nomen sacrum (sacred name) in several early MSS (𝔓^{66} 𝔓^{75} ℵ W), as well as L.

3:15 | everyone who believes will have eternal life in him.

This is the original wording according to the two earliest MSS (𝔓^{75}

B), as well as T W^{s} [seventh century] 083. Two variants on this are "everyone who believes in him will have eternal life" in 086 ℵ f^{1,13} Maj (so KJV), and "everyone who believes on him will have eternal life" in $\mathfrak{P}^{63}$ A. The text, with early documentary support, is the more unusual reading.

3:16 | he gave his one and only Son.
The divine "Son" is written as a nomen sacrum (sacred name) in three early MSS ($\mathfrak{P}^{66}$ ℵ W), as well as L.

3:17 | God did not send his Son into the world to condemn the world.
The divine "Son" is written as a nomen sacrum (sacred name) in two early MSS ($\mathfrak{P}^{66}$ W), as well as L.

3:18 | the one and only Son of God.
The divine "Son" is written as a nomen sacrum (sacred name) in three early MSS ($\mathfrak{P}^{66c}$ $\mathfrak{P}^{75}$ W), as well as L.

3:25 | a dispute between some of John's disciples and a Jew.
This is the original wording according to early and diverse testimony: $\mathfrak{P}^{75}$ ℵ^{2} [seventh century] A B L W^{s} [seventh century] D Ψ 070 086. The final word is "Jews" in $\mathfrak{P}^{66}$ ℵ* Θ f^{1,13} it^{e}. The text has superior documentation.

3:31 | the one who comes from heaven is superior to everyone.
This is the wording in $\mathfrak{P}^{36vid}$ $\mathfrak{P}^{66}$ ℵ^{2} A B L W^{s} [seventh century] Θ Ψ 083 086 33 f^{13} Maj syr^{h,p,s} cop^{bo}. The phrase "is superior to everyone" is omitted in $\mathfrak{P}^{75}$ ℵ* D f^{1} it syr^{c}. The manuscript evidence for both readings is evenly split. The early papyri, $\mathfrak{P}^{66}$ and $\mathfrak{P}^{75}$, are divided, as are ℵ and B, and the ancient Syriac and Coptic versions; thus, they neutralize each other's testimony. Furthermore, good reasons could be given to defend why scribes would be tempted to add the words "is superior to everyone," as a repeat from the first part of the verse, or delete the words because they seemed redundant. Therefore, this is a case where either reading could be original.

3:34 | the One whom God sent speaks the words of God, for he pours out the immeasurable Spirit.
The earliest MSS (𝔓^{66} 𝔓^{75} 𝔓^{80vid} א) and B^{2} [tenth century] C* L W^{s} [seventh century] indicate it is the Son who gives the immeasurable Spirit. Other MSS, mainly later (A C^{2} [sixth century] D Maj), supply the subject, "God," yielding the sense that "God gives the immeasurable Spirit." The divine "Spirit" is written as a nomen sacrum (sacred name) in 𝔓^{66} 𝔓^{75} א B^{c} D W.

3:35 | The Father loves his Son.
The divine "Father" is written as a nomen sacrum (sacred name) in two early MSS (𝔓^{66} W), as well as L. The divine "Son" is written as a nomen sacrum (sacred name) in three early MSS (𝔓^{66} א W), as well as L.

3:36 | the Son.
The divine "Son" is written (both times) as a nomen sacrum (sacred name) in four early MSS (𝔓^{66} 𝔓^{75} א W), as well as L.

4:1 | Jesus knew.
This is the original wording according to the testimony of three early MSS (𝔓^{66*} א D), as well as Θ 086 f^{1}. The variant reading is "the Lord knew" in 𝔓^{66c2} 𝔓^{75} A B C L W^{s} [seventh century] 083 f^{13} Maj. Most likely "Jesus" was changed to "Lord" because the literal wording is awkward: "Jesus knew the Pharisees had heard that Jesus was baptizing." The repetition of "Jesus" was avoided by changing the first occurrence to "Lord." The scribe of 𝔓^{66} wrote the first noun as "Jesus," which was then changed by a corrector to "Lord." This took only two pen strokes (an *iota* changed to a *kappa*) in the Greek because the nomen sacrum for "Jesus" is written as $\overline{\text{IC}}$, whereas the nomen sacrum for "Lord" is written as $\overline{\text{KC}}$.

4:9 | Jews use nothing in common with Samaritans.
This sentence is found in 𝔓^{63} 𝔓^{66} 𝔓^{75} 𝔓^{76} א^{1} A B C L W^{s} [seventh century] Δ Θ Ψ 083 086 33 f^{1,13}. It is omitted in א* D it^{a,b,e,j} cop^{fay}. The textual evidence strongly affirms the inclusion of the sentence.

4:21 | worship the Father.
The divine "Father" is written as a nomen sacrum (sacred name) in four early MSS ($\mathfrak{P}^{66}$ $\mathfrak{P}^{75}$ D W), as well as L.

4:23 | the Father.
The divine "Father" is written as a nomen sacrum (sacred name) in both occurrences in three early MSS ($\mathfrak{P}^{66}$ $\mathfrak{P}^{75}$ W), as well as L.

4:23–24 the Spirit.
The divine "Spirit" is written as a nomen sacrum (sacred name) in all three occurrences in five early MSS ($\mathfrak{P}^{66}$ $\mathfrak{P}^{75}$ ℵ D W).

4:42 | this one is the Savior.
This is the original wording according to early, excellent testimony: $\mathfrak{P}^{66}$ $\mathfrak{P}^{75}$ ℵ B C* W^s [seventh century]. This is worded as "this is the Savior, the Christ" in A C^3 [ninth century] D L Θ Ψ $f^{1,13}$ 33 Maj (so KJV), by way of scribal expansion.

4:49 | Lord, come down before my child dies.
"Lord" is written as a nomen sacrum (sacred name) in early MSS ($\mathfrak{P}^{66}$ $\mathfrak{P}^{75}$ ℵ B D), showing these scribes had the royal official address Jesus as the divine Lord.

5:2 | a pool called Bethsaida.
The original wording is Bethsaida (meaning "house of fish") according to three early MSS ($\mathfrak{P}^{66c}$ $\mathfrak{P}^{75}$ B), and W^s [seventh century]. The name is changed to "Beth-zatha" (meaning "house of mercy") in ℵ (L it^e) 33, and "Bethesda" (also meaning "house of mercy") in A C Θ 078 $f^{1,13}$ Maj.

5:3–4 | omit verses.
The earliest MSS ($\mathfrak{P}^{66}$ $\mathfrak{P}^{75}$ ℵ B) and other MSS (A* C* L T cop) do not include 5:3b–4. Other MSS (A^c C^3 [ninth century] Θ Ψ 078^{vid} Maj it) add 5:3b–4, "waiting for a certain movement of the water, [4]for an angel of the Lord came from time to time and stirred up the water. And the first person to step in after the water was stirred was healed of whatever

disease he had." These words were added by later scribes to help explain why the water bubbled up (5:7).

5:17b-23, 26, 30, 36, 43 | Father.
The divine "Father" is written as a nomen sacrum (sacred name) in some early MSS ($\mathfrak{P}^{66}$ W; once in $\mathfrak{P}^{75}$ in 5:43), as well as L.

5:19–23, 25–26 | Son.
The divine "Son" is written as a nomen sacrum (sacred name) in some early MSS ($\mathfrak{P}^{66}$ א; twice in $\mathfrak{P}^{75}$ in 5:19), as well as L.

5:27 | he is the Son of Man.
"Son of Man," a messianic title (Dan. 7:13–14), is written as a nomen sacrum (sacred name) in four early MSS ($\mathfrak{P}^{66}$ $\mathfrak{P}^{75}$ א W), as well as L.

5:44 | glory of the One and Only.
In Greek, "the One and Only" is *tou monou,* supported by the three earliest MSS ($\mathfrak{P}^{66}$ $\mathfrak{P}^{75}$ B) and W^s [seventh century]. This is worded as "the one and only God" in $\mathfrak{P}^{63vid}$ א A D L Δ Θ Ψ 0210^{vid} $f^{1,13}$ 33 Maj it^e syr. The text, which has early documentation, was expanded by adding "God." The title *tou Monou* is titular in and of itself; it expresses the one who is "the One and Only." Of course, this is God, but "God" doesn't need to be added for the title to make sense.

6:27a | the Son of Man.
"Son of Man," a messianic title (Dan. 7:13–14), is written as a nomen sacrum (sacred name) in two early MSS ($\mathfrak{P}^{75}$ W), as well as L.

6:27b, 37, 40, 44–46, 57 | Father.
The divine "Father" is written as a nomen sacrum (sacred name) in some early MSS ($\mathfrak{P}^{66}$ W; in $\mathfrak{P}^{75}$ in 6:45–46), as well as L.

6:40 | everyone who looks on the Son and believes in him has eternal life.
The divine "Son" is written as a nomen sacrum (sacred name) in some early MSS ($\mathfrak{P}^{66}$ א C), as well as L.

6:42a | Jesus the son of Joseph.

The word "son" is written in full (in *plene*; i.e., not written as a sacred name) in $\mathfrak{P}^{66}$ $\mathfrak{P}^{75}$ B, pointing to one who is a son (not a divine title). This is significant; it indicates that Jesus did not receive his divine Sonship from Joseph.

6:42b | whose father and mother we know.

The words "and mother" are included in $\mathfrak{P}^{66}$ $\mathfrak{P}^{75}$ $\aleph^{c}$ A B D L Maj; they are omitted in ℵ* W. The text has superior documentation.

6:53 | eat the flesh of the Son of Man.

"Son of Man," a messianic title (Dan. 7:13–14), is written as a nomen sacrum (sacred name) in three early MSS ($\mathfrak{P}^{75}$ ℵ W), as well as L.

6:62 | the Son of Man ascending.

"Son of Man," a messianic title (Dan. 7:13–14), is written as a nomen sacrum (sacred name) in four early MSS ($\mathfrak{P}^{66}$ $\mathfrak{P}^{75}$ ℵ W), as well as L.

6:63a | the Spirit is the life-giver.

The scribe of $\mathfrak{P}^{66}$ first began to write out the word *pneuma* in full (in *plene*; i.e., not as a sacred name), which would be translated "spirit" (the spirit is the life-giver), then he changed it to the nomen sacrum (the divine "Spirit"), which yields the translation, "the Spirit is the life-giver." "Spirit" is written as a nomen sacrum (sacred name) also in three early MSS ($\mathfrak{P}^{75}$ ℵ W), as well as L.

6:63b | the words I speak to you are Spirit and life.

"Spirit" is written as a nomen sacrum (sacred name) in four early MSS ($\mathfrak{P}^{66}$ $\mathfrak{P}^{75}$ ℵ W), as well as L. Codex B writes out the word in full (in *plene*; i.e., not as a sacred name), yielding the translation, "the words I speak to you are spirit and life"—a translation reflected in most English translations.

6:69 | you are the Holy One of God.

This is the original wording according to most of the earliest MSS ($\mathfrak{P}^{75}$

ℵ B C* D W). Two significant variant readings are "you are the Christ, the Holy One of God" ($\mathfrak{P}^{66}$ cop) and "you are the Christ, the Son of the living God" (Θ^{c} Ψ 0250 f^{13} syr Maj). The reading of the text is superior to the other variant readings because of its excellent documentary support and because the other variant readings are obvious assimilations to Matt. 16:16 ("the Christ, the Son of the living God") or some derivation thereof.

7:8 | I am not yet going to this festival.

This is the wording according to several early MSS ($\mathfrak{P}^{66}$ $\mathfrak{P}^{75}$ B T W), as well as L Θ Ψ 070 0105 0250 $f^{1,13}$ Maj syr^{h,p} cop^{sa,ac2}. A different reading is, "I am not going to this festival" in ℵ D it syr^{c,s} cop^{bo}. The textual decision is difficult here because the reading of the text has superior documentary support, while the variant is the more difficult reading (Jesus eventually went to this festival) and therefore a candidate for being the original wording.

7:34 | they will seek me and not find me.

This is the reading in three early MSS ($\mathfrak{P}^{75}$ B T), as well as N 0105. A variant reading is, "they will seek me and not find" in four early MSS ($\mathfrak{P}^{66}$ ℵ D W), as well as Θ Ψ $f^{1,13}$ 33 Maj. The textual evidence is evenly split; either reading could be original.

7:39a | He said this about the Spirit.

The divine "Spirit" is written as a nomen sacrum (sacred name) in five early MSS ($\mathfrak{P}^{66}$ $\mathfrak{P}^{75}$ ℵ D W), as well as L.

7:39b | as yet there was no Spirit.

This is the original wording according to four early MSS ($\mathfrak{P}^{66c}$ $\mathfrak{P}^{75}$ ℵ T), as well as Θ Ψ. A variant reading is "as yet there was no Holy Spirit" in $\mathfrak{P}^{66*}$ L W 0105 $f^{1,13}$ 33 Maj. Another variant is "the Spirit had not yet been given" in it^{a,aur,b,c} sy^{c,s,p}. The verb "given" was added by ancient translators (Old Latin and Syriac) to complete the sense. The idea in the Greek is that the Spirit of Jesus was not available to believers until after Jesus had been glorified through death and resurrection. "Spirit" is written as a nomen sacrum (sacred name) in $\mathfrak{P}^{66}$ $\mathfrak{P}^{75}$ ℵ D L W Maj.

7:52 | the prophet does not arise from Galilee.
This is the wording in $\mathfrak{P}^{66*}$ $\mathfrak{P}^{75\text{vid?}}$. A variant reading is, "no prophet arises from Galilee" in $\mathfrak{P}^{66c}$ ℵ B C D Maj. One early manuscript ($\mathfrak{P}^{66*}$) and perhaps another ($\mathfrak{P}^{75\text{vid?}}$—see discussion in Comfort, *NT Text and Translation Commentary*, 285) read "the prophet"—that is, the messianic Prophet predicted by Moses (see Deut. 18:15, 18; John 1:21). The rest of the MSS support the Pharisees saying that "no prophet arises in Galilee." (See next note for further discussion on this.)

7:53–8:11 | omit verses.
The most ancient Greek MSS and other MSS do not include John 7:53–8:11, namely $\mathfrak{P}^{39\text{vid}}$ $\mathfrak{P}^{66}$ $\mathfrak{P}^{75}$ ℵ A^{vid} B C^{vid} L N T W D Θ Ψ 0141 0211 33 565 it$^{\text{a,f}}$ syr$^{\text{c,s,p}}$ cop$^{\text{sa,bo,ach2}}$ geo. Its omission is also attested to by the Diatessaron Origen Chrysostom Cyril Tertullian Cyprian MSS$^{\text{acording to Augustine}}$ MSS$^{\text{according to Jerome}}$. The passage is found in later MSS (with various verse lengths) and in different positions in the Gospels: D (F) G H K M U Γ it$^{\text{aur,c,d,e}}$ syr$^{\text{h,pal}}$ cop^{boMSS} Maj MSS$^{\text{according to Didymus}}$ 7:53–8:11; E 8:2–11 with asterisks; Λ 8:3–11 with asterisks; f^{1} after John 21:25; f^{13} after Luke 21:38 (see note there); 1333c 8:3–11 after Luke 24:53; 225 after John 7:36. The passage, which is clearly a later addition, came from an oral tradition. It does not belong in John's Gospel as part of the original text. (It is printed as an appendix in this book.)

The reader is encouraged to read from John 7:52 to 8:12 as a continuous narrative. John 8:12ff. contains Jesus's rebuttal to the Pharisees who had boldly told Nicodemus that the Scriptures make no mention of the prophet (or even a prophet—see previous note), much less the Christ, being raised up in Galilee (7:52). With respect to this assertion, Jesus made a declaration in which he implied that the Scriptures did speak of the Christ coming from Galilee. He said, "I am the light of the world; he who follows me will not walk in darkness, but will have the light of life." This statement was probably drawn from Isa. 9:1–2: "But there will be no more gloom for her who was in anguish; in earlier times he treated the land of Zebulun and the land of Naphtali with contempt, but later on he will make it glorious, by the way of the sea, on the other side of the Jordan, Galilee of the Gentiles. The people who walk in darkness will see a great light, and the light will shine on those who live in the shadow of death." Both passages contain parallel images. Both Isa. 9:2 and John 8:12 speak about the Messiah coming as the light among those who are walking in darkness and sitting under the shadow of death to give them the light of life.

8:16 | the Father who sent me.

This is the original wording according to several MSS ($\mathfrak{P}^{39}$ $\mathfrak{P}^{66}$ $\mathfrak{P}^{75}$ $\aleph^{c}$ B T W). A variant reading is "the One who sent me" in $\aleph^{*}$ D. The divine "Father" is written as a nomen sacrum (sacred name) in $\mathfrak{P}^{39}$ $\mathfrak{P}^{66}$ L W.

8:18 | the Father who sent me.

The divine "Father" is written as a nomen sacrum (sacred name) in three early MSS ($\mathfrak{P}^{39}$ $\mathfrak{P}^{66}$ W), as well as L.

8:19a | They asked him, "who is your father?"

The name "father" is written in full (in *plene*; i.e., not written as a sacred name) in three early MSS ($\mathfrak{P}^{75}$ $\aleph$ B). The Pharisees wanted to know who Jesus's earthly father was.

8:19b | my Father.

The divine "Father" is written (in both occurrences) as a nomen sacrum (sacred name) in two early MSS ($\mathfrak{P}^{66}$ W), as well as L. Jesus identified his "Father" as being the divine "Father," whom the Pharisees didn't know.

8:25 | I am that which I have told you.

Ancient Greek MSS did not leave any spaces between words; therefore, it is difficult to determine if the text is to be read as O TI ("that which"—lit. "I am that which I've said to you") or OTI ("why"—"why do I speak to you?"). Either reading is viable.

8:27–28 | Father.

The divine "Father" is written in both occurrences as nomina sacra (sacred names) in two early MSS ($\mathfrak{P}^{66}$ W), as well as L.

8:28 | when you lift up the Son of Man.
"Son of Man," a messianic title, is written as a nomen sacrum (sacred name) in three early MSS (𝔓[75] א W), as well as L.

8:36 | if the Son sets you free.
The divine "Son" is written as a nomen sacrum (sacred name) in three early MSS (𝔓[66] 𝔓[75] א), as well as L.

8:38 | I am telling you the things I have seen while with the Father; you should practice the things you have heard from the Father.
The divine "Father" is written in both occurrences as nomina sacra (sacred names) in the early MS, 𝔓[66]. The verb "have heard" is found in 𝔓[75] א[c] B C. It is "have seen" in 𝔓[66] א* 070 0250. Both readings have early documentary support; either could be original.

8:39 | if you were really the children of Abraham, you would be doing what he did.
This is the wording in early MSS (𝔓[75] א B[2] [tenth century] D W), as well as Γ Θ 070 0250. Another reading is "if you are really the children of Abraham, do what he did" in two early MSS (𝔓[66] B*). Both readings have early documentary support; either could be original.

8:41–42 | Father.
The divine "Father" is written as a nomen sacrum (sacred name) in two early MSS (𝔓[66] W), as well as L.

8:44 | your father the devil . . . the father of lies.
The scribe of 𝔓[75] wrote out "father" in full (in *plene*; i.e., not as a sacred name) in both occurrences because this "father," the devil, is not divine.

8:49, 54 | my Father.
The divine "Father" is written as a nomen sacrum (sacred name) in two early MSS (𝔓[66] W), as well as L.

8:57 | How can you say Abraham has seen you?

This is the wording in two early MSS (𝔓^{75} ℵ*), as well as 070 syr^{s} cop$^{sa, ach2}$. A variant reading is, “How can you say you have seen Abraham?” in some early MSS (𝔓^{66} ℵ^{2} [seventh century] A B C D W), as well as Δ (Θ) Ψ f^{1,13} it syr^{p,h,pal}. Both readings have early documentary support; either could be original. Either way, the message is the same: the leaders were arguing that Abraham and Jesus could not have seen each other because they were not contemporaries. In the next verse, Jesus claims that he predated Abraham: “before Abraham was even born, I have always been alive.”

9:4 | we must carry out the tasks assigned us by the one who sent us.

This is the original wording according to four early MSS (𝔓^{66} 𝔓^{75} ℵ* W), as well as L. Two variant readings are “I must carry out the tasks assigned me by the one who sent me” in ℵ^{c} A C, and “we must carry out the tasks assigned us by the one who sent me” in B D. The text, which has the earliest documentation, indicates that Jesus included his disciples as co-sent ones.

9:35 | “Do you believe in the Son of Man?”

This is the original wording according to the earliest MSS (𝔓^{66} 𝔓^{75} ℵ B D W), as well as it^{d} syr^{s} cop. A variant reading is “Do you believe in the Son of God?” in A L Θ Ψ 070 0250 f^{1,13} Maj syr^{p,h}(so KJV). The manuscript support for the text is impressive. It is far more likely that “man” was changed to “God” than vice versa. Later in history, the church sought confession of Jesus’s divine sonship—hence, the change from “the Son of Man” to “the Son of God” in later MSS. “Son of Man,” a messianic title, is a title Jesus used for himself; it has royal and messianic implications (see Dan. 7:13–14). It is written as a nomen sacrum (sacred name) in three early MSS (𝔓^{66} 𝔓^{75} ℵ), as well as L.

9:38–39a | omit verses.

Three early MSS (𝔓^{75} ℵ* W) and it^{b} cop$^{ach2, saMS}$ do not include 9:38–39a. Other MSS read: ^{38}“Yes, Lord, I believe!” the man said. And he worshiped Jesus. ^{39}Then Jesus told him” (𝔓^{66} ℵ^{2} [seventh century] A B

D L Δ Θ Ψ Maj). Though the manuscript evidence is evenly divided, the additional words probably came from early baptismal liturgy in which the person being baptized confesses, "Lord, I believe." (For more on this, see Comfort, *NT Text and Translation Commentary*, 293–294).

10:8 | all who came were thieves and robbers.

This is the original wording according to three early MSS (𝔓^{45vid} 𝔓^{75} ℵ*), as well as Γ Δ Maj it syr^{p,s} cop. A variant reading is "all who came before I did were thieves and robbers" in 𝔓^{66} ℵ^{2} [seventh century] A B D L W Ψ f^{1,13} 33 syr^{h**}. The words "before I did" were added to give the statement better sense. But implicit in the words "all who came" is the idea of claiming to be the Messiah-shepherd.

10:15, 17 | the Father.

The divine "Father" is written as a nomen sacrum (sacred name) in two early MSS (𝔓^{66} W), as well as L.

10:26 | you are not my sheep.

This is the original wording in several early MSS (𝔓^{66}c 𝔓^{75} ℵ B W), as well as L Θ 33. A variant reading is, "you are not my sheep, as I said to you" in 𝔓^{66*} A D Ψ f^{1,13} Maj, by way of scribal expansion.

10:29 | my Father who has given them to me is more powerful than anyone.

This is the original wording in the two earliest MSS (𝔓^{66} 𝔓^{75vid}), as well as f^{1,13} 33 Maj. Two variant readings are "what my Father has given me is more powerful than anything" in B* it cop^{bo}, and "regarding that which my Father has given me, he is greater than all" in ℵ (D) L W. The text has the earliest documentation. The divine "Father" is written as a nomen sacrum (sacred name) in three early MSS (𝔓^{66} A W), as well as L.

10:30, 32 | the Father.

The divine "Father" is written as a nomen sacrum (sacred name) in two early MSS (𝔓^{66} W), as well as L.

10:36a | the Father.

The divine "Father" is written as a nomen sacrum (sacred name) in three early MSS ($\mathfrak{P}^{45}$ $\mathfrak{P}^{66}$ W), as well as L.

10:36b | I am the Son of God.

"Son of God" is written as a nomen sacrum (sacred name) in all the earliest MSS ($\mathfrak{P}^{45}$ $\mathfrak{P}^{66}$ $\mathfrak{P}^{75}$ א B D W), as well as L. Jesus was not claiming to be a son of God; he was claiming to be *the* unique Son of God.

10:37–38 Father.

The divine "Father" is written as a nomen sacrum (sacred name) in three early MSS ($\mathfrak{P}^{45}$ $\mathfrak{P}^{66}$ W), as well as L.

11:4 | so that the Son of God might be glorified.

"Son of God" is written as a nomen sacrum (sacred name) in several early MSS ($\mathfrak{P}^{45}$ $\mathfrak{P}^{75}$ א B D W), as well as L.

11:25 | I am the resurrection and the life.

This is the original wording according to most of the early MSS ($\mathfrak{P}^{66}$ $\mathfrak{P}^{75}$ א A B C D W), as well as L Δ Θ 0250 $f^{1,13}$ 33 cop. A variant reading is "I am the resurrection" in $\mathfrak{P}^{45}$ it^{l} syr^{s}. The text is strongly supported; the scribe of $\mathfrak{P}^{45}$ is known for frequently shortening the text.

11:27 | you are the Christ, the Son of God.

"Christ" is written as a nomen sacrum (sacred name) in all MSS. "Son of God" is written as a nomen sacrum (sacred name) in the earliest MSS ($\mathfrak{P}^{45}$ $\mathfrak{P}^{75}$ א B D W), as well as L.

11:33 | he was agitated in Spirit.

"Spirit" is written as a nomen sacrum (sacred name) in several early MSS ($\mathfrak{P}^{45vid}$ $\mathfrak{P}^{66}$ $\mathfrak{P}^{75vid}$ א W), as well as L. These scribes considered the spirit/Spirit of Jesus to be divine. In codex B, *pneuma* is written in full (in *plene*; i.e., not written as a sacred name), suggesting this scribe was thinking of Jesus's human spirit.

11:41 | "Father, I thank you."
The divine "Father" is written as a nomen sacrum (sacred name) in one early MS ($\mathfrak{P}^{66}$) and L.

12:1 | Bethany, where Lazarus lived.
This is the original wording according to several early MSS ($\mathfrak{P}^{75}$ ℵ B D W). There is a scribal expansion to "Lazarus who had died" in $\mathfrak{P}^{66}$ A D Θ Ψ 0217^{vid} 0250 $f^{1,13}$ 33 Maj.

12:23 | The hour has come for the Son of Man to be glorified.
"Son of Man," a messianic title (Dan. 7:13–14), is written as a nomen sacrum (sacred name) in three early MSS ($\mathfrak{P}^{66}$ $\mathfrak{P}^{75}$ W), as well as L.

12:27–28 | Father.
The divine "Father" is written as a nomen sacrum (sacred name) in two early MSS ($\mathfrak{P}^{66}$ W), as well as L.

12:34 | Who is this Son of Man?
This is the original wording according to early and excellent testimony: $\mathfrak{P}^{66}$ ℵ A B D L W. The sentence is omitted in $\mathfrak{P}^{75}$. The phrase "Son of Man," a messianic title (Dan. 7:13–14), is written (in both occurrences) as a nomen sacrum (sacred name) in early MSS ($\mathfrak{P}^{66}$ ℵ W), as well as L.

12:41 | because he saw his glory.
This is the wording in the earliest MSS ($\mathfrak{P}^{66}$ $\mathfrak{P}^{75}$ ℵ A B), as well as L Θ Ψ 33. A variant on this is, "when he saw his glory" in D f^{13} Maj (so KJV). The reading of the text, which has the best documentary support, is the one John wrote. Isaiah had seen the Lord of glory, and *because* of his vision Isaiah predicted the blindness to come (see Isa. 6:1–10). Later scribes obfuscated the causal (*oti* = because) by using the temporal (*ote* = when), which makes for an easier reading needing little explanation.

12:49–50 | the Father.
The divine "Father" is written as a nomen sacrum (sacred name) in two early MSS ($\mathfrak{P}^{66}$ W), as well as L.

13:1 | the Father.
The divine "Father" is written as a nomen sacrum (sacred name) in three early MSS ($\mathfrak{P}^{66}$ A W), as well as L.

13:2 | the devil already had it in his heart.
This is the original wording according to $\mathfrak{P}^{66}$ $\aleph^{2}$ [seventh century] B L W Ψ 070. Other MSS (A Θ $f^{1,13}$ 33 Maj) read "the devil had already put it into the heart [of Judas]." The original wording indicates that the devil purposed the betrayal; then Judas carried it out.

13:3 | the Father had handed all things over to him.
The divine "Father" is written as a nomen sacrum (sacred name) in three early MSS ($\mathfrak{P}^{66}$ A W), as well as L.

13:10 | he needs only to wash his feet.
This is the original wording according to early and excellent testimony: $\mathfrak{P}^{66}$ B C* (L) W f^{13} $syr^{s,p}$. Another reading is nearly the same: "he has no other need than to wash his feet" ($\mathfrak{P}^{75}$ A C^{3} [ninth century] D Maj). And the statement is omitted in ℵ and Origen. The documentary evidence supports the inclusion of the mention of the foot washing. Jesus was speaking of two kinds of bathing—the first, a bath of the whole body and the second, a foot washing.

13:16 | a servant is not greater than his lord/master.
The word for "lord" or "master" is written in full (in *plene*; i.e., not as a sacred name) in $\mathfrak{P}^{93}$ because the reference here is to a generic master, not the Lord Jesus Christ.

13:21 | Jesus was greatly distressed in his Spirit.
"Spirit" is written as a nomen sacrum (sacred name) in four early MSS ($\mathfrak{P}^{66}$ ℵ D W), as well as L. These scribes considered the Spirit/spirit

of Jesus to be divine. B writes out the word in full (in *plene*; i.e., not as a sacred name), suggesting Jesus's human spirit, which is the way it is translated in most English versions.

13:31 | the Son of Man is glorified.
"Son of Man," a messianic title (Dan. 7:13–14), is written as a nomen sacrum (sacred name) in two early MSS ($\mathfrak{P}^{66}$ W), as well as L.

13:32 | God has been glorified in him.
This is the original wording according to early and excellent testimony: $\mathfrak{P}^{66}$ א* B C* D L W syr^{s,h} cop^{ach}. Another reading is, "God has been glorified in him, and if God has been glorified in him" in א^{2} [seventh century] A C^{2} [sixth century] Θ Ψ 0233 f^{13} Maj it syr^{p} cop^{sa}, by way of scribal expansion.

14:2, 6 | Father.
The divine "Father" is written as a nomen sacrum (sacred name) in two early MSS ($\mathfrak{P}^{66}$ W), as well as L.

14:7 | If you have really known me, you will know my Father.
This is the wording in four early MSS ($\mathfrak{P}^{66}$ א D* W). An alternative wording is "if you had really known me, you would have known my Father" in four early MSS (A B C D^{1}), as well as L Θ Ψ f^{1,13} Maj (so KJV). The documentary evidence is evenly divided. Scribes opted for verbs that presented a promise of future knowledge (as in the reading of the text) or that presented a reproof (as in the variant reading). The divine "Father" is written as nomen sacrum (sacred name) in three early MSS ($\mathfrak{P}^{66}$ Θ W), as well as L.

14:8–10 the Father.
The divine "Father" is written as a nomen sacrum (sacred name) in three early MSS ($\mathfrak{P}^{66}$ Θ W), as well as L.

14:11 | the Father.
The divine "Father" is written as a nomen sacrum (sacred name) in four early MSS ($\mathfrak{P}^{66}$ $\mathfrak{P}^{75}$ Θ W), as well as L.

14:12–13 | the Father.
The divine "Father" is written as a nomen sacrum (sacred name) in three early MSS (𝔓[66] 𝔓[75] Θ), as well as L.

14:16 | I will ask the Father.
The divine "Father" is written as a nomen sacrum (sacred name) in three early MSS (𝔓[75] Θ W), as well as L.

14:17a | the Spirit of truth.
The divine "Spirit" is written as a nomen sacrum (sacred name) in five early MSS (𝔓[66] 𝔓[75] ℵ D W), as well as L.

14:17b | will be indwelling you.
This is the wording in five early MSS (𝔓[66c2] 𝔓[75] ℵ A D), as well as L. Another reading is, "is indwelling you" in four early MSS (𝔓[66*] B D* W). Both readings have substantial support. In context, Jesus was telling his disciples that he would send them the Spirit as the Paraclete, and Jesus added that they should know who "the Paraclete" is because "he abides with you and will be (or, is) in you." If the text originally had two present verbs, this statement could be understood to describe, proleptically, the twofold location of the Spirit in relationship to the believer. In other words, the Spirit is viewed in its future state as present *with and in* the believer. If the text originally had a present tense verb and a future tense verb (as in the text), then Jesus probably meant that the Spirit as present with Jesus (then and there) was *with* the disciples, and, in the future, would be *in* the disciples.

14:20 | I am in my Father.
The divine "Father" is written as a nomen sacrum (sacred name) in four early MSS (𝔓[66] 𝔓[75] Θ W), as well as L.

14:21 | will be loved by my Father.
The divine "Father" is written as a nomen sacrum (sacred name) in three early MSS (𝔓[66] Θ W), as well as L.

14:23–24 | Father.
The divine "Father" is written as a nomen sacrum (sacred name) in two early MSS (𝔓[66] W), as well as L.

14:26 | the Holy Spirit.
The divine "Spirit" is written as a nomen sacrum (sacred name) in three early MSS (𝔓[66] ℵ D), as well as L.

14:28 | the Father.
The divine "Father" is written in both occurrences as a nomen sacrum (sacred name) in two early MSS (𝔓[66vid] D), as well as L.

14:31 | the Father.
The divine "Father" is written in both occurrences as nomina sacra (sacred names) in one early MS (𝔓[66vid]), as well as L.

15:1 | my Father is the vinedresser.
The divine "Father" is written as a nomen sacrum (sacred name) in two early MSS (𝔓[66vid] D), as well as L.

15:8–10 | Father.
The divine "Father" is written as a nomen sacrum (sacred name) in one early MS (𝔓[66]), as well as L.

15:15–16 | Father.
The divine "Father" is written as a nomen sacrum (sacred name) in one early MS (𝔓[66vid]), as well as L.

15:20 | A servant is not greater than his Lord.
"Lord" (Greek *kurios*) is written as a nomen sacrum (sacred name) in two early MSS (𝔓[66] ℵ), but not in two other early MSS, B W (signaling a generic master), which would be rendered as "a servant is not greater than his lord/master."

15:23–24 | my Father.
The divine "Father" is written as a nomen sacrum (sacred name) in one early MS ($\mathfrak{P}^{66}$) and L.

15:25 | it is written in their law.
All MSS except one ($\mathfrak{P}^{66*}$) read "it is written in their law." The original scribe of $\mathfrak{P}^{66}$ wrote "it is written in the law." The scribe may have done this because he perceived Jesus naming the Scriptures as "their law" to be a pejorative statement, wherein Jesus was disassociating himself from the Jews and their Scriptures. Indeed, Jesus had previously used the same kind of language when he labeled the Scriptures as "your law" when speaking to the Jewish leaders (see 8:17 and 10:34 where other scribes deleted "your"). A second corrector added "their" before "law" (see Comfort and Barrett, *Text of Earliest NT Greek MSS*, 450).

15:26a | the Spirit of truth.
The divine "Spirit" is written as a nomen sacrum (sacred name) in two early MSS ($\mathfrak{P}^{22vid}$ $\mathfrak{P}^{66vid}$).

15:26b | who goes out from the Father.
The divine "Father" is written as a nomen sacrum (sacred name) in one early MS ($\mathfrak{P}^{22}$), as well as L.

16:3 | they have not known the Father or me.
The divine "Father" is written as a nomen sacrum (sacred name) in one early MS ($\mathfrak{P}^{66vid}$), as well as L.

16:10 | I am going to the Father.
The divine "Father" is written as a nomen sacrum (sacred name) in one early MS ($\mathfrak{P}^{66vid}$), as well as L.

16:13 | the Spirit of truth.
The divine "Spirit" is written as a nomen sacrum (sacred name) in four early MSS ($\mathfrak{P}^{66vid}$ א D W), as well as L.

16:15a | everything the Father has is mine.
The divine "Father" is written as a nomen sacrum (sacred name) in one early MS ($\mathfrak{P}^{5}$), as well as L.

16:15b
This entire verse is missing in one early MS ($\mathfrak{P}^{66}$), but is extant in three early MSS ($\mathfrak{P}^{5}$ ℵ B), as well as all other MSS.

16:17 | I am going to the Father.
The divine "Father" is written as a nomen sacrum (sacred name) in three early MSS ($\mathfrak{P}^{5}$ $\mathfrak{P}^{66}$ W), as well as L.

16:23 | whatever you ask the Father, he will give it to you in my Name.
This is the original wording according to four early MSS ($\mathfrak{P}^{5vid}$ ℵ B C*), as well as L. A variant reading is, "whatever you ask the Father in my Name, he will give it to you" in five early MSS ($\mathfrak{P}^{22vid}$ A C^{3vid} D W), as well as Θ Ψ f^{13}. Both readings have support from early MSS; however, the text has the earliest testimony and is the harder reading. Because Jesus usually spoke of making petition to the Father in his own name (see 14:13, 14; 15:16; 16:24, 26), it would have been quite natural for scribes to conform this clause to the more usual order. The divine "Father" is written as a nomen sacrum (sacred name) in three early MSS ($\mathfrak{P}^{5vid}$ $\mathfrak{P}^{66vid}$ W), as well as L.

16:25 | I will tell you plainly about the Father.
The divine "Father" is written as a nomen sacrum (sacred name) in four early MSS ($\mathfrak{P}^{5}$ $\mathfrak{P}^{22}$ $\mathfrak{P}^{66}$ W), as well as L.

16:26 | I will ask the Father concerning you.
The phrase "concerning you" is found in five early MSS ($\mathfrak{P}^{22vid}$ ℵ A B D W), but omitted in two early MSS ($\mathfrak{P}^{5vid}$ $\mathfrak{P}^{66}$). The textual evidence is divided; either reading could be original. The divine "Father" is written as a nomen sacrum (sacred name) in three early MSS ($\mathfrak{P}^{22}$ $\mathfrak{P}^{66}$ W), as well as L.

16:27 | you have believed that I came from God.
"God" is the reading in several early MSS ($\mathfrak{P}^{5}$ $\mathfrak{P}^{66vid}$ $\aleph^{*,2}$ [seventh century] A C^{3} [ninth century] W), as well as Θ 33 $f^{1,13}$ Maj; a variant reading is "the Father" in four early MSS ($\aleph^{1}$ B C D), as well as L. The text has early and diverse testimony (for the reading of $\mathfrak{P}^{66vid}$, see Comfort and Barrett, *Text of Earliest NT Greek MSS*, 452). The reading "Father" was probably assimilated from the next verse and/or is a modification intended to make the disciples' revelation more elevated.

16:28 | the Father.
The divine "Father" is written in both occurrences as nomina sacra (sacred names) in two early MSS ($\mathfrak{P}^{5}$ $\mathfrak{P}^{22}$), as well as L.

16:32 | my Father is with me.
The divine "Father" is written as a nomen sacrum (sacred name) in two early MSS ($\mathfrak{P}^{66}$ W), as well as L.

17:1a | Father, the hour has come.
The divine "Father" is written as a nomen sacrum (sacred name) in three early MSS ($\mathfrak{P}^{66vid}$ $\mathfrak{P}^{107vid}$ W), as well as L.

17:1b | glorify your Son.
The divine "Son" is written as a nomen sacrum (sacred name) in two early MSS ($\mathfrak{P}^{66}$ $\aleph$), as well as $\mathfrak{P}^{60}$ L.

17:5 | Father, glorify me.
The divine "Father" is written as a nomen sacrum (sacred name) in two early MSS ($\mathfrak{P}^{66}$ W), as well as L.

17:11a | Holy Father.
The divine "Father" is written as a nomen sacrum (sacred name) in two early MSS ($\mathfrak{P}^{66}$ $\mathfrak{P}^{107vid}$), as well as L.

17:11b | the Name you have given me.

This is the original wording according to the testimony of $\mathfrak{P}^{60}$ $\mathfrak{P}^{66vid}$ $\mathfrak{P}^{107}$ ℵ A B C L W $f^{1,13}$ Maj. A variant reading is, "those [disciples] you have given me" in D^{1} cop^{sa}. The text is strongly supported by early and diverse MSS.

17:12 | the Name you have given me.

This is the original wording according to $\mathfrak{P}^{66c,vid}$ $\aleph^{2}$ B C* W L 33. A variant reading is, "those [disciples] you have given me" in A C^{3} [ninth century] D Δ Θ Ψ $f^{1,13}$ Maj . The text is strongly supported by early and diverse MSS.

17:16 |

The entire verse is included in $\mathfrak{P}^{66*}$ and most other MSS; it is omitted in $\mathfrak{P}^{66c}$ 33. It is possible it was deleted because it was thought to repeat 17:14.

17:21, 24–25 | Father.

The divine "Father" is written as a nomen sacrum (sacred name) in two early MSS ($\mathfrak{P}^{66vid}$ $\mathfrak{P}^{108vid}$), as well as L.

18:11 | Shouldn't I drink the cup the Father has given me?

The divine "Father" is written as a nomen sacrum (sacred name) in two early MSS ($\mathfrak{P}^{66vid}$ W), as well as L.

18:37

Pilate's words are treated as a question in NA^{27} and UBS^{4} and by nearly all translations. But a translation, "you are a king!", is supported by one second-century manuscript, $\mathfrak{P}^{90}$—the inversion (*su ei*) suggesting an emphatic declaration instead of *ei su* (which is more suggestive of interrogation). Jesus's following response suggests that Pilate wasn't asking a question but making a declaration, whether sincere or sarcastic. In effect Jesus was saying "you said it" when he answers, (you said it—I am a king). This is similar to his response in Matt. 26:64 (*su eipas*—"you said [it]").

18:40 | they all shouted.

This is the reading in the earliest MS ($\mathfrak{P}^{66vid}$), as well as K N Ψ $f^{1,13}$ 33. A variant reading is "they shouted again" in $\mathfrak{P}^{60}$ ℵ B L W 0109; another variant is "they all shouted again" in A (D^s) Θ 0250 Maj. The text has the support of $\mathfrak{P}^{66}$, but the variant in $\mathfrak{P}^{60}$, et al., could be the original reading.

19:6 | They shouted, "Crucify him! Crucify him!"

"Crucify" is written as a nomen sacrum (sacred word) in one early MS ($\mathfrak{P}^{66}$); so also in 19:15, 20.

19:7 | he claimed to be the Son of God.

"Son of God" is written as a nomen sacrum (sacred name) in three early MSS ($\mathfrak{P}^{66}$ ℵ B), as well as L.

19:17, 19 | Cross.

"Cross" is written as a nomen sacrum (sacred word) in one early MS ($\mathfrak{P}^{66vid}$), as well as L.

19:20 | written in Hebrew, Latin, and Greek.

This is the original wording according to three early MSS ($\mathfrak{P}^{66vid}$ $\aleph^1$ B), as well as L N Ψ 33. A variant reading is "written in Hebrew, Greek, and Latin" in A D^s Θ f1 Maj. The text has superior support, including that of $\mathfrak{P}^{66}$, whose reading is based on my publication of new fragments of $\mathfrak{P}^{66}$ (see Comfort, "New Reconstructions and Identifications of New Testament Papyri," in *Novum Testamentum* XLI [1999], 3:214–230; see p. 229). Prior to my publication, it could not be said that $\mathfrak{P}^{66}$ preserved this order, for the first two words were completely missing. $\mathfrak{P}^{66}$ now provides the earliest testimony for the reading of the text. Pilate provided a tribute to Jesus's kingship in a trilingual placard that everyone in Palestine could read, for it was written in the three major languages of the day: Hebrew (or, Aramaic—the language of the Jews), Latin (the Roman language, the official language) and Greek (the lingua franca, the common tongue). A change in the order was made to accord with a geographical order going from East to West.

19:25 | standing beside the Cross.
"Cross" is written as a nomen sacrum (sacred word) in one early MS (𝔓^{66vid}), as well as L f^{1,13}.

19:26 | "look at your son."
The word "son" is written in full (in *plene*; i.e., not written as a sacred name) in four early MSS (𝔓^{66} ℵ B W), signaling a generic son. Jesus was asking his mother to look at her new son, the beloved John, who would take care of her from then on. Had Jesus been directing his mother to look at himself, her son, it is likely that "Son" would have been written as a nomen sacrum (sacred name).

19:30 | he gave up his Spirit.
"Spirit" is written as a nomen sacrum (sacred name) in three early MSS (𝔓^{66} ℵ W), as well as L. These scribes considered the Spirit/spirit of Jesus to be divine. This could also indicate that these scribes thought Jesus was giving over his divine Spirit to the believers. Out of his death came life-giving Spirit. The word is written in full (in *plene*; i.e, not written as a sacred name) in B, which would mean that Jesus gave up his human spirit (or, breath) when he expired. Most English versions render it this way. (See note on Matt. 27:50 on a similar expression.)

19:31 | not stay on the Cross on the Sabbath.
"Cross" is written as a nomen sacrum (sacred word) in two early MSS (𝔓^{66vid} D), as well as L f^{1,13}.

19:35 | so that you may continue to believe.
This is the original wording according to the three earliest MSS (𝔓^{66vid} ℵ* B), as well as Ψ. A variant reading is, "so that you may believe" in ℵ^{2} [seventh century] A D^{s} L W Θ f^{1,13} 33 Maj. John was encouraging ongoing faith in Jesus (see note on 20:31.)

20:17, 21 | Father.
The divine "Father" is written in all three occurrences as a nomen sacrum (sacred name) in two early MSS (𝔓^{66} W), as well as L.

20:22 | he breathed on them and said, "Receive the Holy Spirit."
The divine "Spirit" is written as a nomen sacrum (sacred name) in three early MSS ($\mathfrak{P}^{66\text{vid}}$ ℵ W). Jesus imparted the divine Holy Spirit into them, not just holy breath, which would be the meaning if the word *pneuma* was written in full (in *plene*; i.e., not a sacred name).

20:31a | that you may continue to believe.
This is the original reading according to the three earliest MSS ($\mathfrak{P}^{66\text{vid}}$ ℵ* B), as well as Θ 0250. A variant reading is, "that you may come to believe" in ℵ^{2} [seventh century] A C D L W Ψ $f^{1,13}$ 33 Maj. The documentary evidence supports the present subjunctive; this indicates that John wrote his Gospel to inspire ongoing faith in Jesus.

20:31b | that Jesus is the Christ, the Son of God.
"Jesus" and "Christ" are written as nomina sacra (sacred names) in all MSS. "Son of God" is written as a nomen sacrum (sacred name) in five early MSS ($\mathfrak{P}^{66\text{vid}}$ ℵ B D W), as well as L.

21:18 | others will dress you and carry you off.
This is the original wording according to early and excellent testimony: $\mathfrak{P}^{59\text{vid}}$ $\mathfrak{P}^{109\text{vid}}$ ℵ C^{2} D W 33. A variant reading is, "another will dress you and carry you" in A Θ Ψ f^{13} Maj. The documentary evidence supports a reading that indicates that more than one person would be involved in carrying out Peter's death (via crucifixion).

21:24–25 | This is the disciple who testifies concerning these things and who wrote these things. And we know that his testimony his true. There are many other things Jesus did, which if they were written one by one, I suppose the world could not contain the books that would be written.
It is possible that John dictated his epistle to an amanuensis, and then signed off in his own hand at the end of the Gospel—using the personal "I" to identify himself as the author. If so, these last two verses would be in his own handwriting in the autograph. The statement "we know his testimony is true" could have also been in yet another hand—that of

the Ephesian elders affirming the truth of John's Gospel. (History says John wrote this Gospel in Ephesus.) It is also possible that John himself wrote the entire Gospel (the expression "who wrote these things" being taken literally); if so, these verses would be in the same hand as the rest of the Gospel. It should also be noted that codex Sinaiticus originally omitted all of 21:25, and then added it.

End of the Gospel

All MSS except f^1 conclude the Gospel at 21:25. The story of the woman caught in adultery, traditionally placed at the end of John 7 (see note on John 7:53–8:11), is printed here (as in f^1) as follows:

[53]*Each of them went home,* [8]*while Jesus went to the Mount of Olives.*
[2]*Early in the morning he came to the temple. When the people came to*
him, he sat down and began to teach them. [3]*The scribes and the Pharisees*
brought a woman who had been caught in adultery. Making her stand
before all of them, [4]*they told him, "Teacher, this woman was caught in*
the act of committing adultery. [5]*The law of Moses commands us to stone*
such women. But what do you say?" [6]*They were testing him, so as to bring*
some charge against him. Jesus bent down and with his finger wrote on
the ground. [7]*When they persisted in questioning him, he sat up and said*
to them, "Let him who is without sin be the first to throw a stone at her."
8 Once again he bent down and wrote on the ground. [9]*When they heard*
this, they went away, one by one, beginning with the elders. Jesus was left
alone with the woman standing before him. [10]*Jesus sat up and said to her,*
"Woman, where are they now? Has anyone condemned you?"

11 She answered, "No one, Lord."
And Jesus replied, "Neither do I condemn you. Go your way, and don't sin again."

Chapter Five

Acts of the Apostles

ACTS OF THE APOSTLES

Title: Acts of the Apostles
This is the book title according to the two earliest MSS (א B). English versions should not title this simply "Acts," but "Acts of the Apostles."

1:2 | he had given orders by the Holy Spirit.
The divine "Spirit" is written as a nomen sacrum (sacred name) in one early MS (א), as well as $\mathfrak{P}^{74}$.

1:4 | wait there for what my Father promised.
The divine "Father" is written as a nomen sacrum (sacred name) in one early MS ($\mathfrak{P}^{56}$).

1:5 | you will be baptized with the Holy Spirit.
The divine "Spirit" is written as a nomen sacrum (sacred name) in one early MS (א).

1:7 | the times the Father has set.
The divine "Father" is written as a nomen sacrum (sacred name) in one early MS ($\mathfrak{P}^{56vid}$).

1:8 | you will receive power when the Holy Spirit comes upon you.
The divine "Spirit" is written as a nomen sacrum (sacred name) in one early MS (א), as well as $\mathfrak{P}^{74}$.

1:14 | prayer with one accord.
This is the original wording according to early and diverse testimony: $\mathfrak{P}^{74}$ א A B C* D E. Another reading is, "prayer and supplication with one accord" in C^3 [ninth century] 33 1739 Maj, by way of scribal expansion based on Phil. 4:6.

1:16 | the Holy Spirit foretold.
The divine "Spirit" is written as a nomen sacrum (sacred name) in one early MS (א).

1:25 | to take his place in the ministry.
This is the original wording according to early and diverse testimony: 𝔓[74] A B C* D. A variant reading is "to take his share in the ministry" in א C[3] E Maj, by way of scribal assimilation to 1:17.

2:4 | the Spirit.
The divine "Spirit" is written in both occurrences as nomina sacra (sacred names) in two early MSS (א D), as well as 𝔓[74].

2:17 | I will pour out my Spirit.
The divine "Spirit" is written as a nomen sacrum (sacred name) in two early MSS (א D).

2:18 | I will pour out my Spirit.
"Spirit" is written as a nomen sacrum (sacred name) in two early MSS (א D), as well as 𝔓[74].

2:31 | you will not abandon him to Hades.
This is the original wording according to early and diverse testimony: 𝔓[74] 𝔓[91vid] א A B C* D. A variant reading is "you will not abandon his soul to Hades" in C[3] [ninth century] E 33 1739 Maj, by way of scribal assimilation to 2:27.

2:33a | the promise of the Holy Spirit.
The divine "Spirit" is written as a nomen sacrum (sacred name) in four early MSS (𝔓[91vid] א A C).

2:33b | from the Father.
The divine "Father" is written as a nomen sacrum (sacred name) in one early MS (𝔓[91]).

2:34–35 | The Lord said to my Lord.
This comes from Ps. 110:1, which in the Hebrew begins with, "Yahweh said to Elohim"; this became "*Kurios* said to *Kurios*" in the Greek, both names written as nomina sacra (sacred names) in all MSS.

2:38 | the gift of the Holy Spirit.
The divine "Spirit" is written as a nomen sacrum (sacred name) in two early MSS (א D*), as well as $\mathfrak{P}^{74}$.

2:47 | united community.
This is the original wording according to early and diverse testimony: $\mathfrak{P}^{74\text{vid}}$ $\mathfrak{P}^{91\text{vid}}$ א A B C 095. An inferior variant reading is "church" in E 33 Maj. "United community" is a translation of *epi to auto*, which literally means "to the same," suggesting the unity of community. The phrase also appears in 2:44, which is translated as "they were united."

3:6 | in the name of Jesus Christ, the Nazarene, walk.
This is the original wording in the two earliest MSS (א B) and D. A variant reading for the verb is, "rise up and walk" in A C E Ψ 095 33 1739 Maj, by way of scribal gap filling.

3:13 | the God of Abraham, Isaac, and Jacob.
This is the reading in two early MSS (B 0236), as well as E 33 1739 Maj. A variant reading is, "the God of Abraham, the God of Isaac, and the God of Jacob" in four early MSS (א A C D). The textual evidence is evenly divided; either reading could be original.

4:8 | Peter was full of the Holy Spirit.
The divine "Spirit" is written as a nomen sacrum (sacred name) in two early MSS (א D).

4:25 | you who spoke by your Holy Spirit through the mouth of your servant David, our ancestor.
This is the original wording according to early and diverse testimony: $\mathfrak{P}^{74}$ א A B E 33 1739. Two variant readings are "you who spoke by your Holy Spirit through the mouth your servant David" (D), and "you who spoke through the mouth of your servant" (Maj; so KJV). This verse, as it reads in the best MSS, is difficult to translate because God's speaking is both through the Holy Spirit and David's mouth (simultaneously) and because David is called both God's servant and the Jews' father. The text would seem to be

so much simpler if one of each of the options were written, not all four! Consequently, various scribes tried to relieve the text of this heavy load by getting rid of "our father" (as in the first variant) or both "through the Holy Spirit" and "our father" (as in the second variant—so TR). However, most Greek scribes kept the text as is, and this presents the problem of understanding how God spoke though the Holy Spirit and David simultaneously, when it would seem more logical for David (as a prophet) to be the one speaking by the Holy Spirit. If this is what Luke intended (or actually wrote), then the text—as it has come down to us—does not say this. What the text says is that God spoke through the Holy Spirit and David's mouth as through a united oracle. Westcott and Hort (*The New Testament in the Original Greek, Introduction and Appendix*, 92) recognized that the mouth of David is represented as the mouth of the Holy Spirit. This can be affirmed because, according to the Greek, David's "mouth" is in apposition to the "Holy Spirit"; this indicates that David's prophetic utterance (in Ps. 2:1–2) was the same as the Holy Spirit's, which is written as a nomen sacrum (sacred name) in three early MSS (א A D), as well as $\mathfrak{P}^{74}$ 33.

4:31 | they were all filled with the Holy Spirit.

The divine "Spirit" is written as a nomen sacrum (sacred name) in four early MSS ($\mathfrak{P}^{8}$ $\mathfrak{P}^{45}$ א D), as well as $\mathfrak{P}^{74}$.

4:33 | the resurrection of the Lord Jesus.

This is the original reading in two early MSS ($\mathfrak{P}^{8}$ B), as well as Maj syr^{h} cop^{sa}. The name is "Lord Jesus Christ" in D E 1739, and it is "Jesus Christ the Lord" in א A. As often happened in the course of textual transmission, divine names were expanded.

5:3 | lie to the Holy Spirit.

The divine "Spirit" is written as a nomen sacrum (sacred name) in four early MSS ($\mathfrak{P}^{8}$ א A D), as well as $\mathfrak{P}^{74}$.

5:9 | test the Spirit of the Lord.

"Spirit of the Lord" is written as a nomen sacrum (sacred name) in six early MSS ($\mathfrak{P}^{8}$ $\mathfrak{P}^{57vid}$ א A B D).

5:32 | the Holy Spirit whom God has given.
The divine "Spirit" is written as a nomen sacrum (sacred name) in four early MSS (𝔓^{45} ℵ A D), as well as 𝔓^{74} 33.

5:41 | suffer dishonor for the sake of the Name.
This is the original wording according to early and diverse testimony: 𝔓^{74} ℵ A B C (D) 1739. "The Name" was changed in three ways: "his Name" (945 1175); "the Name of Jesus" (Ψ 33 Maj; so KJV), and "the Name of the Lord Jesus" (E). The absolute use of the term "the Name," referring to the all-inclusiveness of Jesus Christ's person, is spoiled here by the additions. The early Christians knew that "the Name" denoted "Jesus Christ." Other NT writers simply said "the Name" and expected their readers to know that this referred to Jesus Christ (see Heb. 13:15; James 2:7; 3 John 7).

6:3 | full of the Spirit and wisdom.
The divine "Spirit" is written as a nomen sacrum (sacred name) in three early MSS (𝔓^{8} ℵ D), as well as 𝔓^{74}. This is written as "the Holy Spirit" in some MSS (A 33 Maj) by way of scribal expansion.

6:5 | full of faith and the Holy Spirit.
The divine "Spirit" is written as a nomen sacrum (sacred name) in two early MSS (𝔓^{8} ℵ), as well as 𝔓^{74}.

6:8 | full of grace and power.
This is the original wording according to early and diverse testimony: 𝔓^{8} 𝔓^{45vid} 𝔓^{74} ℵ B D. Several variations occur: "full of grace and faith" (E); "full of faith, grace, and the Spirit" (Ψ); "full of faith and power" (Maj; so KJV), all scribal alterations.

6:10 | they could not resist the wisdom and the Spirit with which he spoke.
"Spirit" is written as a nomen sacrum (sacred name) in early MSS (𝔓^{8} 𝔓^{45} 0175 ℵ), as well as 𝔓^{74}. This indicates that Stephen was speaking by the power of the divine Spirit. Codex B writes the word *pneuma* in full

(in *plene*; i.e., not written as a sacred name), suggesting the translation "the wisdom and spirit of his speech."

7:18 | another king.

This is the reading in two early MSS ($\mathfrak{P}^{45vid}$ D), as well as E Maj. A variant reading is "another king over Egypt" in four early (ℵ A B C), as well as $\mathfrak{P}^{33vid}$ $\mathfrak{P}^{74}$ Ψ. The textual evidence is divided; either reading could be original.

7:30 | an angel appeared to him.

This is the original wording according to four early MSS (ℵ A B C), as well as $\mathfrak{P}^{74}$. A variant reading is "an angel of the Lord appeared to him" in D E 33 1739 Maj (so KJV), by way of scribal expansion.

7:46 | house of Jacob.

This is the wording according to three early MSS (ℵ* B D), as well as $\mathfrak{P}^{74}$ H 049. A variant reading is "God of Jacob" in two early MSS (A C), as well as $\aleph^{2}$ [seventh century] E 33 1739 Maj syr cop. The documentary evidence slightly favors the text, whereas internal considerations favor the variant. Either reading could be original.

7:51 | You are always resisting the Holy Spirit.

The divine "Spirit" is written as a nomen sacrum (sacred name) in two early MSS (ℵ D), as well as $\mathfrak{P}^{74}$.

7:55 | Stephen, full of the Holy Spirit.

The divine "Spirit" is written as a nomen sacrum (sacred name) in three early MSS ($\mathfrak{P}^{45}$ ℵ D), as well as $\mathfrak{P}^{74}$.

7:56 | the Son of Man standing at the right hand of God.

"Son of Man," a messianic title of Jesus (Dan. 7:13–14), is written as a nomen sacrum (sacred name) in one early MS (ℵ), as well as $\mathfrak{P}^{74}$.

7:59 | receive my spirit.

The rendering "spirit" represents the orthography of B, suggesting the human spirit. Stephen was asking God to receive his spirit once he died. Other MSS ($\mathfrak{P}^{74}$ א D) write *pneuma* as a nomen sacrum (sacred name).

8:15 | they would receive the Holy Spirit.
The divine "Spirit" is written as a nomen sacrum (sacred name) in two early MSS ($\mathfrak{P}^{45}$ א).

8:17 | they received the Holy Spirit.
The divine "Spirit" is written as a nomen sacrum (sacred name) in two early MSS (א D), as well as $\mathfrak{P}^{74}$.

8:18 | he saw that the Holy Spirit was given.
This is the reading according to early and diverse testimony: $\mathfrak{P}^{45}$ $\mathfrak{P}^{74}$ A* C D E Ψ 33 1739 Maj syr cop^{bo}. Some MSS (א A^{c} B cop^{sa}) read "Spirit" instead of "Holy Spirit." The text has superior documentation. The divine "Spirit" is written as a nomen sacrum (sacred name) in three early MSS ($\mathfrak{P}^{45}$ א D).

8:19 | receive the Holy Spirit.
The divine "Spirit" is written as a nomen sacrum (sacred name) in three early MSS ($\mathfrak{P}^{45}$ א D), as well as $\mathfrak{P}^{74}$.

8:25 | had spoken the message of the Lord.
This is the original wording according to four early MSS (א B C D), as well as E 33 1739 Maj. A variant reading is "had spoken the message of God" in $\mathfrak{P}^{74}$ A Ψ. The text has superior documentation.

8:29 | the Spirit.
The divine "Spirit" is written as a nomen sacrum (sacred name) in three early MSS ($\mathfrak{P}^{50}$ א D), as well as $\mathfrak{P}^{74}$.

8:32–33
This comes from Isa. 53:7–8 LXX. That this passage comes from the LXX (Septuagint) proves that the Ethiopian eunuch was reading the Septuagint version of Isaiah. (Reading in ancient times was done out

loud.) The image of a lamb being led to slaughter without uttering a sound is a powerful depiction of the way Jesus faced his trial and persecution.

8:37 | omit verse.

The earliest and best Greek MSS ($\mathfrak{P}^{45}$ $\mathfrak{P}^{74}$ ℵ A B C), as well as syr^{p} cop, do not include 8:37. Other MSS (4^{mg} E 1739 it) add, "And Philip said, 'If you believe with all your heart, you may.' And he replied, 'I believe that the Son of God is Jesus Christ.'" If the verse was an original part of Luke's text, there is no good reason for explaining why it would have been omitted in so many ancient MSS and versions. Rather, this verse is a classic example of scribal gap-filling, in that it supplied the apparent gap left by the unanswered question of the previous verse ("The eunuch said, 'Look, water! What could keep me from being baptized?'"). The interpolation puts an answer on Philip's lips that is derived from ancient Christian baptismal practices. Before being baptized, the new believer had to make a confession of his or her faith in Jesus as the Son of God. A similar addition also worked its way into the text of John 9:38–39 (see note). There is nothing doctrinally wrong with this interpolation; it affirms belief with the heart (in accordance with verses like Rom. 10:9–10) and elicits the response of faith in Jesus Christ as the Son of God (in accordance with verses like John 20:31). But it is not essential that one make such a verbatim confession before being baptized. In fact, the eunuch had made no such confession, but it was obvious to Philip that he believed Jesus was the Christ when the eunuch said, "Look, water! What could keep me from being baptized?" This is part of the beauty of the book of Acts: Many individuals come to faith in Christ in a variety of ways. The church throughout history has had a habit of standardizing the way people express their faith in Christ. It is difficult to know when this interpolation first entered the text, but it could have been as early as the second century, since Irenaeus (*Against Heresies* 3.12.8) quoted part of it. The earliest extant Greek manuscript to include this is E, of the sixth century. Erasmus included the verse in his edition of the Greek New Testament because—even though it was not present in many of the MSS he knew—he considered it to have been omitted by the carelessness of scribes. He based its inclusion on a marginal reading in codex 4. From Erasmus's edition it worked its way into the TR and subsequently the KJV.

8:39 | the Spirit of Lord snatched Philip away.

"Spirit of the Lord" is the original wording according to early MSS (𝔓[45] א A* B C), as well as 𝔓[74] E. The name of the Spirit was changed to "Holy Spirit" in A[c] 1739, by way of scribal conformity to the more usual title. The divine "Spirit" is written as a nomen sacrum (sacred name) in three early MSS (𝔓[45] 𝔓[74] א), as well as L.

9:5 | Who are you, Lord?

"Lord" is written as a nomen sacrum (sacred name) in two early MSS (א B), as well as 𝔓[74] Ψ indicating the scribes thought Paul was addressing the divine Lord. Otherwise, the translation would be, "sir."

9:17 | be filled with the Holy Spirit.

The divine "Spirit" is written as a nomen sacrum (sacred name) in two early MSS (𝔓[45] א), as well as 𝔓[74].

9:20a | he began to proclaim Jesus.

"Jesus" is the original wording according to five early MSS (𝔓[45] א A B C), as well as 𝔓[74]. A variant reading is "the Christ" in H L P. The text has superior documentation. It is significant that Saul was identifying a specific man, Jesus, as the Son of God (see next note). He was not speaking abstractly about the Christ (the Messiah) being the Son of God, as if he wanted to persuade his listeners that the Messiah (as predicted in the OT) would be God's Son, not David's son. Although this is true and implicit in his words, Paul's primary purpose was to identify a man from Nazareth as being God's Son. His audience, who had heard of this man Jesus and knew that Saul was persecuting those who followed Jesus, was shocked to hear that Saul was now proclaiming Jesus to be "the Son of God."

9:20b | This man is the Son of God.

"Son of God" is written as a nomen sacrum (sacred name) in two early MSS (א B), as well as 𝔓[74] L.

9:21 | Everyone was astonished.
This is the original wording according to the earliest MS ($\mathfrak{P}^{45\mathrm{vid}}$) and $\mathfrak{P}^{74}$. A variant reading is, "everyone who heard was astonished" in א A B D 33 Maj, by way of scribal gap filling.

9:31a | the church increased in numbers.
The "church" is the original wording according to four early MSS (א A B C), as well as $\mathfrak{P}^{74}$. This was changed to "churches" in E Maj (so KJV) by way of scribal clarification.

9:31b | encouragement of the Holy Spirit.
The divine "Spirit" is written as a nomen sacrum (sacred name) in one early MS (א), as well as $\mathfrak{P}^{74}$.

9:34 | Jesus Christ heals you.
This is the original wording according to three early MSS (א B* C), as well as $\mathfrak{P}^{74}$. Variant readings on the name are "Jesus the Christ" in $\mathfrak{P}^{53\mathrm{vid}}$ B^{c} E 1739 Maj, "the Lord Jesus Christ" in A, and "the Christ" in 614 1505. The text has superior documentation.

10:4 | What is it, Lord?
"Lord" is written as a nomen sacrum (sacred name) in two early MSS (א B), as well as $\mathfrak{P}^{74}$, suggesting that Cornelius was addressing the Lord through his messenger, the angel.

10:16 | the object was taken up to heaven.
This is the reading in the earliest MS ($\mathfrak{P}^{45}$). Two variants on the verbal expression are, "was taken up again" in D Ψ 33^{vid} 1739 Maj (so KJV), and "was taken up suddenly" in $\mathfrak{P}^{74}$ א A B C E, perhaps both scribal expansions.

10:19a | the Spirit.
The divine "Spirit" is written as a nomen sacrum (sacred name) in three early MSS ($\mathfrak{P}^{45\mathrm{vid}}$ א D), as well as $\mathfrak{P}^{74}$.

10:19b | three men.
This is the wording according to three early MSS (א A C), as well as 𝔓[74]. Other variants are "two men" (B) or "men" (D). According to 10:7, Cornelius sent two of his servants and one soldier, who had served him, to go to Joppa and find Peter. Thus, the reading with "three men" makes the most sense and has excellent documentation. The second variant, though poorly supported, also makes sense. The first variant is the most difficult but could still be plausible if we consider the two servants to be the two men seeking Peter, excluding the soldier, who must be considered as merely accompanying the messengers as an escort.

10:30 | I was praying.
This is the original wording according to four early MSS (א A* B C), as well as 𝔓[74]. A variant reading is, "I was fasting and praying" in 𝔓[50] A[2] (D), by way of scribal expansion.

10:38 | God anointed him with the Holy Spirit.
The divine "Spirit" is written as a nomen sacrum (sacred name) in five early MSS (א A B C D), as well as 𝔓[74]. (The occurrence of a nomen sacrum for "Spirit" in B is rare.)

10:44–45, 47 | the Spirit.
The divine "Spirit" is written as a nomen sacrum (sacred name) in three early MSS (𝔓[127vid] א D), as well as 𝔓[74] L.

10:48 | in the name of Jesus Christ.
This is the original wording according to three early MSS (א A B), as well as 𝔓[74]. The name is changed to "Lord" (H L P), "Lord Jesus" (436 1241), and "Lord Jesus Christ" (D). The text has superior testimony.

11:12a | the Spirit told me.
The divine "Spirit" is written as a nomen sacrum (sacred name) in three early MSS (𝔓[45] א D), as well as 𝔓[74] L.

11:12b | to accompany them.
This is probably the original wording according to two early MSS (𝔓[45vid] D). There are three variant readings: "to accompany them without making a distinction" (א* A B E 33 1739), "to accompany them without hesitation" Maj (so KJV), and "to accompany them without questioning" (𝔓[74]), which are all likely scribal expansions (see 10:20).

11:15–16, 24a the Holy Spirit.
The divine "Spirit" is written as a nomen sacrum (sacred name) in two early MSS (א D), as well as 𝔓[74] L.

11:26 | Christians.
This is written as a nomen sacrum (sacred name) in 𝔓[45]. (א wrote the name as Chrestianous, meaning "kind ones"; see 1 Pet 4:16.)

11:28 | predicted by the Spirit.
The divine "Spirit" is written as a nomen sacrum (sacred name) in two early MSS (א D), as well as 𝔓[74] L.

12:22 | the voice of God.
"God" is written as a nomen sacrum (sacred name) in three early MSS (א B D), as well as 𝔓[74] L. Had the scribes wanted to indicate "a god" (as in many English versions), they could have written out *theos* in full (in *plene*; i.e., not as a sacred name), as in Acts 25:26 (see note). But the people were calling Herod, "God." Having accepted this divine accolade, he was struck by an angel of the Lord with a deadly disease.

12:24 | the message of God.
This is the original wording according to three early MSS (א A D), as well as 𝔓[74]. A variant reading is "the message of the Lord" in B. The text has superior documentation.

12:25 | having fulfilled their mission they returned to Jerusalem.
This is the original wording according to the two earliest MSS (א B), as well as Maj cop[sa]. Other MSS (𝔓[74] A 33) read, "they returned from

Jerusalem, having completed their ministry"; still other MSS (E 1739) read "they returned from Jerusalem to Antioch, having completed their ministry." The reading in א and B has to be translated as in the text above because Paul and Barnabas went to Jerusalem on a relief mission and then returned to Antioch. The other MSS make this clear.

13:2 | the Holy Spirit said.
The divine "Spirit" is written as a nomen sacrum (sacred name) in two early MSS (א D), as well as L.

13:4 | sent out by the Holy Spirit.
The divine "Spirit" is written as a nomen sacrum (sacred name) in one early MS (א), as well as $\mathfrak{P}^{74}$ L.

13:9 | filled with the Holy Spirit.
The divine "Spirit" is written as a nomen sacrum (sacred name) in three early MSS ($\mathfrak{P}^{45}$ א D), as well as $\mathfrak{P}^{74}$ L.

13:18 | he put up with them in the wilderness.
This is the wording according to four early MSS (א B C^2 D). A variant reading is "he cared for them in the wilderness" in other MSS ($\mathfrak{P}^{74}$ A C* E). Since, in the Greek, there is only a one-letter difference (*pi/phi*) between the two readings (*etropophorēsen/ etrophophorēsen*), either reading could have been confused for the other and therefore either reading could be original.

13:33 | the psalms.
This is the reading in the earliest MS ($\mathfrak{P}^{45vid}$). Two variant readings are "the second psalm" ($\mathfrak{P}^{74}$ א A B C) and "the first psalm" (D). The textual evidence is divided between "the psalms" found in the earliest MS ($\mathfrak{P}^{45}$) and "the second psalm" found in other early MSS. The passage quoted is from Psalm 2:7.

13:44 | message of the Lord.
This is the original wording according to two early MSS (א A), as well as

𝔓[74] B[2] [tenth century] 33 1739. Two variant readings are "message of God" (B* C E Maj; so KJV) and "God" (D). The reading of the text has slightly better attestation than the first variant. Furthermore, scribes would be more likely to change "message of the Lord" to "message of God" than vice versa.

13:48 | message of the Lord.
This is the original wording according to four early MSS (𝔓[45] ℵ A C), as well as 𝔓[74] 33. A variant reading is "message of God" in B D E. The reading of the text has better attestation than the variant. Furthermore, scribes would be more likely to change "message of the Lord" to "message of God" than vice versa.

13:52 | filled with joy and the Holy Spirit.
The divine "Spirit" is written as a nomen sacrum (sacred name) in two early MSS (ℵ D), as well as 𝔓[74] L.

14:25 | the message.
This is the original wording according to two early MSS (B D), as well as 1739 Maj. Two variant readings are "the message of the Lord" (ℵ A C 33) and "the message of God" (𝔓[74] E), both scribal expansions.

15:8 | giving them the Holy Spirit.
The divine "Spirit" is written as a nomen sacrum (sacred name) in two early MSS (ℵ D), as well as 𝔓[74] L.

15:20 | abstain from things defiled by idols and from fornication and from what has been strangled and from blood.
The phrase "and from fornication" is omitted in 𝔓[45]. This could reflect the original reading, but since the scribe of 𝔓[45] is known for brevity we cannot be certain.

15:24 | commanded you to do certain things and thereby disturbed you.
This is the original wording according to early and diverse testimony:

$\mathfrak{P}^{33}$ $\mathfrak{P}^{45vid}$ $\mathfrak{P}^{74}$ ℵ B D 33. A variant reading is, "commanded you to be circumcised and keep the law and thereby disturbed you" in C E 1739 Maj, by way of scribal expansion.

15:28 | it seemed best to the Holy Spirit and to us.

The divine "Spirit" is written as a nomen sacrum (sacred name) in two early MSS (ℵ D), as well as $\mathfrak{P}^{33}$ $\mathfrak{P}^{74}$ L.

15:34 | omit verse.

This verse is not included in many MSS, both early and diverse: $\mathfrak{P}^{74}$ ℵ A B E Ψ Maj syr^{p} cop^{bo}. The verse is added in two different forms in other MSS: (1) "But it seemed good to Silas to remain there" (C 33 1739 syr^{h**} cop^{sa}); (2) "But it seemed good to Silas to remain with them, so Judas traveled alone" ($\mathfrak{P}^{127vid}$ D). The extra verse, though it contradicts 15:33, was added to avoid the difficulty in 15:40, which indicates that Silas was still in Antioch. Thus, in trying to solve one problem, another was created.

15:40 | the grace of God.

This is the reading in two early MSS ($\mathfrak{P}^{45}$ C), as well as E 1739 Maj. A variant reading is, "the grace of the Lord" in four early MSS (ℵ A B D), as well as $\mathfrak{P}^{74}$ 33. The textual evidence is split; either reading could be original.

16:7 | the Spirit of Jesus.

This is the original wording according to early and excellent testimony: $\mathfrak{P}^{74}$ ℵ A B C^{2} [sixth century] D E 33 1739. Two variant readings are "the Spirit of the Lord" (C*) and "the Spirit" (Maj; so KJV). The uniqueness of the expression, "the Spirit of Jesus" (strongly supported by the MSS) caused the two variants. In fact, this is the first and only place in the NT where the phrase "the Spirit of Jesus" occurs. Elsewhere, the Spirit is called "the Spirit of Christ" (Rom. 8:9; 1 Pet 1:11) and "the Spirit of Jesus Christ" (Phil. 1:19). The use of the title "Spirit of Jesus" in Acts shows the unity of action between Jesus and the Spirit that permeates this book. During the days of Jesus's earthly ministry, the disciples were directed by Jesus; now, after his resurrection and ascension, by "the Spirit of Jesus." "Spirit" is written as a nomen sacrum (sacred name) in 𝔓[74] א D L.

16:16 | spirit of python.

The word "spirit" is written in full (in *plene*; i.e., not a sacred name) in 𝔓[74] B, indicating this spirit was not divine. 𝔓[45] and 𝔓[127] write "Spirit" as a nomen sacrum (sacred name), suggesting this "Spirit of Python" was a deity.

16:18 | he turned and said to the spirit.

The word "spirit" is written in full (in *plene*; i.e., not a sacred name) in B, indicating this spirit was not divine. 𝔓[45] 𝔓[74] א write "Spirit" as a nomen sacrum (sacred name), probably because this was the Spirit of a deity (namely, Python).

16:31 | Believe in the Lord Jesus.

This is the original wording according to early and excellent testimony: 𝔓[74vid] 𝔓[127] א A B 33. The name is "Lord Jesus Christ" in C D E Ψ 1739 Maj syr cop[sa], by way of scribal expansion.

18:21 | I will return again.

This is the original wording according to three early MSS (א A B), as well as 𝔓[74]. A variant reading is, "I must by all means make the festival in Jerusalem. I will return" in D Ψ Maj (so KJV). Scribes added these words to explain why Paul made such a hasty departure.

18:25 | by the Spirit he spoke and taught.

The divine "Spirit" is written as a nomen sacrum (sacred name) in two early MSS (א D), as well as 𝔓[41] 𝔓[74] L.

19:2 | Holy Spirit.

The divine "Spirit" is written as a nomen sacrum (sacred name) in both occurrences in three early MSS (𝔓[38] א D), as well as 𝔓[41] 𝔓[74] L.

19:6a | the Holy Spirit came upon them.
The divine "Spirit" is written as a nomen sacrum (sacred name) in two early MSS (א D), as well as 𝔓[74] L.

19:21 | Paul decided, in the Spirit, to go to Jerusalem.
"Spirit" is written as a nomen sacrum (sacred name) in two early MSS (א D), as well as L. Another rendering could be, "was compelled in his spirit" (which would reflect the orthography of B, which writes out "spirit" in full). The issue pertains to whether or not Paul was motivated by the divine Spirit or his own inner compulsion (his spirit) to go to Jerusalem (cf. 20:22 and note below).

19:37 | not blasphemers of our god.
The word *theos* is written in full (in *plene*) in three early MSS (א A B), as well as 𝔓[74], indicating these scribes did not think the word was worthy of being a nomen sacrum (sacred name); in other words, they distinguished this "god" from the "Lord God" (which is nearly always written as a nomen sacrum throughout the NT). The feminine article (*tēn*) before *theos* could warrant the translation "goddess" (who was Artemis). Other MSS (D* E[c]) actually read "goddess" (*thean*).

20:22 | compelled by the Spirit.
The divine "Spirit" is written as a nomen sacrum (sacred name) in two early MSS (א D), as well as 𝔓[74] L.

20:23 | the Holy Spirit warns me.
The divine "Spirit" is written as a nomen sacrum (sacred name) in one early MS (א), as well as 𝔓[74] L.

20:28a | the Holy Spirit has made you overseers.
"Spirit" is written as a nomen sacrum (sacred name) in two early MSS (א D), as well as 𝔓[74] L.

20:28b | the church of God which he purchased with his own blood.
This is the original wording according to the two earliest MSS (א B), as

well as cop^{boMS} syr. "God" is replaced with "Lord" in 𝔓^{74} A C* D E 33 1739 cop, and "Lord and God" in C^{3} [ninth century] Maj (so KJV). The reading "God," found in the two earliest MSS (א B), was likely changed to "Lord" because scribes were uncomfortable with the idea of God having blood. The second variant (Lord and God) is a conflation of the two readings. It is possible that the expression "with his own blood" could be rendered "the blood of his Own" or "the blood of his own Son." In other words, it is possible that Luke was thinking of "his own Son" when he wrote, "which God purchased with the blood of his own [*tou idiou*]."

21:1 | Patara.

This is the original wording according to four early MSS (א A B C), as well as 𝔓^{74}. This is expanded to "Patara and Myra" in 𝔓^{41vid} D. The documentary evidence supports the shorter reading. Besides, they couldn't have reached Myra yet, which was another 50 miles away.

21:4 | they told Paul through the Spirit.

The divine "Spirit" is written as a nomen sacrum (sacred name) in one early MS (א), as well as 𝔓^{74} L.

21:11 | the Holy Spirit says this.

"Spirit" is written as a nomen sacrum (sacred name) in one early MS (א), as well as 𝔓^{74} L

21:20 | they praised God.

"God" is the original word according to early and diverse testimony: 𝔓^{74} א A B C E L 33 1739. This was changed to "the Lord" in D Ψ Maj (so KJV). The text has superior documentation.

21:22 | a multitude will surely gather.

This is the reading in three early MSS (א C^{2} [sixth century] D), as well as 𝔓^{74} Maj. It is omitted in two early MSS (B C^{*vid}), as well as 1739 cop. The textual evidence is evenly divided; either reading could be original.

22:8 | Who are you, Lord?
"Lord" is written as a nomen sacrum (sacred name) in three early MSS (ℵ B D), as well as $\mathfrak{P}^{74}$ L, indicating these scribes considered Paul to be speaking to the divine Lord; otherwise, the translation would be "Sir."

22:9 | they saw the light.
This is the original wording according to three early MSS (ℵ A B), as well as $\mathfrak{P}^{74}$ 049 33. A variant reading is, "they saw the light and became afraid" in D E Ψ 1739 Maj (so KJV), by way of scribal expansion.

22:10 | What should I do, Lord?
"Lord" is written as a nomen sacrum (sacred name) in four early MSS (ℵ A B D), as well as $\mathfrak{P}^{74}$ L, indicating these scribes considered Paul to be speaking to the divine Lord; otherwise, the translation would be "Sir."

23:8 | The Pharisees say there is no resurrection, or angel, or Spirit.
"Spirit" is written as a nomen sacrum (sacred name) in one early MS (ℵ), as well as $\mathfrak{P}^{74}$ L, designating the divine Spirit. Codex B writes *pneuma* in full (in *plene*; i.e., not as a sacred name), designating "spirit"—yielding the translation, "they say there is no resurrection, or angel, or spirit."

23:30a | charges against this man.
This is the original reading according to $\mathfrak{P}^{74}$ B. Two variant readings are "charges against this man by them" (ℵ A E), and "charges against this man by the Jews" (Maj; so KJV), both scribal expansions. Some MSS (ℵ E Ψ 1739 Maj) add to this "Farewell." This scribal expansion provides the typical final greeting to a Hellenistic letter.

24:6–8 | so we arrested him.
This is the original wording according to three early MSS (ℵ A B), as well as $\mathfrak{P}^{74}$ H L. This is expanded to, "so we arrested him, and we would have judged him according to our law, [7]but the commander Lysias came and with great force took him out of our hands, [8]commanding his accusers to come before you" (E Ψ Maj 33 1739; so KJV). The earliest

MSS have the shorter text. The extra words are the result of scribal gap filling based on the previous narrative in Acts.

24:15 | there is going to be a resurrection.
This is the original wording according to four early MSS (א A B C), as well as 𝔓74 33 1739. A variant reading is, "there is going to be a resurrection of the dead" in E Ψ Maj (so KJV), by way of scribal expansion.

24:24 | faith in Christ Jesus.
This is the original wording according to early and diverse testimony: 𝔓74 א* B E L Ψ 049 33 1739. The name is shortened to "Christ" in א1 A Cvid H. The text has better textual support than the variant.

25:26 | I have nothing definite to write to my lord about him.
The word "lord" is written in full (in *plene*; i.e., not as a sacred name) in three early MSS (א B C), as well as 𝔓74, indicating that these scribes recognized that *kurios* here is not a divine name but a title ascribed to Caesar.

26:16 | what you have seen of me.
This is the original wording according to two early MSS (B C*), as well as 1739 syr copsa. A variant reading is, "what you have seen" in 𝔓74 א A C2 [sixth century] E. According to the text, the emphasis is on Jesus's revelation of himself to Paul. This could be rendered in full as: "for this purpose I appeared to you, to appoint you a servant and a witness both of the things [wherein] you have seen me and of the things wherein I will appear to you." It is not just that Jesus revealed many things (or, many items) to Paul. Jesus revealed himself in his fullness to Paul so that Paul could preach him among the nations (see Eph. 3:8). The first appearance Jesus made to Paul was on the road to Damascus. It was at this time that Paul saw the risen Christ (see 1 Cor. 15:8). Subsequent to this appearance, Paul received more revelations from Jesus concerning his commission.

27:16 | Cauda.
This is the reading in one early MS (B), as well as 𝔓74 א2 [seventh

century]. A variant reading is "Clauda" in one early MS (א*), as well as 33 1739. The name of this island appears in an Alexandrian form (Cauda) and a Latinized form (Clauda). In Modern Greek it is called Guados; in Italian it is called Gozzo.

28:6 | they said he was God.

"God" is written as a nomen sacrum (sacred name) in two early MSS (א B), as well as $\mathfrak{P}^{74}$ L; otherwise, it would be "a god" if written in full (in *plene*; i.e., not as a sacred name).

28:25 | the Holy Spirit spoke rightly.

The divine "Spirit" is written as a nomen sacrum (sacred name) in one early MS (א), as well as $\mathfrak{P}^{74}$ L.

28:29 | omit verse.

The earliest and best Greek MSS ($\mathfrak{P}^{74}$ א A B E 048 33 1739), as well as syr^{p} and cop, do not include 28:29. It is added (by way of narrative gap filling) in the Majority of MSS (so KJV), which read, "And after he said these things, the Jews went away, arguing greatly among themselves."

Chapter Six

The Epistles of Paul

TO THE ROMANS

Title: To the Romans
This is the wording according to two early MSS (ℵ B), as well as $\mathfrak{P}^{26\text{vid}}$.

1:1 | a servant of Christ Jesus.
This is the wording in two early MSS ($\mathfrak{P}^{10}$ B). Another reading is "Jesus Christ" in two early MSS (ℵ A), as well as $\mathfrak{P}^{26}$ 33 1739 Maj. The textual evidence is divided; either reading could be original.

1:3a | concerning his Son.
The divine "Son" is written as a nomen sacrum (sacred name) in one early MS ($\mathfrak{P}^{10}$), as well as L.

1:3b | son of David.
The expression "son of David" is written in full (in *plene*; i.e., not a sacred name) in two early MSS ($\mathfrak{P}^{10}$ B), but it is written as nomen sacrum (sacred name) in one early MS (ℵ), as well as $\mathfrak{P}^{26}$, because "Son of David" is a royal-messianic title (see 2 Sam. 7:13, 16; Jer. 23:5; Ezek. 37:24).

1:4a | Son of God.
"Son of God" is written as a nomen sacrum (sacred name) in three early MSS ($\mathfrak{P}^{10}$ ℵ B), indicating that Jesus is *the* Son of God, not just a son of God.

1:4b | according to the Holy Spirit.
The divine "Spirit" is written as a nomen sacrum (sacred name) in two early MSS ($\mathfrak{P}^{10}$ ℵ), as well as $\mathfrak{P}^{26}$.

1:7 | our Father.
The divine "Father" is written as a nomen sacrum (sacred name) in two early MSS ($\mathfrak{P}^{10}$ ℵ), as well as L.

1:9a | God, whom I serve in my spirit.
"God" is written as a nomen sacrum (sacred name) in all MSS. The

word "spirit" is written in full (in *plene*; i.e., not a sacred name) in B, suggesting the human spirit. The word *pneuma* is written as nomen sacrum (sacred name) in $\mathfrak{P}^{26}$ ℵ.

1:9b | the gospel of his Son.

The divine "Son" is written as a nomen sacrum (sacred name) in one early MS (ℵ), as well as L.

1:11 | some Spiritual gift.

"Spiritual" is written as nomen sacrum (sacred word) in one early MS (ℵ), as well as L.

2:16 | my gospel through Christ Jesus.

"Christ Jesus" is the original wording according to the two earliest MSS (ℵ* B). Two variants are "Jesus Christ" (ℵ^{1} A 1739 Maj; so KJV) and "Jesus Christ our Lord" (D).

2:29 | circumcision is of the heart by the Spirit.

The divine "Spirit" is written as a nomen sacrum (sacred name) in two early MSS ($\mathfrak{P}^{113}$ ℵ).

3:25 | the belief in his blood.

This is the wording in two early MSS ($\mathfrak{P}^{40vid}$ B), as well as C^{3} [ninth century] D^{2} 33 Maj. Another reading is, "belief in his blood" in four early MSS (ℵ C* D* 0219^{vid}), as well as F G. The textual evidence is evenly divided. The reading with the definite article points to the specific faith/belief in Jesus mentioned previously in 3:22. The reading without the article emphasizes belief as the means to justification.

4:1 | what will we say that Abraham discovered?

This is the wording according to four early MSS ($\mathfrak{P}^{40vid}$ ℵ^{*,2} [seventh century] A C*), as well as 33; other MSS (B 1739) read, "what will we say about Abraham?" It seems likely that "discovered" was originally part of the text—for several reasons. First, the word is present in the earliest witness, $\mathfrak{P}^{40vid}$ (see Comfort and Barrett, *Text of Earliest NT*

Greek MSS, 152). Second, the verb was often used in the LXX in the context of finding grace or finding mercy from God (see Gen. 18:3). Third, the grammar of the sentence requires an infinitive to complete the sense.

4:19 | his own body as already dead.

The reading "his own body as already dead" is found in three early MSS (א A C), as well as D 33 Maj. The word "already" is not found in the earliest MS (B), as well as F G 1739. The manuscript evidence is divided; either reading could be original.

5:1 | we have peace with God.

This is the reading in two early MSS (א^{1} 0220^{vid}), as well as B^{2} [tenth century] F G P 1739^{c}. Another reading is, "let us have peace with God" in four early MSS (א* A B* C), as well as D L 33 1739*. The manuscript evidence is divided; either reading (whether the indicative verb or the subjunctive verb) could be original. (See Comfort, *NT Text and Translation Commentary*, 443, for discussion about the certainty of the reading in 0220, the earliest witness to this verse.)

5:2 | we have access.

This is the original wording according to two early MSS (B 0220), as well as D F G cop^{sa}. A variant reading is, "we have access by faith" in two early MSS (א* C), as well as 33 1739 Maj, by way of scribal expansion.

5:5 | the Holy Spirit was given to us.

The divine "Spirit" is written as a nomen sacrum (sacred name) in one early MS (א).

6:4 | the glory of the Father.

The divine "Father" is written as a nomen sacrum (sacred name) in one early MS (𝔓^{46vid}).

6:11 | Christ Jesus.

This is the original wording according to early and diverse testimony:

𝔓[46] A B D F G 1739*. The name is "Christ Jesus our Lord" in 𝔓[94vid] ℵ C 33 1739[c] Maj—scribal expansion of a divine name (common in the NT Epistles), perhaps influenced by 5:21; 6:23.

7:6a | released from the Law.
This is the original wording according to four early MSS (ℵ A B C), as well as 33 1739. A variant reading is, "released from death" in D F G. The variant is a scribal attempt to build off the previous phrase, "having died to that which held us."

7:6b | the new life of the Spirit.
The divine "Spirit" is written as a nomen sacrum (sacred name) in one early MS (ℵ).

7:14 | the law is Spiritual.
"Spiritual" is written as a nomen sacrum (sacred word) in one early MS (ℵ*).

7:25 | thanks be to God.
This is the wording in two early MSS (B A[1]), as well as C[2] [sixth century]). Another wording is "I thank God" in two early MSS (ℵ* A), as well as 1739. Two other readings are "the grace of God" (D) and "the grace of the Lord" (F G). Either of the first two readings could be original.

8:2, 4–6. 9a | the Spirit.
The divine "Spirit" is written as a nomen sacrum (sacred name) in one early MS (ℵ).

8:9b | the Spirit of Christ.
"Spirit of Christ" is an unique expression the NT (it appears only elsewhere in 1 Pet 1:11); elsewhere we read of "the Spirit of Jesus" (Acts 16:7) and "the Spirit of Jesus Christ" (Phil. 1:19). The risen Christ is united to the Spirit; the Spirit is Christ. "Spirit" is written as a nomen sacrum (sacred name) in three early MSS (ℵ B C).

8:10–11a | the Spirit.
The divine "Spirit" is written as a nomen sacrum (sacred name) in one early MS (א).

8:11b | raised Christ from the dead.
"Christ" is the original wording according to one early MS (B), as well as D² F G. Two variants are "the Christ" in א² [seventh century] 33 Maj, and "Christ Jesus" in א* A (C D*) 1739, both scribal expansions.

8:11c | will make your bodies alive through his Spirit.
This is the wording in three early MSS (א A C). A variant reading is "make your bodies alive because of his Spirit" in one early MS (B), as well as D F G 33 1739 Maj. Either reading could be original. The first indicates agency (God will resurrect believers through the indwelling Spirit); the second indicates cause (God will resurrect believers because they have the Spirit).

8:13 | the Spirit.
The divine "Spirit" is written as a nomen sacrum (sacred name) in one early MS (א).

8:14 | the Spirit of God.
This expression is written as a nomen sacrum (sacred name) in three early MSS (𝔓²⁷ א B).

8:15a | spirit of slavery
The word "spirit" is written in full (in *plene*; i.e., not as a sacred name) in one early MS (B), denoting "a spirit of slavery"; it is written as a nomen sacrum (sacred name) in another early MS (א), denoting "the Spirit of slavery." (Had the first part of the verse been extant in 𝔓⁴⁶ we might expect to see "a spirit of slavery"; see next note).

8:15b | spirit of sonship
The word "spirit" is written in full (in *plene*; i.e., not as a sacred name) in the two earliest MSS (𝔓⁴⁶ B), denoting "a spirit of sonship"; it is

written as a nomen sacrum (sacred name) in three early MSS (א A C), denoting "the Spirit of sonship."

8:15c | we cry, "Abba, father."

The name "father" is written in full (in *plene*; i.e., not as a sacred name) in the two earliest MSS ($\mathfrak{P}^{46}$ B); it is written as a nomen sacrum (sacred name) in two early MSS (א A), yielding the translation, "Abba, Father." ("Abba" means "father" in Aramaic.)

8:16a | the Spirit.

"Spirit" is written as a nomen sacrum (sacred name) in two early MSS ($\mathfrak{P}^{46}$ א).

8:16b | bears witness with our spirit.

The word "spirit" is written in full (in *plene*; i.e., not as a sacred name) in B, denoting "the human spirit."

8:20–21 | the One who subjected it in hope that the creation will be liberated.

This is the original wording according to early and excellent testimony: $\mathfrak{P}^{27vid}$ $\mathfrak{P}^{46}$ A B C D^2 Maj. A variant reading is, "the One who subjected it in hope, because the creation will be liberated" in א D* F G. The text has the earliest documentary support.

8:23a | spiritual firstfruits.

The word "spirit" (*pneuma*) is written in full (in *plene*; i.e., not a sacred name) in $\mathfrak{P}^{46}$ B, suggesting that which is spiritual; it is written as a nomen sacrum (sacred name) in א, which would be rendered as "firstfruits of the Spirit."

8:23b | eagerly expecting the redemption of our bodies.

This is the wording in the two earliest MSS ($\mathfrak{P}^{27vid}$ $\mathfrak{P}^{46}$), as well as D F G. A variant reading is, "eagerly expecting sonship, the redemption of our bodies" in four early MSS (א A B C), as well as 33 1739 Maj. The text has the support of the two earliest MSS.

8:26a | the Spirit.
The divine "Spirit" is written in both occurrences as a nomen sacrum (sacred name) in two early MSS (𝔓^{27vid} ℵ).

8:26b | intercedes.
This is the original wording according to six early MSS (𝔓^{27vid} 𝔓$^{46vid?}$ ℵ* A B D), as well as F G 1739. A variant reading is, "intercedes on our behalf" in ℵ^{2} [seventh century] C 33 Maj (so KJV), by way of scribal expansion.

8:27 | the Spirit intercedes.
The divine "Spirit" is written as a nomen sacrum (sacred name) in two early MSS (𝔓^{46} ℵ).

8:28 | God turns everything to good.
This is the original wording according to three early MSS (𝔓^{46} A B). A variant reading is, "all things work together for good" in ℵ C D F G 33 1739. The two earliest MSS (𝔓^{46} B) support the text. It is God who turns everything to good; it is not just that everything works out for the good.

8:29, 32 | his Son.
The divine "Son" is written as a nomen sacrum (sacred name) in one early MS (𝔓^{46}).

8:34a | Christ Jesus.
This is the reading in three early MSS (ℵ A C), as well as F G L 33. A variant reading is "Christ" in one early MS (B), as well as D 0289 1739. The manuscript evidence is evenly divided; either reading could be original.

8:34b | he rose again.
This is the original wording according to the three earliest MSS (𝔓^{27vid} 𝔓^{46} B), as well as ℵ^{2} [seventh century] D F G 33 Maj. A variant reading is "rose again from the dead" in three early MSS (ℵ* A C), as well as 0289^{vid}, by way of scribal expansion.

8:35 | God's love.

This is the reading in one early MS (א), as well as cop^{sa} . A variant reading is "Christ's love" in one early MS (C), as well as D F G 33 1739 Maj; another is "God's love in Christ Jesus" in one early MS (B). (Though $\mathfrak{P}^{27}$ and $\mathfrak{P}^{46}$ have lacunae at this point, the space allotment in each MS would support one of the first two readings, not the reading in B.)

9:1 | my conscience assures me in the Holy Spirit.

The divine "Spirit" is written as a nomen sacrum (sacred name) in two early MSS ($\mathfrak{P}^{46}$ א).

9:4a | the covenant.

This is the original wording according to the two earliest MSS ($\mathfrak{P}^{46}$ B), as well as D F G. A variant reading is, "the covenants" in two early MSS (א C), as well as 0285 33 1739 Maj (so KJV). According to the two earliest MSS, the Israelites were entrusted with the one Abrahamic covenant.

9:4b | the promise.

This is the wording in the earliest MS ($\mathfrak{P}^{46}$), as well as D F G. A variant reading is "the promises" in two early MSS (א C), as well as 0285 33 Maj. Either reading could be original.

10:3 | their own way of righteousness.

This is the wording in two early MSS ($\mathfrak{P}^{46}$ א), as well as F G 33 Maj. A variant reading is "their own way" in two early MSS (A B), as well as D. Either reading could be original.

10:9 | confess with your mouth the Lord Jesus Christ.

This is the wording in two early MSS ($\mathfrak{P}^{46}$ A)—$\mathfrak{P}^{46}$ being the earliest (second century). A variant reading is "Lord Jesus" in three early MSS (א A B), as well as F G 33 1739 Maj. The textual evidence is divided; either reading could be original.

10:17 | the message of Christ.

This is the original wording according to four early MSS ($\mathfrak{P}^{46vid}$ א* B C), as well as D* 1739. A variant reading is "the message of God" in ℵ[1] A D[1] 33 Maj (so KJV). The manuscript evidence strongly supports the text.

11:6 | grace would no longer be grace.

This is the original wording in four early MSS (𝔓[46] ℵ* A C), as well as D F G 1739 cop. A variant reading is. "grace would no longer be grace. But if it is of works, then it is no longer grace; otherwise work is no longer work" in one early MS (B), as well as ℵ[2] [seventh century] 33[vid] Maj (so KJV). The textual evidence in favor of the shorter reading is impressive. Furthermore, there is no good reason to account for the omission of the second sentence (in the variant) had it been originally in the epistle. Thus, the variant is likely an interpolation created perhaps as early as the fourth century. But this gloss does not help elucidate the passage, which plainly depicts the nature of grace as being a free gift, not a reward for doing work. The gloss adds nothing to this, but rather detracts with the opaque statement, "otherwise work is no longer work."

11:8a | a spirit of stupor.

The word "spirit" is written in full (in *plene*; i.e. not a sacred name) in two early MSS (𝔓[46] B) to denote a kind of spirit—i.e., "a spirit of stupor."

11:17 | the richness of the olive tree.

This is the original reading according to the earliest MS (𝔓[46]), as well as D* F G cop[bo]. Two variant readings are "the root of the richness of the olive tree" (ℵ* B C), and "the root and the richness of the olive tree" (ℵ[2] A D[2] 33 1739 Maj)—both scribal expansions.

12:11a | zealous in Spirit.

"Spirit" is written as a nomen sacrum (sacred name) in two early MSS (𝔓[46] ℵ). Codex B writes out the word *pneuma* in full (in *plene*; i.e., not as a sacred name), suggesting the translation "zealous in spirit."

12:11b | serving the Lord.

This is the original wording according to four early MSS (𝔓[46] ℵ A B), as well as D[2] 1739 Maj. A variant reading is, "serving the opportune time" in D[*, c] F G Latin MSS[according to Origen, Jerome]. At first glance, one could consider that *kurios* (Lord) was mistaken for *kairos* (opportune time), but in ancient MSS *kurios* was written as a nomen sacrum (sacred name). So one word was not confused for the other by scribes. The variant reading *kairos* is likely the result of a scribe (or Latin translator—as evidenced by the comments of Jerome) attempting to make a general exhortation ("serving the Lord") more specific, especially since the surrounding exhortations are quite pointed. Indeed, the two prior exhortations evoke the images of zeal and fervency. What better way to continue the image than by adding a note about being opportunistic?

13:9a | you shall not steal.
This is the original wording according to three early MSS (𝔓[46] A B), as well as D F G L 1739. A variant reading is, "you shall not steal, you shall not bear false witness" in one early MS (א), as well as 048, by way of scribal expansion.

13:14 | Jesus Christ our Lord.
This is the wording according to the earliest MS (𝔓[46]), as well as it[a,t]. There are several variants: "the Lord Jesus Christ" in three early MSS (א A C), as well as D F G 0285[vid] 33 Maj; "Lord Jesus" in 1739; "Christ Jesus" in one early MS (B). The original reading is likely preserved in 𝔓[46] or א, et al.

14:4a | before his own Lord/lord he stands or falls.
"Lord" is written as a nomen sacrum in four early MSS (𝔓[46] א A B), as well as D* F G. However, it is written as "lord" in C L 33 (i.e., *kurios* is written in full, not as a sacred name). In this context, the statement "to their own Lord/lord they stand or fall" is ambiguous; it can refer to the divine Lord or a human lord/master.

14:4b | the Lord is able to make him stand.
"Lord" is the original word according to five early MSS (𝔓[46] א A B C). "God" is the reading in later MSS (D F G 048 33 1739 Maj). The text has superior documentation.

14:6 | those who observe a certain day do so to the Lord.
This is the original wording according to five early MSS (𝔓^{46} א A B, as well as C^{2vid} [sixth century] D F G 048 1739. A variant reading is, "those who observe a certain day do so to the Lord; and those who don't observe a certain day also do so to the Lord" in later MSS (C^{3} [ninth century] 33 Maj; so KJV), by way of scribal expansion.

14:10 | judgment seat of God.
This is the original wording according to four early MSS (א* A B C*), as well as D F G 1739 cop. A variant reading is, "judgment seat of Christ" in א^{c} C^{2} [sixth century] 048 0209 33 Maj (so KJV). The text has very strong documentation.

14:17 | joy in the Holy Spirit.
The divine "Spirit" is written as a nomen sacrum (sacred name) in two early MSS (𝔓^{46vid} א).

14:21 | to stumble, be ensnared, or made weak.
This is the wording in two early MSS (𝔓^{46vid} B), as well as א^{2} [seventh century] D F G 0209 33 Maj syr^{h} cop^{sa}. A variant reading is, "to stumble" in three early MSS (א* A C), as well as 048 1739 syr^{p} cop^{bo}. Both readings have good documentary support; either reading could be original.

14:23
The doxology that appears as 16:25–27 in most MSS is included here in A P 33 both at the end of chapters 14 and 16. It is added here only in Ψ 0209^{vid} Maj MSS$^{\text{acccording to Origen}}$. The doxology also appears at the end of chapter 15 in the earliest MS, 𝔓^{46} (see extensive notes on 15:33 and 16:23 for discussion).

15:13 | the power of the Holy Spirit.
The divine "Spirit" (*pneuma*) is written as a nomen sacrum (sacred name) in two early MSS (א A).

15:16 | sanctified by the Holy Spirit.
The divine "Spirit" (*pneuma*) is written as a nomen sacrum (sacred name) in two early MSS (א A).

15:19 | Spirit of God.
This is the original wording according to two early MSS ($\mathfrak{P}^{46}$ א), as well as D^1 Maj. The name is "Holy Spirit" in A $D^{*,2}$ F G 1739, and "Spirit" in B. Though scribes tended to expand divine titles, the testimony of $\mathfrak{P}^{46}$ with א is followed here. "Spirit" is written as a nomen sacrum (sacred name) in $\mathfrak{P}^{46}$ א A C D F G L.

15:29 | the full blessing of Christ.
This is the original wording according to five early MSS ($\mathfrak{P}^{46}$ א* A B C), as well as 1739. Two variant readings are "the full blessing of the gospel of Christ" ($\aleph^2$ 33 Maj; so KJV), and "the full assurance of the blessing of Christ" (D* F G). The text has the support of the five earliest MSS.

15:30 | through the love of the Spirit.
"Spirit" is written as a nomen sacrum (sacred name) in two early MSS ($\mathfrak{P}^{46}$ א).

15:31 | my ministry.
This is the original wording according to three early MSS ($\mathfrak{P}^{46}$ א C), as well as D^1 33 1739 Maj. A variant reading is, "my bringing of a gift" in one early MS (B), as well as D* F G. The variant is a scribal attempt to explain that Paul's ministry (or, service) to Jerusalem was the bringing of a (monetary) gift.

15:33 | plus 16:25–27 (the concluding doxology)
The earliest MS, $\mathfrak{P}^{46}$ (dated mid-second century), concludes chapter 15 with a four-verse doxology: 15:33 followed by what is normally printed as 16:25–27. $\mathfrak{P}^{46}$, with its doxology after 15:32, probably reflects a form of the epistle that originally had only fifteen chapters, to which chapter sixteen (a separate, accompanying letter) was later appended. $\mathfrak{P}^{46}$ shows a very primitive form of the Pauline text and

corpus as a whole (see Comfort and Barrett, *Text of Earliest NT Greek MSS*, 204–206). As to Romans, 𝔓46 could very well reflect a form of the epistle as compiled by an early editor of Paul's Epistles—that is, one who placed and arranged Paul's Epistles in one codex. This compiler could have seamed together Paul's original complete epistle from 1:1–15:32, which ends with his four-verse doxology (15:33 with what is usually printed as 16:25–27, concluded with a final "amen") and the appended letter of recommendation (chapter 16)—which in 𝔓46 does not have a final benediction. Rather, it ends with a final greeting from Erastus and Quartus (16:23). So the arrangement in 𝔓46 is as follows: (a) 1:1–15:32; (b) 15:33 + 16:25–27, the doxology—concluded with "amen"; (c) 16:1–23, a short letter with recommendations for Phoebe and greetings for and from several believers. The fact that 𝔓46 (with A F G) does not have an "amen" at the end of 15:33 means that 15:33 is immediately followed by the doxology (usually printed as 16:25–27) and becomes the first part of it, as reflected in this translation. As in many doxologies, Paul elevated his language beyond normal prose into poetry. This poetic doxology is syntactically balanced by the three-time occurrence of the Greek preposition *kata* (translated here as "according to"). For further discussion on the doxology, see note on 16:23.

16:22 | I, Tertius, who wrote this epistle, send you my greetings.
Tertius was Paul's amanuensis. Paul had a habit of dictating his epistles to an amanuensis, then signing off in his own handwriting (see 1 Cor. 16:21; Gal. 6:11–18; Col. 4:18; 2 Thess. 3:17–18; Philem. 19–25). In the autograph the readers would have seen two handwritings—that of the amanuensis, followed by the handwriting of Paul.

16:23
The earliest manuscript, 𝔓46 (mid-second century), ends the book of Romans at the end of 16:23 and immediately begins with the book of Hebrews. The doxology (normally printed as 16:25–27) appears at the end of chapter 15 in 𝔓46 (see note there). Some MSS (see below) add a verse here (16:24), as follows: "The grace of our Lord Jesus Christ be

with you all. Amen." Several other MSS add the doxology of 16:25–27 (see note on 15:33).

The various placements of the doxology in the extant MSS are as follows: (1) 1:1–16:23 + doxology ($\mathfrak{P}^{61\text{vid?}}$ ℵ B C D 1739 it^{d} syr^{p} cop [Note: the first extant page of $\mathfrak{P}^{61}$ exhibits portions of Rom. 16:23, with 16:24 vacant, and 16:25–26. Thus, it is certain that the doxology immediately followed 16:23. What is not certain is whether or not $\mathfrak{P}^{61}$ also had the doxology at the end of Rom. 14 and/or 15]); (2) 1:1–15:32 + 15:33 and doxology + 16:1–23 ($\mathfrak{P}^{46}$); (3) 1:1–14:23 + doxology + 15:1–16:23 + doxology (A P 33); (4) 1:1–14:23 + doxology + 15:1–16:24 (L Ψ 0209^{vid} syr^{h} MSS$^{\text{according to Origen}}$ [Origen is said to have known MSS that included the doxology after 14:23]); (5) 1:1–16:24 (F G MSS$^{\text{according to Jerome}}$ [In Codex G, the scribe left a space after 14:23 large enough to contain the doxology, intimating that he knew of MSS that placed it after 14:23 but that it was not so in his exemplar. Jerome indicated he knew of various MSS that did not contain the doxology]) (6) 1:1–14:23 Marcion$^{\text{according to Origen}}$ (According to Rufunius' translation of Origen's *Commentary on Romans* 8.453, Origen said Marcion not only deleted 16:25–27, but also all of chapters 15–16); (7) 1:1–14:23 + 16:24 + doxology (Vulgate MSS (1648 1792 2089) Codex Amiatinus^{vid}; (8) 1:1–16:23 + 16:24 + doxology (Maj, so TR); (9) 1:1–14:23 + doxology + 15:1–33 + doxology + 16:1–23 (1506).

The various placements of the doxology in the last chapters of Romans, as well as the content of chapter 15 and especially chapter 16, have caused textual critics and biblical scholars to ask many questions about the arrangement of Paul's epistle to the Romans. Did it originally have only 14 chapters, to which two more were added? Or did it originally have only 15 chapters, to which the sixteenth was added? Or was it a sixteen-chapter epistle from the very beginning? And to which of these chapters does the doxology belong? As to the position that Romans was originally only fourteen chapters, there is no actual Greek manuscript evidence to support this. What we have is Origen's comment that Marcion's edition of Romans ended at chapter fourteen (#6 above), and there are some clues in a few Latin MSS that this may have been so (#7 and see comments below).

If Origen's words about Marcion's deletion can be trusted (see Westcott and Hort, *The New Testament in the Original Greek, Introduction and Appendix,* 111–113, who have their doubts that Origen meant that all of chapters 15–16 were deleted by Marcion), then it is possible that the purported MSS ending with 14:23 or having the doxology there (#4, #6, #7) reflect Marcion's influence. (The readings #3 and # 9 may also reflect this influence, but not fully.) Marcion would have been prone to delete chapter 15 because (1) it says that "whatever was written in former days was written for our instruction" (15:4); (2) it calls Christ "a servant to the circumcised to show God's truthfulness, to confirm the promises given to the patriarchs" (15:8); and (3) it is full of OT quotations (15:9–12). F. F. Bruce (*The Letter of Paul to the Romans*, 29) said, "such a concentration of material offensive to Marcion can scarcely be paralleled in the Pauline writings." It is possible that Marcion would not need to delete chapter 16 because it might not have been known to him.

The chapter summaries or *capitula* in Codex Amiatinus suggest that 16:25–27 immediately followed 14:1–23 in archetypal MSS. *Capitula* 50 reads "concerning the danger of grieving one's brother with one's food, and showing that the kingdom of God is not food and drink but righteousness and peace and joy in the Holy Spirit," followed by *capitula* 51: "concerning the mystery of God, which was kept in silence before the passion but has been revealed after his passion." Gamble (*History of the Text of Romans*, 123–132) argues for the original positioning of the doxology at 14:23 because putting the doxology at 16:23–25 would violate Paul's normal pattern of a grace benediction appearing at the close of the epistle. At the same time, Gamble argues for the inclusion of 16:24, but this has weak textual support (see #4 above).

Whatever one supposes about the epistle originally ending with chapter 14, the textual evidence stands against it. All extant Greek MSS have chapters 14, 15, and 16. Chapter fifteen is completely contiguous with chapter fourteen, and it is replete with Pauline thought—the likes of which only Marcion would object to. The sixteenth chapter is different in intent and content. The epistle does not need it for any kind of completion inasmuch as Paul came to a natural conclusion in 15:30–33, where he asks the believers for their prayers, especially in anticipation of his coming to them, and then concludes with a benediction: "May the God of peace be with you all. Amen."

What we know as Romans 16 may have been sent as a separate letter of recommendation for Phoebe (with personal greetings included), which was later attached to the rest of the epistle. Or Paul may have made two copies of the epistle, one with chapter sixteen (which may have gone to Ephesus) and one without chapter sixteen (which would have gone to Rome). Interestingly, Codex G does not include "in Rome" in Romans 1:7 and 15, and also has all sixteen chapters without a doxology. Some have thought that this codex could be a witness to an earlier form of the epistle that would not have gone to the Romans (see #5 above). However, the subscription in G indicates that the letter was sent to the Romans.

$\mathfrak{P}^{46}$, with its doxology after 15:32 (see #2 above), probably reflects a form of the epistle that originally had only fifteen chapters, to which chapter sixteen (a separate, accompanying letter) was later appended. $\mathfrak{P}^{46}$, dated in the middle of the second century, shows a very primitive form of the Pauline text and corpus as a whole (see Comfort and Barrett, *Text of Earliest NT Greek MSS*, 204–206). As to Romans, $\mathfrak{P}^{46}$ could very well reflect a form of the epistle as compiled by an early editor of Paul's Epistles—that is, one who placed and arranged Paul's Epistles in one codex. This compiler could have seamed together Paul's original complete epistle from 1:1–15:32 (which ends with his four-verse doxology [15:33 + 16:25–27] and a final "amen") and the accompanying letter of recommendation (chapter 16)—which in $\mathfrak{P}^{46}$ does not have a final benediction. Rather, it ends with a final greeting from Erastus and Quartus (16:23). So the arrangement in $\mathfrak{P}^{46}$ is as follows: 1:1–15:32; 15:33 + 16:25–27, the four-verse doxology—concluded with "amen"; 16:1–23 a short letter with recommendations for Phoebe and greetings from several believers.

The double presence of the doxology in certain MSS (A P 33, see #3)—both at the end of chapter 14 and of chapter 16—indicates that by the fifth century (and thereafter) some scribes were seeing the doxology at the end of both chapters in various exemplars and then copied it accordingly. The same holds true for the scribe of 1509, who must have seen the doxology at the end of chapter 15 (as in $\mathfrak{P}^{46}$) and at the end of chapter 16 (as in several MSS) in certain exemplars.

Some scholars think Paul wrote all sixteen chapters as one unit, which he concluded with his doxology at the end of chapter 16 (as in #1 above). This was then abridged to a fifteen-chapter epistle when it was circulated to other churches, because these churches would not need or be interested in the circumstantial details of chapter 16. But since there is not one extant manuscript that ends with chapter 15, this view has no textual support.

In conclusion, it seems to me that the presence of the doxology appearing at the end of chapter 14 only (as in #4) reflects the influence of Marcion. The presence of the doxology at the end of chapter sixteen reflects the work of a compiler (or compilers) who moved it there when they added chapter sixteen to the main body of the letter. The most likely original arrangement is reflected in $\mathfrak{P}^{46}$ (the earliest manuscript), which has the doxology at the end of chapter 15, to which is appended an extra chapter, which probably was a short letter sent along to Rome with the major epistle (Rom. 1–15)—much in the same way that Paul's letter to Philemon was sent along with his letter to the Colossians. Since this short letter begins with Paul's recommendation of Phoebe, it could very well be that Phoebe carried both epistles (Rom. 1–15; Rom. 16) to the leaders of the church in Rome. This letter of recommendation includes several personal greetings and its own short benediction: "the grace of our Lord Jesus be with you" (16:20). In keeping with his usual practice, Paul probably wrote this benediction in his own hand (see Comfort, *Encountering the Manuscripts*, 7–8), as well as the next verse, where he passes on the greetings of "Timothy, my coworker" (16:21). Tertius, the amanuensis of this final chapter and probably of all Romans, signed off in his own hand (16:22). He may have also passed along greetings from Gaius, Erastus, and Quartus—or, as is in keeping with ancient letter writing, each of these men gave their greeting in their own handwriting (16:23). As such, at the close of the original letter, the Roman Christians would see several different signatures. After this, they would not see the doxology; they would see blank papyrus.

TO THE CORINTHIANS 1

Title: To the Corinthians A [= 1]
This is the wording in the three earliest MSS ($\mathfrak{P}^{46}$ ℵ B).

1:6 | the testimony about Christ.
This is the original wording according to four early MSS ($\mathfrak{P}^{46}$ ℵ A C), as well as B^{2} [tenth century] D 33 1739 Maj cop. The name is "God" in one early MS (B*), as well as F G. The text has superior testimony.

1:8 | the day of our Lord Jesus.
This is the original wording according to the two earliest MSS ($\mathfrak{P}^{46}$ B). The name is expanded to "Lord Jesus Christ" in ℵ A C D F G 33 1739 Maj syr cop (so KJV).

1:9 | fellowship with his Son.
The divine "Son" is written as a nomen sacrum (sacred name) in two early MSS ($\mathfrak{P}^{46vid}$ ℵ).

1:14 | I am thankful.
This is the original wording according to the two earliest MSS (ℵ* B). Two variant readings are "I thank God" (ℵ^{2} C D F G Maj; so KJV), and "I thank my God" (A 33), both scribal expansions.

1:17–18 | the Cross.
"Cross" is written as a nomen sacrum (sacred word) in the earliest MS ($\mathfrak{P}^{46}$).

1:23 | preach Christ Crucified.
The word "Crucified" is written as a nomen sacrum (sacred word) in the earliest MS ($\mathfrak{P}^{46}$).

2:1b | the mystery of God.
This is the original wording according to four early MSS ($\mathfrak{P}^{46vid}$ ℵ* A

C), as well as syr^{p} cop^{bo}. A variant reading is "the testimony of God" according to one early MS (B), as well as ℵ^{2} [seventh century] D F G 33 1739. The two words, "mystery" and "testimony" are very close in Greek (*mustērion/marturion*), but it is doubtful they would have been confused one for the other. The earliest manuscript (𝔓^{46}) clearly reads *mustērion*; I have seen this verse in the actual manuscript. This witness (with ℵ* A C), along with the fact that a major theme in 1 Cor. 2 is God's mysteries being revealed by the Spirit to spiritual people, affirms the reading "mystery."

2:4a | persuasive wisdom.
This is the original wording according to the earliest MS (𝔓^{46}), as well as F G. A variant reading is "persuasive words of wisdom" in two early MSS (ℵ* B), as well as D 33 1739, by way of scribal expansion.

2:4b | demonstration of the Spirit and power.
The divine "Spirit" is written as a nomen sacrum (sacred name) in two early MSS (𝔓^{46} ℵ). Codex B writes out the word *pneuma* in full (in *plene*; i.e., not as a sacred name), suggesting the translation, "demonstration of spirit and power."

2:10 | he has revealed these to us by the spirit, for the spirit searches all things, even the deep things of God.
The word "spirit" (*pneuma*) is written in full (in *plene*; i.e., not as a sacred name) in both occurrences in the two earliest MSS (𝔓^{46} B). The reading in these two MSS shows that the scribes were thinking of the human spirit as being the medium through which the Spirit of God reveals his truths. Other MSS write *pneuma* as nomen sacrum (sacred name), yielding the translation, "he has revealed these to us by the Spirit, for the Spirit searches all things."

2:11a | the man's spirit within him.
The word "spirit" (*pneuma*) is written in full (in *plene*; i.e., not as a sacred name) in the two earliest MSS (𝔓^{46vid} B), denoting the human spirit.

2:11b | Spirit of God.
"Spirit of God" is written as a nomen sacrum (sacred name) in the three earliest MSS ($\mathfrak{P}^{46}$ א B).

2:12a | the spirit of the world.
The word "spirit" (*pneuma*) is written in full (in *plene*; i.e., not as a sacred name) in the two earliest MSS ($\mathfrak{P}^{46}$ B). This is the world's spirit; in contrast to the divine Spirit in 2:12b.

2:12b, 13a | the Spirit.
The divine "Spirit" is written as a nomen sacrum (sacred name) in two early MSS ($\mathfrak{P}^{46}$ א).

2:13b | matching spiritual with spiritual.
This can be rendered as "interpreting spiritual truths with spiritual words," according to three early MSS ($\mathfrak{P}^{46}$ B 0185), which don't write "spiritual [words]" as a nomen sacrum (sacred name). א writes both words for "spiritual" as nomina sacra (sacred names), allowing the translation, "interpreting truths of the Spirit to people of the Spirit" (cf. 3:1). The earliest interpreter of this passage was the scribe of $\mathfrak{P}^{46}$. He wrote *pneumatikois pneumatika sugkrinontes*. Had he wanted to indicate "spiritual people" he would have written *pneumatikois* as a nomen sacrum (sacred word), which is what he did for the same word in 1 Cor. 2:15 and 3:1 (see Comfort and Barrett, *The Text of the Earliest NT Greek Manuscripts*, 253, where the scribe used the nomen sacrum for *pneuma* to denote the "Spirit-people" in 2:15 and 3:1). Because he wrote out the word *pneumatikois* in full (in *plene*; i.e., not as a nomen sacrum) in 2:13, we can be certain his interpretation was "matching/explaining spiritual truths with spiritual words," not "explaining spiritual truths to spiritual people." The scribe's interpretation of the last phrase of 2:13 completely accords with the previous part of the verse, which says, "when we tell you these things, we do not use words that come from human wisdom. Instead, we speak words given to us by the Spirit"—which is perfectly followed by "matching/explaining spiritual truths with spiritual words."

2:14a | the Spirit of God.
"Spirit of God" is written as a nomen sacrum (sacred name) in the three earliest MSS (𝔓^{46} ℵ B).

2:14b | person knowing the Spirit.
This translation is defensible according to the orthography of several early MSS (𝔓^{46} ℵ A C), as well as 1739, which write the expression as a nomen sacrum (sacred name).

2:15a | person knowing the Spirit.
This translation is defensible according to the orthography of several early MSS (𝔓^{46} ℵ A C), as well as D 1739, which write the expression as a nomen sacrum (sacred name).

3:1b | people knowing the Spirit.
This translation is based on the fact that two early MSS (𝔓^{46} ℵ) write this expression *pneumatikois* as a nomen sacrum (sacred name).

3:4 | are you not merely human?
This is the original wording according to five early MSS (𝔓^{46} ℵ* A B C), as well as 048 0289 33 1739. Other MSS (ℵ^{2} [seventh century] Ψ Maj syr; so KJV) substitute "carnal" for the last word. The text has superior documentation.

3:10 | God's grace.
This is the wording in four early MSS (ℵ* A B C), as well as D F G 0289 33 1739. This is shortened to "the grace" in 𝔓^{46} 81 it^{b} Clement. The shorter reading may be original, but there is not enough textual evidence to be sure.

3:16 | the Spirit of God lives in you.
"Spirit of God" is written as a nomen sacrum (sacred name) in the three earliest MSS (𝔓^{46} ℵ B).

4:17 | Christ Jesus.

This is the wording in three early MSS ($\mathfrak{P}^{46}$ ℵ C), as well as D^1 33 1739. Two other readings are “Christ” (A B D^2 Ψ Maj) and “Lord Jesus” (D^* F G). The text and first variant have early and diverse documentation; either could be original.

4:21 | gentleness of the Spirit.

This is a rendering supported by four early MSS ($\mathfrak{P}^{46}$ ℵ A C), as well as D 1739, which write *pneuma* as a nomen sacrum (sacred name). Other MSS (B F G) write out the word *pneuma* in full (in *plene*; i.e., not as a sacred name), prompting the rendering, “a gentle spirit.”

5:3 | I am present in the Spirit.

“Spirit” is written as a nomen sacrum (sacred name) in two early MSS ($\mathfrak{P}^{46}$ ℵ). The reading in B, which does not write it as a nomen sacrum, allows the rendering “I am present in spirit.”

5:4a | Lord Jesus Christ.

This is the wording in two early MSS ($\mathfrak{P}^{46}$ ℵ), as well as D^2 F G 33 Maj. A variant reading is “Lord Jesus” in one early MS (B), as well as D^* 1739. Either reading could be original.

5:4b | my spirit is with you.

This reflects the orthography of B, where *pneuma* is written in full (in *plene*; i.e., not as a sacred name).

5:5a | so that his spirit may be saved.

This reflects of the orthography of B, where *pneuma* is written in full (in *plene*; i.e., not as a sacred name). The phrase could also be rendered “so that the Spirit may be saved,” following the orthography of $\mathfrak{P}^{46}$ ℵ, which write *pneuma* as a nomen sacrum (sacred name).

5:5b | Lord.

This is the original wording according to the two earliest MSS ($\mathfrak{P}^{46}$ B), as well as 1739. The title is expanded to "Lord Jesus" in 𝔓$^{61\text{vid}}$ א Ψ Maj, and "Lord Jesus Christ" in A D F G.

5:7 | sacrificed.

This is the original wording according to five early MSS (𝔓$^{46\text{vid}}$ א* A B C*), as well as 𝔓$^{11\text{vid}}$ D F G 33 1739. Another wording is "sacrificed for us" in later MSS (א^{2} [seventh century] C^{3} [ninth century] Ψ Maj; so KJV), by way of scribal expansion. (The *editio principes* of 𝔓^{46} did not reconstruct this portion of the manuscript, but it is reconstructed in Comfort and Barrett, *Text of Earliest NT Greek MSS*, 257.)

6:11a | Lord Jesus Christ.

This is the original wording according to four early MSS (𝔓^{46} א B C^{vid}), as well as 𝔓$^{11\text{vid}}$ D* 33 1739. A variant reading is "Lord Jesus" in A D^{2} Ψ Maj (so KJV).

6:11b | the Spirit of our God.

The divine "Spirit" is written as a nomen sacrum (sacred name) in two early MSS (𝔓^{46} א).

6:17 | the one united with the Lord is one spirit with him.

The word "spirit" is written in full (in *plene*; i.e., not as a sacred name) in the two earliest MSS (𝔓^{46} B), as well as 𝔓^{11}, designating a spiritual union between the Spirit of God and the human spirit.

6:19 | your body is the temple of the Holy Spirit.

The divine "Spirit" is written as a nomen sacrum (sacred name) in two early MSS (𝔓^{46} א).

7:5 | devote yourselves to prayer.

This is the original wording according to early and diverse MSS: 𝔓$^{11\text{vid}}$ 𝔓^{46} א* A B C D F G Ψ 1739 cop. A variant reading is "devote yourselves to fasting and prayer" in א^{2} [seventh century] Maj syr (so KJV), by way of scribal expansion perhaps influenced by a variant in Mark 9:29 (see note there).

7:34a | virgin.
This is the wording in two early MSS ($\mathfrak{P}^{15}$ B). A variant reading is "unmarried virgin" in three early MSS ($\mathfrak{P}^{46}$ ℵ A), as well as 33 1739. Either reading could be original.

7:34b | both in body and spirit.
This follows the orthography of B where *pneuma* (spirit) is written out in full (in *plene*; i.e., not as a sacred name).

7:40 | the Spirit of God.
This is the wording in five early MSS ($\mathfrak{P}^{46}$ ℵ A B C), as well as D F G 1739. A variant reading is "the Spirit of Christ" in one early MS ($\mathfrak{P}^{15}$), as well as 33. Even though the expression "Spirit of Christ" is rare in the NT (Rom. 8:9; 1 Pet 1:11), textual evidence favors "Spirit of God." "Spirit" is written as a nomen sacrum (sacred name) in $\mathfrak{P}^{15}$ $\mathfrak{P}^{46}$ ℵ.

8:3 | if anyone loves God, this person is recognized by him.
This is the wording in three early MSS ($\mathfrak{P}^{15}$ A B), as well as $\aleph^{2}$ [seventh century] D F G. A variant reading is, "if anyone loves, this person is recognized" in the earliest MS ($\mathfrak{P}^{46}$), as well as Clement. The shorter reading could be original, but there is not enough textual evidence to be certain.

8:6 | there is one God, the Father.
"God" is written as a nomen sacrum (sacred name) in all MSS. "Father" is written as a nomen sacrum (sacred name) in the earliest MS ($\mathfrak{P}^{46}$).

8:12 | wound their conscience.
This is the reading in the earliest MS ($\mathfrak{P}^{46}$), as well as Clement; another reading is "weak conscience" in ℵ A B D 33 1739 Maj, likely scribal expansion.

9:9 | it is written in the Law.
This is the reading in the earliest MS ($\mathfrak{P}^{46}$). All other MSS read "it is

written in the Law of Moses." It is possible that $\mathfrak{P}^{46}$ preserves the original reading and that all other MSS display a scribal expansion.

10:2 | immersed themselves (or, baptized themselves).
This is the original wording according to the two earliest MSS ($\mathfrak{P}^{46}$ B), as well as 1739 Maj Origen. A variant reading is "were immersed (or, were baptized)" in ℵ A C D F G 33. The text has the earliest manuscript support.

10:9 | let us not tempt Christ.
This is the original wording according to the earliest MS ($\mathfrak{P}^{46}$), as well as D F G Ψ 1739 Maj. Two variants on the divine name are "the Lord" (ℵ B C 33) and "God" (A). "Christ" is the more difficult reading, with the earliest support; the reader would not expect Paul to be saying that the Israelites were testing Christ when they were in the wilderness. But we must remember that Paul has already said that the spiritual rock they drank from was "Christ" (10:4), so he pictured the preincarnate Christ as being in the wilderness with the Israelites.

11:24 | my body for you.
This is the original wording according to five early MSS ($\mathfrak{P}^{46}$ ℵ* A B C*), as well as 1739*. Two variant readings in later MSS are "my body broken for you" in $\aleph^{2}$ [seventh century] C^{3} [ninth century] D^{2} F G Ψ 1739^{mg} Maj (so KJV), and "my body sacrificed for you" in D*, both scribal expansions.

11:29a | whoever eats and drinks, eats and drinks judgment to himself.
This is the original wording according to five early MSS ($\mathfrak{P}^{46}$ ℵ* A B C*), as well as 1739 cop. A variant reading of the first phrase is "whoever eats and drink unworthily" in $\aleph^{2}$ [seventh century] C^{c} D F G Maj syr (so KJV), by way of scribal expansion.

11:29b | not discerning the body.
This is the original wording according to five early MSS ($\mathfrak{P}^{46}$ ℵ* A B

C*), as well as 1739 cop. A variant reading is, "not discerning the body of the Lord" in א² [seventh century] C^c D F G Maj syr (so KJV), by way of scribal clarification.

12:3–4, 7–9, 11, 13a | the Spirit.

The divine "Spirit" is written as a nomen sacrum (sacred name) in two early MSS (𝔓⁴⁶ א).

12:9 | the Spirit.

This is the wording in the earliest MS (𝔓⁴⁶). Two other readings are "the one Spirit" in A B 33 1739, and "the same Spirit" in א C³ [ninth century] D F G 0201 Maj (so KJV). It is likely that 𝔓⁴⁶ preserves the original wording and that the other two readings are scribal expansions.

12:10 | to discern spirits.

The idea in the translation is that some have the ability to determine if a prophet is speaking by the Spirit or not. Several MSS (𝔓⁴⁶ א A D) write *pneumatōn* as a nomen sacrum (sacred name), suggesting that some of these scribes may have been thinking of the divine Spirit speaking to each prophet. Other scribes (B F G) wrote out the word *pneumatōn* in full (in *plene*; i.e., not as a sacred name), suggesting that these scribes were thinking of the human spirits of the prophets.

12:13b | one Spirit.

The divine "Spirit" is written in both occurrences as a nomen sacrum (sacred name) in two early MSS (𝔓⁴⁶ א).

13:3 | if I give my body that I may boast.

The verb "boast" (*kauchēsōmai*) is supported by the earliest MSS (𝔓⁴⁶ א A B) and other MSS (048 33 1739 cop MSS^according to Jerome^). It is to be understood that the giving of one's body probably indicates martyrdom. Other MSS (C D F G L Maj; so KJV) have the word *kauthēsōmai* (I may burn)—"If I give my body that I may burn." Martydom via burning at the stake did not happen until about 10 years after Paul wrote 1 Corinthians, during Nero's persecution of Christians in Rome.

13:5 | love is not rude.
This is the original wording according to all MSS but one, namely 𝔓[46] (the earliest MS), which reads "love is not pretentious."

13:8 | love never ends.
This is the original wording according to five early MSS (𝔓[46] ℵ* A B C*), as well as 048 0243 33 1739. A variant reading in later MSS is "love never fails" in ℵ[2] [seventh century] C[3] [ninth century] D F G Ψ Maj (so KJV). The text has superior testimony.

14:2 | he is speaking mysteries of the Spirit.
"Spirit" is written as a nomen sacrum (sacred name) in two early MSS (𝔓[46] ℵ).

14:14 | my spirit prays.
Th word "spirit" is written in full (in *plene*; i.e., not a sacred name) in the two earliest MSS (𝔓[46] B), denoting the human spirit.

14:15a | I will pray in the Spirit.
"Spirit" is written as a nomen sacrum (sacred name) in two early MSS (𝔓[46] ℵ).

14:15b | I will sing in my spirit.
The word "spirit" is written in full (in *plene*; i.e., not a sacred name) in the two earliest MSS (𝔓[46vid] B), denoting the human spirit.

14:16 | praising in the Spirit.
"Spirit" is written as a nomen sacrum (sacred name) in two early MSS (𝔓[46] ℵ).

14:33 | For God is not the author of discord but of harmony, as in all the gatherings of the saints.
This reflects the reading of the three earliest MSS (𝔓[46] ℵ B), contra NA[27] and UBS[4], which join this phrase with the beginning of 14:34. The difference in meaning is significant: harmony is the rule of God for

all the gatherings of the believers (so the translation above). Paul was not saying that women should be silent in all the Christian gatherings, only in Corinth, which must have been experiencing problems with women speaking out of turn during the prophesying.

14:34–35
Some MSS (D F G it[a,b]) place these verses after 14:40, prompting some scholars to deem these verses as a gloss that was added into the text (see full discussion in *NT Text and Translation Commentary*, 518–519). But the earliest MSS ($\mathfrak{P}^{46}$ א A B) place the verses after 14:33.

14:38 | let him be ignorant.
This is the wording in early and diverse MSS: $\mathfrak{P}^{46}$ א[2] [seventh century] A[c] B D[2] Ψ Maj. A variant reading is, "he himself is ignored," also in early and diverse MSS: א* A*vid D (F G) 048 0243 33 1739. Either reading could be original.

15:24 | when he hands over the kingdom to God the Father.
"God" is written as a nomen sacrum (sacred name) in all MSS. "Father" is written as a nomen sacrum (sacred name) in two early MSS ($\mathfrak{P}^{46}$ א).

15:45 | the last Adam became life-giving Spirit.
The divine "Spirit" is written as a nomen sacrum (sacred name) in two early MSS ($\mathfrak{P}^{46}$ א). Jesus, the last Adam, became "life-giving Spirit" in resurrection. There is no article before *pneuma* in the Greek; it does not mean that he became *the* Spirit (as if the Spirit did not exist before Christ's resurrection), but that he became "live-giving Spirit" in his resurrection.

15:46 | the Spiritual.
The word "Spiritual" is written in both occurrences as a nomen sacrum (sacred word) in two early MSS ($\mathfrak{P}^{46}$ א).

15:47 | the second, Spiritual man from heaven.
This is the reading in the earliest MS, 𝔓[46] (where "Spiritual" is written as a nomen sacrum [sacred word]). There are three variant readings on this: "the second man from heaven" (ℵ* B C D* 0243 33), "the second man, the Lord from heaven" (ℵ[2] [seventh century] A D[1] 075 1739[mg]), and "the second man, the heavenly one from heaven" (F G). The textual evidence points to one of the first two readings as being original—the one in 𝔓[46] or the one in ℵ*, et al.

15:49 | let us also express the image of the heavenly man.
This is the original wording according to four early MSS (𝔓[46] ℵ A C), as well as D F G Ψ 075 0243 1730 Maj Clement Origen. A variant reading is, "we will also express the image of the heavenly man" in B I. The documentary evidence strongly supports the text.

15:54a | when the mortal puts on immortality.
This is the wording according to two early MSS (𝔓[46] ℵ*), as well as 088 0243 1739* it cop[bo]. A variant reading is, "when the perishable puts on the imperishable and when the mortal puts on immortality" in later MSS: ℵ[2] [seventh century] (A) B C[2vid] [sixth century] D (33) 1739[c] Maj (so KJV). F and G omit both these clauses due to homoeoteleuton.

16:18 | they refreshed my spirit and yours.
This reflects the orthography of B where *pneuma* is written in full (i.e., not a a sacred name). An alternative rendering is "they have refreshed the Spirit you and I share," based on *pneuma* being written as a nomen sacrum (sacred name) in two early MSS (𝔓[46] ℵ).

16:19 | Aquila and Priscilla greet you heartily in the Lord.
This is the reading in the earliest MS (𝔓[46]), as well as 69 and few other MSS. Most other MSS read, "the churches of Asia greet you; Aquila and Priscilla greet you heartily in the Lord." The shorter reading in 𝔓[46] is possibly original. How could Paul, residing in Ephesus at that time, send greetings from *all* the churches in the province of Asia?

16:21 | I, Paul, send this greeting with my own hand.
Paul had dictated this letter to an amanuensis (see Rom. 16:22) and then signed off in his own handwriting (so also Gal. 6:11–18; Col. 4:18; 2 Thess. 3:17–18; Philem. 19–25). He did so at the end of every epistle (2 Thess. 3:17). The readers of the original writing would have seen two handwritings—that of the amanuensis and that of Paul (16:21–24).

TO THE CORINTHIANS 2

Title: To the Corinthians B [= 2]
This is the wording in the three earliest MSS (𝔓[46] א B).

1:12 | sacredness.
This is the original wording according to the five earliest MSS (𝔓[46] א* A B C), as well as P Ψ 0121 0243 33 1739. A variant reading is "simplicity" in later MSS: א[2] [seventh century] D F G Maj (so KJV), as well as it syr. Although the two words could easily be confused for one another (*hagioteti*/*haploteti*), the text has superior textual support.

1:13 | we did not write to you anything other than what you can read.
This is the original wording according to the two earliest MSS (𝔓[46] B). Most other MSS add to this: "and what you can know."

1:22a | he gave us the Spirit.
The divine "Spirit" is written as a nomen sacrum (sacred name) in two early MSS (𝔓[46] א), as well as 0223.

2:13 | I had no rest in my spirit.
The word "spirit" (*pneuma*) is written in full (in *plene*; i.e., not as a sacred name) in the two earliest MSS (𝔓[46vid] B), denoting the human spirit.

2:17 | we are not like the rest of the people who peddle the word of God for profit.
This is the original wording according to the earliest MS (𝔓[46]), as well as D F G L syr. A variant reading is, "we are not like many people who peddle the word of God for profit" in four early MSS (א A B C), as well as Ψ 0243 33 1739 Maj it cop. The text has the earliest support (𝔓[46]) and is the more difficult reading in that Paul is condemning "the rest of the people," not just "many people."

3:3 | the Spirit of the living God.
The divine "Spirit" is written as a nomen sacrum (sacred name) in two early MSS (𝔓^{46} א).

3:6a | a new covenant, not of letter but of spirit.
The word "spirit" is written in full (in *plene*; i.e., not as a sacred name) in the two earliest MSS (𝔓^{46} B), denoting the spiritual nature of the new covenant. See next note.

3:6b | the Spirit gives life.
The divine "Spirit" is written as a nomen sacrum (sacred name) in two early MSS (𝔓^{46} א). Note how 𝔓^{46} writes "spirit" in the first part of the verse and "Spirit" in the next part to differentiate the two different uses of the word *pneuma* in this verse.

3:17a | the Lord is the Spirit.
The divine "Spirit" is written as a nomen sacrum (sacred name) in three early MSS (𝔓^{46} א I). The resurrected "Lord" is one and the same as "the Spirit."

3:17b | the Spirit of the Lord.
This title is written as a nomen sacrum (sacred name) in four early MSS (𝔓^{46} א B I^{vid}).

3:18 | the Lord, who is the Spirit.
The divine "Spirit" appears as a nomen sacrum (sacred name) in two early MSS (𝔓^{46} א). The resurrected "Lord" is one and the same as "the Spirit."

4:4 | the God of this age.
"God" is written as a nomen sacrum (sacred name) in the three earliest MSS (𝔓^{46vid} א B). The idea is that Satan has usurped God's authority for himself and thereby assumed the position as the God who controls this age. Most translations render this as "god," which is supported by one late manuscript, 365 (twelfth century)—it writes out *theos* in full (i.e., in *plene*, not as a sacred name).

4:5 | your servants through Jesus.
This is the original wording according to four early MSS ($\mathfrak{P}^{46}$ א* A^c C), as well as 0243 33 1739. Two variants are "your servants through Christ" (א^{1}), and "your servants because of Jesus" (A*vid B D F G H Ψ 0209 Maj; so KJV). The reading of the text has early and diverse testimony.

4:6b | the face of Jesus Christ.
This is the original wording according to three early MSS ($\mathfrak{P}^{46}$ א C), as well as H Ψ 0209 1739^c Maj. Two variants on the divine name are "Christ Jesus" (D F G 0243 1739*) and "Jesus" (A B 33). The reading of the text has early and diverse testimony.

4:13 | we have the same spirit of faith.
The word "spirit" (*pneuma*) is written in full (in *plene*, i.e., not as a sacred name) in B, suggesting the human spirit. "Spirit" is written as a nomen sacrum (sacred name) in א, suggesting the translation, "we have the same Spirit of faith."

4:14 | the one who raised up Jesus.
"Jesus" is the original wording according to the two earliest MSS ($\mathfrak{P}^{46}$ B), as well as 0243 33 1739. A variant reading is "Lord Jesus" in א C D F G Ψ Maj, by way of scribal expansion.

5:5 | God, who gave us the Spirit.
"God" is written as a nomen sacrum (sacred name) in all MSS. The divine "Spirit" is written as a nomen sacrum (sacred name) in two early MSS ($\mathfrak{P}^{46}$ א).

5:19 | the gospel of reconciliation.
This is the reading in $\mathfrak{P}^{46}$. Two other readings are, "the message of reconciliation" (א B C Maj) and "the gospel, the message of reconciliation" (D* F G). The original reading is one of the first two readings ($\mathfrak{P}^{46}$ or א et al.).

6:6 | by the Holy Spirit
The divine "Spirit" is written as a nomen sacrum (sacred name) in $\mathfrak{P}^{46}$ א.

6:18 | I will be a father to you.
The word "father" is written in full (in *plene*; i.e., not as a nomen sacrum) in the three earliest MSS (𝔓[46] א B), pointing to one who is a father, not a title.

7:13 | all of you have refreshed his [Titus's] spirit.
The word "spirit" (*pneuma*) is written in full (in *plene*; i.e. not as a sacred name) in the two earliest MSS (𝔓[46] B), denoting the human spirit.

8:21 | we are concerned about what is right not only before God but before people.
"Before God" is the wording of the earliest MS (𝔓[46]), as well as it syr[p]. Nearly all other MSS read, "before the Lord," perhaps in scribal conformity to Prov. 3:4 LXX, the verse alluded to here.

10:1 | Now I, Paul, appeal to you personally.
It is possible that Paul took pen (stylus) in hand and began to write the rest of the epistle (see 13:10), as he did in other epistles (Gal. 6:11–18; 2 Thess. 3:17–18). Some scholars think chapters 10–13 are a separate epistle, perhaps "the sorrowful letter" that Paul refers to in 7:8, which was then appended to the end of chapter 9 by some editor early in the textual history of Paul's epistles.

11:3 | simplicity and purity.
This is the original wording according to the three earliest MSS (𝔓[46] א* B), as well as D[(2)] F G 33. The wording is "simplicity" in א[2] [seventh century] H Ψ 0121 0243 1739 Maj. The text has early and diverse documentation.

11:4 | if you receive a different spirit.
The word "spirit" (pneuma) is written in full (in *plene*; i.e., not as a sacred name) in the two earliest MSS (𝔓[46] B), denoting that which is "spirit," not a divine title.

11:6 | I don't lack knowledge.
This is the wording in the earliest MS (𝔓[46]). All other MSS read, "I

don't lack knowledge, as we have manifested to you in every way." It is possible that 𝔓[46] preserves the original wording.

11:31 | God and Father.

"God" is written as a nomen sacrum (a sacred name) in all MSS. The divine "Father" is written as a nomen sacrum (sacred name) in the earliest MS (𝔓[46]), as well as L 33.

12:18 | Didn't we conduct ourselves in the same Spirit?

"Spirit" is written as a nomen sacrum (sacred name) in two early MSS (𝔓[46] א). The word "spirit" (*pneuma*) is written in full (in *plene*, i.e., not as a sacred name) in B, suggesting the rendering, "in the same spirit."

13:13 | the fellowship of spirit.

In the earliest MS (𝔓[46]) the word for "spirit" (*pneuma*) is written in full (in *plene*; i.e., not as a sacred name), suggesting the spiritual fellowship of the believers, an *espirit de corp*. All other MSS read "the fellowship of the Holy Spirit." The exclusion of "holy" in 𝔓[46] could suggest that the original text was embellished to have a more traditional Trinitarian formula, making the third "person" of the Trinity "the Holy Spirit."

TO THE GALATIANS

Title: To the Galatians
This is the wording in the three earliest MSS ($\mathfrak{P}^{46}$ ℵ B).

1:3–4 | Father.
"Father" is written as a nomen sacrum (sacred name) in early MSS: $\mathfrak{P}^{46}$ (1:4) and $\mathfrak{P}^{51}$ (1:3–4).

1:6 | called you by grace.
This is the wording according to the earliest MS ($\mathfrak{P}^{46vid}$), as well as F* G H^{vid}. Two variant readings are, "called you by the grace of Christ" in four early MSS ($\mathfrak{P}^{51}$ ℵ A B), as well as F^c Ψ 33 1739, and "called you by the grace of Jesus Christ" in D. One of the first two readings is original.

1:8–9
Based on line lengths and page length, it is likely that $\mathfrak{P}^{46}$ did not include 1:9, which reads, "As we have just said, and now say again, if anyone proclaims a message besides that which you received, let that one be cursed!" (For reconstruction of the text of $\mathfrak{P}^{46}$ here, see Comfort and Barrett, *Text of Earliest NT Greek MSS*, 313).

1:15a | the One who set me apart.
This is the original wording according to the earliest MSS ($\mathfrak{P}^{46}$ B), as well as F G. The wording "the One" was changed to "God" in ℵ A D Ψ 0278 33 1739 Maj, by way of scribal clarification.

1:15b | from the time I was in my mother's womb.
This is probably the original wording according to the earliest MS ($\mathfrak{P}^{46}$), as well as 1739 1881. A variant reading adds, "and called me by his grace," in ℵ A B D F G Ψ 33 Maj—probably scribal expansion.

1:16 | reveal his Son in me.
"Son" is written as a nomen sacrum (sacred name) in two early MSS ($\mathfrak{P}^{46}$ ℵ).

2:12 | a certain person . . . came.

This is the reading in $\mathfrak{P}^{46}$ (and some Old Latin MSS). All other MSS read, "certain people . . . came." According to $\mathfrak{P}^{46}$, it was one individual (representing the circumcision party) who caused the problems in Galatia.

2:19 | I have been Crucified with Christ.

The word "Crucified" is written as a nomen sacrum (sacred word) in the earliest MS ($\mathfrak{P}^{46}$).

2:20 | the faithfulness of God and Christ.

This is probably the original wording according to the two earliest MSS ($\mathfrak{P}^{46}$ B), as well as D* F G. A variant reading is, "the faithfulness of the Son of God" in three early MSS (א A C), as well as D^1 Ψ 0278 33 1739 Maj.

3:2–3, 5 | the Spirit.

The divine "Spirit" is written as a nomen sacrum (sacred name) in two early MSS ($\mathfrak{P}^{46}$ א).

3:14 | the blessing of the Spirit.

This is the wording according to the earliest MS ($\mathfrak{P}^{46}$), as well as $D^{*,c}$ F G it^b. A variant reading is "the promise of the Spirit" in five early MSS ($\mathfrak{P}^{99}$ א A B C), as well as D^2 Ψ 0278 33 1739 Maj syr cop. The textual evidence is divided; either reading could be original—and both fit the context: the promised Spirit is a blessing. The divine "Spirit" is written as a nomen sacrum (sacred name) in two early MSS ($\mathfrak{P}^{46vid}$ א).

3:19 | So what is the purpose of the Law of deeds? It was there until the Seed would come.

This is the original wording according to the earliest MS ($\mathfrak{P}^{46}$), as well as F G (which both read "it was established" instead of "it was there"). A variant reading is, "so what is the purpose of the Law? It was added for the sake of the transgression until the Seed should come" (א A B C D^2 Ψ 33 1739 Maj), probably by way of scribal expansion.

3:21 | the promises.

This is the original wording according to the two earliest MSS (𝔓46 B). A variant reading is, "the promises of God" in ℵ A C D (F G) Ψ 33 1739 Maj, by way of scribal expansion.

4:1 | he is lord of everything.

The word "lord" (*kurios*) is written in full (in *plene*; i.e., not as a sacred name) in the earliest MS (𝔓46vid), denoting the one who is "a master" or "owner."

4:2 | until the date set by the father.

The word "father" is written in full (in *plene*; i.e., not as a sacred name) in ℵ B, pointing to an earthly father. 𝔓46 writes it as a nomen sacrum (sacred name), pointing to the divine Father.

4:4 | God sent his Son.

"God" is written as a nomen sacrum (sacred name) in all MSS. "Son" is written as a nomen sacrum (sacred name) in four early MSS (𝔓46 ℵ A C), as well as L 33 1739.

4:6a | the Spirit of his Son.

This is written as a nomen sacrum (sacred name) in three early MSS (ℵ A C). The earliest MS (𝔓46) reads simply "the Spirit."

4:6b | Abba! Father!

"Father" is written as a nomen sacrum (sacred name) in the earliest MS (𝔓46).

4:29; 5:5 | the Spirit.

"Spirit" is written as a nomen sacrum (sacred name) in two early MSS (𝔓46 ℵ).

5:11 | the offense of the Cross.

The word "Cross" is written as a nomen sacrum (sacred word) in the earliest MS (𝔓46).

5:16–18, 22 | the Spirit.
The divine "Spirit" is written as a nomen sacrum (sacred name) in two early MSS (𝔓[46] א).

5:24a | those who belong to Christ.
This is the original wording according to the earliest MS (𝔓[46]), as well as D F G 0122 Maj. The divine name is "Christ Jesus" in א A B C 33 1739, by way of scribal expansion.

5:24b | have Crucified the flesh.
The word "Crucified" is written as a nomen sacrum (sacred word) in the earliest MS (𝔓[46]).

5:25 | the Spirit.
The divine "Spirit" is written in both occurrences as a nomen sacrum (sacred name) in two early MSS (𝔓[46] א).

6:1 | the Spirit of meekness.
The divine "Spirit" is written as a nomen sacrum (sacred name) in two early MSS (𝔓[46] א). Codex B writes out the word in full (in *plene*; i.e., not a sacred name), suggesting the rendering "a spirit of meekness."

6:8 | the Spirit.
The divine "Spirit" is written in both occurrences as a nomen sacrum (sacred name) in two early MSS (𝔓[46] א).

6:11 | different handwriting .
This is the original wording according to the two earliest MSS (𝔓[46] B*), as well as 33. Two variant readings are "diversified handwriting" in 0278 642, and "large handwriting" in א A B[c] C D F G L 1739. At this point in the composition of the epistle, the amanuensis stopped writing and Paul took stylus in hand and wrote out the rest of the epistle (6:11–18) in his own handwriting. (The two different handwritings would be evident in the autograph.) According to 𝔓[46] B* 33, Paul pointed to the fact that the letters would now look "larger" (*hēlikois*). This was

changed in other MSS to say that the letters would look "different" (*poikilois*).

6:12a | persecuted for the Cross.
"Cross" is written as a nomen sacrum (sacred word) in the earliest MS (𝔓[46]).

6:12b | Christ Jesus.
This is the wording in the two earliest MSS (𝔓[46] B). Another reading is "Christ" in three early MSS (א A C), as well as D F G L 33 1739. The manuscript evidence is divided; either reading could be original.

6:14a | the Cross.
"Cross" is written as a nomen sacrum (sacred word) in the earliest MS (𝔓[46]).

6:14b | the world has been Crucified to me.
"Crucified" is written as a nomen sacrum (sacred word) in the earliest MS (𝔓[46]).

6:15 | For neither circumcision nor uncircumcision counts for anything.
This is the original wording in the two earliest MSS (𝔓[46] B), as well as Ψ 33 1739. A variant reading is, "for in Christ Jesus neither circumcision nor uncircumcision counts for anything" in three early MSS (א A C), as well as D F G Maj, by way of scribal harmonization to 5:6.

6:18 | may the grace of our Lord Jesus Christ be with your spirit.
"Lord," "Jesus," and "Christ" are written as nomina sacra (sacred names) in all MSS. Codex B writes out the word *pneuma* in full (in *plene*; i.e., not a sacred name), suggesting the rendering "[grace] be with your spirit." 𝔓[46] writes the word *pneuma* as a nomen sacrum (sacred name) suggesting the rendering "[grace] be with the Spirit you all have."

TO THE EPHESIANS

Title: To the Ephesians
This is the wording in the three earliest MSS (𝔓^{46} ℵ B).

1:1 | to those who are holy.
This is the original wording according to the three earliest MSS (𝔓^{46} ℵ* B), as well as 1739. A variant reading is, "to those in Ephesus who are holy" in ℵ^{2} [seventh century] A B^{2} [tenth century] D F G Ψ 0278 33 Maj it syr cop. According to the evidence of the three earliest MSS, it is obvious that "in Ephesus" was added later in the textual transmission of this letter. The truth is, the epistle known as "Ephesians" was as an encyclical intended for the audience of several churches—likely those in Asia Minor, the same seven churches in Rev. 1:11 (Ephesus, Smyrna, Pergamum, Thyatira, Sardis, Philadelphia, Laodecia), plus Hierapolis and Colossae. The epistle known as "Ephesians," in its content, has all the earmarks of being an encyclical. First, there are no personal exchanges and greetings, which one would expect because Paul had lived in Ephesus for two years. Second, Paul didn't deal with any local situations or problems, which he did in every other epistle. Third, the content of the epistle, especially with regard to the church, is universal in scope. Fourth, in 2:19 Paul spoke of the recipients as being "the households [plural, *oikeioi*] of God," very likely referring to several local churches. Fifth, when Paul told the Colossians to read the epistle coming from Laodecia (Col. 4:16), he must have been referring to the epistle known as Ephesians, an encyclical. Tychicus delivered both the epistle known as "Ephesians" and the epistle to Colossians to these churches (Eph. 6:21–22; Col. 4:7–9). The words "in Ephesus" were added because Ephesus was the leading church in the province.

1:13 | the promised Holy Spirit.
The divine "Spirit" is written as a nomen sacrum (sacred name) in two early MSS (𝔓^{46} ℵ).

1:15 | your trust in the Lord Jesus and in all the holy believers.
This is the original wording according to the four earliest MSS (𝔓[46] א* A B), as well as 33 1739. A variant reading is, "your trust in the Lord Jesus and love for all the holy believers" in א[2] [seventh century] D[2] Ψ Maj (so KJV). The text has superior documentation. Paul was commending the believers for trusting Jesus and other believers.

1:17 | Spirit of wisdom and revelation.
The divine "Spirit" is written as a nomen sacrum (sacred name) in two early MSS (𝔓[46] א). Codex B writes out the word *pneuma* in full (in *plene*; i.e., not as a sacred name), suggesting the rendering "a spirit of wisdom and revelation."

2:1–3
These verses, grammatically speaking, should be connected with the end of chapter 1, otherwise they are just dangling (see note in NET). There is no break between the two chapters in the earliest MS (𝔓[46]). The idea is that Christ fills the church, his body, and (specifically) fills those who were once dead in their trespasses and sins. No other translation makes this connection.

2:15a | he nullified the law of commandments.
"Law of commandments" is the reading in the earliest MS (𝔓[46]). All other MSS read, "law of commandments in dogmas." It is possible that the wording in 𝔓[46] is original and that the other MSS represent scribal clarification—it was not just the laws that were nullified by Christ's death on the cross but the Jewish dogmatic traditions based on the law. But it is possible, according to 𝔓[46], that Paul was boldly stating that the laws themselves were nullified.

2:15b | one common man.
This is the reading in the earliest MS (𝔓[46]), as well as F G. Another reading is "one new man" in three early MSS (א A B), as well as D. The textual evidence is split; either reading could be original and both suit the context.

2:18a | we have access in one Spirit.
The divine "Spirit" is written as a nomen sacrum (sacred name) in two early MSS (𝔓[46] א).

2:18b | to the Father.
The divine "Father" is written as a nomen sacrum (sacred name) in the earliest MS (𝔓[46]).

2:22a | dwelling place of God in Spirit.
"God" is written as a nomen sacrum (sacred name) in all MSS. The divine "Spirit" is written as a nomen sacrum (sacred name) in two early MSS (𝔓[46] א). God inhabits his people via his Spirit.

3:5 | revealed to his holy apostles and apostles by the Spirit.
The divine "Spirit" is written as a nomen sacrum (sacred name) in two early MSS (𝔓[46] א).

3:8 | I am the least of all.
This is the reading in the earliest MS (𝔓[46]). All other MSS read, "I am the least of all the saints." The reading in 𝔓[46] could be original.

3:9 | to enlighten everyone.
This is the reading in three early MSS (𝔓[46] B C), as well as א[2] [seventh century] D F G Ψ 33 Maj. The word "everyone" is omitted in א* A 1739. The text has early and diverse support.

3:14b | I kneel before the Father.
The divine "Father" is written as a nomen sacrum (sacred name) in the earliest MS (𝔓[46]).

3:16 | strengthened with power through the Spirit.
The divine "Spirit" is written as a nomen sacrum (sacred name) in the earliest MS (𝔓[46]).

4:3–4 | Spirit.
The divine "Spirit" is written as a nomen sacrum (sacred name) in two early MSS (𝔓[46] א).

4:6 | Father.
The divine "Father" is written as a nomen sacrum (sacred name) in the earliest MS (𝔓[46]).

4:9a | he descended.
This is the original wording according to early and diverse testimony: 𝔓[46] א* A C* D F G I[vid]. A variant reading is "he first descended" in א[2] [seventh century] B C[3] [ninth century] Ψ Maj, by way of scribal expansion.

4:9b | lower to the earth.
This is the reading according to the earliest MS (𝔓[46]), as well as D* F G. A variant reading is, "to the lower parts of the earth" in א A B C D[2] I Ψ 33 1739 Maj. Both readings have good support; either reading could be original. The first reading speaks of Christ's descent to earth via incarnation. The second reading could speak of Christ's descent into the underworld between his burial and resurrection (see 1 Pet 3:18–19).

4:15 | the headship of Christ.
This is the reading in the earliest MS (𝔓[46]). All other MSS read, "the head, Christ." The reading in 𝔓[46], though unique, is probably not the original wording.

4:23 | be renewed by the Spirit in your mind.
The divine "Spirit" is written as a nomen sacrum (sacred name) in three early MSS (𝔓[46] 𝔓[49] א). Codex B writes out the word *pneuma* in full (in *plene*; i.e., not as a sacred name), suggesting the human spirit and the rendering, "be renewed in the spirit of your mind."

4:30 | do not grieve the Holy Spirit.
The divine "Spirit" is written as a nomen sacrum (sacred name) in four early MSS (𝔓[46] 𝔓[49vid] א I).

5:5 | the kingdom of God.

This is the reading in the earliest MS ($\mathfrak{P}^{46}$). Other readings are "kingdom of God and Christ" (F G), "kingdom of the Christ of God" (1739), and "kingdom of Christ and God" (א A B Maj). The shortest reading in $\mathfrak{P}^{46}$ could be original—the other readings being scribal expansions. Or the reading in $\mathfrak{P}^{46}$ could be the result of scribal conformity to the more usual NT expression, "kingdom of God."

5:9 | the fruit of the light.

This is the reading in four early MSS ($\mathfrak{P}^{49}$ א A B), as well as D* F G 33 1739 it cop. A variant reading is "the fruit of the Spirit" in the earliest MS ($\mathfrak{P}^{46}$), as well as D^2 Ψ Maj (so KJV). The "fruit of light" is a unique expression in the NT, which could have been changed to "fruit of the Spirit," an expression that appears in Gal. 5:22. However, "Spirit" (written as a nomen sacrum [sacred name] in $\mathfrak{P}^{46}$) may have been changed to "light" to accord with the immediate context which speaks of light (5:8, 13). Thus, either reading could be original.

5:14 | Awake, O sleeper. Rise from the dead, and Christ will shine on you.

This three-line poem, known as a tristich, has a metrical rhythm that was especially associated with religious initiation chants. It is likely that early Christians adapted the rhythm for the Christian initiation rite of baptism; the wording is loosely based on Isaiah 60:1. The expressions "wake up" and "rise from the dead" are clearly resurrectional; resurrection and baptism were closely linked in the early church (see Rom. 6:3–4). The hymn could possibly be one of the hymns or spiritual songs Paul speaks of a few verses later (5:18). There is another version of this hymn in the third line according to certain MSS and witnesses (D* it^b Victorinus, Ambrosiaster, Jerome): "O sleeping one, / wake up from the dead, / and Christ will touch you." In his *Commentary on Ephesians* (PL 26, 559a), Jerome interprets the words as addressed by Christ to Adam when releasing him from Hades. Jerome said that Adam was held prisoner directly beneath the place where Christ was crucified, the name Golgotha being derived from Adam's skull, which was thought to be buried there.

5:18 | be filled with the Spirit.
The divine "Spirit" is written as a nomen sacrum (sacred name) in two early MSS ($\mathfrak{P}^{46}$ א).

5:19 | speaking to one another in psalms, hymns, and songs.
"Songs" is probably the original wording according to the two earliest MSS ($\mathfrak{P}^{46}$ B). Two variants are "spiritual songs" (א D F G Ψ 0278 33 1739 Maj it syr cop), and "spiritual songs with grace" (A) by way of scribal conformity to Col. 3:16, a parallel verse.

5:20 | giving thanks to God the Father.
"God" is written as a nomen sacrum (sacred name) in all MSS. The divine "Father" is written as a nomen sacrum (sacred name) in three early MSS ($\mathfrak{P}^{46}$ א I).

5:22 | the wives to their own husbands.
This is the original wording according to the two earliest MSS ($\mathfrak{P}^{46}$ B), as well as Clement MSS$^{\text{according to Jerome}}$. A variant reading is "the wives should submit to their own husbands" in א A I P 0278 33 1739. The text has the earliest testimony ($\mathfrak{P}^{46}$ B Clement).

6:1 | obey your parents in the Lord.
This is the original wording according to $\mathfrak{P}^{46}$ א A D^{1} I^{vid} Ψ 33 1739. Other MSS (B D* F G) do not include "in the Lord." The text has early and diverse testimony.

6:17 | the sword of the Spirit.
The divine "Spirit"is written as a nomen sacrum (sacred name) in two early MSS ($\mathfrak{P}^{46}$ א).

6:18 | pray at all times in the Spirit.
The divine "Spirit" is written as a nomen sacrum (sacred name) in two early MSS ($\mathfrak{P}^{46}$ א).

6:19 | that I may boldly make known the mystery.

"Mystery" is the original wording according to the two earliest MSS (𝔓[46vid] B), as well as F G it[b]. A variant reading is, "the mystery of the gospel" in ℵ A D I Ψ 0278 33 1739 Maj syr cop, probably by way of scribal expansion. (The reconstruction of the lines in 𝔓[46] allow for "mystery" to fit the space as opposed to "mystery of the gospel.")

6:21 | Tychicus will make known to you everything.

The epistle known as Ephesians was an encyclical that also went to Colossae (see Col. 4:16, and see note on Eph. 1:1). According to Col. 4:7–9, Tychicus also delivered the epistle from Paul to the Colossians. It is possible that he was the amanuensis for the epistle known as "Ephesians," as well as Colossians.

TO THE PHILIPPIANS

Title: To the Philippians
This is the wording in the four earliest MSS (𝔓^{46} א A B*).

1:2 | our Father.
The divine "Father" is written as a nomen sacrum in two early MSS (𝔓^{46vid} I).

1:11 | to God's glory and my praise.
This is the wording in the earliest MS (𝔓^{46}). Two variant readings are "to the glory and praise of God" (א A B D^{2} I Ψ 0278 33 1738 Maj it syr cop), and "to the glory and praise of Christ" (D*). The unusualness of the reading in 𝔓^{46} may have prompted the two variants. But Paul was known to speak of the believers giving him cause to boast on the day of Christ (2 Cor. 1:14; Phil. 2:16; 1 Thess. 2:19–20).

1:14 | the message.
This is the original wording according to the earliest MS (𝔓^{46}), as well as D^{2} 1739 Maj. Two variants are "the message of God" (א A B D* P 048^{vid} 33), and "the message of the Lord" (F G), both scribal expansions.

1:19 | Spirit of Jesus Christ.
This is a unique expression in the NT; it highlights the fact that Jesus Christ is united to the Spirit—to experience the Spirit of Jesus Christ is to experience Jesus Christ. "Spirit of Jesus Christ" is written as a nomen sacrum (sacred name) in three early MSS (𝔓^{46} א B).

1:27 | standing firm in one Spirit.
The divine "Spirit" is written as a nomen sacrum (sacred name) in two early MSS (𝔓^{46} א).

2:6–11
This section is a poem or hymn about Christ. Its poeticalness comes from the language and meter; in the original writing and in ancient copies it was

not set in poetic lines, as is done in the modern critical edition of the Greek New Testament known as *Novum Testamentum Graece*. The poem celebrates the truth that Christ, though equal with God in life and substance, surrendered that equality to become the Father's servant in the sacrificial acts of incarnation and redemption. For doing so, the Father has highly exalted him and given him the Name above every name in the universe.

2:11 | the Father.
The divine "Father" is written as a nomen sacrum (sacred name) in two early MSS ($\mathfrak{P}^{46}$ א).

2:21 | Jesus Christ.
This is the original wording according to four early MSS ($\mathfrak{P}^{46}$ א A C), as well as D F G. A variant reading is "Christ Jesus" in B 0278 Maj (so KJV).

2:26 | he was yearning to send word to you all.
This is the wording in the earliest MS ($\mathfrak{P}^{46}$). Two other readings are "he was yearning to see you all" (א* A C D I^{vid} 33), and "he was yearning for you all" (א^2 [seventh century] F G Ψ 1739 Maj). It is possible that $\mathfrak{P}^{46}$ preserves the original wording, but the textual evidence favors the first of the two variants (in א*, et al,).

2:30 | the work of Christ.
This is the original wording according to the two earliest MSS ($\mathfrak{P}^{46}$ B), as well as F G 0278. A variant reading is "the work of the Lord" in א A P 075 33.

3:3 | worshiping in spirit.
This is the wording according to the earliest MS ($\mathfrak{P}^{46}$). Two variants are "worshiping in God's Spirit" (א* A B C D^2 F G 0278^{vid} 33 1739), and "worshiping God in spirit" (א^2 [seventh century] D* P Ψ 075). It is possible that the bare expression in $\mathfrak{P}^{46}$ (wherein *pneuma* [spirit] is written out in full [i.e., not as a sacred name], signifying the human spirit) was amplified in one of two ways.

3:12 | or already been made righteous.

This is the reading in the earliest MS (𝔓[46]), as well as D (F G). It is omitted in ℵ A B C Ψ 33 1739 Maj. The reading of 𝔓[46] et al. is likely original and was then deleted because it would have struck scribes as being a non-Pauline statement (inasmuch as Paul proclaimed justification by faith as an accomplished fact throughout his epistles). But the kind of justification Paul was seeking here was the prize of fully knowing Christ and participating in the ultimate resurrection, which would justify his entire spiritual pursuit (as is made evident in the previous verses).

3:13b | I do not consider myself to have laid hold.

This is the original wording according to the two earliest MSS (𝔓[46] B), as well as D^2 F G Ψ Maj. A variant reading is, "I do not consider myself to have laid hold yet" in 𝔓[61vid] ℵ A D* P 33, by way of scribal expansion.

3:18 | enemies of the Cross.

"Cross" is written as a nomen sacrum (sacred word) in the earliest MS (𝔓[46]).

4:3b | the rest of my coworkers.

This is the wording in four early MSS (𝔓[46] ℵ[c] B C), as well as D F G. A variant reading is, "my coworkers and the rest" in two early MSS (𝔓[16vid] ℵ*). Either reading could be original.

4:13 | the One empowering me.

This is the original wording according to four early MSS (ℵ* A B I), as well as D* 33 1739 it cop. A variant reading is, "the One empowering me, Christ" in ℵ[2] [seventh century] D^2 (F G) Ψ Maj syr (so KJV), by way of scribal expansion.

4:20 | our Father.

The divine "Father" is written as a nomen sacrum (sacred name) in the earliest MS (𝔓[46]).

4:23a | may the grace of the Lord Jesus Christ be experienced by the Spirit you all have.

This rendering reflects the fact that the earliest MSS write *pneuma* (Spirit) as a nomen sacrum (sacred name): 𝔓^{46} א B (a rare occurrence in this MS). The idea is that Jesus Christ is experienced in the Spirit.

4:23b | Amen.

"Amen" is included in three early MSS (𝔓^{46} א A), as well as D Ψ 33 1739^{c} Maj syr cop^{bo}. The word is omitted in one early MS (B), as well as F G 1739* it^{b} cop^{sa} . The textual evidence casts doubts on the inclusion of "amen," as does the fact that "amen" was frequently added by scribes at the end of epistles. In fact, a final "amen" to an epistle is only certain in Gal. 6:18 and Jude 25.

TO THE COLOSSIANS

Title: To the Colossians
This is the wording of the three earliest MSS ($\mathfrak{P}^{46}$ א B).

1:2b | God our Father.
This is the original wording according to the two earliest MSS ($\mathfrak{P}^{46vid}$ B), as well as D L Ψ 33 1739. A variant reading is, "God our Father and Lord Jesus Christ" in four early MSS (א A C I), as well as F G 075 Maj, by way of scribal expansion influenced by all of Paul's other epistles (Rom. 1:7; 1 Cor. 1:3; 2 Cor. 1:2; Gal. 1:3; Eph. 1:2; Phil. 1:2; 1 Thess. 1:1; 2 Thess. 1:1; 1 Tim. 1:2; 2 Tim. 1:2; Titus 1:4; Philem. 3). The divine "Father" is written as a nomen sacrum (sacred name) in two early MSS ($\mathfrak{P}^{46vid}$ א).

1:8 | your love in the Spirit.
"Spirit" is written as a nomen sacrum (sacred name) in two early MSS ($\mathfrak{P}^{46}$ א). Codex B writes the word in full (not as a sacred name), suggesting the rendering "the love you have for others in spirit."

1:15–20
This section is a poem or hymn about Christ. Its poeticalness comes from the language and meter; in the original writing and in ancient copies it was not set in poetic lines, as is done in the modern critical edition of the Greek New Testament known as *Novum Testamentum Graece*. The poem celebrates Christ as being the image of the invisible God and as having preeminence in the natural creation (he is the "premier" of all creation in that every living thing was created through him) and in the new creation (he is the "firstborn" of the dead via his resurrection). All the fullness of God dwells in him.

1:20 | the blood of his Cross.
"Cross" appears as a nomen sacrum (sacred word) in the earliest MS ($\mathfrak{P}^{46}$).

1:27 | the wealth of this mystery.
This is the reading in $\mathfrak{P}^{46}$. All other MSS read, "the wealth of the glory

of this mystery." The reading in $\mathfrak{P}^{46}$ may represent the original wording, which was then expanded.

2:2 | the mystery of God, Christ (**or, the mystery of God—namely, Christ**).

This is the original wording according to the two earliest MSS ($\mathfrak{P}^{46}$ B). There are several variant readings: "the mystery of God, which is Christ" (D*), "the mystery of God" (D^1 H P), "the mystery of Christ" (81 1739), "the mystery of God, Father of Christ" (א* A C 048^{vid}), "the mystery of God, even the Father of Christ" ($א^2$ [seventh century] Ψ 0208), and "the mystery of God and of the Father and of Christ" (D^2 Maj). Among the myriad variations, the testimony of the two earliest MSS ($\mathfrak{P}^{46}$ B) is to be followed; Christ is God's mystery—now revealed.

2:5 | I am present with you in the Spirit.

"Spirit" is written as a nomen sacrum (sacred name) in two early MSS ($\mathfrak{P}^{46}$ א). Codex B writes out the word in full (in *plene*; i.e., not as a sacred name), suggesting the translation, "I am with you in spirit."

2:18 | delving into things which he has seen.

This is the original wording according to four early MSS ($\mathfrak{P}^{46}$ א* A B), as well as D* F G 33 1739. Other MSS ($א^2$ [seventh century] C D^1 Ψ 075 0278 Maj) read "delving into things which he has not seen." Strong documentary support affirms that Paul was writing about "visions."

3:6 | God's anger comes against these things.

This is the original wording according to the two earliest MSS ($\mathfrak{P}^{46}$ B). A variant reading is, "because of these things, God's anger comes on the sons of disobedience" in four early MSS (א A C I), as well as D F G H Ψ 33 1739 Maj. This is scribal conformity to Eph. 5:6, a parallel verse.

3:13 | the Lord has forgiven you.

"Lord" is the original wording according to three early MSS ($\mathfrak{P}^{46}$

A B), as well as D* F G. Two variant readings are "Christ" (א[2] [seventh century] C D[1] Ψ 1739) and "God" (א*). The text has superior documentation.

3:16 | the word of Christ.

This is the original wording according to early and diverse testimony: 𝔓[46] א[2] [seventh century] B C[2] [sixth century] D F G Ψ 1739 Maj. Two variants are "the word of the Lord" (א* I) and "the word of God" (A C* 33). The text has superior testimony.

3:22a | obey your earthly masters.

This is probably the original wording according to the earliest MS (𝔓[46]), as well as 075 0278. A variant reading is, "obey your earthly masters in everything you do" in four early MSS (א A B C), as well as D F G 33 1739 Maj—perhaps scribal expansion.

3:22b, 4:1

"Lord" and "master" translate the same word in Greek: *kurios*. This would be evident to the original hearers/readers of the epistle. In these verses the earliest MSS (𝔓[46] א B) write *kurios* as a nomen sacrum (sacred name), denoting the "Lord" or "Master."

4:8 | so that I may know how you are.

This is the wording in two early MSS (𝔓[46] C), as well as א[2] [seventh century] D[1] Ψ 1739 Maj. Another reading is, "so that you may know how we are" in three early MSS (א* A B), as well as D*,c F G 048. The textual evidence is evenly split; either reading could be original.

4:11 | Jesus who is called Justus.

The scribes of א and B wrote out the name "Jesus" in full (in *plene*; i.e., not as a sacred name) because this is not Jesus Christ of Nazareth, whose name is always written as a nomen sacrum (sacred name) elsewhere.

4:15 | Nympha and the church that meets in her house.

This is the original wording according to the earliest MS (B), as well as

0278 1739*. Two variant readings are "Nympha and the church that meets in their house" (ℵ A C 33), and "Nymphan and the church that meet in his house" (D F G Ψ Maj; so KJV). The textual evidence favors the fact that a woman (Nympha) is noted here. The church met in the home of a Christian sister named Nympha.

4:16 | the epistle from Laodecia.

The epistle coming from Laodecia was very likely an encyclical written by Paul, probably the one known as "Ephesians" (see note on Eph. 1:1). Tychicus, Paul's emissary, likely brought both the epistle of Ephesians and the epistle of Colossians to these churches (Eph. 6:21–22; Col. 4:7–8).

4:18 | I, Paul, write this greeting in my own hand.

Paul customarily dictated his epistles to an amanuensis (see Rom. 16:22), and then signed off in his own handwriting (see 1 Cor. 16:21–24; Gal. 6:11–18; 2 Thess. 3:17–18; Philem. 19–25). Readers of the original epistle would see two different handwritings—that of the amanuensis and that of Paul's.

TO THE THESSALONIANS 1

Title: To the Thessalonians A [= 1]
This is the wording in the three earliest MSS (𝔓[30] א B).

1:1a | the Father.
The divine "Father" is written as a nomen sacrum (sacred name) in two early MSS (𝔓[46] I).

1:1b | Grace to you and peace.
This is the original wording according to the two earliest MSS (𝔓[46vid] B), as well as F G Ψ 0278. A variant reading is, "grace to you and peace from God our Father and the Lord Jesus Christ" in three early MSS (א A I), as well as (D) 33 Maj. This is scribal expansion influenced by Rom. 1:7; 1 Cor. 1:3; 2 Cor. 1:2; Gal. 1:3; Eph. 1:2; Phil. 1:2; 2 Thess. 1:2; 1 Tim. 1:2; 2 Tim. 1:2; Titus 1:4.

1:3 | Father.
The divine "Father" is written as a nomen sacrum (sacred name) in one early MS (𝔓[65vid]).

1:5–6 | the Holy Spirit.
The divine "Spirit" is written as a nomen sacrum (sacred name) in two early MSS (𝔓[65vid] א).

1:10 | wait for his Son from heaven.
The divine "Son" is written as a nomen sacrum (sacred name) in three early MSS (𝔓[46] 𝔓[65vid] א).

2:7 | we became little children.
This is the original wording, where the Greek for "little children" is *nēpioi*, according to five early MSS (𝔓[65] א* B C* I), as well as D* F G Ψ*. A variant reading is "we became gentle," where the Greek for "gentle" is *ēpioi*, according to א[2] [seventh century] A C[2] [sixth century] D[2] Ψ[c] 0278 33 1739 Maj. The Greek word *nēpioi* has the best documentation,

both early ($\mathfrak{P}^{65}$ being the earliest, as well as א B) and diverse. It was changed (note the correctors of א C D Ψ) to the easier reading by dropping the *nu*—easier, because it doesn't require the reader to deal with a sudden shift of metaphor, from the apostles being like "children" to them being a like "a nursing mother." But the manuscript evidence supports this sudden shift. The thrust of the dual image is that the apostles were not overbearing toward the Thessalonians—rather, they cared for them.

2:18 | For we wanted to come to you (I, Paul, tried again and again).
It seems clear enough that Paul and Silvanus were speaking together up to this point in the epistle (see 1:1–2:17); then Paul spoke out in his own voice here. He does so again at 3:5 and 5:27. It is possible that he wrote this in his own hand.

3:2a | we sent Timothy.
This not only shows that Paul *and* Silvanus sent Timothy, it indicates Paul and Silvanus were coauthors of the epistle.

3:2b | Timothy, our brother and coworker
This is the reading in one MS (B). There are several variants on the last word: "servant of God" (א A P Ψ), "servant of God and our coworker" (D^2 Maj), "servant and coworker of God" (F G), "coworker of God" (D* 33). The simplest reading, "coworker," is found in B, but several other MSS call him a "servant of God" and/or "coworker of God." The original reading is difficult to discern.

3:13 | with all his holy believers.
This is the original wording according to early and diverse testimony: $א^2$ [seventh century] B D^2 F G Ψ 1739. Some MSS (א* A D*) add "amen" by way of scribal expansion.

5:4 | overtake you as if you were thieves.
This is the reading in two early MSS (A B). Another reading is, "overtake you like a thief" in one early MS (א), as well as D F G 33 1739 Maj.

If the first reading is original, we see Paul and Silvanus offering a turn of phrase, shifting the metaphor from "you know that the day of the Lord comes as a thief in the night" (5:2) to "be careful that the day of the Lord would not overtake you as if you were thieves" (5:4). The idea is that the Thessalonians were being warned not to be caught in the act of living in darkness. The alternate reading needs no explanation. Either could be original.

5:19 | Do not extinguish the Spirit.
The divine "Spirit" is written as a nomen sacrum (sacred name) in three early MSS ($\mathfrak{P}^{30vid}$ א I).

5:23 | may your spirit and soul and body be kept blameless.
The word "spirit" is written in full (in *plene*; i.e., not as a sacred name) in B, denoting the human spirit.

TO THE THESSALONIANS 2

Title: To the Thessalonians B [= 2]
This is the wording in the three earliest MSS ($\mathfrak{P}^{30}$ א B*).

1:1a | our Father.
The divine "Father" is written as a nomen sacrum (sacred name) in the earliest MS ($\mathfrak{P}^{30vid}$).

1:1b | Lord Jesus.
This is the reading in the earliest MS ($\mathfrak{P}^{30}$). All other MSS read, "Lord Jesus Christ," probably by way of scribal expansion. (See Comfort and Barrett, *Text of Earliest NT Greek MSS*, 131, for reconstruction of $\mathfrak{P}^{30}$.)

1:2 | the Father.
The divine "Father" is written as a nomen sacrum (sacred name) in the earliest MS ($\mathfrak{P}^{30vid}$).

1:12 | glorify the name of our Lord Jesus.
This is the reading in the two earliest MSS (א B), as well as D K L Ψ 0111. A variant on the name is "Lord Jesus Christ" in A F G P 0278, by way of scribal expansion. The last words of the verse read, "the grace of our God and Lord, Jesus Christ." According to a grammatical rule, wherein one definite article governs two nouns joined by *kai* (known as the Granville Sharpe rule), "Jesus Christ" is identified as both "God" and "Lord" in the statement.

2:2 | do not be disturbed by any kind of spirit or message or letter.
The word "spirit" (*pneuma*) is written in full (in *plene*; i.e. , not as a sacred name) in B, denoting the spirit of a prophet.

2:3 | man of lawlessness.
This is the reading according to the two earliest MSS (א B), as well as 0278 1739 cop. A variant reading is, "man of sin" in A D F G Ψ Maj

it syr. The text has superior attestation. "The man of lawlessness" is the rebellious antichrist.

2:4 | presenting himself as God.
"God" is written as a nomen sacrum (sacred name) in the two earliest MSS (א B). Had these scribes wanted to convey "god" (as in the rendering "every so-called god"—common in many translations), they could have written the word *theos* in full (in *plene*; i.e., not as a sacred name).

2:8a | the Lord Jesus will destroy.
"Lord Jesus" is the reading in two early MSS (א A), as well as D* F G L^c 33. A variant reading is "Lord" in one early MS (B), as well as D^2 1739 Maj. The textual evidence is evenly split; either rendering could be original.

2:8b | by the spirit of his mouth (or, **by the breath of his mouth**).
The word *pneuma* is "spirit" (*pneumati*) in B, which writes the word in full (in *plene*; i.e., not as a sacred name). Codex א writes this as a nomen sacrum (sacred name), denoting the divine Spirit, which suggests the rendering, "whom the Lord Jesus will destroy by the Spirit coming out of his mouth."

2:13a | chose you as first fruits.
This is the reading in one early MS (B), as well as F G 33 1739. A variant reading is, "chose you from the beginning" in one early MS (א), as well as D Ψ Maj. The first reading follows the Greek word *aparchēn* (first fruits); the second follows *ap archēs* (from beginning). The documentary evidence is divided, as are external arguments. Paul had a habit of calling the first converts in a certain geographical region the "first fruits" (Rom. 16:5; 1 Cor. 16:15), and the Thessalonians were among the first converts in Europe. But the variant reading also has legitimacy because it was customary for Paul to speak of God's selection of his elect before the foundation of the world (see Eph. 1:4; 2 Tim. 1:9)—i.e., from the beginning.

2:13b | sanctification by the Spirit.
The divine "Spirit" is written as a nomen sacrum (sacred name) in one early MS (א).

3:6 | according to the tradition you received.
This is the reading in one early MS (B), as well as F G. A variant reading is, "according to the tradition they received" in two early MSS (א* A), as well as D 33. The variant reading is referring to the idle brothers. The documentary evidence is divided; either reading could be original.

3:17 | I, Paul, write this greeting with my own hand.
The epistle, up to this point, had been dictated to an amanuensis (cf. Rom. 16:22)—unless Silvanus himself wrote it. Paul signed off in his own handwriting, as at the end of every epistle. This is made explicit in 1 Cor. 16:21; Gal. 6:11; Col. 4:18; here (2 Thess. 3:18); Philem. 19. In the autograph, one could see the different handwriting.

TO TIMOTHY 1

Title: To Timothy A [=1]
This is the wording according to two early MSS (א I), as well as (D F G) 33 1739*.

1:17a | indestructible, invisible.
This is the reading in the earliest MS (א). D* reads, "immortal, invisible." F and G read, "indestructible, invisible, immortal." The Greek behind "indestructible" is *aphthartos*; it denotes that which cannot be corrupted and does not perish. Greek philosophers applied this characteristic to the soul (as opposed to the body). "Invisible" means that which cannot be seen with the mortal eye (*a* + *horatos*; cf. Col. 1:15).

1:17b | the only God.
This is the original wording according to two early MSS (א* A), as well as D* F G H* 33 1739 cop. A variant reading is "the only wise God" in א² [seventh century] D¹ Hᶜ Ψ Maj (so KJV), by way of scribal expansion influenced by Rom. 16:27. The statement "he alone is God" (lit. "the only God") is distinctively Jewish (as opposed to the polytheism of the non-Jewish world).

3:16a | great is the mystery of godliness: who was manifested in the flesh.
This is the original reading supported by the earliest MSS (א* A* C*), as well as F G 33. Other MSS read "which" (D*) or "God" (אᶜ Aᶜ C² [sixth century] D² Ψ 1739). The documentation evidence supporting "who" (or "he who") is very strong; many MSS were corrected to read "God"—clearly the result of scribal emendation. Obviously, the pronoun "who" refers to Jesus Christ, God incarnate.

3:16b | was justified by the Spirit.
The divine "Spirit" is written as a nomen sacrum (sacred name) in the earliest MS (א). In the Greek, this passage is immediately recognizable as a poem, which was very likely sung as a creedal hymn. Each line is

structured the same: a passive voice verb (each ending in *theta/eta*), followed by the proposition *en* (in five of the six lines), followed by a noun in the dative case. The beauty of the poem is that readers can read it as a pithy chronology of Jesus's life and ministry from the first line to the last (manifested in flesh . . . taken up in glory), or each of the three couplets can be read as *first* presenting Jesus's life on earth:

1a manifested in flesh (via incarnation)
2a seen by angels (after his birth, in the wilderness, garden of Gethsemane)
3a believed (by some) in this world

followed by his life after death and resurrection:

1b justified by the Spirit (via his resurrection into spiritual life)
2b proclaimed among nations (by the apostles and so on)
3b taken up in glory (his present exultant state)

4:1 | the Spirit expressly says.
The divine "Spirit" is written as a nomen sacrum (sacred name) in two early MSS (א I).

4:10 | we work hard and struggle.
The word "struggle" (Greek, *agōnizometha*) is the original word according to three early MSS (א* A C), as well as F G Ψ 33. A variant reading of the second verb is, "are reproached" (Greek, *oneidizometha*) in א^{2} [seventh century] D 0241^{vid} 1739 Maj it syr cop (so KJV). Not only does "struggle" (or, "agonize") have superior attestation, it better suits the context which speaks of "training" (Greek, *gumnazō*; 4:8). Both words (*agōnizometha* and *gumnazō*) were used in athletic contexts.

5:5 | has set her hope on the Lord.
This is the reading in one early MS (א*), as well as D*. A variant reading is, "has set her hope on God" in two early MSS (A C), as well as א^{2}

[seventh century] D^2 F G P Ψ 048 1739 it syr cop. Either reading could be original.

6:13 | who gives life to everything.

This is the reading in all MSS exept one. The Greek is *zōogonountos ta panta.* The one MS is א, which reads, "who makes everything alive" (Greek, *zōopoiountos ta panta*).

6:15–16

This section is a poem or hymn about Christ's epiphany. Its poeticalness comes from the language and meter; in the original writing and in ancient copies it was not set in poetic lines, as is done in the modern critical edition of the Greek New Testament known as *Novum Testamentum Graece*. The first stanza of Paul's encomia of Christ's epiphany simulates language of the hymns of praise in the Psalter (Ps. 136:3) and applies it to Christ (so also Rev. 17:14). The second stanza has the richest language, wherein Paul exalts Christ as the only one who has "immortality" (the Greek term is an *alpha*-private plus *thanatos* – *athanatos,* the negation of death). The confession that Christ alone is intrinsically immortal is found only here in the NT. His immortality is magnified by the fact that mere mortals cannot access the light he inhabits and cannot see him (cf. Exod. 33:20; John 1:18). His epiphany contrasts with Greek mythology where so-called immortal gods made epiphanies.

6:21 | Grace be with you all.

The word "you" is plural in Greek. Though Paul wrote this epistle to Timothy personally, Paul had a larger audience in mind—namely, the church in Ephesus, which Timothy was serving at this time. (The same plural occurs in 2 Tim. 4:22; Titus 3:15; Philem. 25.) Many MSS (א* A D* F G 33 1739*) end here; some MSS ($א^2$ [seventh century] D^1 Ψ 1739^c Maj) add "amen" at the end of the verse by way of scribal expansion.

TO TIMOTHY 2

Title: To Timothy B [=2]
This is the wording in the two earliest MSS (א C), as well as (D F G) 33.

1:7 | God did not give us the Spirit of fear.
"Spirit" is written as a nomen sacrum (sacred name) in the earliest MS (א).

1:10 | the epiphany of our Savior, Christ Jesus.
This is the original wording according to two early MSS (א* A), as well as D 81. The name is inverted to "Jesus Christ" in א^2 [seventh century] C D^2 F G Ψ 33. And the name is "God" in I. Clearly, Paul had Jesus's epiphany in mind, not God's (per se). The poem (1:9–10) springs out of another exhortation (see previous poem in 1 Tim. 6:14–16) from Paul to Timothy. As in the previous poem, the mention of Christ's epiphany sparked exalted language, especially in the last stanza. I would use the phrases "snuffed out death" and "lit the path to amaranthine" to highlight the contrast. The Greek participle behind "snuffed out" (*katargeō*) has the sense of "abolish, wipe out" (see 1 Cor. 15:26, 53–54; 2 Thess. 2:8; Heb. 2:14). The phrase "lit the path" translates the aorist participle *phōtisantos*, from *phōtizō*, "bring to light," "reveal" (cf. Eph. 3:9). The line is literally, "brought life and incorruptibility to light." The words "life" and "incorruptibility" form a single idea: "life incorruptible," which I think is more felicitously translated as "amaranthine life." The two words form a hendiadys, a literary device wherein a single idea is expressed by means of two words joined by "and."

1:11 | I was appointed a preacher and apostle and teacher.
"Teacher" is the original wording according to three early MSS (א* A I). There are two variant readings: "minister" (33) and "teacher of the Gentiles" (א^2 [seventh century] C D F G Ψ 1739 Maj it syr cop; so KJV)—a scribal expansion.

1:14 | the Holy Spirit who lives within us.
The divine "Spirit" is written as a nomen sacrum (sacred name) in the earliest MS (א).

2:14 | charge them before God.
This is the original wording according to two early MSS (א C), as well as F G. A variant reading is, "charge them before the Lord" in A D Ψ 048 1739.

2:18 | who say that a resurrection has already occurred.
This is probably the original wording according to one early MS (א), as well as F G 048 33. A variant reading is, "who say that the resurrection has already occurred" in two early MSS (A C), as well as D Ψ 1739 Maj, by way of scribal clarification. Scribes wanted to make it clear that Hymenaeus and Philetus were falsely claiming that the great resurrection had already occurred.

3:15 | you have known sacred writings.
This is the original wording according to one early MSS (א), as well as C^{2vid} [sixth century] D* F G 33. A variant reading is "you have known the sacred writings" in two early MSS (A C*), as well as D^1 Ψ 1739 Maj, by way of scribal clarification. But there is probably no difference in meaning; both expressions refer to the Old Testament scriptures, which are called God-inspired (Greek, *theopneustos*) in the next verse (3:16).

4:10 | Crescens went to Gaul.
"Gaul" is the wording in two early MSS (א C). The word is "Galatia" in one early MS (A), as well as D F G L Ψ 33 1739. The two words could be easily confused for one another: Gallian/Galatian. If Gallian (= Gaul) is original, however, it probably refers to the same area, for in the early centuries of the Christian era the Roman province Galatia was commonly known as Gaul or Gallia—named after the Gallic mercenaries who settled there (see NEBmg).

4:22a | The Lord be with your spirit.
"Lord" is the original wording according to the earliest MS (א*), as well as F G 33 1739. Two variant readings are "Lord Jesus" (A) and "Lord Jesus Christ" ($א^2$ [seventh century] C D Ψ Maj; so KJV), both scribal expansions.

4:22b | Grace be with you all.

The Greek pronoun is plural, suggesting Paul had an audience larger than Timothy in mind—perhaps the church in Ephesus, where Timothy was ministering at the time. Later MSS (א^2 [seventh century] D Ψ 1739^c Maj) add "amen" at the end of the verse by way of scribal expansion; it is not included in the three earliest MSS (א* A C), as well as F G 33 1739*.

TO TITUS

Title: To Titus
This is the wording in two early MSS (א C), as well as 𝔓^{61vid} (D F G) 33.

1:4 | the Father.
"Father" is written as a nomen sacrum (sacred name) in **א**.

2:5 | those who work in their own homes.
This is the original wording according to four early MSS (א* A C I), as well as D G Ψ 33. A variant reading is, "those who care for their own homes" in א^{2} [seventh century] D^{2} H 1739 Maj (so KJV). The difference in meaning is slight.

2:7a | in your teaching don't express envy.
This is the wording in the earliest MS (𝔓^{32}), as well as F G. There are two other readings: "in your teaching have integrity" (א* A C D* 33 1739) and "in your teaching express sincerity" (א^{2} [seventh century] D^{1} Ψ Maj; so KJV). The original reading is either that in 𝔓^{32}, et al., or **א**, et al.

2:7b | be serious.
This is the original wording according to the four earliest MSS (𝔓^{32vid} א A C), as well as D* F G 33 1739. A variant reading is "be serious, incorruptible" in D^{2} Ψ Maj (so KJV), by way of scribal expansion influenced by 2 Tim. 1:10.

2:13 | our great God and Savior, Jesus Christ.
This is the original wording according to two early MSS (A C), as well as א^{2} [seventh century] D Ψ 0278 33 Maj it syr. Another reading is, "our great God and Savior, Christ Jesus" in one early MS (א*), as well as F G. In both readings the Greek grammar makes it very clear that Jesus Christ (or Christ Jesus) is God and Savior. The rule is when one article governs two nouns joined by *kai*, the referent is the same person (the Granville Sharp rule).

3:5 | through the washing of regeneration and renewal of the Holy Spirit.

This is the reading according to the earliest MS (א). Other MSS (D* F G) add another preposition (*dia*) to make this two separate experiences (the washing of regeneration *and* the renewal of the Holy Spirit). According to the original text, the Holy Spirit (which is written as a nomen sacrum in א) enacts the washing of regeneration, which is the renewal. "Regeneration" translates *palingenesia*, which is used for cosmic renewal (after the flood – 1 Clement 9:4; in the future age of the Messiah – Matt. 19:28), or for the experience of a complete change of life ("regenesis"). This and Matthew 19:28 are the only biblical uses of this word. The word was used widely in the ancient world for many different kinds of renewal. Its use in Titus 3:5 probably refers to the individual's incorporation into the cosmic renewal with a view to its future completion. Paul also calls this regeneration a "renewing."

3:15 | Grace be with you all.

The Greek pronoun is plural, suggesting Paul had an audience larger than Titus in mind—perhaps the churches in Crete, where Titus was ministering at the time. Some later MSS ($א^2$ [seventh century] D^1 F G H Ψ 0278 Maj; so KJV) add "amen" at the end of the verse by way of scribal expansion; it is not included in the three earliest MSS (א* A C), as well as D* 048 33 1739.

TO PHILEMON

Title: To Philemon
This is the wording according to three early MSS (ℵ A C), as well as (D) 33.

1:3 | Father.
The divine "Father" is written as a nomen sacrum (sacred name) in the earliest MS (ℵ).

1:6a | every blessing that belongs to you.
The pronoun is "you" in one early MS (ℵ), as well as $\mathfrak{P}^{61}$ F G P 33. The pronoun is "us" in two early MSS (A C), as well as D Ψ 048^{vid} Maj. The textual evidence is evenly divided; either reading could be original.

1:6b | in Christ.
"Christ" is the original reading according to the three earliest MSS (ℵ* A C), as well as $\mathfrak{P}^{61}$ 33. A variant reading is "Christ Jesus" in ℵ^{2} [seventh century] D F G 1739 Maj—scribal expansion of a divine name.

1:19 | I, Paul, write this with my own hand: I will repay it. And I won't mention that you owe me your very soul!
Paul had just asked Philemon to liberate Onesimus from slavery (1:16), as well as to charge him (Paul) with any amount Onesimus owed Philemon (1:18). Up to this point Paul was dictating the letter to an amanuensis. Then Paul took pen (stylus) in hand and wrote verse 19 in his own hand. If we had the original writing (the autograph) we would see a different handwriting here. It is possible that Paul continued writing out the rest of the letter in his own hand, as he did in Galatians 6:11–18.

1:25 | Grace be with you all.
This is probably the original reading according to the earliest MS, $\mathfrak{P}^{87}$ (second century). All other MSS read, "the grace of the Lord Jesus Christ be with your spirit." Several MSS (ℵ C D^{1} Ψ 0278 1739^{c} Maj; so KJV) add "amen" at the end of the verse by way of scribal expansion; it is not included in $\mathfrak{P}^{87}$ A D* 048^{vid} 33 1739*.

Chapter Seven

Hebrews

TO THE HEBREWS

Title: To the Hebrews
This is the wording in three early MSS (𝔓^{46} ℵ I). The book of Hebrews immediately follows Romans in 𝔓^{46}, and very likely in 𝔓^{13} (according to the pagination). Codex I places Hebrews after 2 Thessalonians and before 1 Timothy. Many early Christians thought Paul wrote Hebrews, but most modern commentators, noting the non-Pauline style of Hebrews, attribute the book to some other author, such as Apollos (an intellectual Jewish Christian).

1:1 | the ancestors.
This is the reading in four early MSS (𝔓^{46*} ℵ A B), as well as D Maj. Another reading is, "our ancestors" in two early MSS (𝔓^{12} 𝔓^{46c}). The second reading indicates that the author probably considered himself a Jew.

1:2 | he has spoken to us in a son.
The word "son" is written in full (in *plene*; i.e., not as a sacred name) in four early MSS (𝔓^{46} ℵ B I), pointing to one who is a son, not a divine title—cf. 1:5, 8 where the nomen sacrum (sacred name) is used.

1:3 | by himself cleansed sins.
This is the reading in the earliest MS (𝔓^{46}), as well as D* H^{c} 0243 0278 1739 Maj. The phrase "by himself" is omitted in three early MSS (ℵ A B), as well as D^{1} H* P Ψ 33. The textual evidence is divided; either reading could be original.

1:5 | my Son.
The divine "Son" is written in both occurrences as a nomen sacrum (sacred name) in two early MSS (𝔓^{46} ℵ).

1:8a | the Son.
The divine "Son" is written as a nomen sacrum (sacred name) in three early MSS (𝔓^{46} 𝔓^{114vid} ℵ).

1:8b | his kingdom.

This is the original wording according to the three earliest MSS (𝔓[46] ℵ B). A variant reading is, "your kingdom," in A D Ψ 0243 0278 33 1739 Maj.

1:9 | O God, your God.

The first "O God" is a vocative in the Greek—the Son is being addressed as "God"; the second statement "your God" refers to God the Father. Both occurrences of "God" are written as nomina sacra (sacred names) in the earliest MSS (𝔓[46] 𝔓[114] ℵ B I).

1:1–13

Novum Testamentum Graece (NA[27]) sets the first chapter of Hebrews in poetic format, but doesn't begin the poem until verse 3. However, the poem should begin in 1:1. Note the rhythmical balance between 1:1 | and 1:2:

A In multiple portions and multifarious ways
  B God spoke through the prophets to our ancestors;
A' in these last days
  B' he has spoken to us in the Son.

The first line of the first stanza mirrors the alliteration of the words *polumerōs* (meaning "many shares, allotments, portions") and *polutropōs* (meaning "many ways"—varied, diverse). The poetic description of the Son begins thereafter. Two of the most succinct and sublime expressions of the Son's eternal being are found in the words "the radiant aura of his glory" (*apaugasma tēs doxēs*) and "the presentation of his essence" (*charaktēr tēs hupostaseōs*).

After the first stanza, the rest of the poem is a pastiche taken from the following OT verses: v. 5 from Psalm 2:7; 2 Samuel 7:14; v. 6 from the Greek version of Deuteronomy 32:43; v. 7 from the Greek version of Psalm 104:4; vv. 8–9 from Psalm 45:6–7; vv. 10–12 from the Greek version of Psalm 105:25–27; v. 13 from Psalm 110:1.

2:3 | was confirmed to us by those who heard him.
This places the author of Hebrews as a second-generation Christian who heard the message of Christ from the apostles.

2:4 | gifts of the Holy Spirit.
The divine "Spirit" is written as a nomen sacrum (sacred name) in two early MSS ($\mathfrak{P}^{46}$ ℵ).

2:6 | the Son of Man.
"Son of Man" is written as a nomen sacrum (sacred name) in three early MSS ($\mathfrak{P}^{46}$ ℵ I), pointing to Jesus as "the Son of Man," his favorite self-identification in the Gospels; it was a messianic title (Dan. 7:13–14). The expression "son of man" is written in full (in *plene*; i.e., not a sacred name) in B, suggesting that the expression is a name for humanity in general. In 2:6, the author of Hebrews was thinking of Jesus as the Son of Man representing humanity.

2:7 | crowned him with glory and honor.
This is the original wording according to the two earliest MSS ($\mathfrak{P}^{46}$ B), as well as D^2 Maj. A variant reading is, "crowned him with glory and honor, and you set him over the works of your hands" in three early MSS (ℵ A C), as well as D* Ψ 33 1739, by way of scribal expansion influenced by Ps. 8:7.

2:8 | he subjected all things.
This is the original wording according to the two earliest MSS ($\mathfrak{P}^{46}$ B). An expanded reading is, "he subjected all things to him" in ℵ A C D Ψ 33 1739 Maj.

3:2 | as Moses was in his house.
This is the original wording according to the three earliest MSS ($\mathfrak{P}^{13}$ $\mathfrak{P}^{46vid}$ B). A variant reading is, "as Moses was in his entire house" in ℵ A C D Ψ 33 1739 Maj, by way of scribal expansion influenced by 3:5.

3:6a | Christ as the Son over his house.
"Son" is written as a nomen sacrum (sacred name) in $\mathfrak{P}^{46}$ ℵ I, pointing to a divine title; it is written in full (in *plene*; i.e., not as a sacred name) in $\mathfrak{P}^{13}$ B, pointing to one who is "a son," not a title. Both "the Son" and "a son" fit the context, as is evident in various English translations.

3:6b | we hold firmly to our hope.
This is the original wording according to the three earliest MSS ($\mathfrak{P}^{13}$ $\mathfrak{P}^{46}$ B). A variant reading is, "we hold firmly to our hope until the end" in three early MSS (ℵ A C), as well as D Ψ 33 1739 Maj, by way of scribal expansion influenced by 3:14.

3:7 | the Holy Spirit says.
The divine "Spirit" is written as a nomen sacrum (sacred name) in three early MSS ($\mathfrak{P}^{13vid}$ $\mathfrak{P}^{46}$ ℵ).

3:18 | those who were disobedient.
This is the original wording according to early and diverse testimony: $\mathfrak{P}^{13}$ ℵ A B C D Maj. $\mathfrak{P}^{46}$ reads "those who were unbelieving" (see notes on 4:6, 11; 11:31).

4:2 | they were not united in faith with those who heard the message.
This is the original wording according to early and diverse testimony: $\mathfrak{P}^{13}$ $\mathfrak{P}^{46}$ A B C Ψ 33 1739 $it^{t,v}$ syr^{h}. Two variant readings are, "those who heard did not combine the message with faith" (ℵ $it^{b,d}$ syr^{p}), and "they were not united with the faith of those who heard the message" (D syr^{hmg}). Both NA^{27} and UBS^{4} cite $\mathfrak{P}^{13vid}$, as opposed to $\mathfrak{P}^{13}$, but the reading is certain: *sugkekerasmenous* (see Comfort and Barrett, *Text of Earliest NT Greek MSS*, 86), meaning "combine," which agrees grammatically with *ekeinous* ("those ones"). The idea is not that faith wasn't combined with the hearing of the message, but that the people did not join in the faith of *those who heard* God's good message about entering the promised land—namely, the message of Joshua and Caleb, who told the people they could conquer the land. In other words, the Israelites, who heard the word through these men, did not share *their* faith.

4:3 | we have not entered into rest.
This is the original wording according to the three earliest MSS ($\mathfrak{P}^{13vid}$ $\mathfrak{P}^{46}$ B), as well as D*. A variant reading is, "we have not entered into the rest" in three early MSS (א A C), as well as D^{1} Ψ 33 1739 Maj.

4:6 | they did not enter because of unbelief.
This is the wording in two early MSS ($\mathfrak{P}^{46}$ א*). The last word is "disobedience" in $א^{c}$ A B C D Ψ 33 1739 Maj. ($\mathfrak{P}^{13}$ could support either reading; there is a lacuna at this word with two letters showing, which concur with either Greek word: *apistian* [unbelief], *apeitheian* [disobedience]). The scribe of $\mathfrak{P}^{46}$ chose the word "unbelief" over "disobedience" in four verses in Hebrews (3:18; 4:6, 11; 11:31).

4:11 | the same example of unbelief.
This is the wording of the two earliest MSS ($\mathfrak{P}^{13vid}$ $\mathfrak{P}^{46}$). The last word is "disobedience" in א A B C D Ψ 33 1739 Maj. (See Comfort and Barrett, *Text of Earliest NT Greek MSS*, 87, for the reconstruction of $\mathfrak{P}^{13}$.) (See notes on 3:18; 4:6; 11:31.)

4:12 | dividing soul and Spirit.
"Spirit" (*pneuma*) is written as a nomen sacrum (sacred name) in three early MSS ($\mathfrak{P}^{13}$ $\mathfrak{P}^{46}$ א). The word *pneuma* is written in full (in *plene*; i.e., not as a sacred name) in B, suggesting the human spirit and the translation, "dividing soul and spirit."

4:14 | the Son of God.
"Son of God" is written as a nomen sacrum (sacred name) in four early MSS ($\mathfrak{P}^{46}$ א B I).

5:5 | You are my Son.
The divine "Son" is written as a nomen sacrum (sacred name) in the earliest MS ($\mathfrak{P}^{46}$), pointing to a title. It is written in full (in *plene*; i.e. not as a sacred name) in two early MSS (א B), pointing to a position of a son.

5:8 | though he was the Son.
"Son" is written as a nomen sacrum (sacred name) in two early MSS ($\mathfrak{P}^{46vid}$ א), pointing to a divine title. It is written in full (in *plene*; i.e., not as a sacred name) in one early MS (B), pointing to the position of one who is a son, and yielding the translation, "though he was a son."

6:4 | partakers of the Holy Spirit.
The divine "Spirit" is written as a nomen sacrum (sacred name) in two early MSS ($\mathfrak{P}^{46}$ א).

6:6a | they are Crucifying.
"Crucifying" is written as a nomen sacrum (sacred word) in the earliest MS ($\mathfrak{P}^{46}$).

6:6b | the Son of God.
"Son of God" is written as a nomen sacrum (sacred name) in the three earliest MSS ($\mathfrak{P}^{46}$ א B).

7:3 | he is like the Son of God.
"Son of God" is written as a nomen sacrum (sacred name) in the three earliest MSS ($\mathfrak{P}^{46}$ א B). Note that Melchizedek is said to be "like" the Son of God, not that he was a preincarnate manifestation of *the* Son of God.

7:28a | the law appoints priests.
This is the reading according to two early MSS ($\mathfrak{P}^{46vid}$ I^{vid}), as well as D syr^{p} cop^{sa}. A variant reading is "the law appoints high priests" in four early MSS (א A B C), as well as Ψ 33 1739. The manuscript evidence is divided; either reading could be original.

7:28b | the law appoints a son made perfect forever.
The word "son" is written in full (in *plene*; i.e., not as a sacred name) in four early MSS ($\mathfrak{P}^{46}$ א B I), pointing to one who is a son, not a title.

8:4 | There are those who offer gifts prescribed by the law.
This statement indicates that this epistle was written while priests were

functioning in the Temple in Jerusalem. This had to be before AD 70, when the Temple was destroyed.

8:8 | God, finding fault, says to them.
This is the wording according to early and diverse testimony: $\mathfrak{P}^{46}$ $\aleph^{2}$ [seventh century] B D^{2} 1739 Maj. A variant reading is, "God, finding fault with them, says," also with early and diverse testimony: $\aleph^{*}$ A D I Ψ 33. Either reading could be original.

9:2 | the holy place.
This is the reading in ($\aleph$ B) D^{2} (I) 0278 33 1739 Maj. A variant reading is "the holy of holies" in $\mathfrak{P}^{46}$ A D*.

9:8 | the Holy Spirit is making clear.
The divine "Spirit" is written as a nomen sacrum (sacred name) in two early MSS ($\mathfrak{P}^{46}$ $\aleph$).

9:9 | This is a symbol for the present time, when gifts and sacrifices are being offered that cannot perfect the conscience of the worshiper.
This verse indicates that the writer of Hebrews was addressing a current situation; priests in the Temple offering sacrifices (see note on 8:4).

9:11 | the good things that have come.
This is the original wording according to the two earliest MSS ($\mathfrak{P}^{46}$ B), as well as D* 1739. A variant reading is, "the good things about to come" in $\aleph$ A D^{2} I^{vid} 33 Maj, by way of scribes making the statement pertain to future blessings.

9:14a | through an eternal spirit he offered himself to God.
The phrase "eternal spirit" is the original wording found in five early MSS ($\mathfrak{P}^{17vid}$ $\mathfrak{P}^{46}$ $\aleph^{*}$ A B), as well as D^{2} 33 1739 Maj. It is "Holy Spirit" in $\aleph^{2}$ [seventh century] D* P cop^{bo}. The word "spirit" is written in full (in *plene*; i.e., not as a sacred name) in two early MSS ($\mathfrak{P}^{46}$ B), pointing to Christ's eternal spirit. This indicates that Christ entered into eternity by virtue of being made alive in his spirit (see 1 Pet 3:18), and then resurrecting and

ascending. The word "Spirit" is written as a nomen sacrum (sacred name) in two early MSS ($\mathfrak{P}^{17}$ ℵ), suggesting the eternal Spirit of God working in Jesus to bring about his resurrection and ascension.

9:14b | worship the living God.
This is the original wording according to three early MSS ($\mathfrak{P}^{46vid}$ ℵ B), as well as D 33 1739 Maj. A variant is "worship the living and true God" in A P 0278, by way of scribal expansion influenced by 1 Thess 1:9.

10:9 | I have come to do your will.
This is the original wording according to four early MSS ($\mathfrak{P}^{46}$ ℵ* A C), as well as D Ψ 33. A variant reading is, "I have come, O God, to do your will" in ℵ^{2} [seventh century] 0278^{vid} 1739 Maj, by way of scribal assimilation to 10:7.

10:11 | every priest.
This is the original wording according to the three earliest MSS ($\mathfrak{P}^{46}$ $\mathfrak{P}^{79vid}$ ℵ), as well as D Ψ 33 1739 Maj cop^{bo}. A variant reading is "high priest" in A C P 0278 cop^{sa}.

10:15 | the Holy Spirit testifies.
The divine "Spirit" is written as a nomen sacrum (sacred name) in two early MSS ($\mathfrak{P}^{46}$ ℵ).

10:29a | whoever has contempt for the Son of God.
"Son of God" is written as a nomen sacrum (sacred name) in one early MS ($\mathfrak{P}^{46}$), as well as $\mathfrak{P}^{79}$.

10:29b | insults the Spirit of grace.
"Spirit" is written as a nomen sacrum (sacred name) in two early MSS ($\mathfrak{P}^{46}$ ℵ), as well as $\mathfrak{P}^{79}$.

10:30 | and again.
This is the original wording according to three early MSS ($\mathfrak{P}^{13vid}$ $\mathfrak{P}^{46}$ ℵ*), as well as D* Ψ 33 1739. A variant reading is, "and again

the Lord says" in $\aleph^{2}$ [seventh century] A D^{2} Maj, by way of scribal expansion.

10:34 | you suffered with those in chains.

This is the reading in the earliest MS ($\mathfrak{P}^{46}$) and Ψ (where the Greek is *desmois*). This was changed to "my chains" in ℵ D^{2} Maj—pointing to Paul's chains (i.e., Paul's imprisonment; cf. Phil. 1:7; Col. 4:18). Many early Christians thought Paul wrote Hebrews; indeed, in $\mathfrak{P}^{46}$ it is placed in the codex between Romans and 1 Corinthians. (Most modern commentators do not think Hebrews is Pauline in style.) Other MSS (A D* H 33 1739) read "prisoners" (Greek, *desmiois*)—with one *iota* of a difference. Either reading could have been confused for the other.

10:38 | my righteous one.

This is the reading in three early MSS ($\mathfrak{P}^{46}$ ℵ A), as well as H* 33 1739. A variant reading is, "the righteous one" in two early MSS ($\mathfrak{P}^{13}$ I), as well as D^{2} H^{c} Ψ. The textual evidence is divided; either reading could be original.

11:1

$\mathfrak{P}^{13}$ reads "faith is the storehouse of things hoped for, the evidence of things not seen." (For correct reconstruction of the text, see Comfort and Barrett, *Text of Earliest NT Greek MSS*, 89.) All other MSS support the translation, "faith is the substance of things hoped for, the evidence of things not seen."

11:11a | By faith, he, even though past age—and Sarah herself being barren—received power to beget.

This is most likely the original wording according to the earliest MS ($\mathfrak{P}^{46}$), as well as D* Ψ. A variant reading is, "by faith even Sarah herself, though past age, received power to conceive from a seed" in three early MSS ($\mathfrak{P}^{13vid}$ ℵ A), as well as D^{2} 33 Maj. Yet another variant is, "by faith even Sarah herself, the barren one, received power to conceive" in D^{1} 1739. The verse seems to refer to both Abraham and Sarah (as in $\mathfrak{P}^{46}$ etc.) because the Greek term *katabolēn spermatos*, means "to lay down seed" or "to deposit seed" (BAGD, 515)—the activity of a male—of which Sarah was the recipient. The masculine participle in 11:12 (*nenekrōmenou*—"he being as dead") also points to the subject being Abraham.

11:12 | sand on the shore of the sea.

This is the original wording according to four early MSS ($\mathfrak{P}^{13}$ $\mathfrak{P}^{46c}$ א A), as well as 33 1739 Maj. A variant reading is, "sand on the sea" in $\mathfrak{P}^{46*}$ D* Ψ.

11:31

All MSS except $\mathfrak{P}^{46}$ read "disobedient." $\mathfrak{P}^{46}$ reads, "unbelieving." The scribe of $\mathfrak{P}^{46}$ chose the word "unbelieving" over "disobedient" four times in Hebrews (3:18; 4:6, 11; 11:31; see notes).

11:32 | What more shall I say? Time will fail me.

This statement suggests that the epistle to the Hebrews was originally written as a sermon, which was delivered orally. Limited by time of delivery, the writer decided to cut short his catalog of believers.

11:37 | they were sawn in two.

This is the reading in the earliest MS ($\mathfrak{P}^{46}$), as well as syr^{p} cop^{sa}. Two variants on this are, "they were tested, they were sawn in two" (א D* L P 048 33), and "they were sawn in two, they were tested" ($\mathfrak{P}^{13vid}$ A D^{c} Ψ 1739), probably both scribal expansions.

12:1 | the sin that distracts.

This is the reading in the earliest MS ($\mathfrak{P}^{46}$), as well as 1739. A variant reading is, "the sin that entangles" in three early MSS ($\mathfrak{P}^{13}$ א A), as well as D Maj it cop syr. Either reading could be original.

12:2a | he endured the Cross.

"Cross" written as a nomen sacrum (sacred word) in the earliest MS ($\mathfrak{P}^{46}$).

12:3 | opposition from sinners, working against themselves.

This is the original wording according to the three earliest MSS ($\mathfrak{P}^{13}$

$\mathfrak{P}^{46}$ ℵ*), as well as D* 33 1739*. A variation is, "opposition from sinners working against him" in A D^{2} P Ψ* 1739^{c} Maj. The documentary evidence strongly supports the text, which indicates that people (the sinners) only hurt themselves by opposing Jesus.

12:5, 7 | a son.

The word "son" is written in full (in *plene*; i.e., not as a sacred name) in the three earliest MSS ($\mathfrak{P}^{13}$ $\mathfrak{P}^{46}$ ℵ), pointing to one who is a son, not a title.

12:7b, 9 | father.

The word "father" is written in full (in *plene*; i.e., not as a sacred name) in the three earliest MSS ($\mathfrak{P}^{13}$ $\mathfrak{P}^{46}$ ℵ), pointing to one who is a father, not a title.

13:10 | those who serve in the tabernacle.

This statement indicates that priests were serving in the tabernacle (a synonym for the Temple) at the time of writing. Thus, the writing must be before AD 70.

13:21 | to whom be glory forever.

This is the original wording according to the earliest MS ($\mathfrak{P}^{46}$), as well as C^{3} [ninth century] D Ψ. The last expression is "forever and ever" in three early MSS (ℵ A C*), as well as 0243 0285 33 1739 Maj. Either reading could be original.

13:25 | grace be with you all.

This is the original wording according to three early MSS ($\mathfrak{P}^{46}$ ℵ* I^{vid}), as well as 33. Several MSS ($ℵ^{2}$ [seventh century] A C D H 1739 Maj) add "amen" by way of scribal expansion.

Chapter Eight

The General Epistles

EPISTLE OF JAMES

Title: Epistle of James
This is the wording in the two earliest MSS (ℵ B).

1:17a | father of luminaries.
The word "father" is written in full (in *plene*; i.e., not as a sacred name) in the three earliest MSS ($\mathfrak{P}^{23}$ ℵ B), pointing to one who fathers, one who originates things—in this case, God fathered the luminaries.

1:17b | with whom there is no variation or turning of the shadow.
This is the reading in $\mathfrak{P}^{23}$, the earliest MS. Two variant readings are "with whom there is no variation which consists in the turning of the shadow" ($\aleph^{*}$ B), and "with whom there is no variation or turning of the shadow" ($\aleph^{2}$ [seventh century] A C 1739 Maj). The reading of $\mathfrak{P}^{23}$ signifies that father God is both changeless and timeless (the turning of the shadow referring to the movement of the shadow on a sun dial). The variants indicate that God is changeless—the images referring to the motions of heavenly luminaries causing variation in light and darkness and thereby casting shifting shadows.

2:2 | if someone comes into your synagogue.
That James spoke of their assembly as a "synagogue" indicates he was writing to Jewish Christians who were probably still practicing their Judaism to some extent.

2:5 | heirs of the kingdom.
This is the original wording according to three early MSS ($\aleph^{1}$ B C), as well as 33 1739 Maj. A variant reading is "heirs of the promise" in $\aleph^{*}$ A, by way of scribal conformity to Heb. 6:17.

2:20 | faith without works is useless.
The word "useless" is the original word according to two early MSS (B C*), as well as 1739. There are two variants for the last word: "empty"

($\mathfrak{P}^{74}$) and "dead" (א A C^2 [sixth century] P Ψ 33 Maj), which probably shows assimilation to 2:17, 26.

2:26 | the body without the Spirit is dead.
"Spirit" is written as a nomen sacrum (sacred name) in two early MSS ($\mathfrak{P}^{20}$ א), as well as $\mathfrak{P}^{54}$, denoting the divine Spirit. The word *pneuma* is written in full (in *plene*; i.e., not as a sacred name) in B, denoting the human spirit or breath—suggesting the translations, "just as the body without spirit is dead" or "just as the body without breath is dead."

3:9 | the Lord and Father.
"Lord" is the original word according to five early MSS ($\mathfrak{P}^{20}$ א A B C), as well as P Ψ 33 1739. It was changed to "God" in the majority of MSS (so KJV). "Lord" is written as a nomen sacrum (sacred name) in all MSS. "Father" is written as a nomen sacrum (sacred name) in the earliest MS ($\mathfrak{P}^{20vid}$).

4:4 | adulteresses.
This is the original word according to the four earliest MSS ($\mathfrak{P}^{100}$ א* A B), as well as 33 1739. A variant reading is "adulterers and adulteresses" in א^2 [seventh century] P Ψ Maj, by way of scribal expansion. The feminine "adulteresses" refers to any and all (whether male or female) who turn away from God and go after other gods.

4:5 | God longs jealously for the Spirit he placed to live within us.
The divine "Spirit" is written as a nomen sacrum (sacred name) in two early MSS ($\mathfrak{P}^{100vid}$ א), suggesting the translation above. Codex B writes out the word *pneuma* in full (in *plene*; i.e., not as a sacred name), denoting the human spirit, and yielding the translation, "God longs jealously for the spirit he placed within us."

5:19 | if anyone among you wanders from the truth.
The words "the truth" are original according to two early MSS (A B), as well as P 048^{vid} 1739 Maj. Two variants are "the way" ($\mathfrak{P}^{74}$), and "the way of the truth" (33 א).

THE EPISTLE OF PETER 1

Title: The Epistle of Peter A [=1]
This is the wording in three early MSS (𝔓[72] א A), as well as 33.

1:2a | the foreknowledge of God the Father.
"God" is written as a nomen sacrum (sacred name) in all MSS. The divine "Father" is written as a nomen sacrum (sacred name) in the earliest MS (𝔓[72]).

1:2b | set apart by the Spirit.
The divine "Spirit" is written as a nomen sacrum (sacred name) in two early MSS (𝔓[72] א).

1:3 | God and Father.
"God" is written as a nomen sacrum (sacred name) in all MSS. The divine "Father" is written as a nomen sacrum (sacred name) in the earliest MS (𝔓[72]).

1:11 | the Spirit of Christ.
This is the original wording according to four early MSS (𝔓[72] א A C), as well as P 048. A variant reading is "the Spirit" in B. The "Spirit of Christ" is written as a nomen sacrum (sacred name) in two early MSS (𝔓[72] א). Peter spoke of the Spirit of Christ indwelling the OT prophets who lived before the incarnation of the Son of God, when he became Jesus Christ of Nazareth. This means the Spirit of Christ existed before the incarnation; it also suggests that the Spirit of Christ is not bound by time—i.e., the Spirit of Christ is eternal. The scribe of B obfuscates these realities by making the title simply "the Spirit."

1:17 | the Father.
The divine "Father" is written as a nomen sacrum (sacred name) in the earliest MS (𝔓[72]).

1:22 | a pure heart.
The wording "a pure heart" is the original wording according to three early MSS (𝔓[72] ℵ* C), as well as P Ψ 33 1739 Maj. Two variant readings are "a true heart" (ℵ[2] [seventh century]) and "with heart" (A B). The text has solid testimony.

2:3 | if you have tasted that the Lord is Christ.
This is the wording in the earliest MS (𝔓[72]), as well as K L 049 33. A variant reading is, "if you have tasted that the Lord is good" in four early MSS (ℵ A B C), as well as Ψ 1739 Maj. Though one would think the two words ("Christ" and "good") could be easily confused for each other in the Greek (*christos* = Christ and *chrestos* = good), the name of Christ was always written in MSS, from early in the textual tradition, as a nomen sacrum (XPC in 𝔓[72]). So, if there was some confusion, it must have happened as early as the first century. The exemplar the scribe of 𝔓[72] used must have had "Christ" written as a nomen sacrum.

2:21 | Christ suffered for you.
This is the wording in four early MSS (𝔓[72] A B C), as well as P 33. A variant reading is, "Christ died for you" in two early MSS (𝔓[81] ℵ), as well as Ψ. Both readings, each of which has early documentary support, could be original. And one could argue, on internal grounds, for either reading—"suffered" was changed to "died" because that is the more usual NT expression; "died" was changed to "suffered" to suit the immediate context.

3:4 | quietness inspired by the Spirit.
This translates "quietness of Spirit/spirit." 𝔓[72] and ℵ write "Spirit" as a nomen sacrum (sacred name); B writes out the word in full (in *plene*; i.e., not as a sacred name), denoting the human spirit—"quietness of spirit."

3:6 | Sarah obeyed Abraham, calling him "lord."
The word "lord" follows the orthography of B, which writes the name *kurion* in full (in *plene*; i.e., not as a sacred name—as in 𝔓[72] 𝔓[81vid] ℵ).

This shows that the scribe of B broke from his normal pattern of writing a nomen sacrum (sacred name) for *kurion*, and instead, wrote out the word in full. This clearly indicates the interpretation of the scribe that Sarah called her husband "lord," not "Lord," since Abraham was not divine.

3:7 | grace of life.

This is the original wording according to three early MSS ($\mathfrak{P}^{81vid}$ B C*), as well as P Ψ 33 1739 Maj. Two variant readings are "grace of eternal life" ($\mathfrak{P}^{72}$), and "multifarious grace of life" (א A C^2 [sixth century]). $\mathfrak{P}^{72}$ identifies the "life" as being "eternal," which it is, and **א**, et. al, add an adjective ("multifarious") influenced by 4:10.

3:14 | do not fear their terror.

This is the original wording according to the two earliest MSS ($\mathfrak{P}^{72}$ B). Scribes expanded the reading to, "do not fear their terror or be afraid" (א A C P Ψ 33 1739 Maj).

3:15 | set apart Christ as Lord in your hearts.

This is the original reading according to early and diverse testimony: $\mathfrak{P}^{72}$ א A B C Ψ 33 1739. Instead of "Lord," some MSS read "God" (P Maj; so KJV).

3:18a | Christ died for sins.

This is the original wording according to four early MSS ($\mathfrak{P}^{72}$ א A C), as well as L Ψ 33 1739. A variant reading is, "Christ suffered for sins" in one early MS (B), as well as P Maj, by way of scribal conformity to the context, which is speaking of suffering, and/or conformity to 4:1.

3:18b | made alive by the Spirit.

"Spirit" is written as a nomen sacrum (sacred name) in two early MSS ($\mathfrak{P}^{72}$ א); it is written in full (in *plene*; i.e., not as a sacred name) in one early MS (B), suggesting the translation "made alive in spirit" (referring to Jesus's human spirit or a spiritual experience).

4:6 | they may live by the Spirit.
"Spirit" (*pneuma*) is written as a nomen sacrum (sacred name) in two early MSS (𝔓^{72} ℵ^{vid}). Codex B writes the word in full (in *plene*; i.e., not as a sacred name), suggesting the rendering "may live in spirit."

4:14a | the Spirit of glory.
This is the original wording according to the two earliest MSS (𝔓^{72} B), as well as K L Ψ. A variant reading is "the Spirit of glory and power" in two early MSS (ℵ A), as well as P 33 1739, by way of scribal expansion. "Spirit" is written as a nomen sacrum (sacred name) in two early MSS (𝔓^{72} ℵ).

4:14b | the Spirit of God.
"Spirit of God" is written as a nomen sacrum (sacred name) in the three earliest MSS (𝔓^{72} ℵ B).

4:16 | if you suffer as a Christian.
"Christian" is spelled *christianos* in two early MSS (𝔓^{72} ℵ^{c}), meaning one who belongs to "Christ." "Christian" is spelled *chrēstianos* in ℵ* (also in Acts 11:26; 26:28), meaning one who belongs to "chrestus," meaning "the kind one." The Roman historian Tacitus (perhaps misunderstanding that Jesus was called the "Christ" [*christos*], meaning "the anointed one") called him *chrēstus*, meaning "the kind one" (see *Annals* 15.44). (Codex B spells the name as *chreistianos*.)

5:1 | Christ's sufferings.
This is the reading in all MSS except 𝔓^{72}, which reads "God's sufferings." The extraordinary reading in 𝔓^{72} indicates that Jesus was viewed as God incarnate, susceptible to suffering.

5:2 | exercising oversight.
This is the original reading according to two early MSS (𝔓^{72} A), as well as ℵ^{2} [seventh century] P Ψ 33 1739. The expression is omitted in two fourth-century MSS (ℵ* B). The word *episkopountes* was deleted in ℵ* and B probably because later in church history (by the fourth century)

this was the function of a bishop (overseer), not an elder. In the early church, the elders were one and the same as the overseers.

5:10a | eternal glory in Christ.
This is probably the original reading according to three early MSS (א B 0206^{vid}). The name is expanded to "Christ Jesus" in two early MSS (𝔓^{72} A), as well as P Ψ 33 1739 Maj.

5:10b | restore, confirm, and establish.
This is the reading in the earliest MS (𝔓^{72}). Another reading is "restore, confirm, and strengthen" in three early MSS (A B 0206^{vid}), as well as Ψ. Yet another reading is, "restore, confirm, strengthen, and establish" in one early MS (א), as well as 33^{vid} 1739*. Either of the first two readings could be original; the third is likely an expansion.

5:12 | Through Silvanus, whom I know to be a faithful brother, I have written to you briefly.
Silvanus (also known as Silas) was Peter's amanuensis. Likely, Peter dictated the epistle (whether in Aramaic or Greek) and Silvanus put it into the words we read in 1 Peter. Or it is possible that Peter gave him the thoughts he wanted to express, and Silvanus thereafter composed the letter. Silvanus, the coauthor of 1 and 2 Thessalonians, was an experienced writer. It is likely that Peter took pen (stylus) in hand at this point, and wrote the rest of the letter in his own handwriting. In the original letter (the autograph) we would see two different handwritings—that of Silvanus and that of Peter.

5:14 | Greet one another with a loving kiss.
The epistle ends here in the earliest MS (𝔓^{72}). Several MSS add, "Peace be to all who are in Christ" (א [adds "Jesus" after "Christ"] A B Ψ 33 1739 Maj), to which some MSS append "amen" (א P 1739^{c} Maj) by way of scribal expansion.

THE EPISTLE OF PETER 2

Title: The Epistle of Peter B [= 2]
This is the wording in two early MSS (𝔓72 C), as well as 33.

1:1 | our God and Savior, Jesus Christ.
This is the original wording according to three early MSS (𝔓72 A B), as well as Maj. A variant reading is "our Lord and Savior, Jesus Christ" in א Ψ. According to the Greek grammar, it is more than clear that Peter was naming "Jesus Christ" as both "God" and "Savior." There is one definite article for the two nouns joined by *kai*; the Granville Sharp rule indicates that the so-named person ("Jesus Christ") is both "God" and Savior" (cf. 1:11; 2:20).

1:2 | God and Jesus our Lord.
This is the reading in all MSS except 𝔓72, which reads, "God, Jesus our Lord." The reading of 𝔓72 indicates that "God" is "Jesus our Lord" (see previous note).

1:3 | he called us through his own glory and virtue.
This is the reading in two early MSS (𝔓72 B), as well as 0209vid Maj. A variant reading is, "he called us to his own glory and virtue" in א A C P Ψ 33 1739. There is a one letter difference between the two readings: *dia* (through) and *idia* (to his own). Though either reading could be original, the reading of the text has the earliest testimony (𝔓72 B), which suggests that believers were attracted though Christ's glory and virtue to respond to God's call of salvation.

1:17a | the Father.
The divine "Father" is written as a nomen sacrum (sacred name) in the earliest MS (𝔓72).

1:17b | my beloved Son.
The divine "Son" is written as a nomen sacrum (sacred name) in one early MS (א). The name is written in full (in *plene*; i.e., not as a sacred

name) in two early MSS ($\mathfrak{P}^{72}$ B), pointing to one who is a son, not a title.

1:21 | the Holy Spirit.
The divine "Spirit" is written as a nomen sacrum (sacred name) in two early MSS ($\mathfrak{P}^{72}$ א).

2:4 | he locked them up in chains.
The word "chains" is found in the earliest MS ($\mathfrak{P}^{72}$), as well as P Ψ 33 1739 Maj syr. This is substituted by "pits" in four early MSS (א A B C). The two words are very similar in Greek (*seirais* = chains; *sirois* = pits), and could easily be confused for one another. Therefore, either reading could be original, and both suit the context.

2:6 | he condemed them.
This is probably the original wording according to three early MSS ($\mathfrak{P}^{72*}$ B C*), as well as 1739. A variant reading is, "condemned them to destruction" in four early MSS ($\mathfrak{P}^{72mg}$ א A C^2 [sixth century]), as well as Ψ 33 Maj—probably scribal expansion.

2:11 | bring slanderous judgment against them from the Lord.
This is the reading in the earliest MS ($\mathfrak{P}^{72}$). Two variant readings are "bring slanderous judgment against them before the Lord" (א B C P 1739 Maj) and "bring slanderous judgment against them" (A Ψ 33). The first or second readings ($\mathfrak{P}^{72}$ or א, et al.) could be original; both are exegetically defensible. The angels can bring judgment against the glorious ones "from the Lord" or "before the Lord."

2:13 | indulging in deceptions.
This is the original wording according to four early MSS ($\mathfrak{P}^{72}$ א A* C), as well as 33 Maj syr^{h} cop^{bo}. A variant reading is "indulging in love feasts" in two early MSS (A^c B), as well as Ψ. Though either word could be easily confused for the other (*apatais* = deceptions; *agapais* = love feasts), the variant was influenced by Jude 12, a parallel passage.

3:10 | the earth and its works will be found out.

This is the reading in two early MSS (א B), as well as P 0156^{vid} 1739^{vid}. There are three variations on the verb: "will be found destroyed" ($\mathfrak{P}^{72}$), "will be burned up" (A 048 33 1739^{mg}), "will disappear" (C). The variants are scribal clarifications of a difficult text that speaks of what will happen to the earth as the result of God's judgment.

3:18

The final word is "amen" in four early MSS ($\mathfrak{P}^{72}$ א A C), as well as P Ψ 33 1739^{c} Maj. It is omitted in B 1739*. It is likely the original epistle did not have "amen" as the final word. Scribes had a propensity for adding it to the end of the epistles.

JOHN 1

Title: John A [= 1].
This is the wording in the three earliest MSS (א A B).

1:5 | this is the message we heard from him.
The words "the message" are original according to three early MSS (א*,1 A B), as well as Maj. Two variants are "the promise" (C P 33 1739) and "the love of the promise" (א2 [seventh century] Ψ).

1:7 | Jesus his Son.
"Jesus" is written as a nomen sacrum (sacred name) in all MSS. The divine "Son" is written as a nomen sacrum (sacred name) in one early MS (א).

2:14 | the word of God.
This is the original wording according to nearly all MSS: 𝔓74 א A C L P Ψ 33 1739 Maj. This is reduced to "the word" in B.

2:22–23 | the Father and the Son.
The divine "Father" and "Son" are written as nomina sacra (sacred names) in one early MS (א).

3:5 | you know that Jesus was revealed to take away sins.
The original wording is "you know" according to three early MSS (A B C), as well as P Ψ 33 1739 Maj. A variant reading is "we know" in one early MS (א).

3:8 | the Son of God was revealed.
"Son of God" is written as a nomen sacrum (sacred name) in two early MSS (א B).

3:21 | beloved friends.
This is the original wording according to most MSS: A B C Ψ 33 1739 Maj. A variant reading is "brothers" in one early MS (א).

3:23 | his Son.
"Son" is written as a nomen sacrum (sacred name) in one early MS (א).

3:24 | the Spirit he has given us.
The divine "Spirit" is written as a nomen sacrum (sacred name) in one early MS (א).

4:1 | do not believe every spirit.
The word "spirit" (*pneuma*) is written in full (in *plene*; i.e., not as a sacred name) in B. The "spirit" refers to the spirits of various prophets.

4:2 | the Spirit of God.
"Spirit of God" is written as a nomen sacrum (sacred name) in two early MSS (א B).

4:3a | the spirit of the antichrist.
The word "spirit" (*pneuma*) is written in full (in *plene*; i.e., not as a sacred name) in B.

4:3b | confess Jesus.
This is the original wording according to two early MSS (A B), as well as 1739. A variant reading is, "confess Jesus come in the flesh" in one early MS (א), as well as Ψ (33) Maj (so KJV), by way of scribal expansion influenced by the previous verse (4:2).

4:6a | the Spirit of truth.
The divine "Spirit" is written as a nomen sacrum (sacred name) in one early MS (א).

4:6b | the spirit of deceit.
The word "spirit" (*pneuma*) is written in full (in *plene*; i.e., not as a sacred name) in B.

4:9–10 | Son.
The divine "Son" is written as a nomen sacrum (sacred name) in one early MS (א).

4:13 | he has given us of his Spirit.
The divine "Spirit" is written as a nomen sacrum (sacred name) in one early MS (א).

4:14 | the Son.
The divine "Son" is written as a nomen sacrum (sacred name) in one early MS ($\mathfrak{P}^{9vid}$).

4:15a | Jesus.
This is the original wording according to most MSS: $\mathfrak{P}^{74}$ א A 33 1739 Maj. The name is "Jesus Christ" in B.

4:15b | the Son of God.
"Son of God" is written as a nomen sacrum (sacred name) in three early MSS ($\mathfrak{P}^{9}$ א B).

5:5 | the Son of God.
"Son of God" is written as a nomen sacrum (sacred name) in two early MSS (א B).

5:6 | the Spirit.
The divine "Spirit" is written in both occurrences as a nomen sacrum (sacred name) in one early MS (א).

5:7–8 | So we have three witnesses—[8] the Spirit, the water, and the blood—and all three agree.
This is the wording in the earliest MSS (א A B), as well as Ψ, and several early versions (Syriac, Coptic, Armenian, Ethiopic, Old Latin). Some late MSS ([61 629 in part] 88 221 429 636 918 2318) read, "so there are three testifying in heaven: the Father, the Word, and the Holy Spirit. And these three are one. [8] And there are three that testify on earth: the

Spirit, the water, and the blood, and these three have one testimony." This expanded passage called the "heavenly witness" passage or *Comma Johanneum*, came from a gloss on 5:8 which explained that the three elements (water, blood, and Spirit), symbolize the Trinity (the Father, the Word [Son], and the Spirit). The gloss showed up in the writings of Latin fathers in North Africa and Italy (as part of the text of the epistle) from the fifth century onward, and it found its way into more and more copies of the Latin Vulgate. (The original translation of Jerome did not include it.) "The heavenly witnesses" passage has not been found in the text of any Greek manuscript prior to the fourteenth century. The passage as written by John has nothing to do with the Trinity, but with the three critical phases in Jesus's life where he was manifested as God incarnate, the Son of God in human form. This was made evident at his baptism (= the water), his death (= the blood), and his resurrection (= the Spirit). At his baptism, the man Jesus was declared God's beloved Son (see Matt. 3:16–17). At his crucifixion, a man spilling blood was recognized by others as "God's Son" (see Mark 15:39). In resurrection, he was designated as the Son of God in power (Rom. 1:3–4). This trifold testimony is unified in one aspect: each event demonstrated that the man Jesus was the divine Son of God.

The word *pneuma* (Spirit) is written as a nomen sacrum in א, denoting the divine Spirit. The word is written in full (in *plene*; i.e., not as a sacred name) in B, suggesting the translation "spirit."

5:9 | his Son.

The divine "Son" is written as a nomen sacrum (sacred name) in one early MS (א).

5:10a | the Son of God.

"Son of God" is written as a nomen sacrum (sacred name) in two early MSS (א B).

5:10b, 12a | Son.

The divine "Son" is written as a nomen sacrum (sacred name) in one early MS (א).

5:12b, 13 | Son of God.
"Son of God" is written as a nomen sacrum (sacred name) in two early MSS (א B).

5:18 | the One born of God keeps him.
Either John was speaking of Jesus, "the One born of God," or the believer, "the one born of God." If the latter, the reader would expect the text to say "keeps himself," which is the reading in two early MSS (א A^c), as well as P Ψ 33 1739 Maj. However, two early MSS (A* B) read "keeps him." Thus, the most likely reading is that Jesus, as "the One born of God," preserves (keeps) the believer.

5:20 | the Son of God has come.
"Son of God" is written as a nomen sacrum (sacred name) in two early MSS (א B). The grammar in the Greek makes it clear that the Son of God, Jesus Christ, is identified as "the true God and eternal life."

JOHN 2

Title: John B [= 2]
This is the wording in three early MSS (ℵ A B).

1:3a | the Father.
The divine "Father" is written in both occurrences as a nomen sacrum (sacred name) in one early MS (0232).

1:3b | from Jesus Christ.
This is the original reading according to three early MSS (A B 0232). The name is "Lord Jesus Christ" one early MS (ℵ), as well as P 33 Maj, by way of scribal expansion.

1:3c | the Son.
The divine "Son" is written as a nomen sacrum (sacred name) in two early MSS (0232 ℵ).

1:4 | the Father commanded us.
The divine "Father" is written as a nomen sacrum (sacred name) in one early MS (0232).

1:8 | so that you do not lose what you worked for.
This is the original wording according to three early MSS (ℵ A 0232^{vid}), as well as Ψ 33 1739. A variant reading is, "so that you do not lose what we [i.e., the apostles] worked for" in one early MS (B). The text has superior testimony.

1:9a | the Father and the Son.
The divine "Father" is written as a nomen sacrum (sacred name) in one early MS (0232^{vid}). The divine "Son" is written as a nomen sacrum (sacred name) in two early MSS (0232^{vid} ℵ).

1:12 | Though I have many other things I want to write to you, I do not want to do so with paper and ink.

This indicates that John himself penned this letter. The entire epistle would have fit on one sheet of papyrus (front and back).

JOHN 3

Title: John Γ [= 3]
This is the wording according to the three earliest MSS (א A B).

1:9 | I wrote something to the church.
This probably refers to the epistle known as 1 John.

1:13 | I have many things I want to write to you, but I do not want to write to you with pen and ink.
This indicates that John himself penned this letter. The entire epistle would have fit on one sheet of papyrus (front and back).

THE EPISTLE OF JUDE

Title: The Epistle of Jude
This is the wording in two early MSS ($\mathfrak{P}^{72}$ A), as well as 33 1739.

1:1 | the Father.
The divine "Father" is written as a nomen sacrum (sacred name) in one early MS ($\mathfrak{P}^{72}$).

1:4 | our only Master and Lord, Jesus Christ.
This is the original wording according to five early MSS ($\mathfrak{P}^{78}$ א A B C), as well as 33 1739. Two variant readings are "God, the only Master, and our Lord Jesus Christ" (P Ψ Maj) and "our Master and our Lord Jesus Christ" ($\mathfrak{P}^{72c}$). The text has superior documentation.

1:5 | Jesus saved them out of Egypt.
This is the reading in two early MSS (A B), as well as 33 1739 2344. The earliest MS ($\mathfrak{P}^{72}$) reads "God, who is Christ [lit. "God Christ"] saved them out of Egypt." Two variants are "the Lord saved them out of Egypt" (א C* Ψ), and "God saved them out of Egypt" (C^{2}). According to the textual evidence, the original text either reads "Jesus" or "God who is Christ" (which could also be rendered "Messiah God"). Either reading is remarkable because it places Jesus Christ present at the exodus and thereafter. Some have suggested that "Jesus" (*Iēsous*) should be "Joshua," but Joshua was not Israel's leader at the time of the exodus.

1:19–20 | Spirit, Holy Spirit.
The divine "Spirit" is written as a nomen sacrum (sacred name) in two early MSS ($\mathfrak{P}^{72}$ א).

1:22–23 | And snatch some from the fire, and show mercy with fear to others who have doubts.
This is the reading in the earliest MS ($\mathfrak{P}^{72}$). There are several variants: (1) "and show mercy to some who have doubts—save them by snatching them from the fire; and to some show mercy with fear" (B); (2) "and

have mercy on some, making a difference, and others, save with fear, pulling them out of the fire" (Maj; so KJV); (3) "and reprove some who have doubts [or, who dispute] and in fear save some from fire" (C*); (4) "and show mercy to some who have doubts [or, who dispute], and save some, snatching them from the fire, and to some show mercy with fear" (א); (5) "and reprove some who have doubts [or, who dispute], and save some, snatching them from the fire, and to some show mercy with fear" (A). The short reading in 𝔓[72] (which is nearly the same in B) could be original. If so, the other variants are scribal expansions.

Chapter Nine

The Revelation of John

THE REVELATION OF JOHN

Title: The Revelation of John
This is the wording in the two earliest MSS (א A).

1:4 | the seven Spirits.
This could also be rendered "the seven-fold Spirit," which is suggested by the nomen sacrum (sacred name) form in one early MS (א). The earliest MS ($\mathfrak{P}^{18}$), however, writes this as "the seven Spirits."

1:6a | priests to God and his father.
"God" is written as a nomen sacrum (sacred name) in all MSS. The wording "father" follows the orthography of the earliest MS ($\mathfrak{P}^{18}$), which does not write it as a nomen sacrum (sacred name), pointing to one who is a father (not a title). One early MS (א) writes "Father" as a nomen sacrum (sacred name).

1:6b | forever.
This is the original wording according to two early MSS ($\mathfrak{P}^{18}$ A), as well as P. A variant reading is "forever and ever" in two early MSS (א C), as well as Maj, by way of scribal expansion.

1:8 | the Alpha and the Omega.
This is the original wording according to three early MSS ($א^{1}$ A C). A variant reading is, "the Alpha and Omega, the beginning and the end" according to $א^{*,2}$ [seventh century] Maj^{A} it cop^{bo}, by way of scribal expansion influenced by 21:6 and 22:13, parallel verses.

1:10 | I was in the Spirit.
The divine "Spirit" is written as a nomen sacrum (sacred name) in one early MS (א).

1:13 | the Son of Man.
"Son of Man," a messianic title (Dan. 7:13–14), is written as a nomen sacrum (sacred name) in one early MS (א).

1:18 | forever and ever.
This is the original wording according to four early MSS (𝔓[98vid] א* A C), as well as P. A variant reading is, "forever and ever, amen" in א[1] Maj, by way of scribal expansion.

2:7, 11, 17 | the Spirit says.
The divine "Spirit" is written as a nomen sacrum (sacred name) in one early MS (א).

2:18 | the Son of God.
"Son of God" is written as a nomen sacrum (sacred name) in one early MS (א).

2:28 | from my Father.
The divine "Father" is written as a nomen sacrum (sacred name) in one early MS (𝔓[115vid]).

2:29 | the Spirit says.
The divine "Spirit" is written as a nomen sacrum (sacred name) in two early MSS (𝔓[115vid] א).

3:1 | the seven Spirits of God.
This could also be rendered "the seven-fold Spirit of God," which is suggested by the nomen sacrum (sacred name) form in one early MS (א).

3:6, 13 | the Spirit says.
The divine "Spirit" is written as a nomen sacrum (sacred name) in one early MS (א).

3:21 | sat down with my Father on his throne.
The divine "Father" is written as a nomen sacrum (sacred name) in two early MSS (0169 א).

3:22 | the Spirit says.
The divine "Spirit" is written as a nomen sacrum (sacred name) in two early MSS (0169 א).

4:2a | I was in the Spirit.
The divine "Spirit" is written as a nomen sacrum (sacred name) in two early MSS (0169 א).

4:5 | the seven Spirits of God.
This could also be rendered "seven-fold Spirit of God" according to one early MS (א), which writes "Spirit" as a nomen sacrum (sacred name).

4:11 | Lord, O Lord and our God.
This is the wording in one early MS (א). All other MSS read, "our Lord and God."

5:6 | the seven Spirits of God.
This could also be rendered, "the sevenfold Spirit of God," which is suggested by the nomen sacrum (sacred name) form in two early MSS ($\mathfrak{P}^{24}$ א).

9:2 | And when he opened the shaft of the abyss.
This is the original wording according to three early MSS ($\mathfrak{P}^{115vid}$ A 0207), as well as Maj. The words are omitted in one early MS (א).

9:20 | demons and idols.
This is the original wording according to three early MSS ($\mathfrak{P}^{115}$ א A), as well as Maj. One early MS ($\mathfrak{P}^{47}$) omits "and idols."

9:21 | sexual immorality and stealing.
This is the original wording according to three early MSS ($\mathfrak{P}^{115vid}$ א C). One early MS ($\mathfrak{P}^{47}$) omits "and stealing."

10:2 | little book.
This is the original wording according to four early MSS ($\mathfrak{P}^{85vid}$ $\mathfrak{P}^{115vid}$

$\aleph^{1}$ C*), as well as Maj^{A}. A variant reading is "book" in one early MS ($\mathfrak{P}^{47}$), as well as Maj^{K}. The description strongly suggests he was holding a small codex (which could be held open in one hand), not a scroll (which would require two hands to hold it open).

10:8 | little book.
This is the original wording according to two early MSS ($\mathfrak{P}^{115vid}$ $\aleph$), as well as Maj. A variant reading is "book" in two early MSS (A C). See note on 10:2.

10:10a | little book.
This is the original wording according to four early MSS ($\mathfrak{P}^{47c}$ $\mathfrak{P}^{115vid}$ A C), as well as Maj^{A}. A variant reading is "book" in two early MSS ($\mathfrak{P}^{47*vid}$ $\aleph$).

10:10b | my stomach became bitter.
This is probably the original wording according to three early MSS ($\mathfrak{P}^{47}$ A C), as well as Maj. Two variant readings are "my stomach became full" in two early MSS ($\mathfrak{P}^{115vid}$ $\aleph$*) and "my stomach became full and bitter" in $\aleph^{1}$.

11:8a | this is Spiritually called Sodom and Egypt.
The word "spiritually" is written as a nomen sacrum (sacred word) in two early MSS ($\mathfrak{P}^{115vid}$ $\aleph$).

11:8b | where their Lord was also Crucified.
"Lord" is written as a nomen sacrum in all MSS. "Crucified" is written as a nomen sacrum (sacred word) in two early MSS ($\mathfrak{P}^{47}$ $\aleph$).

11:11 | the Spirit of life from God.
The divine "Spirit" is written as a nomen sacrum (sacred name) in the three earliest MSS ($\mathfrak{P}^{47}$ $\mathfrak{P}^{115}$ $\aleph$).

11:19 | the ark of his covenant.
This is the original wording according to three early MSS ($\mathfrak{P}^{115vid}$ A C).

Two variant readings are "the ark of the covenant of the Lord" in one early MS ($\mathfrak{P}^{47}$), as well as Maj^{K}, and "the ark of the covenant of God" in one early MS (א), both scribal expansions.

12:9 | the ancient serpent.
This is the original wording according to four early MSS ($\mathfrak{P}^{115}$ א A C). A variant reading is "the serpent" in one early MS ($\mathfrak{P}^{47}$).

13:1 | a blasphemous name.
This is probably the original reading according to three early MSS ($\mathfrak{P}^{47}$ א C). A variant reading is, "blasphemous names" in two early MSS ($\mathfrak{P}^{115vid}$ A), as well as Maj^{K}.

13:6 | his dwelling place, that is, those who dwell in heaven.
This is the original wording according to three early MSS ($\mathfrak{P}^{115vid}$ א* A). Two variant readings are "his dwelling place in heaven" in one early MS ($\mathfrak{P}^{47}$), and "his dwelling place and those who dwell in heaven" in א^{2} [seventh century] Maj^{A}. God's dwelling place is his people. He lives in them and they live in him.

13:7 | the creature was allowed to war against the saints and conquer them.
This is probably the original wording according to two early MSS ($\mathfrak{P}^{115vid}$ א). The clause is omitted in three early MSS ($\mathfrak{P}^{47}$ A C), as well as Maj^{A}. Though the textual evidence is evenly divided, it is likely that the scribes of $\mathfrak{P}^{47}$, et al., deleted the phrase because it says that the creature conquered the saints.

13:15 | to give breath to the image of the first creature.
One early MS ($\mathfrak{P}^{115vid}$) writes out the word *pneuma* in full (in *plene*; i.e., not as a sacred name), suggesting "breath" or "spirit." Two early MSS ($\mathfrak{P}^{47}$ א) write it as a nomen sacrum (sacred name), suggesting "the Spirit."

13:18b | his number is 616.
This is the wording in two early MSS ($\mathfrak{P}^{115}$ C), as well as $MSS^{according}$

$^{\text{to Irenaeus}}$. A variant reading is "his number is 666" in two early MSS ($\mathfrak{P}^{47}$ א), as well as P Maj MSS$^{\text{according to Irenaeus}}$. Either reading could be original. Irenaeus, writing in the second century (*Against Heresies* 5.30), knew of the two readings; so both were very early. Whichever one John wrote, they both symbolize Caesar Nero. Through gematria (a method whereby letters of an alphabet signify various numbers), the Hebrew translation of "Caesar Nero" is signified by "616," and "Caesar Neron" is signified by "666." Caesar Nero persecuted Christians. Those who received his "mark" were exempt from this persecution.

14:1 | The name of his Father.
The divine "Father" is written as a nomen sacrum (sacred name) in the three earliest MSS ($\mathfrak{P}^{47}$ $\mathfrak{P}^{115\text{vid}}$ א).

14:6 | I saw another angel.
The original wording is "another angel" according to four early MSS ($\mathfrak{P}^{115\text{vid}}$ א^{2} [seventh century] A C). A variant reading is "an angel" in two early MSS ($\mathfrak{P}^{47}$ א*), as well as Maj.

14:13 | the Spirit says.
The divine "Spirit" is written as a nomen sacrum (sacred name) in the three earliest MSS ($\mathfrak{P}^{47}$ $\mathfrak{P}^{115\text{vid}}$ א).

14:14 | one like the Son of Man.
"Son of Man," a messianic title, is written as a nomen sacrum (sacred name) in two early MSS ($\mathfrak{P}^{115\text{vid}}$ א), with clear reference to Jesus according to the prophecy in Dan. 7:13–14. One early MS ($\mathfrak{P}^{47}$) writes the words in full (in *plene*; i.e., not as a sacred name), suggesting the translation "one like a son of man."

15:3 | King of the ages.
This is probably the original reading according to three early MSS ($\mathfrak{P}^{47}$ א^{*,2} [seventh century] C). A variant reading is "king of nations" in two early MSS (א^{1} A), as well as Maj . Although it could be argued that the expression "king of the ages [*aiōnōn*]" was borrowed from 1 Tim. 1:17,

it has the impressive support of $\mathfrak{P}^{47}$ א^{*,2} C. The reading "king of the nations [*ethnōn*]" appears to be the result of scribal assimilation to the next verse, which speaks of the "nations" fearing God.

15:7 | the four Zoa [living creatures].
This is the original wording according to four early MSS ($\mathfrak{P}^{115}$ א A C). One early MS ($\mathfrak{P}^{47}$) reads simply "the four."

16:11 | they still refused to repent of their deeds.
This is the original wording according to three early MSS ($\mathfrak{P}^{47}$ A C), as well as Maj. A variant reading is "they still refused to change" in one early MS (א).

17:3 | he carried me away in the Spirit.
The divine "Spirit" is written as a nomen sacrum (sacred name) in two early MSS ($\mathfrak{P}^{47vid}$ א).

18:2 | a prison of wicked, detestable birds.
This is the original wording according to two early MSS (א C), as well as Maj. A variant reading is "a prison of wicked birds and a prison of detestable creatures" in one early MS (A) by way of scribal expansion.

18:22 | craftsmen of every kind and trade will never work in you again.
This is probably the original wording according to one early MS (א), as well as syr^{ph} cop^{bo}. A variant reading is, "craftsmen of every kind and trade will never work in you again. The sounds of a mill will never be heard in you again!" in two early MSS (A C), as well as Maj, perhaps by way of scribal expansion.

19:10 | the Spirit of prophecy.
The divine "Spirit" is written as a nomen sacrum (sacred name) in one early MS (א).

20:5 | This is the first resurrection.
This is the reading in one early MS (א), as well as Maj^{K}. A variant reading in two early MSS (A C) is "The rest of the dead did not come to life until the thousand years were finished. This is the first resurrection." The omission in א may have been accidental; but if intentional, it eliminates the problem of explaining how certain Christians (i.e., the martyrs of 20:4) are allowed to participate in the first resurrection and the millennial kingdom, while others (i.e., those who are not martyrs) have to wait until after the millennium to experience resurrection. If the reading in א is original, then the longer text could be a scribal gloss that found its way into the text.

21:10 | he took me away in the Spirit.
The divine "Spirit" is written as a nomen sacrum (sacred name) in one early MS (א).

22:17 | the Spirit and the bride say, "Come."
The divine "Spirit" is written as a nomen sacrum (sacred name) in one early MS (א).

22:21a | the grace of the Lord Jesus be with the saints.
This is the reading in one early MS (א). Two variant readings are, "the grace of the Lord Jesus be with all the saints" in Maj syr cop, and "the grace of the Lord Jesus be with you all" in A—probably both scribal expansions.

22:21b
"Amen" is found in one early MS (א), as well as Maj syr cop, but omitted in one early MS (A) and other MSS. It is probably a scribal addition.

Select Bibliography

Bibliography of transcriptions of actual manuscripts appears in the first chapter of this volume with each manuscript. There is also footnoted bibliography for writings about the dates of the early papyri. The following bibliography pertains to volumes I used in preparing the rest of the book.

Aland, Kurt, and Barbara Aland. 1987. *The Text of the New Testament*. Grand Rapids: Eerdmans.

Aland, Kurt, Barbara; J. Karavidopoulos, C. Martini, B. Metzger. 2001. *Novum Testamentum Graece* (26th ed, 8th printing). Stuttgart: Deutsche Bibelgesellschaft.

Aland, Kurt, Barbara; J. Karavidopoulos, C. Martini, B. Metzger. 1993. *The Greek New Testament* (4th rev. ed.). Stuttgart: Deutsche Bibelgesellschaft.

Bell, Harold I., and T. C. Skeat. 1935. *Fragments of an Unknown Gospel and Other Early Christian Papyri*. London: British Library.

Bruce, F. F. 1985. *The Letter of Paul to the Romans*, 2nd ed. Grand Rapids: Eerdmans.

______. 1989. *The Canon of Scripture*. Grand Rapids: Eerdmans.

Colwell, E. 1965. "Scribal Habits in Early Papyri: A Study in the Corruption of the Text." Pages 370–389 in *The Bible in Modern Scholarship*, editor J. P. Hyatt. Nashville: Abingdon.

______. 1969. "Hort Redivivus: A Plea and a Program." Pages 148–171 in *Studies in Methodology in Textual Criticism of the New Testament*, editor E. Colwell. Leiden: E. J. Brill.

Comfort, Philip W. 2004. "Scribes as Readers: Looking at New Testament Textual Criticism according to Reader Reception Analysis." *Neotestamentica* 38.1:28–53.

______. 2005. *Encountering the Manuscripts: An Introduction to New Testament Paleography and Textual Criticism*. Nashville: Broadman & Holman.

______. 2008. *New Testament Text and Translation Commentary*. Wheaton: Tyndale House Publishers.

Comfort, Philip, and David Barrett 2001. *The Text of the Earliest New Testament Greek Manuscripts*. Wheaton: Tyndale House Publishers.

Elliott, J. Keith 1989. *A Bibliography of Greek New Testament Manuscripts*. Cambridge: Cambridge University Press.

Epp, Eldon J. 1966. *The Theological Tendency of Codex Bezae Cantabrigiensis in Acts*. Cambridge: Cambridge University Press.

______. 1981. "The Ascension in the Textual Tradition of Luke-Acts." Pages 131–145 in *New Testament Textual Criticism: Its Significance for Exegesis*, editors E. Epp and G. Fee. Oxford: Claredon.

Farmer, William. 1974. *The Last Twelve Verses of Mark*. Cambridge: Cambridge University Press.

Fee, Gordon. 1974. "$\mathfrak{P}^{75}$, $\mathfrak{P}^{66}$, and Origen: The Myth of the Early Textual Recension in Alexandria." Pages 19–45 in *New Dimensions in New Testament Study*, editors, R. Longenecker and M. Tenney. Grand Rapids: Zondervan.

Gamble, Harry. 1977. *The Textual History of the Letter to the Romans.* Studies and Documents 42. Grand Rapids: Eerdmans.

______. 1995. *Books and Readers in the Early Church*. New Haven: Yale University Press.

Holmes, Michael. 2002. "The Case for Reasoned Eclecticism." Pages 77–100 in *Rethinking New Testament Textual Criticism*, editor, D. Black. Grand Rapids: Baker.

Metzger, Bruce. 1977. *The Early Versions of the New Testament.* Oxford: Clarendon.

______. 1992. *The Text of the New Testament: Its Transmission, Corruption, and Restoration*, 3rd ed. Oxford: Oxford University Press.

______. 1994. *A Textual Commentary on the Greek New Testament*, 2nd ed. New York: United Bible Societies.

Porter, Calvin. 1962. "Papyrus Bodmer XV ($\mathfrak{P}^{75}$) and the Text of Codex Vaticanus." *Journal of Biblical Literature* 81:363–376.

Richards, E. Randolph. 1991. *The Secretary in the Letters of Paul.* Tubingen: J. C. B. Mohr.

Skeat, T. C. 1938. "The Lilies of the Field." *Zeitschrift für die neutestamentliche Wissenschaft* 37:211–214.

______. 1997. "The Oldest Manuscript of the Four Gospels?" *New Testament Studies* 43:1–34.

Tregelles, Samuel P. 1854. *An Account of the Printed Text of the Greek New Testament*. London: Samuel Bagster and Sons.

Westcott, Brooke F., and Fenton J. A. Hort 1881. *The New Testament in the Original Greek*. Cambridge: Macmillan.

______. 1882. *The New Testament in the Original Greek, Introduction and Appendix*. New York: Harper & Brothers.

Appendix

The Significance of the Nomina Sacra (Sacred Names)

This appendix provides a continued discussion of the Nomina Sacra as presented in chapter two. It details each nomen sacrum and addresses its significance in the New Testament.

Lord: $\overline{\mathrm{KC}}$ for KϒPIOC (*Kurios*)

In this book, the title for *kurios* is written as "Lord." This reflects the fact that the divine title (nomen sacrum) for *kurios* (Lord) was consistently written in a special way ($\overline{\mathrm{KC}}$) throughout the second and third century. This is evidenced by the following second-century and third-century New Testament manuscripts: $\mathfrak{P}^{1}$, $\mathfrak{P}^{4+64+67}$, $\mathfrak{P}^{5}$, $\mathfrak{P}^{9}$, $\mathfrak{P}^{13}$, $\mathfrak{P}^{20}$, $\mathfrak{P}^{27}$, $\mathfrak{P}^{30}$, $\mathfrak{P}^{35}$, $\mathfrak{P}^{37}$, $\mathfrak{P}^{38}$, $\mathfrak{P}^{45}$, $\mathfrak{P}^{46}$, $\mathfrak{P}^{47}$, $\mathfrak{P}^{49+65}$, $\mathfrak{P}^{53}$, $\mathfrak{P}^{66}$, $\mathfrak{P}^{72}$, $\mathfrak{P}^{75}$, $\mathfrak{P}^{78}$, $\mathfrak{P}^{91}$, $\mathfrak{P}^{92}$, $\mathfrak{P}^{100}$, 0171, 0189. This is also the case with several Christian Old Testament Greek manuscripts—noting just the second-century documents: P. Chester Beatty VI, Numbers and Deuteronomy; P. Chester Beatty VII, Isaiah; P. Chester Beatty VIII, Jeremiah; P. Baden (4.56), Exodus, Deuteronomy; P. Antinoopolis 1.7: Psalms. And this is also the case with other Christian writings—noting also just the second-century documents: P. Geneva 253 (Christian homily), P. Egerton 2 (unknown Gospel).

To name Jesus as "Lord" was no small matter to a Jewish Christian, who would have clearly understood that Yahweh has the same title.

Indeed, the title *kurios* appears nearly 6,000 times in the Septuagint as a translation of YHWH. The presence of the nomen sacrum $\overline{\mathrm{KC}}$ in New Testament writings was a way for Christians to show that the title *kurios*, assigned to Yahweh in the Old Testament, was now ascribed to Jesus. In other words, the nomen sacrum $\overline{\mathrm{KC}}$ would signal that Jesus was worthy of as much sacred reverence as was given to Yahweh.

Furthermore, the era in which the nomen sacrum for *kurios* (Lord) was created was an era in which each Caesar was considered to be "Lord." Christians stood alone in calling a man from Nazareth their "Lord." It must have had special significance for readers of the New Testament text; to see $\overline{\mathrm{KC}}$ in a line of text was to see a symbol that represented Jesus as Lord. Only those who knew the special written form would know this. Outsiders, picking up a New Testament book, would not immediately understand that $\overline{\mathrm{KC}}$ = *kurios*. And even if they eventually figured this out, they would not have appreciated what it meant that "the Lord" = Jesus. I am not saying that the nomina sacra were created to conceal Jesus's identity from outsiders, as if the Christians were trying to hide their beliefs behind some indecipherable code. What I am saying is that the nomina sacra were intended to be understood only by the initiates—i.e., those trained to read and decode the New Testament writings for their congregations.

In writing *kurios* as $\overline{\mathrm{KC}}$, the New Testament writers and scribes were signaling that Jesus was the divine Lord, superior to Caesar and any god. Furthermore, the nomen sacrum indicated a distinction between Jesus's lordship and that of others who were masters and landowners, for which the term *kurios* (written in *plene*) was also used (see notes on Rom. 14:4a; Col. 3:22b–4:1).

Jesus: $\overline{\mathrm{IH}}$ or $\overline{\mathrm{IC}}$ or $\overline{\mathrm{IHC}}$ for IHCOΥC (*Iēsous*)

In this book in the New Testament, the title for *Iesous* is written as "Jesus." The name "Jesus" was treated as a nomen sacrum very early in the written tradition of the Christian church. Very likely it was the second nomina sacra to be created—following right behind (if not concurrent with) "Lord." This should not surprise us, because the Messiah's personal name had divine significance from his very inception, and it only grew in significance throughout the course of Jesus's ministry and thereafter in the church. To this day, one needs only to hear the name "Jesus," and the identity is known. Who else in history is so well-known by a single name?

Before the incarnation, Joseph was told by an angel that he should name his son "Jesus" because "he will save his people from their sins" (see Matt. 1:20). This name signifies two important aspects about the Savior: first, it means that he is Yahweh; second, it means that he is the Savior. This is his first name. It is his primary name. He is Jesus; he is Yahweh the Savior.

During his days on earth, Jesus was known by his contemporaries as Jesus of Nazareth. This created problems for Jesus because it was expected that the Messiah should come from Bethlehem, the city of David. Shortly after Jesus began his ministry, a man named Philip told his friend, Nathaniel, that he had found the Messiah predicted by Moses and the prophets. But when Philip named him "Jesus of Nazareth," Nathaniel retorted, "Can anything good come from Nazareth?" (see John 1:45–46). Moses had written about him in the law (Deut. 18:15–18), and the prophets had foretold his coming. The prophets, however, never said that he would come from Nazareth. The Messiah was to be born in Bethlehem (Micah 5:2). Jesus was, in fact, born in Bethlehem (Matt. 2:1), but his parents had to flee to Egypt and later return to Galilee, where Jesus was raised in the obscure town of Nazareth (Matt. 2:13–23). This gave Jesus the reputation of being a Galilean, specifically a Nazarene from the hill country of Nazareth. This was a cause of stumbling for many Jews, because they could not accept a Messiah who had not come from Bethlehem. And since Jesus never told them this, they continued to believe that he was reared from birth as a Galilean, as a Nazarene.

Throughout his ministry the Jewish leaders refused to believe that Jesus was the Messiah because he was called Jesus of Nazareth. He suffered the opprobrium of being known as a Galilean and a Nazarene, not a Judean or a Bethlehemite. One of his greatest sufferings was to be misunderstood as to his true identity. However, Jesus never once discussed his Bethlehemic birth; rather, he always pointed to his divine, heavenly origin. If a person knew the One he came from, he would know that Jesus was the Christ. When Nicodemus tried to defend Jesus before the Sanhedrin, they retorted sarcastically, "Are you from Galilee, too? Look into it, and you will find that a prophet does not come out of Galilee" (John 7:51–52). This is as much to say, "If not even a prophet is mentioned in the Scriptures to come from Galilee, how much less the Christ?" So, the Pharisees and religious rulers were confident that they could reject Jesus as having any claim to Messiahship because of his Galilean origin. But they were wrong on two counts: (1) Jesus had been born in Bethlehem, the city of David (Luke 2:4–11), and therefore had legal claim to the Messiahship (Micah 5:2); (2) the Scriptures do speak of the Messiah as a "great light" arising in Galilee (see Isa. 9:1–7; Matt. 4:13–16).

Nevertheless, the stigma "of Nazareth" stuck with Jesus throughout his ministry and throughout the earliest days of the church. The earliest believers had an uphill battle to fight when they began to proclaim their faith in Jesus of Nazareth. They could not tell people, "believe in Jesus"; they had to specify which Jesus they should believe in, so as to distinguish him from other people with the same name. In the very first sermon preached by Peter to a multitude of Jews in Jerusalem, Peter told them about Jesus of Nazareth:

> Jesus of Nazareth, a man attested to you by God with deeds of power, wonders, and signs that God did through him among you, as you yourselves know—this man, handed over to you according to the definite plan and foreknowledge of God, you crucified and killed by the hands of those outside the law. . . . This Jesus God raised up, and of that all of us are witnesses . . . Therefore let the entire house of Israel know with certainty that God has made him both Lord and Messiah, this Jesus whom you crucified (Acts 2:22–23).

When the apostles preached and performed miracles in Jerusalem, they continued to identify Jesus as "Jesus of Nazareth" (Acts 3:6, 13; 4:10; 6:14). They proclaimed that it was "this Jesus"—this Jesus of Nazareth—who was the Messiah (Acts 5:42). The distinction "of

Nazareth" was important because there were many other Jews with the name "Jesus" inasmuch as "Jesus" was the Greek form of "Joshua"—and Joshua was a very popular name.

After the time of Jesus's ministry and the early years of the church, there was hardly any more mention of "Jesus of Nazareth" because there was no need to distinguish the Nazarene Jesus from others with that name. For example, in all the New Testament Epistles he is known simply as "Jesus" or "Jesus Christ" or "the Lord Jesus." All the readers, being Christians, knew who was being talked about. By contrast, in the Gospels and Acts it was important to distinguish Jesus of Nazareth, the Messiah, from all others with that name. One clear-cut way to do that was to make "Jesus" a nomen sacrum. This would immediately demarcate and denote "Jesus the Savior." Furthermore, the writing of this name as a nomen sacrum uplifted the name to divine status. He was not just any Jesus; he was Jesus—Yahweh the Savior, God come to earth to save his people from their sins. In virtually every verse where the name "Jesus" appears in the New Testament, it is written as a nomen sacrum. The other person named "Jesus" in the New Testament, a Christian brother known by Paul, is not written as a nomen sacrum in codex Sinaiticus and codex Vaticanus (see note on Col. 4:11).

Christ: $\overline{\text{XP}}$ or $\overline{\text{XC}}$ or $\overline{\text{XPC}}$ for XPICTOC (*Christos*)

In this book, the title for *Christos* is written as "Christ." In the New Testament the title "Christ" is often used in combination with the name "Jesus," as "Jesus Christ" (Matt. 1:1; Mark 1:1; Rom. 1:4) and "Christ Jesus" (Rom. 1:1; 1 Cor. 1:1). It is also used alone as the one favored title for Jesus: "the Christ" (John 20:31; Rom. 15:3; Heb. 3:6; 5:5; 1 Pet. 1:11, 19). The Gospels portray Jesus as accepting the title and role of the Christ at the time of his anointing, which occurred at his baptism. At this time, he was anointed into the threefold office of prophet, priest, and king. At his baptism by John, Jesus received the outpouring of the Spirit and thereafter was directed by the Spirit throughout his ministry (Matt. 3:16—4:17).

The confession of the disciples voiced by Peter and approved by Jesus is: "You are the Christ, the Son of the living God" (Matt. 16:16).

The earliest Christians proclaimed that Jesus was and is the Christ (Acts 2:36; 3:18–20; 9:22; 28:23, 31). This is the earliest (Matt. 16:16) and most basic article of the Christian confession (1 Cor. 1:23; 1 John 5:1); it affirms that Jesus perfectly fulfilled the role of anointed prophet, priest, and king as the servant of God for his people (Luke 7:16, 1 Cor. 15:25; Heb. 7:22–28; Rev. 19:16). The title "Christ" occurs about 530 times in the New Testament; Paul used the title more than any other writer (about 380 times). Since Paul used this title so profusely in his epistles, which are all dated between AD 49–65, it stands to reason that "Christ" was a very popular title for Jesus in the early years of the church.

God: $\overline{\Theta C}$ for ΘΕΟC (*theos*)

In this book, the title for *theos* is written as "God." In all the earliest manuscripts of the Greek New Testament, the word *theos* is written as a divine title (nomen sacrum), when the reference is to "God." There is not one New Testament manuscript that I know of where *theos* is written out in full when it designates "God." By contrast, in secular Greek literature, the word *theos* is written out in full; it is not written as a nomen sacrum.[1] The only place where *theos* is written in full (in *plene*) in the manuscripts of the New Testament is when the text of Acts speaks of the Greek god Artemis (see note on Acts 19:37). The New Testament writers and scribes distinguished their writings from secular writings and from the Jewish writings by making *theos* a nomen sacrum. All Greek texts of the Old Testament prepared by Jews have the word *theos* written out in full (in *plene*). Papyrus Fouad 266, mentioned before, is a good example. While Yahweh is written as a Tetragrammaton in paleo-Hebrew script, the word for "God" (*theos*) is not contracted.

There is another significant feature worth noting: the nomen sacrum for *theos* was used by all the Christian scribes when the term applied to God the Father *and* when it applied to God the Son. There was no distinction. And why should there be? The New Testament writers unquestionably considered Jesus, the Son of God, to be God. This is explicitly asserted in several passages, many of which are found in John's writings. It is John who tells us that "the Word was God." Not only was the Word with God from eternity, he was himself God from eternity (John 1:1). This is asserted at the beginning of the prologue to John's Gospel and at the end of the prologue (1:18), where the Son is again called the "only God" (*monogenēs theos*).[2]

In the Gospel of John narrative, Jesus declares that he existed before Abraham even came into being (8:58), and he asserts that he and the Father are one (10:30)—an assertion that the Jewish leaders undeniably understood as a claim to deity (10:31–33), for they attempted to stone him for blasphemy. At the end of the narrative, Thomas sees the risen Christ, believes in him, and proclaims, "My Lord and my God" (20:28). At the end of John's first epistle, he says that Jesus is "the true God and eternal life."[3]

Paul and Peter also affirm the deity of Jesus—each of them calling him "God." In the book of Romans, Paul praises Jesus Christ, saying, "Christ himself was a Jew as far as human nature is concerned. And he is God, who rules over everything and is worthy of eternal praise! Amen" (9:5)![4] In Philippians 2:6, Paul says that Jesus Christ was in the very form (or substance) "God," and in Colossians 1:19 and 2:9 he says that "all God's fullness dwells in him [Christ] bodily." In Titus 2:13, he identifies Jesus as "our God and Savior."[5] Peter also named Jesus as "God and Savior" in 2 Peter 1:1. And in the next verse, he says Jesus is "our God and Lord."[6] In all of the passages just mentioned, the Christian scribes always used the nomen sacrum form for the term "God."

The Jewish leaders of Jerusalem considered it blasphemous for Jesus to claim equality with God. On more than one occasion, they wanted to stone him for his claims. Jesus told the Jewish leaders, "I and the Father are one" (John 10:30). These leaders immediately understood that he was claiming deity for himself; they wanted to stone him for his blasphemy. How could he, a mere man, make himself God?! Jesus argued that it was not blasphemous to call himself the Son of God when, in fact, he was the One whom the Father consecrated and sent into the world. Furthermore, was it not true that other men had been called "gods" in the Scripture? On occasion, God had called the judges of Israel "gods," inasmuch as they were his representatives. In Psalm 82 the supreme God is said to rise in judgment against those whom he calls "gods" (Hebrew, *elohim*), because they had failed to show justice to the helpless and oppressed. These "gods" were those who were the official representatives and commissioned agents of God. If God called them "gods," why was it blasphemous for Jesus, the One consecrated by the Father and sent into the world, to say, "I am God's Son." The Jews could not argue against this because it stands written in the irrefragable Scriptures (i.e., the Scriptures are an entire entity from which no one can remove any portion). But Jesus was greater than those men who received messages from God, for he himself was the very message from God to men. And whereas they were earthly men selected by God to represent him, the Son of God came from heaven as the consecrated one, dedicated to do God's will on earth. Jesus was therefore justified in calling himself the Son of God, equal with the Father—even though the Jewish leaders considered this blasphemy.

These affirmations of Jesus's deity clearly speak against the modern notion that Jesus never claimed to be God, or even the Son of God. Many moderns say that such acclamations came only from the lips of others, not from Jesus himself. First of all, Jesus did acclaim to be the I Am. His audience, devout Jews, clearly understood this as a claim to deity because they wanted to stone him—the punishment for blasphemy (see John 8:54–58). Second, he claimed that he was the one who came from heaven and was going back to heaven (see John 3:13; 6:33). Third, he asserted that "I and the Father are one"—an assertion his Jewish audience understood to be a claim to deity (see discussion above on John 10). Fourth, the Father himself declared that Jesus was the Son of God (see Matt. 3:17; 17:5—and parallel passages). There is no more profound, authoritative voice than the Father's! Fifth, Jesus never denounced or corrected others who called him the Son of God—or even God himself!

With respect to the use of the nomen sacrum for *theos*, not one of the early Christian manuscripts (second to fourth century) makes a written distinction between the Father being called "God" and the Son being called "God." In other words, in all instances where *theos* is used of deity, whether referring to the Father or to the Son, it is written as a nomen sacrum. This also applies to those passages where exegetes have typically made arguments about articular *theos* meaning "the God" or "God himself," in contrast to anarthrous *theos* meaning deity or divinity. The usual understanding about the use of the article before *theos* is that it designates individuality and divine personality—i.e., it denotes the personhood of God, making it titular. By contrast, the absense of the article before *theos* is supposed to signal divine essence.[7] These distinctions, however, may not have been recognized by the earliest scribes if the writing of the nomen sacrum for "God" always designated a title—regardless of whether or not it had an article. In other words, it is well worth asking if the nomen sacrum form, in and of itself, communicated so powerful a signal that the distinctions between anarthrous *theos* and arthrous *theos* were subsequently blurred.

Spirit: $\overline{\text{ΠΝΑ}}$ for ΠΝΕΥΜΑ (*pneuma*)

In this book, the divine title for *pneuma* is written as "Spirit." This is the fifth divine title. When one reads the literature on divine titles (nomina sacra), it is clear that most scholars think that the four divine titles discussed above ("Lord," "Jesus," "Christ," and "God") were the primary titles to be written as nomina sacra and that all other titles were developed later. But the evidence of the extant manuscripts strongly suggests that the "Spirit" was also written as a nomen sacrum very early in the transmission of the text, if not from the beginning. If *pneuma* was not among the earliest nomina sacra, then scribes, beginning in the early second century, began to make exegetical decisions as to whether it should be written as a nomen sacrum, representing the divine Spirit, or written out in full (in *plene*), so as to designate another aspect of the *pneuma*, such as the human spirit, evil spirit, or a spiritual condition.

When we look at all the manuscripts of the second and third centuries where the title *pneuma* (Spirit) occurs, it is written as a nomen sacrum. This is evident in the following second-century, Christian Old Testament and New Testament manuscripts:

P. Chester Beatty VI, Numbers-Deuteronomy
P. Chester Beatty VII, Isaiah
P. Chester Beatty VIII, Jeremiah

P. Chester Beatty IX–X, Ezekiel, Daniel, Esther
PSI VIII.921, Psalms
$\mathfrak{P}^{4}$+$\mathfrak{P}^{64}$+$\mathfrak{P}^{67}$, Matthew and Luke
$\mathfrak{P}^{20}$, James
$\mathfrak{P}^{27}$, Romans
$\mathfrak{P}^{46}$, Paul's Epistles (in nearly all occasions, discussed below)
$\mathfrak{P}^{66}$, John (in all cases except one, discussed below)
$\mathfrak{P}^{75}$, Luke and John

In the other second-century New Testament manuscripts, the word *pneuma* (spirit) is not extant. The evidence of the third-century manuscripts is as follows:

Freer Manuscripts, Minor Prophets
$\mathfrak{P}^{5}$, John
$\mathfrak{P}^{15}$+$\mathfrak{P}^{16}$, 1 Corinthians and Philippians
$\mathfrak{P}^{17}$, Hebrews
$\mathfrak{P}^{24}$, Revelation
$\mathfrak{P}^{30}$, 1 and 2 Thessalonians
$\mathfrak{P}^{38}$, Acts
$\mathfrak{P}^{45}$, Gospels and Acts
$\mathfrak{P}^{47}$, Revelation
$\mathfrak{P}^{50}$, Acts
$\mathfrak{P}^{72}$, 1 and 2 Peter, Jude
$\mathfrak{P}^{101}$, Matthew
$\mathfrak{P}^{106}$, John
$\mathfrak{P}^{113}$, Romans
$\mathfrak{P}^{115}$, Revelation
0171, Matthew and Luke
0189, Acts

The early scribes consistently used the nomen sacrum form for *pneuma* when designating the divine Spirit. (The word *pneuma* was written out only when designating some other kind of spirit, such as evil spirits.) The only exception to this is that the scribe of $\mathfrak{P}^{46}$, in about ten occurrences, did not write *pneuma* as a nomen sacrum where one would expect the word to denote the divine Spirit. (This is discussed at length below). What this could indicate is that $\mathfrak{P}^{46}$ is, in fact, a very early manuscript, which shows the formation of the nomen sacrum for *pneuma* in early transition—most times being written as a divine title, sometimes being written out in full (in *plene*). If this is the case, then there is evidence to suggest that the nomen sacrum for "Spirit" was developed after the nomina sacra for "Lord," "Jesus," "Christ," and "God."

Aside from the phenomenon of $\mathfrak{P}^{46}$, all the other manuscripts indicate that the title "Spirit" was treated as a sacred name as early as were the names "Lord," "Jesus," "Christ," and "God." There is good reason for this. The Spirit was extremely important to the early believers because they considered the Spirit to be the Spirit of the risen Christ—the Spirit of Jesus making himself real to the believers in his spiritual form. From the writings of the New Testament (which are explained below), we gather that the early Christians considered Jesus to be present with them and in them via his Spirit. Thus, they honored the title "Spirit" by writing it as a nomen sacrum.

When Jesus arose from dead, three significant things happened to him. He was glorified, transfigured, and he became spirit. All three happened simultaneously. When he was resurrected, he was glorified (see Luke 24:26). At the same time, his body was transfigured into a glorious one (Phil. 3:21). Equally so—and quite mysteriously—he became life-giving spirit (1 Cor. 15:45). Paul did not say Jesus became "the Spirit"—as if the second person of the Trinity became the third, but that Jesus became spirit in the sense that his mortal existence and form were metamorphosed into a spiritual existence and form. Jesus's person was not changed through the resurrection, only his form. Christ, via resurrection, appropriated a new, spiritual form (while still retaining a body—a glorified one) that enabled him to commence a new spiritual existence. 1 Peter 3:18 says that Jesus was "put to death in the flesh, quickened in the spirit."

With this new spiritual existence, Christ, as spirit and through the Holy Spirit, could indwell millions of believers simultaneously. Before the resurrection, Jesus was limited by his mortal body; after his resurrection, Jesus could be experienced illimitably by all his believers. Before his resurrection, Christ could dwell only among his believers; after his resurrection, he could dwell in his believers. Because Christ became spirit through resurrection, he can be experienced by those he indwells. Prior to the resurrection the disciples could not experience Christ indwelling them because he was still a man limited by his human body. But after the resurrection there was a great change: Jesus's form changed, so he could then (and now) indwell the believers.

The Lord Jesus entered into a new kind of existence when he was raised from the dead because he was glorified and simuitaneously became spirit—or, to coin a phrase, he was "pneumafied" (from the Greek word for "spirit," *pneuma*.) It appears that when he arose, the indwelling Spirit penetrated and saturated his body so as to constitute his entire being with spirit. This is not my teaching alone; several noted Christian authors have advanced the same description of the Lord's resurrection. In fact, a great deal of study in the area of pneumatology (the study of the Spirit) points out that the risen Christ and the Spirit were united via Christ's resurrection.

William Milligan, the author of the best English classic on the subject of the resurrection, said that the risen Christ is spirit. In that classic, called *The Resurrection of our Lord*, he wrote the following:

> The condition of our Lord after His Resurrection was viewed by the sacred writers as essentially a state of *pneuma* (spirit). Not indeed that our Lord had then no body, for it is the constant lesson of Scripture that a body was possessed by him; but that the deepest, the fundamental characteristic of His state, interpenetrating even the body, and moulding it into a complete adaptation to and harmony with His spirit, was *pneuma*. In other words, it is proposed to inquire whether the word *pneuma* in the New Testament is not used as a short description of what our Lord was after His Resurrection, in contrast with what He was during the days of His humiliation upon earth.[8]

Milligan went on from there to show that several scriptures affirm that the resurrected Christ is spirit. He cited 1 Corinthians 6:17 to show that the believer who is joined with the risen Lord must be joined to him as spirit because he who is joined to the Lord is said to be "one spirit" with him. He used 2 Corinthians 3:17–18 to demonstrate that the Lord who is the Spirit is none other than the risen Christ. He also employed 1 Timothy 3:16, Romans 1:3–4, and Hebrews 9:14 to prove that the risen Lord is spirit (see pages 248–56). In these pages Milligan cites Franz Delitzsch who said that the divine personality in Christ "at the Resurrection interpenetrated, and as it were, absorbed the flesh so that He is now altogether spirit." Richard Gaffins, a modern writer, had this to say about Christ's resurrection:

> Christ (as incarnate) experiences a spiritual qualification and transformation so thorough, and endowment with the Spirit so complete that as a result they can now be equated. This unprecedented possession of the Spirit and the accompanying change in Christ result in a unity so close that not only can it be said simply that the Spirit makes alive, but also that Christ as Spirit makes alive.[9]

This is why Paul often speaks of the Spirit and Christ synonymously. This is evident in Romans 8:9–10. The terms "Spirit of God," "Spirit of Christ," and "Christ" are all used interchangeably. The Spirit of God is the Spirit of Christ and the Spirit of Christ is Christ. David Somerville said,

> Being "in Christ" and being "in the Spirit" are the same thing; and in the thought of the apostle, "Christ," "the Spirit of Christ," and "the Spirit of God" are practically synonymous. At the resurrection Christ became a Life-giving Spirit to mankind.[10]

In these verses it is evident that Paul identifies the Spirit with Christ because in Christian experience they are absolutely identical. There is no such thing as an experience of Christ apart from the Spirit. Only the inexperienced would say or think that the two can be separated. The separation and/or distinction does exist in Trinitarian theology—and for very good reasons, but the separation is nearly nonexistent in actual experience. Ever since the beginning of the Christian church, the believers have experienced Christ through his Spirit—the Spirit of Christ. It is in this light that Paul can say, "Now the Lord is the Spirit . . . and we are being transformed into the [Lord's] image by the Lord, who is the Spirit" (2 Cor. 3:17–18).

All this discussion about Christ being experienced in, by, and as the Spirit affirms why the earliest scribes decided to dignify and even deify the term *pneuma* by writing it as a nomen sacrum. To the early Christians, the "Spirit" was identified with Christ and vice versa. Therefore, just as "Christ" was worthy of a divine title, so was the "Spirit." The early believers signaled the Spirit's deity by writing *pneuma* as a nomen sacrum. They distinguished the divine Spirit from any other spirit—the human spirit, evil spirits, or even the wind—by not writing these as nomen sacrum. The best English equivalent to this is the way in which a capital letter "S" is used by Bible translators for God's Spirit and a small letter "s" is used for the human spirit or some other kind of spirit.

Translators and interpreters have been perplexed about how to render the word *pneuma* in certain verses in the New Testament. Does the particular passage indicate the divine Spirit, the human spirit, or another spirit? In several such places the translator has the option of capitalizing it or not; either way, his or her rendering necessitates an interpretation. Thus, a translator may have wished that the original writers had made the distinction. Interestingly, it is possible that they *did* make the orthographic distinction by writing the divine Spirit as as nomen sacrum and by writing out any other spirit as *pneuma*. Since we do not have the autographs, we are not certain if this distinction came from the New Testament authors themselves, or if it was the invention of the earliest scribes. What we do know is that the distinction shows up in the earliest New Testament manuscripts, many of which date in the second century. To be specific, the distinction between the divine Spirit written as a nomen sacrum and the human spirit written in full appears in several of the earliest New Testament manuscripts: $\mathfrak{P}^{45}$, $\mathfrak{P}^{46}$, $\mathfrak{P}^{66}$, $\mathfrak{P}^{75}$. There are also several notes about the translation of *pneuma* throughout this book. These are discussed below in the section "Scribes as Interpreters of the Nomina Sacra."

Other Prominent Divine Names: Father, Son, Son of God, Son of Man, Son of David

There were four basic nomen sacrum in the earliest New Testament manuscripts: "Lord," "Jesus," "Christ," "God," soon followed by "Spirit." Beyond these primary five, there were several others, but these others were definitely not part of the original group because we do not see them consistently written as nomina sacra in all the earliest manuscripts. In other words, only certain scribes in the second and third centuries decided to write the names "Father" and "Son" as nomina sacra. Others chose not to do so at all. And still other scribes did so on some occasions and not on others.

Some of the earliest New Testament manuscripts showed their respect for the divine names, "Father" and "Son," by writing them as nomina sacra. The nomen sacrum for "Son" is found in $\mathfrak{P}^{1}$, $\mathfrak{P}^{9}$, $\mathfrak{P}^{40}$, $\mathfrak{P}^{45}$ (in part), $\mathfrak{P}^{46}$ (in part), $\mathfrak{P}^{66}$ (in part), $\mathfrak{P}^{75}$ (in part), $\mathfrak{P}^{101}$, $\mathfrak{P}^{107}$, and $\mathfrak{P}^{114}$. The nomen sacrum for "Father" is found in $\mathfrak{P}^{5}$, $\mathfrak{P}^{22}$, $\mathfrak{P}^{27}$, $\mathfrak{P}^{39}$, $\mathfrak{P}^{45}$ (in part), $\mathfrak{P}^{46}$ (in part), $\mathfrak{P}^{47}$, $\mathfrak{P}^{53}$, $\mathfrak{P}^{66}$ (in part), $\mathfrak{P}^{72}$, $\mathfrak{P}^{75}$ (in part), $\mathfrak{P}^{91}$, and $\mathfrak{P}^{107}$. The notation "in part" signifies that the manuscript displays the title both in *plene* form (fully written out) and nomen sacrum form. It should also be noted that where a manuscript displays a nomen sacrum for either "Son" or "Father" only, the other name is not extant, so I cannot determine if the scribe used only one or the other. The only exception to this is found in $\mathfrak{P}^{72}$, where the scribe consistently used a nomen sacrum for "Father," whereas "Son" in its one occurrence (2 Pet 1:17) is not written as a nomen sacrum.

This fluctuation in the second and third century manuscripts concerning the names "Father" and "Son" could reflect the theological developments of the time. In the second and third centuries of the church, Christian theologians were exploring the mysteries of the Triune God. During this period, the theologians described God as being one God in three Persons (or *personae*). These three persons were identified as God the Father, God the Son, and God the Spirit. In the previous section, we examined at length the early Christian concept of the Spirit. To their way of thinking, the "Spirit" was the invisible presence of Jesus. But what did they think of the terms "Father" and "Son"? It seems they were considered in two ways: (1) as descriptive nouns for the Father-Son relationship presented in Scriptures, and (2) as solitary titles—"the Father" and "the Son." A verse that shows a descriptive use of "father" and "son" is Hebrews 1:5, which reads in the RSV as, "I will be to him a father and he shall be to me a son" (note the lower case of "father" and "son"). A verse that shows the titular use of both names is 2 John 9—"he who abides in the doctrine of Christ . . . has both the Father and the Son."

When the manuscripts write "Father" as a nomen sacrum (sacred name), this translation renders it as "Father." When the manuscripts do not write "Father" as a nomen sacrum but it is clearly pointing to the divine Father, this translation renders it as "Father." When the manuscripts write "Son" as a nomen sacrum (sacred name), this translation renders it as "Son." When the manuscripts do not write "Son" as a nomen sacrum but it is clearly pointing to the divine Son, this book renders it as "Son." This applies to all the titles which have "Son" in the name: Son of God, Son of Man, and Son of David.

Father: $\overline{\Pi P}$ or $\overline{\Pi T P}$ for ΠΑΤΗΡ (*pater*)

In this book, the divine title for *pater* is written as Father, when it is written as a nomen sacrum. There are other nomina sacra forms present in early manuscripts than the two listed above, thereby revealing that the form of this nomen sacrum was not fixed. Furthermore, various scribes wrote the name sometimes as a nomen sacrum and sometimes not. For example, the scribe of $\mathfrak{P}^{45}$ sometimes wrote out *pater* (Father/father) as a nomen sacrum and sometimes in full. So also for the scribes of $\mathfrak{P}^{46}$ and $\mathfrak{P}^{75}$. This fluctuation probably shows that the scribes were not yet comfortable with writing this name as a nomen sacrum. The fluctuation, however, could have been on purpose: the nomen sacrum for *pater* denoting "the Father" (written in this book as the Father), while the name written out in full (i.e., not as a nomen sacrum) denoting one who is a father by nature and action (i.e., father God). When the name is not written as a nomen sacrum, it is written in this commentary as "father." All such instances are noted. Furthermore, on occasion, scribes distinguish God the Father from human fathers by writing the former as nomen sacrum ("Father") and the latter in full ("father").

Son: $\overline{\text{ΥC}}$ for $\overline{\text{ΥΙΟC}}$ (*huios*); **Son of God** (*huios tou theou*)

In this book, the divine title for *huios* is written as Son. As was previously stated, this divine name was not one of the five names to be written as nomina sacra in early times. We know this because they do not appear in sacral form in some of the earliest manuscripts (such as $\mathfrak{P}^{4}+\mathfrak{P}^{64}+\mathfrak{P}^{67}$) and because in several other manuscripts of the second and third century ($\mathfrak{P}^{45}$, $\mathfrak{P}^{46}$, $\mathfrak{P}^{66}$, $\mathfrak{P}^{75}$) the scribes fluctuated between writing out the full name and writing it as a nomen sacrum, even when it was clear that it was a divine title. This fluctuation shows that the scribes were not yet comfortable with writing this name as a nomen sacrum. The fluctuation, however, could have been on purpose: the nomen sacrum for *huios* denoting "the Son" (written in this commentary as the Son), while the name written out in full (i.e., not as a nomen sacrum) denoting one who is a son by nature and action. When the name is not written as a nomen sacrum, it is written in this book as "son." All such instances are noted. Furthermore, on occasion, scribes distinguish God the Son from human sons by writing the former as a nomen sacrum ("Son") and the latter in full ("son").

Son of Man: $\overline{\text{ΥΙΟC ΤΟΥ ΑΝΟΥ}}$ or $\overline{\text{ΥC ΤΟΥ ΑΝΘΡΟΠΟΥ}}$ or $\overline{\text{ΥC ΤΟΥ ΑΝΟΥ}}$ (*huios tou anthrōpou*)

In this book, the divine title for *huios tou anthrōpou* is written as the Son of Man when it is written as a nomen sacrum. In the early manuscripts sometimes just *huios* (Son) was contracted; other times just *anthrōpou* (man); and other times both words.[11] The divine title "Son of Man" was one of the earliest nomina sacra. However, it is doubtful that it was part of the original writings inasmuch as it does not show up consistently in the earliest papyrus manuscripts. In other words, some of the second-century scribes made it a nomen sacrum and some did not. The title is composed of two words that were written as nomen sacrum by themselves: *huios* (son—see above discussion) and *anthropos* (man). There is plenty of evidence among the literary papyri to show that *anthropos* (man, humanity) was being abbreviated by the first century.

When Jesus spoke of himself, he used the enigmatic title, "the Son of Man." This was his way of saying that he was the Messiah without coming out directly and saying, "I am the Messiah." If he told the Jewish people directly, "I am the Messiah," they would have thought he was claiming to be the next "Maccabean" revolutionary leader and deliverer, come to set them free from Roman military rule. So Jesus used a title borrowed from Ezekiel and Daniel. In the book of Ezekiel, the prophet was referred to as "Son of Man" 90 times. Often, God addressed Ezekiel as "son of man"; in the same breath, God called him "son of dust." As such, it pointed to Ezekiel's humanity. It also pointed to Ezekiel's position as a servant. Thus, in adopting this term for himself, Jesus was adopting a term that emphasized that he had become a man to carry out service to God (see Phil. 2:5–11).

This is one side of the coin. The other side shows that "Son of Man" is a divine title, taken from Daniel 7:13–14. This passage describes a vision of one "like a son of man" who "comes with the clouds" into the presence of "the Ancient of Days," who gives him the universal and eternal kingdom of God. Jesus repeatedly quoted parts of this text in his teachings (Matt. 16:27; 19:28), especially about his second coming:

The sign of the coming of the Son of Man will appear in the heavens, and there will be deep mourning among all the nations of the earth. And they will see the Son of Man arrive on the clouds of heaven with power and great glory (Matthew 24:30, NLT).

Then again, Jesus quoted this passage in his trial before the Sanhedrin:

Then the high priest said to him, "I demand in the name of the living God that you tell us whether you are the Messiah, the Son of God."

Jesus replied, "Yes, it is as you say. And in the future you will see me, the Son of Man, sitting at God's right hand in the place of power and coming back on the clouds of heaven."

> Then the high priest tore his clothing to show his horror, shouting, "Blasphemy! Why do we need other witnesses? You have all heard his blasphemy." (Matt. 26:63–65, NLT)

Clearly, Jesus understood the passage in Daniel about "the Son of Man" to be a title for the Christ, the Son of God. Evidently, the high priest also understood the passage in this way, for he considered it blasphemy for Jesus to have applied the passage to himself.

In the Gospels, the term "Son of Man" is used by Jesus about 80 times as a mysterious, indirect way of speaking about himself as the Messiah (Matthew, 32 times; Mark, 14 times; Luke, 26 times; John, 10 times).[12] In all these texts, Jesus was always the speaker, and no one ever addressed him as "Son of Man." For several New Testament scribes, there was no question of interpreting this expression as a messianic title in the Gospels. Many of the early Gospel manuscripts exhibit the title as a nomen sacrum—namely, $\mathfrak{P}^{45}$, $\mathfrak{P}^{66}$, and $\mathfrak{P}^{75}$ (though not consistently). The scribe of $\mathfrak{P}^{4}$+$\mathfrak{P}^{64}$+$\mathfrak{P}^{67}$ wrote out this title in full (see Luke 6:5). $\mathfrak{P}^{1}$ and $\mathfrak{P}^{5}$ have no extant portion that contains the title, "the Son of Man."

The effect of writing "Son of Man" as a nomen sacrum is the same as when Jesus first used it: the correct identification could be made only by the initiates. Only those who knew Jesus's messianic identity could understood what "Son of Man" meant. Only Christian scribes and readers (lectors) would recognize that $\overline{\text{ΥC}}$ $\overline{\text{ΤΟΥ}}$ $\overline{\text{ΑΝΟΥ}}$ signified "the Son of Man." What better way to write it? The mystery inherent in the term is thereby sustained.

Son of David: $\overline{\text{ΥC ΤΟΥ ΔΑΥΙΔ}}$ (*huios tou Dauid)*

In this book, the divine title for *huios tou Dauid* is written as the Son of David. The very first verse of the New Testament (Matt. 1:1) in the earliest papyrus for this portion ($\mathfrak{P}^{1}$) shows the title "Son of David" written as a nomen sacrum (sacred name). Thereafter throughout the Gospels this name is almost always written as nomen sacrum in codices Siniaticus (א), Ephraemi Rescriptus (C), and Regius (L): Matthew 9:27; 12:23; 15:22; 20:30–31; 21:9, 15; Mark 12:35; Luke 18:38;

20:41. In its extant portion, 𝔓[45] shows it written as a nomen sacrum in Matthew 20:30. When Jesus was addressed as "the Son of David," it was virtually the same as being addressed as the Messiah or the Christ because it was common Jewish knowledge that the Messiah would be David's son (see 2 Sam. 7:11–16).

Scribes as Interpreters of the Nomina Sacra

There are a few instances when the scribes chose *not* to write the nomina sacra form of *theos*, *kurios*, *Iēsous*, *patēr*, *huios*, and *pneuma*. These instances are described below.

I know of only one occurrence where *theos* (God) is written in full in the New Testament manuscripts. In Acts 19:37, 𝔓[74] א B C write *theos* in full (in *plene*) in reference to the god Artemis. (Most English translations render this as "goddess" because *theos* is preceded by the feminine article.)

There are only a few instances where *kurios* (Lord) is written in full in the New Testament manuscripts. In Luke 16:1–8 (the story of the shrewd manager) the word *kurios* is written in full in 16:3 (𝔓[75] L), 16:5a (B D), and 16:5b (f^1). The *kurios* in Gospel parables invariably represents the divine *kurios*, the Lord Jesus or Lord God. In this parable, however, various scribes wrote out the word *kurios* (in *plene*) at least one time, thereby suggesting they were thinking this *kurios* was not the Lord God but a human master. In Acts 25:26 "Caesar" is designated as *kurios*. Significantly, several manuscripts (𝔓[74] א B C) write out the word (in *plene*) to indicate this should be understood as "lord." In 1 Peter 3:16 Sarah called her husband *kurios*. Interestingly, the scribe of B wrote out the word in full (in *plene*) to indicate she was calling him "lord," not "Lord."

The name *Iēsous* (Jesus) is written as a nomen sacrum in all manuscripts throughout the entire New Testament. There are only two exceptions, where the "Jesus" being named is not Jesus of Nazareth, but another "Jesus." In Acts 13:6 the person "Bar-Jesus" is not written as a nomen sacrum in any manuscript; and in Col. 4:11, with reference to the person named "Jesus who is called Justus," the scribes of א and B wrote out "Jesus" in full (in *plene*).

The name *patēr* (Father) is usually, but not always, written as a nomen sacrum in the New Testament manuscripts, even when the reference is clearly the divine Father. Aside from a few instances when scribes wanted to designate a human father (e.g., John 8:19a in $\mathfrak{P}^{75}$) by not writing a nomen sacrum, they also did the same in indicating "one who is a father" or "one who is an originator"—as in 2 Cor. 6:18 where it says "I will be to you a father" ($\mathfrak{P}^{46}$ א B), in Heb. 12:9 which speaks of "the father of spirits" ($\mathfrak{P}^{13}$ $\mathfrak{P}^{46}$ א), and in James 1:17 which has the expression "father of lights" ($\mathfrak{P}^{23}$ א B). On another occasion, the scribe of $\mathfrak{P}^{75}$ wrote out *patēr* (father) when Jesus was referring to "the father" of the Jewish leaders (who wanted to kill him) as being Satan (John 8:44).

The name *huios* (Son) is usually, but not always, written as a nomen sacrum in the New Testament manuscripts, even when the reference is clearly the divine Son. Interestingly, several scribes designated the *huios* in various parables as being the divine Son by writing a nomen sacrum, when they could have written the word out in full (see Matt. 21:37–38; 33–46; Mark 12:6; Luke 20:9–19 in most MSS). In the book of Hebrews, the writer often points to Jesus's superiority on the basis that he was "a son" (as opposed to an angel, etc.). Scribes keyed in on this, and wrote out *huios* in full (in *plene*) on a few occasions: Heb. 1:2 ("he has spoken to us in a son," so $\mathfrak{P}^{46}$ א B I) and Heb. 7:28 ("a son has been perfected forever," so $\mathfrak{P}^{46}$ א B I). In Heb. 3:6, the manuscripts are divided; some scribes ($\mathfrak{P}^{46}$ א I) call him "the Son" ("Christ as the Son over his house") and some ($\mathfrak{P}^{13}$ B) call him "a son" ("a son over his house").

There is more variation when we examine the name *pneuma* (Spirit). For the most part, scribes used the nomen sacrum for *pneuma* if it refered to the divine Spirit. They also used it when it referred to the spirit of Jesus—whether his indwelling divine Spirit or his human spirit. In the following verses all manuscripts have the *pneuma* of Jesus written as a nomen sacrum: Matt. 27:50 (where he gave up his Spirit at death), Mark 2:8 (where he perceived in his Spirit), Mark 8:12 (where he sighed deeply in his Spirit), Luke 23:46 (where he gave up his Spirit to the Father in death), John 11:33 (where he was agitated in his Spirit), John 13:21 (where he was deeply troubled in his Spirit), and John 19:30 (where he gave over his Spirit in death). In all these verses, modern translations have the small letter "s" word, "spirit," to indicate Jesus's human spirit. Scribes could have replicated this by writing out the word *pneuma* in full (in *plene*), and not writing it as a nomen sacrum. But they always chose to make the *pneuma* of Jesus divine.

In many other verses, scribes wrote out the word *pneuma* (in *plene*) to designate the human spirit or a spirit that was not divine (as in "the spirit of Python," Acts 16:16–18). In some verses, there appears both the nomen sacrum for the divine Spirit and the *plene* form for the human spirit, so as to distinguish the two. This occurs in John 3:6, where the scribe of 𝔓[66] wrote "that which is born of the SPIRIT [nomen sacrum] is spirit [plene form]." By writing it this way, the scribe was clearly indicating that he thought the passage means that "the divine Spirit regenerates the human spirit."

Another noteworthy passage is 1 Cor. 2:10–12, where scribes differentiated between the divine Spirit (by writing it as a nomen sacrum) and the human spirit or another spirit (by writing it in *plene* form). The verses can be rendered as follows:

> 10 God has revealed them [the deep things] through the spirit [*plene*] (so 𝔓[46] B), for the spirit [*plene*] searches all things, even the deep things of God (so 𝔓[46] B).
>
> 11 Who knows the human being better than the human spirit in them [*plene*] (so 𝔓[46vid] B), and who knows God better than the Spirit [nomen sacrum] of God (so 𝔓[46] א).
>
> 12 We have not received the spirit [*plene*] of the world (so 𝔓[46] B), but we have the Spirit (nomen sacrum] that comes from God (so 𝔓[46] א).

Yet another passage is 1 Cor. 14:14–16, where scribes differentiated between the divine Spirit (by writing it as a nomen sacrum) and the human spirit (by writing it in *plene* form). The verses can be rendered as follows:

> 14 For if I pray in an unknown language, my spirit [*plene*] prays (so $\mathfrak{P}^{46}$ B), while my mind cannot grasp what I am praying.
>
> 15 What should I do? I will join in prayer with the Spirit [nomen sacrum] (so $\mathfrak{P}^{46}$ ℵ) and also pray with my mind. I will sing in my spirit [*plene*], and also sing with my mind (so $\mathfrak{P}^{46vid}$ B).
>
> 16 Otherwise, if you praise in the Spirit [nomen sacrum] (so $\mathfrak{P}^{46}$ ℵ), how will the one sitting nearby say "amen" to your thanksgiving?

There is one more verse where the two forms of the Spirit (nomen sacrum and *plene*) appear. In 2 Cor. 3:6, the text reads in $\mathfrak{P}^{46}$: "He [God] has qualified us to be ministers of the new covenant, not of letter but of spirit [*plene*], for the letter kills, but the Spirit [nomen sacrum] gives life." Clearly the scribe of $\mathfrak{P}^{46}$ was distinguishing the meanings of *pneuma* in this passage.

The scribe of $\mathfrak{P}^{46}$ on other occasions used the *plene* form of *pneuma* to indicate a spirit that was not clearly the divine Spirit. In Rom. 8:15 he wrote, "a spirit of sonship"; in Rom. 11:8 he wrote "a spirit of numbness" had overtaken Israel; in 1 Cor. 6:17 he wrote that the person who is joined to the Lord "is one spirit" with him; and in 2 Cor. 2:13 he wrote that Paul said, "I had no peace in my spirit."

As can be gleaned from the foregoing discussion, the scribe of $\mathfrak{P}^{46}$ was especially active in his interpretation of *pneuma*—most times writing it as a nomen sacrum, but sometimes writing it in full (in *plene*) to denote the human spirit or another spirit different than the divine Spirit. Translators today engage in the same kind of interpretation when they capitalize "Spirit," or decide not to capitalize it. Translators today have much to learn from the ancient scribes.

Endnotes

1. I know of only one exception to this: the manuscript PSI XI 1200 (second century) has the nomen sacrum for *theos*. Since the nomina sacra is a Christian invention, it stands to reason that a Christian scribe prepared this text.

2. According to superior manuscript evidence, the text reads *monogenēs theos*, which means "an only One, God" or "God, the only begotten." This is supported by $\mathfrak{P}^{66}$ ℵ* B C* L. A few other manuscripts ($\mathfrak{P}^{75}$ $\aleph^{1}$ 33) read *ho monogenēs theos* (the only begotten God). All other manuscripts, most of which are quite late, read *ho monogenēs huios* (the only begotten Son). The manuscript evidence for the first reading (basically supported by the second reading) is superior to the evidence for the third reading. The papyri ($\mathfrak{P}^{66}$ and $\mathfrak{P}^{75}$—which adds the article *ho*), the earliest uncials (ℵ B C), and some early versions (Coptic and Syriac) support the first reading.
3. This verse reads, "And we know that the Son of God has come and has given us understanding so that we may know him who is true, and we are in him who is true, in his Son, Jesus Christ. This one is the true God and eternal life." In Greek, the deictic pronoun "this one" (*houtos*), refers to the nearest noun, which in this case is "Jesus Christ." Thus, the grammar indicates that Jesus Christ is "the true God and eternal life."
4. The translations that support this rendering are NRSV, NIV, NLT.
5. In the Greek, there is one article governing the two titles "God" and "Savior Jesus Christ" joined by the conjunction *kai* ("and"). According to a Greek grammatical rule (called the "Granville Sharpe Rule"—see Dana and Mantey, *A Manual Grammar of the Greek New Testament*, 146–153), this structure indicates that the two nouns describe one person. In this case, Jesus Christ is both God and Savior (as is translated in most modern versions: NASB, RSV, NRSV, NIV, NASB, NLT).
6. The "Granville Sharpe Rule" also applies to the first two verses of 2 Peter.
7. Dana and Mantey, 129–130.
8. William Milligan, *The Resurrection of our Lord* (1884), 246.
9. Richard Gaffins, *The Centrality of the Resurrection* (1978), 87.
10. David Somerville, *St. Paul's Conception of Christ*, 117.
11. For examples of the different ways of writing this title, see $\mathfrak{P}^{45}$ (Matt. 26:2, 24; Luke 9:58; 11:30; 12:10); $\mathfrak{P}^{66}$ (John 1:51; 9:35; 12:34); $\mathfrak{P}^{75}$ (Luke 6:5, 22; 9:22, 26; 11:30; John 6:27; 12:23).
12. It stands to reason that the title "Son of Man" basically passed out of use after the age of the Gospels because the term was used only by Jesus speaking of himself (except when others were responding to a statement he made about "the Son of Man"—as in the question, "Who is this Son

of Man?"). While Jesus was alive on earth, this was his veiled way of claiming to be the Christ. After his death, resurrection, and ascension, he was clearly manifested and vindicated as the Christ, the Son of God. Thereafter, there was no need for his believers to call him the "Son of Man," when they could forthrightly call him "the Christ." Thus, all the New Testament writers, when speaking of his life after resurrection, proclaimed Jesus to be "the Christ." At the same time, the Christian writers showed their reverence for the name Jesus used for himself by making "the Son of Man" a nomen sacrum.